COMMENTARY ON ACTS 5

COMMENTARY ON ACTS 5

STEPHEN MANLEY

COMMENTARY ON ACTS 5
© 2024 by Stephen Manley

Published by Cross Style Press
Lebanon, Tennessee
CrossStyle.org

All rights reserved. No part of this book may be reproduced in any form without prior permission from the publisher, except for brief quotations.

Scripture taken from the New King James Version®. Copyright © 1982 by Thomas Nelson, Inc. Used by permission. All rights reserved.

ISBN (Print): 978-1-957219-02-8
ISBN (eBook): 978-1-957219-05-9

Printed in the United States of America.

CrossStyle.org

CONTENTS

The Agreed Resolve Continued – Acts 5:1-11

Acts 5:1-11	All In	3
Acts 5:1-2	Embezzlement	12
Acts 5:3	The Great War	21
Acts 5:3	What Happened?	30
Acts 5:3	Why Am I Defeated?	38
Acts 5:3-4	Lying to God	47
Acts 5:4	Making a Place	55
Acts 5:5	Consequence of Hearing	64
Acts 5:5, 11	Great Fear	73
Acts 5:6	Removal	82
Acts 5:7	I Didn't Know	91
Acts 5:8	A Critical Moment	100
Acts 5:9-10	An Agreement	109
Acts 5:10	Breathing	118
Acts 5:11	A Fearing Church	127

Another Review: Another Summary – Acts 5:12-16

Acts 5:12-16	Another Summary	139
Acts 5:12	Your Hands	148
Acts 5:12	One Accord	157
Acts 5:13	High Standard	166
Acts 5:14	Others – Others – Others	175
Acts 5:15	Your Shadow	184
Acts 5:16	Confrontation	193

Adversity Repeated – Acts 5:17-21

Acts 5:17-21	Adversity Repeated	205
Acts 5:17	Positive or Negative	214
Acts 5:18	Shut Up	223
Acts 5:19	A Contrast	232
Acts 5:20	Parable of Pentecost	241
Acts 5:20	Words of Life	250
Acts 5:21	Futility	259
Acts 5:21	Consistency	268

Apostle's Restatement: The Unexplainable – Acts 5:22-32

Acts 5:22-32	The Unexplainable	279
Acts 5:22	Divine Protection	289

Acts 5:23	Seeking / Finding	299
Acts 5:23	Security	308
Acts 5:24	What's Going On?	317
Acts 5:25	God's Placement	326
Acts 5:26	Fearless	335
Acts 5:27	Exposed	345
Acts 5:28	Unexpected Testimony	354
Acts 5:29	Compelled	364
Acts 5:30	A Proper Answer	373
Acts 5:30	Resurrection	383
Acts 5:31	Restoration	392
Acts 5:31	The Place	401
Acts 5:31	The Position – Prince	411
Acts 5:31	The Purpose – Savior	420
Acts 5:32	These Things	429
Acts 5:32	Life Consuming	438
Acts 5:32	Jesus Only	447

Advice Rejected: Agreement – Acts 5:33-42

Acts 5:33-42	Agreement	459
Acts 5:33	Two Realms	469
Acts 5:34	Spiritual Wisdom	478

Acts 5:35	Take Heed	487
Acts 5:36-37	A Rebellious Pattern	496
Acts 5:38-39	The End Result	505
Acts 5:38-39	A Certainty	514
Acts 5:40	Who Is In Charge	523
Acts 5:41	What?	532
Acts 5:42	No Change	541

About the Author   551

PART ONE
ACTS 5:1-11

THE AGREED RESOLVE CONTINUED

Acts 5:1-11

ALL IN

"But a certain man named Ananias, with Sapphira his wife, sold a possession. And he kept back part of the proceeds, his wife also being aware of it, and brought a certain part and laid it at the apostles' feet. But Peter said, 'Ananias, why has Satan filled your heart to lie to the Holy Spirit and keep back part of the price of the land for yourself? While it remained, was it not your own? And after it was sold, was it not in your own control? Why have you conceived this thing in your heart? You have not lied to men but to God.' Then Ananias, hearing these words, fell down and breathed his last. So great fear came upon all those who heard these things. And the young men arose and wrapped him up, carried him out, and buried him. Now it was about three hours later when his wife came in, not knowing what had happened. And Peter answered her, 'Tell me whether you sold the land for so much?' She said, 'Yes, for so much.' Then Peter said to her, 'How is it that you have agreed together to test the Spirit of the Lord? Look, the feet of those who have buried your husband are at the door, and they will carry you out.' Then immediately she fell down at his feet and breathed her last. And the young men came in and found her dead, and carrying her out, buried her by her husband. So great fear came upon all the church and upon all who heard these things'"
(Acts 5:1-11).

Part One: The Agreed Resolve Continued

Our passage is the first paragraph in Acts chapter five, and Luke connects it to the ending of Acts chapter four. He visualized for us the state of the early Church in the two illustrations at the end of Acts four and the beginning of Acts five. These new believers clustered in Jerusalem, were converted Jews, who populated the early Church. Luke reported that they ate together in their houses, used the temple as their base for evangelizing Jerusalem, and found favor with the people there. These believers sold their possessions and shared with everyone who had a need. There was tremendous growth among their numbers for God added to the church daily those whom He saved (Acts 2:43-47).

Luke gave an update to his first report (Acts 4:32-35), writing that the members were continuing in the same pattern. The early Church was of one heart and one soul, had all things in common, and, with generous hearts, sold their lands and houses, distributing the proceeds to anyone who had need. ***"Neither did anyone say that any of the things he possessed was his own, but they had all things in common"*** (Acts 4:32). Then Luke gives two illustrations to picture this for us. The first one is Barnabas (Acts 4:36 - 37), a Son of Encouragement, who sold his land and brought the money to the apostles for the Church's use. The second illustration is Ananias and Sapphira (Acts 5:1-11), who had a different outcome. The first illustration is positive, and the second one is negative.

Luke's report, on the state of the early Church, reveals the captivating theme of their complete commitment. This commitment is a consistent theme accepted throughout the history of the Church. True examples of this commitment are the stoning of Stephen, the first martyr (Acts 7:54-60), and the killing of James (Acts 12:2). Saul of Tarsus captured men and women and brought them bound to Jerusalem (Acts 9:1-2). Despite the persecution, the early Church continued to expand and won multitudes to Jesus. Everyone understood that involvement with this Jesus must be total and without compromise.

The dedication of these Christians to Jesus was CONCRETE. Their physical lives became the platform upon which God demonstrated their faith. One expression Luke highlighted was the early Church's dedication to God in the selling of their houses and lands. The issue in the lives of Ananias and Sapphira was a condition of the heart (Acts 5:4), but the catalyst for the condition was money (Acts 5:3). Complete loyalty to Jesus engages the materialistic life. That firm commitment interacts with every physical activity. Because of the total dedication of the early church to Jesus, no one said that any of the things he possessed was his own (Acts 4:32).

COMPASSION dominated the Christian's relationship with others. While compassion is a condition of the heart, we express it in the physical realm. The early church expressed the sincere desire to help those among them who had need. Luke showed the extent of this compassion by saying, ***"Nor was there anyone among them who lacked"*** (Acts 4:34). Seven men ***"of good reputation, full of the Holy Spirit and wisdom"*** were appointed by the early church to oversee the daily distribution (Acts 6:3). Their complete dedication to Jesus gave them God's compassionate heart for others.

We see the same completeness in their COMMUNICATION. The driving force of the Christian's heart is the proclamation of the Gospel. Everyone must know the truth about Jesus. Luke described the early Church's proclamation as bold (Acts 4:31), with great power (Acts 4:33), and with signs and wonders (Acts 5:12). The persecution from the Sanhedrin was because of their proclamation. The threat was ***"not to speak at all nor teach in the name of Jesus"*** (Acts 4:18). The leaders of Israel were not upset that they were preaching, but that their preaching focused on Jesus. The Sanhedrin would not tolerate such dedication and complete focus on the resurrected Lord. However, Peter's response was, ***"For we cannot but speak the things which we have seen and heard"*** (Acts 4:20).

Part One: The Agreed Resolve Continued

The Christian's commitment to Jesus was not merely a belief system, but their belief engulfed them! They had to share Jesus with everyone they met. The Person of Jesus dominated every area of their lives.

We have to understand that the Good News about Jesus must engage every area of life, or we are not Christian. Christianity is never half-hearted, part-time, or lukewarm. A lukewarm Christian is like dry water. Listen to the words Jesus declared to the Church. ***"I know your works, that you are neither cold nor hot. I could wish you were cold or hot. So then, because you are lukewarm, and neither cold nor hot, I will vomit you out of My mouth"*** (Revelation 3:15-16). Jesus will not tolerate lukewarmness. The Bible does not have a standard of knowledge we must achieve to be called Christian. The New Testament does not list a renewed ten commandments for Christianity. We no longer have to meet religious activities such as sacrifices, ceremonies, or mechanical participation to be Christian. The beginning and ending steps to become Christian, and to remain a Christian, are the same. We are to be complete. Jesus said, ***"'You shall love the Lord your God with all your heart, with all your soul, and with all your mind.' This is the first and great commandment. And the second is like it: 'You shall love your neighbor as yourself.' On these two commandments hang all the Law and the Prophets"*** (Matthew 22:37-40). Can anyone read this and conclude that God accepts partial surrender? We must focus entirely on Jesus!

Luke's concern was that we understand the passionate state of the early Church. They were wholly committed to Jesus. Everything in their lives was controlled by Him, even their safety. These believers never wavered in their response to good or evil, and their love for Jesus took dominance over their financial security. Luke writes to convince us of this by presenting the two practical illustrations in our study, one positive (Acts 4:36-37) and one negative (Acts 5:1-11). Each illustration informs us of the necessity of a complete response to Jesus. Why is a radical response necessary? Why does Christianity demand totality?

Nature of the Relationship

Christianity is a relationship with Jesus. You must understand this truth completely! You are not a Christian because of what you do, but because of whose you are! If we view Christianity as things we do, we will allow "better" and "worse" Christians. You might say, "I am not the best Christian in the world, but I am Christian." That statement comes from a person who thinks they are Christian because of the things they do or not do. Those persons determine their Christianity by how much of the list they achieve. Christianity is not activities to do but a relationship with Jesus!

Relationships vary in levels and degrees of intimacy. However, God established the criteria of Christian relationship by His nature. John wrote, **"This is the message which we have heard from Him and declare to you, that God is light and in Him is no darkness at all"** (1 John 1:5). Light is the nature of God, not an activity or something He created. John did not propose two opposite forces - light and darkness. In the context of the verse, darkness is merely the absence of light. In other words, within the nature and character of God, light is never absent. In God, there is **"no"** (meaning "not") darkness **"at all"** (in the Greek language, a compound word - "not" and "one," means "no one," "nothing," or "not at all."). Darkness has no place in a relationship between God and me. If darkness is the absence of light, there is no place in the relationship where God is not! The relationship is complete!

The early Church held Ananias and Sapphira in high esteem. Luke included them in the description of the believers and considered them to be a part of everything. They felt the leadership of the Holy Spirit in sharing their finances for the needs of others. This couple was a part of this body of believers, but we cannot measure their relationship with Jesus by their outward actions. Their hearts were incomplete, and that incompleteness was darkness, which is the absence of light, the nature of God. When a person has a vacancy of Jesus' presence, something else will fill that hole. ***But Peter said, "Ananias, why has Satan filled your heart to lie to the Holy Spirit and keep back part of the price of the land for yourself? While it remained, was it not your own? And after it was sold, was it not in your own control? Why have you conceived this thing in your heart? You have not lied to men but to God"*** (Acts 5:3-4). Satan loves the heart that has an absence of light. The problem was in Ananias' heart. The problem was not his action but the incompleteness of his heart.

You cannot have a relationship with Jesus and be half-hearted. When we allow God to merge our helpless nature with God's Divine nature, He brings completeness in the fusion, creating a new creature. This relationship requires both God and I abandon ourselves, surrendering totally to each other. If God's love is complete for you, your love must be complete for Him. If He opens Himself to you, you must open yourself to Him. The nature of this relationship demands unreserved commitment.

Nature of the Reality

When we understand the merger of the relationship, we will see the reality of this intimacy. Ananias and Sapphira were involved in a business transaction. Peter said they controlled the land they owned, and the proceeds belonged to them. They could do whatever they wished with their profits. A problem arose when they allowed deceit into their spiritual relationship. It seems Ananias and Sapphira viewed their relationship with God only in the physical. They were physically involved in the general beliefs of the church, the activities of fellowship and worship, and wanted inclusion in the generous giving. However, they forgot that the merger in the spiritual relationship is with One who knows everything. It is not that God knows everything because He is omniscient. He participates in the activities with the one with whom He merges.

In a discussion about sexual immorality, Paul said, ***"Do you not know that your bodies are members of Christ? Shall I then take the members of Christ and make them members of a harlot? Certainly not! Or do you not know that he who is joined to a harlot is one body with her? For 'the two,' He says, 'shall become one flesh.' But he who is joined to the Lord is one spirit with Him"*** (1 Corinthians 6:15-17). The Kingdom person is beyond one with a particular belief system. This person is not one who participates in certain acceptable activities. The essence of Christianity is a merger with the Trinity God!

Luke used the terminology, ***"filled with the Holy Spirit"*** (Acts 4:8, 31). The Greek word "pimplemi," translated ***"filled,"*** regarding a person, means to be wholly imbued, affected, influenced with, or by something. John used "pimplemi" to describe the action of the soldiers at the cross. ***"Now a vessel full of sour wine was sitting there; and they filled*** (pimplemi) ***a sponge with sour wine, put it on hyssop, and put it to His mouth"*** (John 19:29). This Greek word is a saturation concept. You cannot partially fill a sponge. The substance you place the sponge in will permeate its entirety. It will be complete!

Peter confronted Ananias with the deception. Ananias was not merged with Jesus because ***"Satan filled"*** his heart to lie to the Holy Spirit (Acts 5:3). Peter used the Greek word "pleroo," which is the idea of a container being filled completely. Ananias was not merged, under the control of, or influenced by the Spirit of Jesus, but by Satan. This filling is focused on the **"heart,"** the core of the spiritual life. It is the determining factor of all that happens throughout the person. The demonic nature of self-centeredness completely saturated the heart of Ananias and influenced his physical actions. A merger with Satan allows him to compartmentalize our lives. Its control system affects each compartment. In other words, the financial culture influences my finances, my cultural pleasures control physical habits and activities, and the norms of my world dictate my sexuality. None of this is true in the spiritual realm if I wholly merge with Jesus. When I am under the control of Jesus' Lordship, He will not delegate anything to compartments in my life. Jesus is Lord of all, or He is not Lord at all! In the Sermon on the Mount, Jesus said, **"No one can serve two masters; for either he will hate the one and love the other, or else he will be loyal to the one and despise the other. You cannot serve God and mammon"** (Matthew 6:24).

We cannot have a relationship with Jesus unless we merge with Him in total abandon. Intimacy and oneness with Jesus only come with total trust, total surrender, and total reliance. There are no half Christians, no partial disciples, or somewhat spiritual Christian people. The relationship with Jesus demands a total commitment of the heart, which brings every area of life under the control of His Lordship!

Nature of the Results

Luke presents two illustrations to give us a visual picture of the complete Christian experience. Barnabas, Son of Encouragement (Acts 4:36-37), is the first illustration. Barnabas was the image of life, fulfillment, and destiny, mentioned twenty-three times in the Book of Acts. He was a vital part of the missionary endeavors of the early Church, fulfilling the destiny God created for him. He played a crucial role in shaping and molding the life of the Apostle Paul. None of this could have happened in his life if he were not merged with the Divine nature and completely abandoned to Jesus.

In contrast to the positive illustration of Barnabas, Luke gives the negative illustration of Ananias and Sapphira (Acts 5:1-11). Luke gives no information about the details of their lives, but he indicates they were heavily involved in the functions of the early Church. Others looked on them as "good people," without judgment or suspicions about their Christian lives. The fact that they sold their property and made a donation to the ministry indicates some level of commitment. However, they were not abandoned to Jesus, leaving their merger incomplete. This incompleteness ended in, ***"Then Ananias, hearing these words, fell down and breathed his last"*** (Acts 5:5).

Please do not focus merely on the physical death of Ananias. His spiritual death proceeded his physical death. Satan filled Ananias' heart (Acts 5:3). Everything that happens in the spiritual realm displays itself in the physical. Ananias and Sapphira did not fulfill God's destiny for their lives. They eliminated themselves from God's plan to evangelize their world because they were not completely committed. Their lack of commitment removed them from the scene. They may have served the church on earth for a few years, but because they did not merge with God in abandonment, that affected their eternal lives. When we do not abandon our lives to Jesus, absolute death is our outcome. No one survives the condition of half-hearted or lukewarm! Get in or get out is the cry of the Christian faith!

Acts 5:1-2

EMBEZZLEMENT

"But a certain man named Ananias, with Sapphira his wife, sold a possession. And he kept back part of the proceeds, his wife also being aware of it, and brought a certain part and laid it at the apostles' feet"
(Acts 5:1-2).

Joshua, the leader of Israel, responsible for getting the people into the promised land, led the first encounter into victory. The guiding hand of Jehovah conquered Jericho. Joshua and his army arose early each morning for seven days and marched around the city seven times. On the seventh day, the priests blew their trumpets, and the people shouted simultaneously. The walls of Jericho fell flat, and Israel marched into the city (Joshua 6).

From Jericho, Joshua sent spies to their second challenge, the city of Ai. The report from the spies was encouraging. Ai was a small city, and the Israelites would not need their entire force to conquer it. However, their attack was a disaster. The small force in the town of Ai utterly defeated the army of Israel. ***"Then Joshua tore his clothes, and fell to the earth on his face before the ark of the Lord until evening, he and the elders of Israel; and they put dust on their heads"*** (Joshua 7:6). They discovered that someone had sinned during the battle of

Jericho. Achan confessed, *"When I saw among the spoils a beautiful Babylonian garment, two hundred shekels of silver, and a wedge of gold weighing fifty shekels, I coveted them and took them"* (Joshua 7:21). Stoning was the penalty for disobedience; therefore, the people stoned Achan, his family, and sheep, and burned all his possessions.

"But the children of Israel committed a trespass regarding the accursed things, for Achan the son of Carmi, the son of Zabdi, the son of Zerah, of the tribe of Judah, took of the accursed things" (Joshua 7:1). We must understand the words chosen to describe this tragic event. The writer used the Greek word "nosphizomai," translated *"took of the accursed things,"* which is used often in the Septuagint, the Greek translation of the Old Testament originally written in Hebrew. But "nosphizomai," used only three times in the New Testament, was used by Luke twice in the story of Ananias and Sapphire (Acts 5:1-11). The underlying meaning of "nosphizomai" is "to embezzle, keep back something, which belongs to another," precisely what Achan did. Joshua commanded the people not to take any spoils from Jericho's conquest, calling the spoils *"the accursed things"* (Joshua 6:17-19). All silver, gold, and bronze vessels and iron were dedicated to God and brought into the treasury of the Lord. Achan had stolen or embezzled from the Lord.

The writer of the story also says that Israel *"committed a trespass regarding the accursed things,"* using the Hebrew word "m'l." It carries the idea of someone acting unfaithfully, used to describe a wife's adultery (Numbers 5:12-13). The trespass is not a trite or superficial mistake, because this action embodies deep betrayal and rebellion, taking everything holy in God's sight and treating it like trash. There are no words to describe further the evil they committed. This sin by Achan is comparable to the sin of Ananias and Sapphire.

Luke uses the Greek word "nosphizomai" to describe the

sin of Ananias and Sapphira. This couple sold their land. ***"And he*** (Ananias) ***kept back part of the proceeds*** (nosphizomai), ***his wife also being aware of it, and brought a certain part and laid it at the apostle's feet. But Peter said, 'Ananias, why has Satan filled your heart to lie to the Holy Spirit and keep back part*** (nosphizomai) ***of the price of the land for yourself'"*** (Acts 5:2, 3)? Luke used this word twice in our passage, and it means "to embezzle, keep back something which belongs to another." The consequence of Ananias and Sapphira's sin would end the same as Achan's sin.

We must understand this spiritual concept. In spiritual experience, our physical possessions are involved. God designed the physical as the platform on which the spiritual demonstrates itself. Nothing is exclusive to the physical or the spiritual because of the interaction between the two. The physical actions of my life will always reveal my spiritual condition. That revelation is how I know who I am.

Let us investigate this concept of the physical revealing the spiritual as presented in our story.

Possession

The central issue of embezzlement is ownership. We do not embezzle from ourselves. Peter addressed this issue in his remarks to Ananias. ***"While it remained, was it not your own? And after it was sold, was it not in your own control"*** (Acts 5:4)? These questions require the obvious positive answer. When Ananias and Sapphira owned their land, they could do with it as they pleased without the guilt of embezzlement. Even after they sold the property they possessed the sale price. They sinned when they shifted ownership of the land to Jesus but kept some of the selling price for themselves; that is embezzlement.

Ananias and Sapphire were in good standing with the church. They belonged to a group of people who were of *"one heart and one soul"* (Acts 4:32). We understand the context of their possessions for *"neither did anyone say that any of the things he possessed was his own but they had all things in common"* (Acts 4:32). Ananias and Sapphire were professed members of this body of believers. Ananias brought the money from the sale of their land and proposed that the amount given was the selling price, but it was not. They proposed that the land belonged to the Lord, therefore, the total proceeds belonged to the Lord. They stole or embezzled from funds that were not theirs.

Our passage of study faces us with the concept of God's call to total surrender and one hundred percent commitment. The early church believed that God is a Tyrant (Acts 4:24), in a positive, not negative, sense. *"Lord, You are God, who made heaven and earth and the sea, and all that is in them"* (Acts 4:24). If you are a Christian, this Creator Tyrant will be Lord of your life. All of you will be His! A Christian cannot partially surrender, or divide his heart into compartments, some for himself and some for God. There is only one category of Christian, the person whose destiny, life, and physical possessions belong to the sovereign Christ. If you deviate from complete surrender, you are an embezzler.

Ananias and Sapphira isolated their hearts to their possessions. When discussing surrender, one issue consistently appears. Someone will always say, "I surrender something to Jesus, but then I take it back. How can I continually surrender it to Him?" The person asking this question suffers from the Ananias and Sapphire syndrome, which is embezzlement. When you commit your life to Jesus, it is no longer yours. You do not influence it; you do not own it or have control over it. If you steal it back from God, you are a thief! You have committed spiritual adultery and cheated on Jesus.

What if we do not surrender all to Jesus? Then we are not Christians, which is the primary idea of this passage. A human must involve all his being to merge with the Divine. God must possess everything to flow His resource through human personality. The Gospel must engage the entire life, or the person is not Christian. The Scriptures never present Christianity as half-hearted, part-time, or lukewarm. According to the Bible, there is no standard of knowledge we must achieve to be called Christian. There are no religious sacrifices, ceremonies, or mechanical actions to carry out to be Christian. Jesus calls us to completeness. ***"You shall love the Lord your God with all your heart, with all your soul, and with all your mind"*** (Matthew 22:37). Christianity is all-inclusive!

Listen again to the admonition of the Apostle Paul. ***"Or do you not know that your body is the temple of the Holy Spirit who is in you, whom you have from God, and you are not your own"*** (1 Corinthians 6:19)? The members of my flesh are not mine and have no right to dominate my activities. My physical drives belong to God, and I must not embezzle them from God for self-satisfaction. If I do so, I am stealing from the Divine. On Pentecost Day, the disciples received the fullness of the Holy Spirit. The Spirit did not fill a specific area but saturated their entire beings with the presence of Jesus. This merger with God is so complete that we are considered a new creature (2 Corinthians 5:17).

Private

Peter accused Ananias of lying to the Holy Spirit. "To lie," by its definition, is hiding the truth from someone. Such action paints a picture of the heart of sin. Sin wants to be done in secret, desiring darkness, which is in every activity and intent of sin. On the internet, it is the dark web; in the city, it is dark allies. Sin cannot tolerate the light. *"And this is the condemnation, that the light has come into the world, and men loved darkness rather than light, because their deeds were evil. For everyone practicing evil hates the light and does not come to the light, lest his deeds should be exposed"* (John 3:19-20).

Achan sinned when he took the valuable clothing, silver, and gold, and buried it in his tent. He did not wear the garments proudly but hid them. He did not pay his bills to debt-free but hid the money for fear of exposure. Ananias did not declare his cleverness in acquiring extra money; he kept it in secret. How ridiculous was Ananias to embezzle from God and think He would not know? How could Achan believe God would not recognize his embezzlement and reveal it to Israel? Yet, this is a consistent pattern in our lives. Consider this passage in Hebrews. *"For the word of God is living and powerful, and sharper than any two-edged sword, piercing even the division of soul and spirit, and of joints and marrow, and is a discerner of the thoughts and intents of the heart. And there is no creature hidden from His sight, but all things are naked and open to the eyes of Him to whom we must give account"* (Hebrews 4:12-13). Notice that the *"word of God"* refers to *"His"* and *"Him."* The Word of God (logos) is the living Christ to whom all things are known! Is it not foolish to think that what we do not see in the physical world is also hidden in the spiritual?

The foolishness of thinking God does not know removes all excuses and rationalizations. A father, excusing himself, was quick to say, "What I do is my private business." He believed his secret sin involved only him and was acceptable, thinking no one else was affected. Yet, he did not hide his sin. His sin exposed his wife and children to the evil he allowed in his home, which also affected his extended family and neighbors.

Part One: The Agreed Resolve Continued

Achan's secret sin caused Israel's defeat at Ai. Ananias and Sapphira's secret sin affected the witness of the early Church to their community.

The Christian lives in the fullness of Christ's Spirit, indwelling in a relationship of total openness. The merger of my mind, emotions, and will with God's can only exist without secrets. He is involved in all my activities, with repentance as the first call to become a Christian (Acts 2:37-38). We define repentance as "giving up a former thought to embrace a new thought." The former thought is my secret sin, where I determine all my thoughts, actions, and attitudes. The new thought is my openness to Jesus, now involving Him in every transaction of my life. We have no secrets!

Purpose

Ananias and Sapphira said they had given all the proceeds from the sale to God, but they kept some of it for themselves. Achan kept some of the spoils from Jericho and hid them in his tent. In each instance, the money was not the issue. Did Ananias and Sapphira's embezzlement deprive God of His needed funding? Did God need the silver and gold Achan embezzled? Was the sin of Ananias, Sapphira, and Achan from greed, embezzlement, unfaithfulness, or lying? We must understand the nature of all sinful deeds!

The deeds of sin are a symptom of sin's nature. It is easy to focus on the activity and miss the heart of the matter. The deed cannot define sin, and the commission of the deed is not what places it in the category of sinfulness. If the act determined the deed as a sin, we could make a list of sinful deeds and avoid them. If I follow the list, I am free from sin. But the issue of sin is the nature of sin; the nature of sin is self-centered and self-sovereign. When this nature drives the deed, it is a sin. The best deed on our best day could be our most sinful act. The deed action is not the problem; the problem is the nature or motive causing the action.

Forgiveness is a major theme of the Gospels. John wrote, ***"If we confess our sins, He is faithful and just to forgive us our sins and to cleanse us from all unrighteousness"*** (1 John 1:9). Jesus is the provision for the forgiveness of all sin. I would never belittle or demean the wonder of God's forgiveness. His forgiveness is the core of His heart of love, which required His amazing sacrifice. God's forgiveness of sin is constant, and I should never question it.

The second part of the verse is just as important. Jesus wants ***"to cleanse us from all unrighteousness."*** This cleansing includes the profound, intertwined, selfishness that influences all my being's attitudes and actions. Forgiveness becomes trite and superficial if God does not cleanse me. Paul referred to this cleansing as crucifixion or death. ***"And those who are Christ's have crucified the flesh with its passions and desires"*** (Galatians 5:24). Forgiveness does not resolve the nature of sin. This nature must die. Paul said this about himself, ***"I have been crucified with Christ; it is no longer I who live, but Christ lives in me; and the life which I now live in the flesh I live by faith in the Son of God, who loved me and gave Himself for me"*** (Galatians 2:20).

The problem in the hearts of Ananias and Sapphira was the self-centered nature of sin, and their embezzlement resulted from this nature. Self-centeredness is a destructive nature, and Ananias and Sapphira died as a result. Self desperately tries to win and save, but always loses and destroys. Jesus said. ***"For whoever desires to save his life will lose it, but whoever loses his life for My sake will find it"*** (Matthew 16:25). Consider the depth of such a statement! The pattern of our culture is the opposite of Jesus' declaration. We think we must fight for ourselves to save our lives, to guard, defend, and protect

Part One: The Agreed Resolve Continued

to survive in our world. BUT when Jesus is involved, everything changes. When we lose our lives to the One who holds our destiny, then we begin to live.

The death of Ananias and Sapphire was not simply embezzlement or an act of sin. It was not about a simple lie that God could forgive. Amid their exposure to the fullness of the Spirit and merging with God's nature, they chose to live for themselves. No one can survive such a destructive decision. God calls us to examine ourselves. What is the purpose of my life? Do my selfish ambitions primarily drive me? There must be completeness in my surrender to Christ. I cannot merely surrender things or issues to Him; He must possess me!

Acts 5:3

THE GREAT WAR

"But Peter said, Ananias, why has Satan filled your heart to lie to the Holy Spirit and keep back part of the price of the land for yourself"
(Acts 5:1-2).

    In our previous studies in the Book of Acts, we discovered this writing is volume two of one book written by Luke. Volume one is the Gospel of Luke portraying the life of Christ. He does not present two themes, but each volume introduces one concept. If we do not continually understand and view all circumstances in light of this concept, all is lost! Luke's idea is the essence of God's Spirit filling humanity and pushing back (defeating) the force of evil dominating the world.

    In volume one, God emptied Himself of every advantage He had as God and became a helpless man. He did not give up being God; He surrendered everything that distinguished Him from us. The Spirit of God filled Jesus. Each miracle invaded demonic territory, pushing back and conquering evil forces. Satan's every attack from the wilderness temptation (Luke 4:1-13) to the Garden of Gethsemane (Luke 22:39-46) was a spiritual war raging on a physical stage. Luke presents Jesus as the Conqueror as He ascends to the right hand of the

Father (Luke 24:51). But Jesus did not conquer because He is God (although He is); Jesus conquered because He is a helpless man filled with God! Even then, we might quickly dismiss this victory because He is Jesus. Therefore, Luke presents to us the disciples, mean and hateful, just like us. But then God filled them with the same Spirit He filled Jesus (Acts 2:1-4). The same spiritual conflict that confronted Jesus we now see in the lives of the early Church.

The lame beggar's healing miracle at the Gate Beautiful stimulated a massive gathering in the temple. As Peter addressed this audience, he greatly disturbed the leaders of Israel (Acts 4:2). These leaders interrogated Peter and John in a courtroom. The apostles' speaking about Jesus, and their constant focus on Him, disturbed the Sanhedrin. This threat began the persecution of the early Church and scattered them from Jerusalem into their known world. Amid these dire circumstances, **"the place where they were assembled together was shaken; and they were all filled with the Holy Spirit"** (Acts 4:31). In our study of Ananias and Sapphire, Luke portrays the opposite picture. **"Satan filled your heart to lie to the Holy Spirit"** (Acts 5:3).

Luke presents to us the proposition of the Scriptures. We can only rightly understand the story of the human race in light of the two forces operating in this world. Each story in the Scriptures points us back to the cosmic conflict between God's forces and the Devil and his forces, the battle from the beginning of Genesis to the end of Revelation! But this is not just a theory or historical presentation. What happens to us and our world depends solely on which of these two powers dominate us. There is a simplicity to the truth of life. There is no philosophy to master or discipline to achieve. Our hearts are either filled by Satan or the Holy Spirit.

The tragedy for us is that we tend to live our lives, never realizing this conflict. In my first year in evangelism, I worked part-time as a caseworker for the social welfare department in our county. I was dismayed by their approach to the problems we faced. The leaders of the program repeatedly stated that the environment was the problem. If we could physically improve the living environment of those we worked with, the destructive activities of evil would cease. They did not recognize the cosmic war in the spiritual realm. They persisted in treating the human problem in terms of their understanding, They considered the war a social problem, and human beings alone were to solve it. However, far from being solved, the troubles of the world grow worse. It is a spiritual problem, a gigantic battle between the power of God and Satan's power. Again, we face this reality in the story of Ananias and Sapphire. What did the early Church believe?

Satan

Peter believed the spiritual battle was not influence or an attitude, not merely a force in the universe. He thought the conflict resulted from a living entity or individual called "Satan." Peter turned to Ananias and said, *"Ananias, why has Satan filled your heart to lie to the Holy Spirit and keep back part of the price of the land for yourself"* (Acts 5:3)? Luke reported that the early Church *"continued steadfastly in the apostles' doctrine and fellowship"* (Acts 2:42). The teaching and doctrine of the early Church contained the real existence of Satan.

If anyone was aware of this reality, it was Jesus. The Holy Spirit filled Jesus and led Him into the wilderness (Luke 4:1), where the Devil tempted Him for forty days. The spiritual battle was so encompassing that Jesus forgot about food. Addressing the Devil, Jesus said, *"Get behind Me, Satan"* (Luke 4:8)! The physical and spiritual involvement of this temptation was beyond measure, and convincing Jesus that Satan was an attitude in our world was not possible. Satan was a mastermind, plotting, and controlling an aggressive war against God.

Satan is a legal name referring to an "accuser," "slanderer," "calumniator," or "adversary" in court. Three times in the Old Testament, Satan appeared in the heavenly court as a supernatural accuser of humankind. Satan stood at God's right hand to accuse Joshua, the High Priest, but God spurned his accusation (Zechariah 3:1-10). In Job, Satan, before God and among the heavenly council, functioned as more than an accuser and questioned the sincerity of Job's righteousness. God gave Satan control over sickness, death, and nature to test Job (Job 1-2).

According to the Scriptures, the Devil is a real person with distinct personality traits. The Apostle Paul attributed the Devil with intelligence (2 Corinthians 11:3). Elsewhere in the Scriptures, the writers ascribe emotional desire (2 Timothy 3:6), jealousy (Job 1:8-9), hatred (1 Peter 5:8), anger (Revelation 12:12), and will, to the Devil. Luke and John the Revelator said the Devil commands (Luke 4:3, 9) and leads rebellions (Revelation 12:1-3). From the first chapter in the Bible, the author describes Satan as a personal enemy of God and a deceiver of humans (Genesis 3:1). 19 out of 27 New Testament books refer to Satan (and four more to demons). In the Gospels, Jesus believed in a real and personal Satan, making 25 of the 29 references to Satan.

Before you run away in fear, let me remind you that Satan is a created being, a fallen angel. Jesus saw Satan *"fall like lightning from heaven"* (Luke 10:18). God has already judged Satan (John 16:11), and, at the Last Judgement, Satan, and all those who belong to him, will depart into the eternal fire (Matthew 25:41). Jude gave a brief allusion to the fall of the angels (Jude 1:6), but John gave a fuller account of this fall in the Book of Revelation (12:7-9). John said, *"Then I saw an angel of the Lord coming down from heaven, having the key to the bottomless pit and a great chain in his hand. He laid hold of the dragon, that serpent of old, who is the Devil and Satan, and bound him for a thousand years; and he cast him into the bottomless pit, and shut him up and set a seal on him"* (Revelation 20:1-3).

Spirit of Jesus

However, there is another important reality in our passage! Peter asked, *"Ananias, why has Satan filled your heart to lie to the Holy Spirit"* (Acts 5:3)? While Satan was involved, do not overlook the overarching presence of the Holy Spirit. As sure as Satan is a real fallen angel, so the Holy Spirit is real, the third Person of the Trinity. The Scriptures do not use the word "Trinity," but the concept is everywhere. In the Old Testament, each time "God" is used, it is a translation of the Hebrew word "Elohim," which is always plural. In the creation story, God said, *"Let Us make man in Our image"* (Genesis 1:26). When we see the Old Testament revealed in the New Testament, the picture of the Father, Son, and Holy Spirit becomes apparent. Each Person of the Trinity is operational in personality, fulfilling a role in the redemption of fallen man.

God's speech is powerful, and His creative word has personality form. This creative person is Jesus, the Word (John 1:1). But imagine Jesus, the Word, having such a commanding presence that He takes the personality form of the Holy Spirit, the Spirit of Jesus. When we receive the Spirit of Jesus, we become Christian (Galatians 3:2-3). When God baptizes us with the Holy Spirit, we become a member of the body of Christ (1 Corinthians 12:13). If we do not *"have the Spirit of Christ,"* we do not belong to Jesus, and we are not a Christian (Romans 8:9). Only when the Spirit of Jesus indwells, us do we become sons of God, and we can call on

God as Father (Romans 8:14-17). The Divine seal bonding God and the believer is now the Spirit of Jesus, not circumcision or baptism (2 Corinthians 1:22; Ephesians 1:13-14).

Therefore, the Holy Spirit is the Spirit of Jesus (Acts 16:7; Romans 8:9; Galatians 4:6; Philippians 1:19; 1 Peter 1:11)! How can we recognize the voice of the Spirit? The Holy Spirit always bears witness to Jesus (John 15:26; 16:13-14; Acts 5:32; 1 Corinthians 12:3; 1 John 4:2; 5:7-8; Revelations 19:10). The Holy Spirit filled and empowered Jesus in humanity. We must recognize the Spirit as the Spirit of sonship. It is this Spirit who inspires the same lifestyle of the cross and the same relationship with God as Father that Jesus enjoyed (Romans 8:15-17; Galatians 4:6-7). The Holy Spirit transforms us into the image of God and makes us like Jesus (2 Corinthians 3:18), meaning when we receive the Spirit of Jesus, we experience Christ's crucifixion, as well as His resurrection (Romans 8:17; 2 Corinthians 4:7-12, 16-18, Galatians 2:20; Philippians 3:10-11). The demonstration of Christ's Spirit through me is not that He transforms my physical weakness, but instead reveals His power in my weakness; it is life through death (2 Corinthians 12:9-10). To know the Spirit is to experience Jesus (John 14:16-28). No one can know Jesus apart from the Spirit, and no one can experience the Spirit without knowing Jesus' character and lifestyle. That relationship is what Ananias missed!

Stage

We must understand that our passage (Acts 5:1-11) is a part of the last section of chapter four. Luke declares the state of the Church, not a new subject in the story of Ananias and Sapphira. The early Church was mostly confined to Jerusalem and was under the threat of persecution. How healthy is a church in such a situation? Luke's report says the condition of the Church was much the same as it was after Pentecost (Acts 2:40-47). He makes a strong emphasis on materialism, the physical world. He does not measure the Church's strength in terms of miracles, numbers, or buildings, but reveals the depth of their spiritual lives on the stage of materialism.

"Now the multitude of those who believed were of one heart and one soul; neither did anyone say that any of the things he possessed was his own" (Acts 4:32). Luke continued, saying this was more than a general attitude among the early Church members. ***"Nor was there anyone among them who lacked; for all who were possessors of lands or houses sold them, and brought the proceeds of the things that were sold"*** (Acts 4:34). He gave a positive illustration (Acts 4:36-37) about Barnabas, a "Son of Encouragement," who displayed his spiritual life through his attitude about his materialism. Ananias and Sapphire were Luke's negative illustration of the same (Acts 5:1-11).

God intimately linked the spiritual world with the physical world. The spiritual world does not eliminate or discount the physical world; instead, the spiritual always displays itself on the physical stage. The cross of Jesus is the convincing demonstration of this truth! While the spiritual war raged in the heavenly realms, God made it visible through Christ's suffering and bleeding. What you and I are inward, we will reveal outwardly. A sinful act must stimulate us to investigate our spiritual lives. Ananias and Sapphire embezzled the funds from the sale of their property. In this physical activity, they displayed the condition of their inner hearts.

Our physical actions display our hearts. The physical practices and accepted norms in our society are the physical manifestations of our community's spiritual condition. The low moral standards of today's society speak to the decay in our spiritual lives. It is past time that we get concerned about this!

Script

Peter asked, ***"Ananias, why has Satan filled your heart to lie to the Holy Spirit and keep back part of the price of the land for yourself"*** (Acts 5:3)? Every movie or play has a script to describe the action, conversations, and emotions the actors will play out in the film or drama. In the real-life event of Ananias and Sapphire, Satan wrote the script in their hearts, and he played it on the physical stage of their lives.

Peter used the Greek word "pleroo," the same Greek word used for the Holy Spirit filling the believers at Pentecost (Acts 2:2). "Pleroo" paints the picture of a filled container, used in the sense of prophecy. A prophecy in the Old Testament was completed or fulfilled in an event in the New Testament. At Pentecost, the believer was the container, and the content filling the container was the Holy Spirit. Now the reverse happened in Ananias and Sapphira.

The prophet Jeremiah foretold of Pentecost, speaking of it as a new covenant. God said, ***"But this is the covenant that I will make with the house of Israel after those days, says the Lord: I will put my law in their minds, and write it on their hearts; and I will be their God, and they shall be My people"*** (Jeremiah 31:33). The law of God would no longer be on tablets of stone but would be the script of the heart. It would describe the reactions, emotions, attitudes, and actions of the physical, displayed as the drama unfolds. The script of the heart is the director of physical activities.

Peter proposed that Satan was the author and director of the script he placed in the hearts of Ananias and Sapphire. Therefore, we see the great war again, not about one act of embezzlement, or one deceitful lie, but it is about our response and allegiance to Jesus. Are we going to come under His influence? Will we allow Him to govern us by His direction?

Who is going to write the script in our hearts for our lives? Each one of us has seen enough of the fulfilled script to know how the drama ends. Satan's script is always destruction. We see it in our society, but we also know it in our lives. The Scriptures tell us how our script will end, which is the message of our passage.

On the one hand, ***"they were all filled with the Holy Spirit, and they spoke the word of God with boldness"*** (Acts 4:31). On the other hand, ***"Satan filled your heart to lie to the Holy Spirit"*** (Acts 5:3). The revelation of death and destruction is always in the drama.

God gives you a challenge and a call for your life. You must choose a side because you cannot dwell in both! Ananias and Sapphire tried and failed because they did not get the message of total surrender. Who is filling your heart?

Acts 5:3

WHAT HAPPENED?

"But Peter said, Ananias, why has Satan filled your heart to lie to the Holy Spirit and keep back part of the price of the land for yourself" (Acts 5:3).

The most common question asked by humanity is, "Why?" We ask "why" of each other and do not fear to ask it of God. The human mind cannot tolerate life's circumstances without knowing the reason. We can suffer pain and discomfort if it comes with a purpose. A mother embraces the pain of childbirth because she knows it brings her baby. To know God, He calls us to go beyond understanding and reason; He calls us to faith! Faith is invoking God's activity instead of ours. When we live under His influence, He requires us to trust Him even though we do not understand His actions, the "why." "**And we know that all things work together for good to those who love God, to those who are the called according to His purpose**" (Romans 8:28). Trust without knowing "why" makes this Scripture real in our lives.

Peter found the issue of "why" more difficult in human relationships. What was the rhyme or reason for the embezzlement and lies of Ananias and Sapphira? "***Ananias,*** *why has Satan filled your heart?" "Ananias, why* did you think *to lie to the Holy Spirit? "Ananias, why* did you embezzle money *and keep part of the price of the land for yourself?" "Why have you conceived this thing in your heart?"* Who can believe these actions?

    Peter's amazement is somewhat embarrassing in light of his denial of Christ three times. Why did Peter follow afar when they led Jesus to the high priest's house (Luke 22:54)? Why was Peter offended when a servant girl recognized him as a disciple (Luke 22:56-57)? Why did Peter boldly declare he did not know Jesus (Luke 22:57)? Later, someone else said he was a disciple, yet he denied that also. Peter failed a second chance to embrace the truth! An hour later, another person confidently affirmed Peter as a disciple because he was a Galilean (Luke 22:59). Why did Peter continue to deny when presented with this third opportunity to stand with Jesus (Luke 22:60)?

    Perhaps Peter's response to Ananias was not so surprising after all. He possibly identified with a heart that had lost its way. Peter surely remembered the crowing of the rooster Jesus used to confront him with the truth of his denial (Luke 22:60). How could Peter forget Jesus' face of compassion and forgiveness looking at Him (Luke 22:61)? Was Peter the rooster making Ananias aware of his sin?

    We should not condemn Peter, Ananias, or Sapphira without asking ourselves, "why?" Confronting the failures of my past brings me to the question, "why?" Why did I yield to temptation when God has given adequate resources for victory? The spiritual riches of Christ are mine, so why do I live in spiritual poverty? Jesus never fails, so why do I worry about menial things? Jesus has a plan for my life, then why do I stress? Why do I hate when God is love? Jesus has forgiven me; why do I not forgive others or myself? Why do I blame God for the circumstances I created? Why do I live in discontent when Jesus is all I need?

Part One: The Agreed Resolve Continued

In the English language, "why" is an adverb when used as a question. "Why" reaches into the verb of the sentence and directs it. The direction is always the purpose of the verb's action. Ananias and Sapphira radically altered their activity; they embezzled funds that belonged to God. The question of "why" deals with the reason for this change. When we examine the passage, there does not seem to be a systematic answer suggested by Peter, but in the context of the event, we find insight that helps us!

Remember

"Remember" is a consistent call throughout the Scriptures! Joseph was in an overwhelming dilemma. Whatever decision he made would have dire consequences. Mary was with child, and Joseph could not marry her because he would identify with her sin. It appeared she had been unfaithful to him during the betrothal period. Why would she do such a thing when they had such a bright future together? Joseph believed the best solution was to put her away secretly. He knew it was not ideal, but it was the best he could do under the circumstances.

In the night hour, the angel of the Lord appeared to him and said, **"Joseph, son of David, do not be afraid to take to you Mary your wife, for that which is conceived in her is of the Holy Spirit"** (Matthew 1:20). The angel of the Lord called Joseph to remember. How can Joseph conquer the fear seeking to dominate his life? Is there a purpose or reason for what appears to be Mary's unfaithfulness and betrayal? He must remember! He is a son of David!

Matthew began his Gospel with the genealogy of Joseph. He was in the lineage of people who consistently experienced the mighty movement of God's hand. These people knew the PROTECTION of God. Over and over again, God used His resource to rescue them, established a covenant with Abraham pledging His loyalty and protection. As a shepherd and as a soldier, King David knew God's deliverance from wild animals and evil men. Many kings of Israel did not serve God, but God always protected a remnant of His people for redemption. Joseph need not panic because the same God was moving on his behalf. He must remember!

Joseph's lineage was not only protected by God, but they also knew the PROVISION of God. From Egypt's wilderness to Joseph's present moment, God always provided for the Israelites. God provided manna from the sky, quail in the bush, and water from a rock. Why would God bring the Israelites to this moment without resources? God's provisions in the battle against the enemy of Israel were always adequate, and He provided prophets that they might hear. Was this hour for Joseph any different? He needs to remember!

Joseph's lineage knew not only the protection and provision of God but also the PLAN of God. God fulfilled His plan with Joseph, His climax to a forty-two generation genealogy. God worked this plan for two thousand years; will He fail now? Joseph was at the heart of God's plan. What problem could be so big as to overshadow God using Joseph to fulfill His dream? God connected everything as He moved through the history of humanity to redeem the world.

In the story of Ananias and Sapphira's betrayal, Judas comes to mind. Judas was a disciple of Christ for three years, intimately connected to Jesus in the flesh. He was in on the late-night discussions, and God filled him with the power for ministry. He saw the miracles, listened to Jesus' teachings, and witnessed Jesus conquering demons. If you were there with Judas as he held 30 pieces of silver, would you not want to ask, "Why?"

With his knowledge about Judas, Peter asked Ananias and Sapphira, "Why?" The leaders of Israel thrust persecution on the early Church. When threatened never to speak Jesus' name

Part One: The Agreed Resolve Continued

again, theses believers rejoiced in the Trinity God, who was in charge. These people went to prayer and aligned themselves with Jesus' crucifixion. They asked God for boldness to continue to proclaim Jesus' name, and that God increase everything in which they were involved. ***"And when they had prayed, the place where they were assembled together was shaken; and they were all filled with the Holy Spirit, and they spoke the Word of God with boldness"*** (Acts 4:31). Did Ananias and Sapphira forget that moment? They were a part of ***"the multitude of those who believed were of one heart and one soul"*** (Acts 4:32). How could they forget? The group's unity caused ***"neither did anyone say that any of the things he possessed was his own, but they had all things in common"*** (Acts 4:32). Ananias and Sapphira had ministered alongside the disciples. ***"And with great power the apostles gave witness to the resurrection of the Lord Jesus. And great grace was upon them all"*** (Acts 4:33). It is also quite possible that Ananias and Sapphira were present for the resurrection appearances of Jesus.

We do not wonder at Peter's asking, "Why?" Ananias and Sapphira sat under the apostles' daily teachings, and they experienced the signs and wonders of the Holy Spirit. They undoubtedly participated in the witness of the living Christ. We think God transformed them into a personal encounter with Jesus. Barnabas, the Son of Encouragement (Acts 4:36), must have moved them with his generosity. You would think their involvement in the early Church pushed them to godliness and obedience. Why were they so disobedient?

The tricky part of this study comes in its application to our lives. God hounds us with His prevenient grace. God has blessed us with His confrontation of truth, and He has captured our lives, laying the Scriptures in our hands and making it available to our hearts. We have known the power of God in answered prayer. We should be the most persuasive witnesses for the

Gospel in our communities. Why would we be half-hearted or ever deviate from His will?

Response

The nature of the question "why" assumes responsibility for the response. Do you answer the "why" with a list of excuses and rationalizations to justify your response? Your justifications prove you had a choice in the situation. Peter assumed these things about Ananias when he asked, *"Why has Satan filled your heart? Why did you lie to the Holy Spirit? Why did you keep back part of the price of the land for yourself? Why have you conceived this thing in your heart?"* Ananias and Sapphira lied and embezzled in response to Satan.

Peter asked, *"Why have you conceived this thing in your heart"* (Acts 5:4). The Greek word "tithemi" is translated *"have you conceived,"* used in the sense of "to move and set into a certain place or abstract location." Peter's unawareness of the many things involved is at the heart of his question, "Why?" "Tithemi" means to take something and purposely put it in a location. Jesus used this imagery to discuss the new Kingdom as the light of the world. *"Nor do they light a lamp and put* (tithemi) *it under a basket"* (Matthew 5:15). "Tithemi" is in the indicative mood, a simple statement of fact, and the aorist tense focused on the act rather than the time of the action. "Tithemi" is in the middle voice, which speaks to personal preference.

Although we do not know why this sin occurred in the hearts of Ananias and Sapphira, we do know they committed the act. If we had the outlined steps that took them to their place of sin, we might never fall into the same trap. How do you go from the Spirit of Jesus' filling to Satan's filling, from a generous heart to embezzlement? Herein lies the difficulty! There is no formula or steps to follow because it is not relational. Every person is different and must guard their committed relationship with Jesus. If we vary even a little from our love and focus on Christ, our deviation will destroy us.

The story of Ananias and Sapphira is a reminder of the spiritual war in which we live. The answer to "why" was in their lack of total involvement and merger with Jesus. Often there are people committed to a church movement, and while they believe in Jesus, their focus is their importance. They thrive on their good deed of compassionate ministry, but they do not wholly commit and merge with Jesus. The moment Jesus becomes less than a total focus, destruction is inevitable. Ananias and Sapphira took their loyalty and placed (tithemi) it somewhere other than Jesus. Even though it may have seemed logical and sensible to them in their materialistic state, their spiritual world collapsed.

The sin of Ananias and Sapphira holds a strong message for us. We cannot allow anything to distract us from Jesus, not His program, His benefits, His gifts, His organization, or even His doctrine. Jesus must capture us by His person! Any movement away from a focus on Jesus will have drastic consequences.

Results

Our response to Jesus will determine the consequence of our physical and spiritual lives. Luke proclaimed this boldly with two illustrations, contrasting life and death. This contrast may seem extreme, but we must carefully consider it in light of eternity. Luke's difference is between a heart abandoned to Jesus (Barnabas) and hearts partially given (Ananias and Sapphira). Each heart was in the Church fellowship and present at Pentecost when God shook the place they assembled and poured out His Holy Spirit. They all were involved in speaking the Word of God boldly (Acts 4:31). Luke's contrast is not between religious and non-religious, believers and non-believers, or professing Christians and non-professing Christians. We do not see the results in the political aspect of church life, such as serving on the church board. The results are a contrast between life and death!

Luke positively illustrates the first part of the contrast with Barnabas (Acts 4:36-37). He was a Son of Encouragement, who greatly influenced his world. Luke refers to him 23 times in the Book of Acts as a crucial leader in world evangelization. We must not see results concerning his leadership, evangelism, or encouragement, but in his fulfillment of the destiny and unique plan Jesus had for him.

The negative illustration is the contrast of Ananias and Sapphira's lack of abandonment to Jesus. Their actions left them with nothing but death, caused by their half-heartedness. They lost everything they had hoped to gain. They eliminated their spiritual lives and lost all their influence. They never achieved the destiny and plan Jesus had for them. Their destruction and death were immediate.

We might miss the truth of this contrast because when we lie to the Holy Spirit, our physical death is not immediate. We either conclude that we get by, or it does not apply to us. We view this New Testament story as meant for that time or not properly recorded. We miss the power of the contrast and discard the principle of truth. Any hesitation of heart or lack of surrender will erupt in death no matter how well hidden. The hidden things will destroy spiritual influence, home relationships, physical existence, and, most of all, the fulfillment of Jesus' dreams for our lives. Everywhere in the New Testament is the call to abandon our lives to Jesus. There is never room for partial commitment. Jesus calls us to absolute surrender, where spiritual growth happens because we are entirely His. Jesus must be our all in all, and we must focus on Him. In light of His focus of commitment on us, could we do anything else?

Acts 5:3

WHY AM I DEFEATED?

"But Peter said, Ananias, why has Satan filled your heart to lie to the Holy Spirit and keep back part of the price of the land for yourself"
(Acts 5:3).

"Counseling" is a significant business in our society. Whatever your difficulty, there are specialized counselors to meet every need, such as marriage, addiction, abuse, eating disorders, and trauma. The list is inexhaustible. Counseling defined refers to guidance or advice provided to help someone resolve difficulties and decide issues. The heart of such counseling is to discover "why?" How did I get into this trouble? What is the core reason for the decision I made creating my problem? I need to know, "why?"

In a sense, we might consider Peter counseling Ananias, who was not a willing participant. The Holy Spirit used Peter to confront Ananias with "why?" How could Ananias, with his spiritual experience, living in a spiritual atmosphere, decide to disobey? What caused his response? Undoubtedly Ananias saw miracles daily, shared in ministry, and knew God's power in him to affect others. He had embraced the praise and worship of the early Church. Then he was caught in the act of embezzlement. How did he get there?

One of the first things we learn about counseling is that we do not judge or condemn the counselee. The person may have committed a horrible act, but the counselor does not tell them how bad they are but asks questions to lead the person to a conclusion. That is what Peter did with Ananias. Listen to the conversation. ***"Ananias, why has Satan filled your heart to lie to the Holy Spirit and keep back part of the price of the land for yourself? While it remained, was it not your own? And after it was sold, was it not in your control? Why have you conceived this thing in your heart? You have not lied to men but to God"*** (Acts 5:3-4).

The grammar formation of Peter's question is crucial because it gives us the structure of our study. Peter's intension was to bring Ananias to the heart of his problem to find the "why?" Peter's aim was not to blame or cause guilt but to discover the core of Ananias' problem. Peter's concern was not about not receiving the full sale price or the amount of money embezzled. We must not read into the passage a motive of destruction or punishment from Peter. Peter was filled with the Holy Spirit and had the heart of Christ. He wanted to be redemptive to Ananias. Although Ananias' death was immediate, there is no indication in our passage that Peter caused it. In fact, "the revelation of truth" is attached to the end of Ananias. ***"Then Ananias, hearing these words, fell down and breathed his last"*** (Acts 5:6). Ananias' response to the convicting revelation of truth caused his death.

In our sentence, ***"Ananias"*** is a proper name used as a vocative, a noun used for direct address. The actual subject of the sentence is ***"Satan,"*** and the main verb is ***"has filled,"*** a translation of the Greek verb "pleroo." "Pleroo" is the verb used to describe the filling of the Holy Spirit at Pentecost (Acts 2:2). This verb is in the aorist tense, which focuses on the action of the verb, not when the filling occurred. The Greek word "kardia," translated ***"heart,"*** is an accusative, which acts as a direct object. The ***"heart"*** received the action of the filling. "Pseudomai" is the Greek word translated "to lie to," the first infinitive verb in the sentence, giving purpose to the principal verb or the filling of the heart. ***"To keep back part for yourself"*** is translated from the Greek word "nosphizo," also an infinitive verb. "Nosphizo" points to the second purpose of the heart filling. Peter directly addresses Ananias in the form of a question. Satan is the prime mover. He acted on the internal core of Ananias' being. Ananias' sin did not come from without but from within him. The internal movement in Ananias' heart stimulated his physical action, which had a twofold purpose. Ananias' deception enveloped his relationship with others, but ultimately he tried to deceive God. Although Peter's statement was bold, he intended to ask, "why?" Why would Ananias allow Satan to fill him? Why would he respond to Satan's prompting? We need to carefully view Peter's question and apply it to our lives.

Person

In the previous study, we discovered "The Great War" that rages between God's forces and the forces of Satan. We must never lose sight of this real battle. It is easy for us to become enthralled in the physical circumstances of life and forget the spiritual warfare. We see the war between the forces of good and evil fought on the stage of our physical conditions. Peter's question to Ananias presents the proposition of the principal enemy. We do not battle against a mere force or even an attitude. Although the power and attitude of evil are factors in the battle, the problem is Satan. We can easily focus on solving a physical problem or correcting a physical circumstance, but good and evil have enlisted us in the war, an actual reality. Though we blame our responses on the things that surround our lives, that is misplaced blame. We have an enemy!

There is no way we can legitimately ignore the statements of Paul. ***"Finally, my brethren, be strong in the Lord and in the power of His might. Put on the whole armor of God, that you may be able to stand against the wiles of the devil. For we do not wrestle against flesh and blood, but against principalities, against powers, against the rulers of the darkness of this age, against spiritual hosts of wickedness in the heavenly places"*** (Ephesians 6:10-12). That which happened in Ananias' life was not an attitude of greed he should have conquered or a financial need he should have solved. It was not even that he chose the wrong thing. Ananias participated in the war between God and Satan!

When the leaders of Israel threatened the Christians, the battle raged in persecution. Would this change the focus of the early Church as they tried to survive? Would it not be more profitable to create a program where they could embrace Jesus as a side issue? Maybe they could take a less offensive approach to evangelism. As the early Church prospered, the war raged on. Satan will allow anything as long as Jesus is not central. The battle is not about methodology, materialism, theological differences, or organizational structure; the war is between Satan and God! There are only two sides, and we have allegiance to one or the other. Ananias realized the truth as stated by Jesus, ***"No one can serve two masters; for either he will hate the one and love the other, or else he will be loyal to one and despise the other. You cannot serve God and mammon"*** (Matthew 6:24).

Pleroo

Peter highlighted Satan as the prime mover in Ananias' spiritual battle. We discover Satan's role or function in Ananias' war in the main verb ***"has filled,"*** a translation of the Greek word "pleroo." "Pleroo" describes a container and content. Someone places content into the container until it is full, which is the Greek word used consistently for the fulfillment of prophecy. In the beginning of his Gospel account, Matthew records four Christmas narratives, interpreting each narrative to tell us the Christmas story completes or fulfills (pleroo) prophecy of old (Matthew 1:22; 2:5, 15, 17, and 23). The prophet Jeremiah records the Trinity God saying,

> *"Am I a God near at hand," says the Lord,*
> *"And not a God afar off?*
> *Can anyone hide himself in secret places,*
> *So I shall not see him?" says the Lord;*
> *Do I not fill (pleroo) heaven and earth? Says the Lord*
> *(Jeremiah 23:23-24).*

However, perhaps the most meaningful use of the word is in Peter's description of Pentecost! Luke pictures the outpouring of the Holy Spirit as a sound that comes from heaven, ***"and it filled*** (pleroo) ***the whole house where they were sitting"*** (Acts 2:2). The believer is the container, and the Spirit is the content. We are the temple of the Holy Spirit (1 Corinthians 3:16). Did Ananias and Sapphira not experience the filling of the Spirit? What would have changed their lives from the usual Jewish practice to embrace Jesus as the Messiah? Did they not believe they were in one accord with the early Church (Acts 4:32)? They were participants in the early Church's ministry, which was why God prompted them to sell their property and give the proceeds to the ministry. What changed the condition of their hearts?

The main verb in our sentence is ***"has filled,"*** which is in the indicative mood (Acts 5:3), a simple statement of fact without argument. We will not debate that Ananias and

Sapphira embezzled and lied to God. ***"Has filled"*** is in the aorist tense, focused on the verb's action instead of the time when it happened. Peter's concern was not about when Satan filled Ananias' heart, but that it happened. Peter used the active voice of this verb. Satan was responsible for filling Ananias' heart. Satan's act does not negate the response of Ananias but highlights the aggressive plotting of Satan to infiltrate and destroy. We are at war!

The imagery of ***"has filled"*** (pleroo) is "coming under the influence," true for the evil of Satan and the goodness of God. "Pleroo" describes a person controlled by that which fills him completely. The early Church's event described in the New Testament completes the foretelling of the Old Testament. When we complete something, we do not look for future or additional facts. We complete it! Again, we face the fact there are no half or partial Christians. Satan and Jesus cannot fill you at the same time. Our filling is all or nothing! We are either all in or all out!

Platform

Satan filled the ***"heart."*** The ***"heart"*** is the platform or the stage upon which the spiritual battle takes place and where the spiritual displays itself in physical activity. We know who we are inside by our outward actions, but the war's battlefield is the ***"heart."*** Luke verifies this by his sentence structure. The Greek word "kardia," translated heart, is in the accusative, comparable to the English direct object, which receives the action of the main verb. In the case of Ananias and Sapphira, Satan filled the container (their hearts), and their hearts received the effect of the filling. "Kardia" is never used in the New Testament for the physical organ we call the heart, but "kardia" represents the core of the human being figuratively. The heart (kardia) is the seat of affection and expresses the appetite of the person.

It is significant to note that Satan did not fill Ananias' heart with himself. We must make a distinction between "filled with Jesus" and "filled with Satan." Satan cannot fill us in the way Jesus fills us. Jesus' Spirit is omnipresent, everywhere at one time. Satan is a created angel and does not have this attribute. Therefore, Satan is limited to space and cannot possess everyone at one time. Think of the wonder that the Spirit of Jesus can fill you and me simultaneously! Satan can only fill one heart at a time.

It is essential to understand that because of Satan's selfish nature, he does not give himself to anyone. He may possess us, but we never possess him. In contrast, the Trinity God opens His redemptive nature to us and invites us to be a part of who He is! In openness, Jesus shares His personhood with us; He has us, but we also have Him. The merger between who Jesus is and who I am forms the new creature. God births sons! Satan never has sons, only slaves. Although Satan can indeed father us, he can never birth us (John 8:44). We do not have his nature in the sense that he shares it with us. We have his nature when we are the re-enactment of his disobedience. Therefore, our fallen self-centered nature is like his. It is a mystery that we can become the sons of God!

Something dramatic happened in the hearts of Ananias and Sapphira. Satan implemented his thought and intent through the hearts of this couple. He did not fill their hearts with himself, but in the process, they reverted to their rebellious, self-centered natures. Temptations no long came from without; their temptation came from within them. The self-centered greed that Jesus' Spirit conquered within the believers (Acts 4:32) now dominates the hearts of Ananias and Sapphira again. The spiritual war staged itself in the hearts of this couple, the result of many decisions and acts of disobedience before their fall.

Purpose

Peter said that Satan **"has filled"** (pleroo) the heart of Ananias. Ananias' **"heart"** received the filling. Because Satan could not be the content of what filled Ananias' heart, what did he put into the core of Ananias' being? The answer is in the next phrase, **"to lie to the Holy Spirit"** (Acts 5:3). The Greek verb "pseudomai," translated **"to lie to,"** is an infinitive verb, used in this case to give purpose to the verbal action of filling. Satan filled the self-centered heart of Ananias with the temptation to lie. Jesus said the same about the Pharisees. ***"You are of our father the devil, and the desires of your father you want to do. He was a murderer from the beginning, and does not stand in the truth, because there is no truth in him. When he speaks a lie, he speaks from his own resources, for he is a liar and the father of it"*** (John 8:44). Satan's interaction with Ananias was deception.

The **"Holy Spirit"** in our verse is in the accusative. Ananias received the action of this infinitive verb, **"to lie to"** (pseudomai). Peter restated David's cry as he wept over his sin.

> *"For I acknowledge my transgressions,*
> *And my sin is always before me.*
> *Against You, You only, have I sinned,*
> *And done this evil in Your sight"* (Psalms 51:3-4).

All sin is an act of rebellion within the context of the war between God and Satan. Indeed, Ananias' sin harmed the early Church. Ananias lied to Peter, but ultimately in the spiritual realm, the sin and rebellion were against God!

Part One: The Agreed Resolve Continued

Proclamation

There is a second purpose to the filling, as stated by Peter. He said, ***"and keep back part of the price of the land for yourself"*** (Acts 5:3). The Greek word "nosphizo," translated ***"keep back for yourself,"*** is also an infinitive verb, which gives purpose to the main verb ***"has filled."*** Satan's action on Ananias' heart caused him to lie to the Holy Spirit, and his physical demonstration was embezzlement. ***"For yourself"*** is added because the infinitive verb is in the middle voice, meaning the action is on behalf of self. The consistent pattern is all sin and rebellion are against God and influenced by Satan. Every sin is deception and is an expression of the person's heart. Sin is expressed on the physical stage of life and is always self-centered, which is the motive and nature of all sin.

The Scriptures are clear that the death of Ananias and Sapphira is not the response our redemptive God desires. What was true for Ananias and Sapphira is also true for you and me. This story of rebellion is not sinning from the streets; it is a revelation of incomplete surrender in the hearts of church people. God does not tolerate sin from the street or in the pew. The forgiving, redemptive Jesus is reaching out to us again.

Acts 5:3-4

LYING TO GOD

"But Peter said, Ananias, why has Satan filled your heart to lie to the Holy Spirit and keep back part of the price of the land for yourself? While it remained, was it not your own? Why have you conceived this thing in your heart? You have not lied to men but to God" (Acts 5:3-4).

Music is the heart's expression of every religious movement. To teach the theology of holiness, John and Charles Wesley wrote words to the bar tunes of their day, teaching truth through music. Expressing the heart through music was also true for the Israelites. Can you imagine several thousand men chanting songs, proclaiming the truth of Jehovah in Jerusalem's temple? The Book of Psalms is a compilation of that music. The Hebrew title for the Psalms is "Tehillim," meaning "praise." The Greek title for the translation of the Old Testament is "Psalmoi," meaning "songs to be accompanied by stringed instruments." The Book of Psalms contains 150 psalms divided into five sections, each having a benediction and final blessing.

The attributes of God fill the songs of the Psalms. For instance, God is transcendent, which means He is different and independent from His creation. The essence and nature of God's being are greater and higher, above and beyond, anything He has created. The Israelites filled their songs with declarations of God's otherness. All of His judgments come from His transcendent greatness (Psalm 10:5).

God is unchangeable! The attributes of God do not change in His perfection or His purpose for humanity.

"I will sing of the mercies of the Lord forever;
With my mouth I will make known
your faithfulness to all generations.
For I have said, 'Mercy shall be built up forever;
Your faithfulness You shall establish in the very heavens'"
(Psalm 89:1-2)

The remainder of this Psalm echoes this great attribute of God.

God is Omnipotent! He is all-powerful and has the highest authority over all things and all creatures.

"He counts the number of stars;
He calls them by name.
Great is our Lord, and mighty in power;
His understanding is infinite" (Psalm 147:4-5).

"Come and see the works of God;
He is awesome in His doing toward the sons of men.
He turned the sea into dry land;
They went through the river on foot.
There we will rejoice in Him.
He rules by His power forever" (Psalm 66:5-7).

God is omniscient! He possesses complete and perfect knowledge of all things. The Psalms declare that God knows everything about our human life. Before my mother's womb, God involved Himself in shaping my life for His destiny. God is

God, and He has searched me and knows me. I can hide nothing from Him. Darkness is as light to God, and no one can hide from Him (Psalm 139). God knows what could have happened and what will happen. He is aware of the past, and all that will happen in the future because He planned the future.

> *"Praise the Lord!*
> *Praise the Lord in His sanctuary;*
> *Praise Him in His mighty firmament!*
> *Praise Him for His mighty acts:*
> *Praise Him according to His excellent greatness!*
> *Praise Him with the sound of the trumpet;*
> *Praise Him with the lute and harp!*
> *Praise Him with the timbrel and dance;*
> *Praise Him with stringed instruments and flutes!*
> *Praise Him with loud cymbals;*
> *Praise Him with clashing cymbals!*
> *Let everything that has breath praise the Lord.*
> *Praise the Lord!"* (Psalm 150).

What else can be said? In light of the immensity of what we do not know about God, what we do know is startling! Should we not live in a state of awe? Should we not always stretch to comprehend more of His greatness?

Luke introduces Ananias and Sapphira to us in our passage (Acts 5:1-11), the only place we see them in the Scriptures. We have no information about their background, ages, social status, or tribal connection. Though we know little about them, what we do know is significant. This couple in the early Church were CONSECRATED JEWS. They lived in Jerusalem to participate in the celebrations and worship as good Israelites. The temple worship, annual feast days, and daily hours of prayer made up a consistent part of the schedule. The Old Testament Scriptures made up the core of their education from childhood to the present moment, and they focused their belief in Jehovah. All the attributes of God highlighted in the Book of Psalms was their faith. They sang the Psalms they had committed to memory.

However, we must add that they were CONVERTED JEWS. They lived in the expectation that Jehovah would send a Messiah, revealing their belief in Him. Following the crucifixion, resurrection, and Pentecost, they embraced Jesus as that Messiah. Were they among the Jews converted at Pentecost? The Holy Spirit used Peter to explain Pentecost and 3,000 converted to Christianity (Acts 2:41). The gathering cried out, **"Men and brethren, what shall we do?"** (Acts 2:37). This crowd realized the truth; they had participated in the crucifixion of Jesus, but His resurrection's reality cut them to the heart (Acts 2:37). Were Ananias and Sapphira in that crowd? Had they joined the call to "Crucify Him?" We do not know, but Jesus had won their hearts! They became a part of the early Church, experiencing the apostles' teaching and breaking bread from house to house (Acts 2:24-47). They certainly knew the persecution applied to the early Church. Peter and John explained the severity of punishment expected if anyone preached or taught in the name of Jesus. Ananias and Sapphira decided to risk everything to embrace the commitment of the early Church to stick with Jesus.

We know their decision because Ananias and Sapphira were CONTRIBUTING JEWS. They had some wealth because they decided to sell one of their possessions (Acts 5:1). No human pressure or requirement made them make such a sacrifice. However, the Holy Spirit, who was within them may have. This couple had a desire to contribute to the thriving ministry of the early Church. The needs of the people moved them, and they responded. Should we not applaud their actions. Are not the church and those who are needy always grateful for the generous response prompted by the Holy Spirit?

However, as the story of Ananias and Sapphira unfolds, everything is upside down, in reverse, and definitely in chaos. Instead of generosity, there is stinginess. Instead of truth, there is deception. Instead of commitment, there is a compromise. Instead of Jesus conquering the heart, Satan wins a victory. How could it be? What has happened? Peter asks, "Why?" ***"Ananias, why has Satan filled your heart to lie to the Holy Spirit and keep back part of the price of the land for yourself?*** (Acts 5:3). ***"Why have you conceived this thing in your heart? You have not lied to men but to God"*** (Acts 5:4).

Have you thought of lying to God? What transition would you need to make in your belief about God to do such a thing? Would you not have to change your relationship with Him? It is impossible to maintain intimacy and oneness with God and have a wall of deception. If Christianity defined is my nature, and God's nature merged, how can I possibly lie to Him? We have to conclude we cannot deceive God but only ourselves. This discussion leads us to a review.

The Attribute

The Book of Psalms strongly influenced Ananias' concept of God and His character. Every Sabbath Ananias would chant and sing his beliefs about God with other worshipers. The temple air resounded with the declaration of God's "abiding presence." God is unchangeable! Jehovah God is "all-powerful," omnipotent. Jehovah was the same in Ananias' day as he was in Moses' day. Old Testament stories of deliverance shaped everything Ananias believed about God. God's power and greatness could not be measured. God Jehovah is "all-knowing," omniscient. Ananias sang Psalms declaring man can hide nothing from God. Why would he attempt to hide something from someone who knows everything? Jehovah God is "above all things," transcendent.

Part One: The Agreed Resolve Continued

God is separated from and not determined by that which He created, which was Ananias' throbbing heart's belief.

All the things Ananias believed about God expanded into the complete revelation of Jesus. The Old Testament stories moved into the daily acknowledgment of truth as Ananias experienced the life of Christ in His world. The transcendent God became flesh! Ananias must have witnessed the miracles of Jesus and heard Him preach the truth. The Spirit of Jesus had come to indwell Ananias as he embraced the mystery of Pentecost. He knew the intimacy of God Jehovah about which he continually sang.

How could Ananias conceive in his heart the idea of lying to the Holy Spirit? Is this not what Peter was asking him? What happened to Ananias' belief? Did he no longer believe God was all-knowing? Did he think he could hide the sale amount of the property from God? Did Ananias believe God had changed? How do you describe the actions of a man who, in the face of an all-knowing God, acts as if He knows nothing?

But let us not demean Ananias without coming to terms with this in our lives? Is not the denial of who God is the essence of every deed of sin? Peter knew the miracle power of God flowing through Jesus for three years. The raising of several people from the dead were spectacular moments within his time with Jesus. Peter was convinced and boldly pledged his support to Jesus (Matthew 26:35). But in the crisis moment in the Garden of Gethsemane, Peter drew a sword to defend himself. Why did he not rely on Jesus? After all he saw demonstrated in Jesus, how could he so easily set that aside?

This analysis is convicting for us all. We propose confidence and faith in the greatness of our God only to live in anxiety over trivial issues in comparison to Jesus! We sing the songs and declare the theology of our faith only to deny the reality of it in our daily lives. We proclaim the omniscience of God only to plot how we might deceive Him. To live in sin, we

Lying to God | Acts 5:3-4

must demean and belittle the character of who God is! Sin makes no sense in light of the nature and attitude of God. **"Come now, and let us reason together. Says the Lord"** (Isaiah 1:18). Has not every deviation from God's will for your life ended in destruction? Each time we do our desires, our selfish intent, does not it bring us pain and destruction? Paul described the world of the god of this age as blinding. He said, **"But even if our gospel is veiled, it is veiled to those who are perishing, whose minds the god of this age has blinded, who do not believe, lest the light of the gospel of the glory of Christ, who is the image of God, should shine on them"** (2 Corinthians 4:3-4). Do the sensible thing and embrace the character of God; live accordingly! How can we lie to an omniscient God?

Attitude

Ananias and Sapphira's attitude of faith and commitment were undoubtedly strong. To embrace Jesus and know the filling of His Spirit repeatedly as they did must have strengthened their confidence in God. Did they not receive blessing after blessing and benefit upon benefit from Him? Were their lives not enriched in every way due to Christ and His Church? Think of the support of the body of Christ represented in Jerusalem. Was there any question in their hearts about the goodness of God? Did they not know as Jehovah God had provided for their forefathers in the Old Testament, He was abundantly able to provide for them in their hour?

However, beyond such a recognition of the Old Testament, this couple knew the fullness of the indwelt God. It is one thing to celebrate events of the ancient past; it is another thing to experience the same God moving in your life. Had they not experienced miracles as great as those of ancient days? Did not they know the presence of God in ways beyond thunder and lightning on Mt. Sinai? God provided for them and worked on their behalf. They trusted Him even in persecution.

Why did they need to lie to the Holy Spirit and provide for themselves? Could their provision be better than His? Did they have a resource beyond God's supply? Was the small amount of profit enough to merit their lives? Again, we must not be demeaning or belittle them until we have carefully looked at our life's experience. How often have we trusted ourselves instead of God? We embrace anxiety and fear rather than confidence and faith, which points to our lack of trust in Him. We live in the temporal instead of the eternal. How amazing is it that we have not ceased breathing in death as they did!

Arrogance

Perhaps the arrogance of our selfish pride is the bottom line of the matter. Is it the answer to Peter's cry of "Why?" How difficult is it for us to embrace our helplessness and live in the constant awareness of such a state? Yet, this is where the full reality of Jesus' presence is known. Nothing else makes any sense. It is the solution to every problem; it is the answer to every question. It is clarity to every confusion.

It is the completeness of surrender Jesus requires of us. Does not our passage teach us again that there are no half-hearted attempts in Christianity? We must either trust Him or trust ourselves. The call is for our total abandonment to Jesus!

Acts 5:4

MAKING A PLACE

"While it remained, was it not your own? And after it was sold, was it not in your own control? Why have you conceived this thing in your heart? You have not lied to men but to God" (Acts 5:4).

Peter confronted Ananias and Sapphira about their participation in the ministry of the early Church. This couple displayed no inconsistencies in their lives until this financial transaction. Peter's concern was not about the amount of money they received, but that embezzlement and deception were involved in their actions. Peter asked this decisive question, **"Why have you conceived this thing in your heart"** (Acts 5:4)? Another translation uses the word **"contrived,"** a translation of the Greek word "tithemi," used 100 times in the New Testament. "Tithemi" focuses on the action of setting, putting, or placing a person or thing. Often it is used to assign a place or make room for something. Peter asked Ananias, "Why did you make room in your heart?"

In the same conversation, Peter asked, **"Ananias, why has Satan filled your heart to lie to the Holy Spirit and keep back part of the price of the land for yourself"** (Acts 5:3)? Peter indicates that Satan, the father of all lies, instigated the deception. Satan stimulated the deception in the core of Ananias' being, his heart. But Satan could not have placed it there unless Ananias made a place (tithemi) for it. Although the old statement, "the devil made me do it," may have some validity, it is never without a willing response from the person. Ananias opened his heart and made room for Satan's activity.

In searching the Septuagint, the Greek version of the Old Testament, for the use of "tithemi," the results were astounding. In over one-fourth of the occurrences, the Trinity God is the subject of the action. God is responsible for all creation; in fact, He made a place (tithemi); He set creation. God took the sun, moon, and stars and **"set them (tithemi) in the firmament of the heavens to give light to the earth"** (Genesis 1:17). The picture of what God did in creation extended to our salvation! It is God who "made" (tithemi)" Abraham the father of many nations (Genesis 17:5). God made a place (tithemi) for the descendants of Jacob as numerous as the sand of the sea (Genesis 32:12). God made (tithemi) David king and established (tithemi) his throne forever (Psalms 89:4) and appointed (tithemi) Jeremiah both prophet (Jeremiah 1:5) and servant (Isaiah 49:2). Our God made a place (tithemi) in His heart for us!

The New Testament is filled with the truth of "tithemi," "to assign a place, or make room for something." Paul quoted the Old Testament to describe the Jew's rejection of Jesus. As he did, he gave insight into God's heart for the redemption of man.

> *"Behold, I lay (tithemi) in Zion*
> *a stumbling stone and rock of offense,*
> *And whoever believes on Him will not be put to shame"*
> *(Romans 9:33).*

The Trinity God carved out of His heart a place for redemption in the Man called Jesus. Throughout the New Testament, Paul calls us to be "in Christ," the heart of God. Jesus is the visible image of the invisible heart of God. We can and must dwell in God's heart! In Paul's epistle to the Thessalonians, he said, *"For God did not appoint us* (tithemi) *to wrath, but to obtain salvation through our Lord Jesus Christ, who died for us, that whether we work or sleep, we should live together with Him"* (1 Thessalonians 5:9-10). The Trinity God made a place for us in His heart. It is not a place of condemnation or judgment; it is a place of salvation, safety from all destruction. This place is Jesus! Regardless of our circumstances, we live in the security of Him, our place.

"Living in our place" seems to be the single message of Paul to the Jews of his day. On his first missionary journey, he entered Antioch in Pisidia. He found the opportunity to preach in the synagogue on the Sabbath day. After his message, the Gentiles begged Paul to give this message to them. On the following Sabbath, *"almost the whole city came together to hear the word of God"* (Acts 13:44). Paul said that the Jews were to hear the message first, but they rejected it. Therefore, *"we turn to the Gentiles. For so the Lord has commanded us: 'I have set* (tithemi) *you a light to the Gentiles, that you should be for salvation to the ends of the earth'"* (Acts 13:46-47).

Our redemptive God contrived within His being a place for us. God placed before us a place of light and righteousness.

Paul presents the Church as the body of Christ. There are many members but only one body, Divinely constructed! *"But now God has set* (tithemi) *the members, each one of them, in the body just as He pleased"* (1 Corinthians 12:18). He describes it as *"God has appointed* (tithemi) *these in the church"* (1 Corinthians 12:28). It is amazing! God created the human body; He creatively constructed each functioning element of the human being and put it in place. In His redemptive heart, He creatively makes a place for you and puts you in that place. God birthed you out of the dreams of His heart. Notice the progression! He creatively carved out a place in His heart and then created you to fit in that place. God birthed you out of His creative dreams and plan.

Paul proposed this placement to Timothy. ***"And I thank Christ Jesus our Lord who has enabled me, because He counted me faithful, putting*** (tithemi) ***me into this ministry"*** (1 Timothy 1:12). Paul described himself as a blasphemer, persecutor, and an insolent man. Yet, he ***"was appointed*** (tithemi) ***a preacher and an apostle"*** (1 Timothy 2:7). Do not easily discard this reality. God has "tithemi" you in His heart. He contrived, cut out a place, and carved your image within Himself. He proceeded to create you from that carving and dream; He placed you in His heart for the fulfillment of His dreams! "In His heart" is the message of the Gospel!

Role

The heart of sin is rebellion against the role for which God created us! Ananias and Sapphira were not bad people in the sense of evil, sinful activities of the world. They could have done anything they wanted with the money from the sale of their land. Then where was the problem? The Trinity God had cut out a place (tithemi) for them. They were not ordinary members of the early Church or nameless people in Jerusalem who gave their lives to Jesus. They were destined, appointed (tithemi) by God. We do not know the long-range eternal dreams of God for them. They had a simple yet profound involvement. If they could not be faithful in the dreams of God in the small things, how could they be trusted in the more important things to come?

The Trinity God carved out a place for Ananias and Sapphira in His heart. They had the opportunity to partake in God's dreams for the needy in the early Church. Would they participate in God's role dreamed and destined for them? It is crucial to hold in mind the progression. God did not save Ananias and Sapphira and then try to use them for His glory. He carved out a place in His inner heart full of destiny and dreams and shaped Ananias and Sapphira for those dreams. God did not create them and invent a plan. He contrived (tithemi) a plan and created them in the form of that plan. The selling of their property was only a small incident in the eternal plan!

But Ananias and Sapphira were not willing! They contrived (tithemi) in their hearts a plan and tried to fit God into it. They refused the destiny of their creation to implement their desires. They were not against God, nor did they disbelieve in Him. They were willing to utilize God and His benefits in their designed plan. They usurped the position of the Creator and determined their destiny, which is the heart of every sin! Ananias and Sapphira contrived (tithemi) in their hearts and set destiny in the place (tithemi) of their choosing. They played the role of God.

The early Church considered the betrayal of Judas in this same manner. They expressed this during their first recorded business meeting (Acts 1:15-26). Ministry, in this case, the role of the apostle, was a separate item and existed distinct from the apostle himself. The Trinity God carved out of His heart (tithemi) the role of the apostle for redemption. Having established and firmly setting this position, He needed someone who could fit this assignment. You might think of this ministry as a chair. Having made the chair of apostleship, God needed someone to sit in that chair. Not everyone could fulfill its requirements. He would need to create a person-shaped like that chair. The sin of Judas was he did not stay in his chair. He did not like the destiny in which God placed him. Judas vacated his chair and proceeded to create his place (tithemi). His sin included thirty pieces of silver, the kiss of betrayal, and hanging himself; however, these were mere details of his created destiny. But the loss was not the brief years of his life, but what God planned for eternity. Judas set it all aside *"that he might go to his own place"* (Acts 1:25).

Ananias and Sapphira followed the sinful pattern of Judas. What was God's eternal plan for their lives? God carved it out in His heart and created them uniquely for such a role. Like Judas, they did not accept their role but carved out of their hearts their design. As with Judas, it was a place of destruction. It was a lie. Above all, deception filled them, and what they sought did not meet their unique creation. It did not fulfill who they were!

Reservation

Our passage is strong in concept. The early Church had a standard belief about the role of ministry. Ministry was a place, office, spot, or space separate from the person functioning in ministry. God did not create a person and call him to ministry, and that person had the responsibility to develop and build the ministry. Instead, God carved a dream out of His heart, and to fulfill that dream, someone with unique and specific elements must be present. God created those elements in the person! You are one of the critical aspects He created to fulfill His dream. God created the uniqueness of your personality so He could fill you and accomplish His heart's dream. He did not create you and invent a plan for you. He carved out a dream in His redemptive heart, and He birthed, shaped, and put you in place to fulfill that dream.

Therefore, the ministry is not what you create by skill, talent, or performance. We do not measure the success of ministry by numbers, size, finances, or apparent increase. Your complete surrender determines ministry characterized by dependency, resting, and intimacy. How visible is the image of the invisible God seen through you? Any expression of self-centeredness blurs the image, and your self-performance of talent and ability produce confusion for those viewing. Your focus is to remain in the place reserved for you in God's heart. He created you in the shape of that reservation. You fit there; it is home! Do not leave your place!

Paul leaves no doubt about our place. It is not a geographic location such as a mission field or city. It is Jesus! Everything God dreams for you in fulfilling your destiny, He placed in Jesus. Listen to the familiar verse, ***"Blessed be the God and Father of our Lord Jesus Christ, who has blessed us with every spiritual blessing in the heavenly places in Christ"*** (Ephesians 1:3). Jesus is your reservation. The Trinity God carved out, set in place, and reserved a chair. When He created the person who could adequately fill that chair, it was you! But it was you in Christ, Jesus filling your uniqueness that fills the chair. Your unique personality filled with Jesus gives an expression of the Trinity God that no other can demonstrate.

Your reservation is ***"in Christ"*** (Ephesians 1:3-14). God chose you; before Him, in His love, you are holy and without blame. You are His son. You are the praise and glory of grace in Him. He accepts you as His beloved; you find your redemption in Jesus, even the forgiveness of sin. The riches of God's grace are in Jesus. All wisdom and prudence toward us are in Him. Jesus' good pleasure, which the Trinity God purposed, is in Him. We become the fulfillment of the mystery of God's will in Jesus. Our inheritance is in Jesus; our destiny, according to His purpose, is that God works all things according to the counsel of His will, which is only in Him. Jesus is the truth!

God's dream, from which He birthed you, is the reservation. Do not think in terms of earthly life-span, because your reservation is eternal in the expanse. Eighty years of life on earth is not His destiny for you. Your experience on earth is hardly the beginning. We have only begun to dip our toes in the pool of His dream. We must think long-range. Ananias and Sapphira were shortsighted. They would not rest in their reservation, but declared their own place; it began with a little financial gain that they lost in death.

Raw Material

Embezzlement, lying to God, deceiving others, and allowing Satan to fill your heart are all elements of sin that lead to destruction. We should all be horrified at the presence of any of these elements. However, the Scriptures do not present these aspects as the core of sin. There is a raw material that allows us to demonstrate these aspects. Redemption is not the elimination of these elements, but the abolishment of the raw material. This raw material of sin is not a substance or a "thing" that we can surgically remove. It is an attitude or approach to life, fundamental to each person, expressed and produced by it. This raw material is dominant and present, becoming the ingredient in every expression of life.

In our passage, the raw material is in the Greek word "tithemi." "Tithemi" is man's attempt to play the role of God in his life. As if he is God, a human being goes into his heart to reserve a place of his making. He establishes his dream and determines his destiny. However, God already established this for the human being in His Divine heart. It is God's role, defined by His nature of love. God created the human being in the shape of that destiny, designed for His filling. He birthed the unique qualities of that person to give the expression of fulfillment. The raw material of sin is man's rejection of that destiny. Therefore, the human being goes into his own heart and reserves a place shaped by his self-centered nature. Then, he will express his self-destiny in every act of living, which is the raw material of sin.

Ananias embezzled a portion of his land's selling price. That embezzlement was an expression of his self-centered nature, determining his destiny. His lie was not the core issue.

He appeared to embrace the completeness of Christian faith but instead utilized it for self-centered destiny. His actions were not the raw material, but all were off-springs of the core issue. Ananias and Sapphira usurped the sovereign position of God. They fought against the essence of their creation. What a tragedy!

It is evident; we are all guilty of this raw material. We must run with all of our might back to the completeness of Christ's call. We must abandon ourselves without hesitation to our destiny found in His dream. We must come home to the safety of His design. Our call is to merge with His nature and a new focus on Him. Rejection only means destruction.

Acts 5:5

CONSEQUENCE OF HEARING

> *"Then Ananias, hearing these words, fell down and breathed his last. So great fear came upon all those who heard these things"*
> *(Acts 5:5).*

There is controversy clustered around the story of Ananias and Sapphira, and the lack of details has fostered theological disputes. Due to the story's gaps, a person can inject his theological bias into the Scriptures. This lack of information suggests the story might not be historically correct, raising questions about its authenticity.

However, the purpose of Luke's writing answers all of these supposed problems. Luke writes to declare and demonstrate the Spirit-filled life. It is a declaration of the New Covenant where God and man merge into a new creature. We know that Luke wrote his Gospel account and the Book of Acts at the same time as one book. He did not propose two themes. In the Gospel of Luke, he presented the New Covenant as seen in one Man, the prototype. Jesus is the first Kingdom person; a man merged with the nature of God. The Trinity God displayed His heart in Jesus; He is the visible image of the invisible God.

The Book of Acts is not an alternate theme. Perhaps we can

accept Jesus as living a Spirit-filled life, but are we on His level? We shake our heads at the disciples' display of self-centeredness. The contrast between the disciples and Jesus is so vast it seems it could never be bridged. Luke's first chapter in the Book of Acts prepares us for the Holy Spirit's outpouring in chapter two. The Holy Spirit fills a group of mean, nasty people, just like us with the Spirit of Jesus. As the Trinity God merged the Man Jesus with His nature, so He merged the disciples with the same nature. The power, purpose, and program of redemption flowed from their lives because they were kingdom people. God birthed the early Church from the completeness of this merger and displayed the reality of the new kingdom creature in hundreds of transformed lives. But then we come to Ananias and Sapphira, who knew the fulness of Jesus but ended up dead.

Luke did not write a historical account with the cultural involvement of his day. In our passage, Ananias heard the words of confrontation from Peter. ***"Then Ananias, hearing these words, fell down and breathed his last"*** (Acts 5:5). Some scholars have pointed out that Peter did not give Ananias a chance to repent; God simply struck him dead. But this theological suggestion is an interpretation and not a statement of the passage. Everything we know about the character of God through Jesus (Gospels) demands the opportunity for response. The fact that Luke did not state that opportunity does not mean it should not be assumed. The passage does not say that God struck Ananias and his wife, Sapphira, dead. Death did take place, but Luke does not tell us the cause.

Another actively debated issue in our passage is the burial of Ananias and Sapphira. It seems strange that they buried Ananias without the presence of his wife, Sapphira. However, in the Greek language, none of the verbs (***"arose," "wrapped him up," "carried him out," "buried him"***) are in the present tense. They are all in the Greek aorist tense, often translated in the past tense. However, here it is a focus on the action of the verb instead of the time it occurred. Luke used the same Greek tense for the death and burial of Sapphira. He never used this tense to tell us when an event or action occurred, but only that it happened. Luke is not relaying information about the burial process, but he reveals serious violations against the merger between God and man. It would be wise for all of us to focus on the story's purpose instead of the historical details.

The story's purpose is the focus of our passage. ***"Then Ananias, hearing these words, fell down and breathed his last"*** (Acts 5:5). ***"Then"*** is a translation of the Greek word "de," a continuative conjunction with contrast as the primary function. However, "de" can mean to add to something already in place. In our passage, we must interpret the meaning. As a contrast, Peter confronted Ananias with truth, but Ananias had no response of repentance. Instead, the death of rebellion against the blaring light of God brought physical death. As a continuation of ideas, there is a weaker but the same thought. When truth is presented but does not get a proper response, it always produces death.

The main verb of the statement's translation is ***"breathed his last"*** (ekpsycho). It is in the aorist tense, which highlights the occurrence of the action and ignores the time element. "Ekpsycho" is a combination of "ek," which is "from" or "out" and "psycho," which most often refers to "soul." There are seven different words used for "dying." They are used over 400 times in the New Testament. However, "ekpsycho" is used only by Luke and only three times. As a doctor, Luke gave details. The emphasis is not just on Ananias' death but on the "soul" of his being. What Ananias heard affects the core of his system.

"Ananias" is the subject of the sentence. The two remaining verbs in the sentence are participles, ***"hearing"*** and ***"fell down."*** Luke used both verbs as adverbs to modify ***"breathed his last."*** The Greek word translated ***"fell down"*** is "pipto," which often has the connotation of worship. As used in our passage, "pipto" has the action of falling down, indicating Ananias recognized the truth of Peter's confrontation. Ananias did not repent but admitted to the state in which he and his wife had fallen. The parallel to this is Judas. As the leaders of Israel led Jesus in His beaten condition, Judas became aware of the terribleness of his betrayal. He went to the leaders with his confession, saying, ***"I have sinned by betraying innocent blood"*** (Matthew 27:4). When the leaders of Israel gave no resolve, in a sense, Judas responded just like Ananias. He fell down by throwing down the thirty pieces of silver and went and hanged himself (Matthew 27:5).

The Revealing
The Verb

Now we come to the pivotal issue of our passage. The problem is the verb Luke used as a participle, **"hearing,"** modifying **"breathed his last." "Hearing"** is the translation for the Greek word "akouo." In the English and the Greek language, "hearing" is a physical action of sound waves penetrating a person's ears, communicating information to the person's mind. "Akouo" is a general use of the word, which we find in the Scriptures. "***So when he heard*** (akouo) ***about Jesus, he sent elders of the Jews to Him, pleading with Him to come and heal his servant***" (Luke 7:3). The centurion physically heard the news about Jesus. In Jesus' conversation with Nicodemus, He explained, ***"The wind blows where it wishes, and you hear*** (akouo) ***the sound of it"*** (John 3:8).

According to the Greek lexicons, while "akouo" involves physical action of the ears, it generally means "to come to know." Engaged in the hearing is the communication of information or revelation. Ananias is in the state of receiving revelation. Luke distinctly stated this revelation using "akuou" as

Part One: The Agreed Resolve Continued

a participle in the nominative form. The verb "hearing" modifies and gives content to ***"breathed his last."*** The subject of the sentence is Ananias, who is the hearing one! People could say many things about Ananias, but not at this moment. At this moment, the focus is on the wonder that God is communicating truth to Ananias.

The communication of truth is throughout the New Testament. Paul declared that anyone who calls on the name of the Lord would find salvation. Then he asked a question. ***"How then shall they call on Him in whom they have not believed? And how shall they believe in Him of whom they have not heard*** (akouo)***? And how shall they hear*** (akouo) ***without a preacher?"*** (Acts 10:14). He concludes his thought by saying, ***"So then faith comes by hearing*** (akouo) ***and hearing*** (akuou) ***by the word of God"*** (Romans 10:17). The emphasis is not on sound waves coming into a person's ears but on the communication and understanding of truth; it is the revelation of truth!

The Gospel accounts give no record and seemingly no concern about the physical appearance of Jesus. The first Christians showed no interest in such matters. How tall was Jesus? Was He slender or muscular? The Gospels focus on what Jesus said and did. What He did was spoken repeatedly; thus, it became hearing. Even when seeing is referenced, it is the seeing of His acts revealing the nature of His mission. The parables Jesus told that portray action are parables of hearing (akuou). The writers of the Gospels filled their accounts with what people saw; however, what they saw usually acquired significance in what they heard. In the Christmas narratives (Matthew 1, 2), the Angel of the Lord confronted Joseph in the night hour. The significance of this story is in Joseph's obedience to what he heard. In the baptism account of Jesus, the critical happening is the voice of the Father speaking (Matthew 3:17). The Mount of Transfiguration climaxes in the sound of the Father speaking revelation about His Son (Matthew 17:5).

"Hearing" (akuou) becomes the content and context of our passage. Ananias is the person hearing. Luke does not give us an exact word for word quote of what Peter said to Ananias. What we have is a summary statement of questions that display the heart of Peter's communication. Think about the accumulated hearing Ananias and Sapphira received throughout their time in the early Church. Luke writes that the early Church ***"continued steadfastly in the apostles' doctrine and fellowship, in the breaking of bread, and in prayers"*** (Acts 2:42). He even said they continued ***"daily with one accord"*** (Acts 2:46). ***"And with great power the apostles gave witness to the resurrection of the Lord Jesus"*** (Acts 4:33). Ananias and Sapphira had received much truth!

In our passage, the Greek word "akouo" is in the present tense. The main verb translated ***"breathed his last,"*** as well as the participle verb ***"fell down,"*** are in the aorist tense. The present tense depicts something that is happening in the present and has continual action; it is the action in the process. Ananias is in the state of hearing, and all the truth he has heard is thundering back into his life. There is a powerful revelation happening. I do not need to describe this to you. We have all had this happen to us. The amazing grace of God captures us, revealing spiritual truth. We are unable to deny or refute it. We are in a state of revelation, which brings us to our next reality.

Revelation
The Direct Object

The participle verb "akuou" has an accusative. An accusative in the Greek language is like a direct object in English. This direct object receives the action of the verb. The ***"hearing"*** directly acts upon ***"these words."*** Ananias is in the state of hearing. Peter is confronting, and God is revealing the truth to Ananias contained in ***"these words."*** The questions and statements of Peter are in verses three and four, but the truth is in the complete story. ***"These words"*** are a summary without extended detail or explanation. The focus of "akuou" is in its revealing thrust.

In the Old Testament, the rabbi connected hearing (akuou) with the Scriptures. The duty of man was to hear God, and the method by which man heard was the Scriptures. ***"And Moses called all Israel and said to them: 'Hear, O Israel, the statutes and judgments which I speak in your hearing today, that you may learn them and be careful to observe them"*** (Deuteronomy 5:1). In the following chapter, Moses focused on the great commandment of the Scriptures. ***"Hear, O Israel: The Lord our God the Lord is one! You shall love the Lord your God with all your heart, with all your soul, and with all your strength"*** (Deuteronomy 6:4-5). The hearing (akuou) acts upon the Scriptures and brings revelation to human life. The emphasis is not on seeing God, for no one will see God, but upon hearing Him through the Scriptures!

"These words" bespeaks the revelation that comes to Ananias' heart. ***"These"*** is a translation of the Greek word "toutous," a demonstrative pronoun. "Toutous" singles out an object or person and often acts as an adjective. The revelation Ananias and Sapphira experienced contained all the truth Peter taught through the Scriptures. Would this revelation not also include everything they studied in the Old Testament and learned through their Jewish culture? The present words of Peter highlighted and focused Ananias on the revelation of the Word!

"Words" is a translation of the Greek word "logos." "Laleo" is the Greek word that focuses on the act of speaking. "Lego" is the Greek word focusing on the content of the words spoken. The root word for "logos" is "lego." The emphasis is not on the tone of voice or the length of speech, and there is no desire to highlight the effectiveness of Peter's commanding voice. The focus is on the words of the revelation! Jesus is the content!

The Response
The Indirect Object

The "revealing hearing (akuou)" brought revelation (toutous logos) to Ananias. God moves through His word and brings salvation to every person who responds. Although there is no recorded appeal from Peter to Ananias for repentance, it is innately present in the *"hearing these words."* To deny this reality would be to deny the essential nature of revelation, the heart of God. This story maintains the primary message of the Gospel. *"For God so loved the world that He gave"* (John 3:16). Yes, God gave His Son, who is the "revealing hearing" of His person and nature. The result of the hearing is an advanced and complete revelation of God's heart. ***"For God did not send His Son into the world to condemn the world, but that the world through Him might be saved"*** (John 3:17).

To not apply the reality of God's confrontation of Ananias, through Peter, would be an unforgivable violation of God's revelation! God did not strike Ananias dead as a punishment for his embezzlement or lying to the Holy Spirit. There is no place in the story (Acts 5:1-11) that indicates this. The story is of the loving heart of the Father trying to reach a child who has strayed. The Father is desperate and will not allow Ananias to continue, but confronts him with truth from the Word, which brings conviction and possible conversion.

Again, we see a parallel between Ananias' experience and Judas. When Judas realized the result of his betrayal of Jesus, the truth confronted him. Aware of his sin, Judas cried out to the leader of Israel, ***"I have sinned by betraying innocent***

blood" (Matthew 27:4). The leaders responded with no concern. ***"What is that to us? You see to it! Then he threw down the pieces of silver in the temple and departed, and went and hanged himself"*** (Matthew 27:4-5). Revelation confronted Ananias and Judas, making them deeply aware of their sin. The response in each case was death! Please, do not attribute to God the death of either man. Is God able and willing to forgive (Matthew 12:31)? Absolutely!

In the case of both Ananias and Judas, it was not just repentance for a single act. The deed of sin for each was only an expression of the lack of their heart's surrender. Ananias had not merged with Jesus and allowed Him to invade every area of his life; Ananias had not come under the influence of Jesus. He had not found his security in Christ alone, and his sin expressed this vacancy. We are brought again to the central theme and message of the story. Jesus is Lord of all, or He is not Lord at all. It is all or nothing. Feeble attempts only work when we define Christianity as "doing." We can do better at some times than others. But Christianity is a merger with God's nature. All of God must indwell and permeate all that I am so that I can be like Him!

Acts 5:5, 11

GREAT FEAR

"Then Ananias, hearing these words, fell down and breathed his last. So great fear came upon all those who heard these things" (Acts 5:5). "So great fear came upon all the church and upon all who heard these things" (Acts 5:11).

"So great fear came upon all those who heard these things" (Acts 5:5). It is easy to understand the group reaction as the news spread about the death of Ananias. He had embezzled money from God and the church; his death exposed his sin. We might view this casually except ***"great fear"*** is repeated in the story's last verse. The climax of the story is the response of fear in the church and all who heard the news. Luke further highlights it by the adjective ***"great,"*** a translation of the Greek word "megas." "Megas" means out of the ordinary in degree, magnitude, or effect.

The Greek word "phobos," translated ***"fear,"*** is our word "phobia." "Phobos" is used forty-seven times in the New Testament, fourteen times in the Gospels. In either verb or noun form, "phobos" means panic-stricken terror. One example of this word's use was when Jesus walked on water in the middle of the night (Matthew 14:26). It was probably three o'clock in

Part One: The Agreed Resolve Continued

the morning, and the disciples had battled the storm all night. Dead tired, they could not go forward or backward. They bailed water with all their strength, trying to keep the boat afloat. The storm waves crashed over the sides of the boat. Suddenly looking up, they saw a ghostly figure skipping from one storm wave to another, causing them great fear. What English word could adequately describe what the disciples felt? Perhaps terror, fright, or scared out of their wits would be a proper interpretation.

Seasoned, elite Roman guards experience the same fear. The angel of the Lord descended, causing an earthquake. The angel rolled the stone away from the empty tomb. His countenance was like lightning, and his clothing was white as snow. **"And the guards shook for fear** (phobos) **of him, and became like dead men"** (Matthew 28:4). Our passage does not say that **"fear"** was a reaction of Ananias and Sapphira, but I wonder if this was a cause of their death? We often view fear in the Scriptures as an independent power that "befalls" human beings (Luke 1:12, 65). It "fills" them (Luke 5:26), "oppresses" them (Luke 7:16), "seizes" them (Luke 8:37), or "comes upon" them (Acts 5:5, 11). Seventy-five times in the New Testament, the writers state admonishment as, "Do not fear!" Fear is a common problem, and we need frequent reminders.

However, **"fear"** (phobos) also describes a fundamental attitude man has toward God. The Scriptures repeatedly tell us to fear the Lord! There are many exhortations to fear the Lord in the Book of Psalms.

> ***"Let all the earth fear the Lord;***
> ***Let all the inhabitants of the world stand in awe of Him"***
> *(Psalms 33:8).*

> ***"Oh, fear the Lord, you His saints!***
> ***There is no want to those who fear Him"*** *(Psalms 34:9).*

Great Fear | Acts 5:5, 11

Luke emphasizes the reaction of astonishment and fear because of Jesus' deeds. After the healing of the paralytic, the witnesses are ***"all amazed, and they glorified God and were filled with fear*** (phobos)***, saying, 'We have seen strange things today'"*** (Luke 5:26). Awe filled all of them! The events surrounding the birth of Christ caused fear within many hearts. Can you imagine being in the fields in the quiet of night only to have an angel of the Lord stand before you and the glory of the Lord to shine around you? The Scriptures report that the shepherds ***"were greatly afraid*** (phobos)***"*** (Luke 2:9).

What is the tone or severity of fear in our passage? You might take the extreme terrorized approach, a result of a casual reading in the English translation. Ananias and Sapphira embezzled funds from God and the church. They sold land and claimed they gave the entire proceeds. In reality, they lied, but as Peter said, the lie was not to men but to God. The result was both Ananias and Sapphira died. Those of the early Church talked of this among themselves, and all of Jerusalem would have known the details. You know what happens to stories as people repeat them. Before long, everyone knew if you joined the early Church and made one slip, God would strike you dead. ***"So great fear*** (phobos) ***came upon all the church and upon all who heard these things"*** (Acts 5:11).

However, the fear held by the early Church did not seem to terrorize Jerusalem. Luke reported, ***"And believers were increasingly added to the Lord, multitudes of both men and women"*** (Acts 5:14). They were bringing their sick into the streets in the hope that as Peter passed by, his shadow might fall on them. The populous of Jerusalem held the early Church in awe and respect, causing many not to join because of this wonderment (Acts 5:13). The outsiders knew that becoming a part of the early Church meant total commitment. There were no half-hearted, part-time members of the early Church! Everyone understood Jesus is Lord! If you were going to be in a relationship with Jesus, He had to maintain this position in your life. ***"He cannot deny Himself"*** (2 Timothy 2:13).

The fear that gripped Jerusalem resulted from awe and reverence. The Sanhedrin understood how Jerusalem felt when they captured Peter, John, and the healed beggar from the Gate Beautiful. These leaders could not deny the miracle of the well-known, healed beggar standing before them. He had begged at the temple gate for nearly forty years. Everyone was in awe over God's movement through the apostles. The Sanhedrin could not punish the apostles because of the people since they all glorified God for the miracle (Acts 4:21). Despite the threat of persecution, the "fear" continued to increase as God moved on Ananias and Sapphira.

Let me propose to you the foundation of this concept. This idea is not a theological bias but is the expression of the New Testament. We must interpret every story in light of all the Scriptures. We have to compare our passage with other passages to maintain the proper focus on truth. Only when we set aside our personal bias can we hear the clear communication from the Spirit of God.

Positive Principle

Our story has a positive principle operating within it. This principle is interwoven in all of the Scriptures and becomes the fundamental understanding of the universe's working mechanics. This principle is an expression of God's heart. If God birthed everything in creation from His thoughts, this has to be the fundamental principle of His heart. This principle is so complicated that one statement cannot reveal its entirety. Yet, it is so simple that every statement of truth about God makes it known, meaning the Bible does not give us a one-sentence description. If so, we would comprehend that one statement and think we knew it all. But God keeps us on the edge of revelation by this positive principle revealing itself in practical interaction with Him. If we get even a small glimpse of this principle, we experience the confidence to enter into a merger with God. This principle is the source of our hunger and thirst for righteousness.

Here is the principle. Fulfillment in the human experience is in righteousness; destruction in the human experience is in sin. The soul of a human being thrives in perfect love and deteriorates in division and hate. Absolute dependence on the Trinity God is the fertile soil of growth; independence is cancer that rots human life in decay. The human character advances on the strength of faith and shrinks in suspicion and skepticism. The road to victory is paved with bleeding, suffering, and dying; self-centeredness paves the way to defeat. Any expression of selfish desire for personal safety or betterment brings ruin and dissatisfaction. This principle of redemption is always a focus on others. "How to be safe" is never the theme, but this principle calls us to risk ourselves. This principle is not about the elimination of suffering, opposition, or battles. It does not cease to work in strife and upset. Instead, this principle is the attitude within the pain, resistance, and conflicts that the world cannot defeat!

In light of this principle, we understand what happened in the lives of Ananias and Sapphira. They violated this principle the moment they thought in terms of "get, grab, keep, protect, and save," entering into death. Even if they continued to breathe, they would have lived in death. The early Church and the Jerusalem community began to understand this principle, and they were in awe (phobos). When such an awareness of ***"fear"*** happens, you either get in or get out. The "awesomeness" either brings you to a total embrace of the principle or repels you to stay your distance.

There are many expressions of this principle. ***"For the wages of sin is death, but the gift of God is eternal life in***

Christ Jesus our Lord" (Romans 6:23). God is not mad; there is no desire in His heart to punish you. He weeps over the wages that you earn by the rebellion in your heart. He is so desirous that we have life that He offers it as a gift. No one needs to be without this amazing life. ***"For whoever desires to save his life will lose it, but whoever loses his life for My sake will find it"*** (Matthew 16:25). Losing one's life is the opposite of the selfish heart that always seeks its own way. Self-centeredness always ends up in the loss of everything. It is in giving that we get, in losing that we win, in surrender we receive, and in dying that we live, all the message of the cross. No wonder Paul cried, ***"For the message of the cross is foolishness to those who are perishing, but to us who are being saved it is the power of God"*** (1 Corinthians 1:18). We shape our lives by the things we merit, earn, or achieve. We compete, conquer, or compare, the only things that make sense to our selfish worldly minds. Indeed, the god of this world has blinded us (2 Corinthians 4:3). However, each of us ends at the finish line broken, empty, and without hope. ***"For by grace you have been saved through faith, and that not of yourselves; it is the gift of God, not of works, lest anyone should boast"*** (Ephesians 2:8-9). The gift is abundant, flowing from God's heart. This gift is the fundamental principle of the universe!

Ananias and Sapphira lived and died in the context of this spiritual principle. God wept over this couple who heard and embraced the positive principle, yet ended in death. He was not mad; He did not strike them dead. It is reality, the decisive principle by which God created all things.

Positive Person

The focus of this positive principle is on Jesus. The Bible does not propose an idea, a proverb, or a bumper sticker slogan.

This principle is not like the law of gravity operating on one's life but is impersonal. It is not a law of the universe at all. This principle is a Person. The Trinity God placed His heart (the way He thinks and functions) in Jesus. All creation comes through Jesus (Colossians 1:16). Therefore, everything has Jesus's fingerprints on it. He is the visible representation of this positive principle. Thus, the Living Christ confronts us, not an impersonal law.

Paul exposed this truth when he said that we are *"in Him." "Even when we were dead in trespasses, made us alive together with Christ (by grace you have been saved), and raised us up together; and made us sit together in the heavenly places in Christ"* (Ephesians 2:5-6). You are seated and surrounded by Jesus. It is in this positive position, in this positive Person, that the positive principle works. All fulfillment, spiritual blessings, spiritual growth, and prosperity are working in your life. Outside of this position are darkness, destruction, decay, and ruin.

What a fantastic picture of completeness! We are not seated in some far corner of God's concern. He does not visit us with the necessary elements for life. He does not send angels to give us what we need. He places us in His heart! We are at the center of His concern and desires, not a part-time hobby receiving His attention occasionally. We fulfill His dreams. God seats us in Christ, the heart of God demonstrated in the flesh. It is "in Christ," we know God. "In Christ" is the principle of life that operates in us. It is "in Christ" that God accomplishes all of His dreams for us.

Do you see the singularity in this reality? My focus must be on Jesus, desiring, or seeking nothing outside of Him. The needs of my life must not be my concern, for only Jesus can fulfill them. The difficulty seems to be in our focus. We believe in Jesus, but not in Him alone. We play the role of Ananias and Sapphira, wanting to be a part of the church, the mission, and the purpose of helping others. But we are not all in! We allow Jesus to be the source of our salvation, but not our finances. Jesus is good for our eternal destiny but not for our daily routine. Jesus is not all in all to us.

Positive Production

The positive Person of the positive principle wants a relationship with you. In the intimacy of His person, you will find life and fulfillment; outside of a relationship with Him, you will find death and destruction. A person does not have a choice on the result; a person only has a choice about intimacy with Jesus. Jesus attempted to explain this to the scribes and Pharisees. He illustrated it with a tree and its fruit. ***"Either make the tree good and its fruit good, or else make the tree bad and its fruit bad; for a tree is known by its fruit"*** (Matthew 12:33). A good tree cannot produce bad fruit, and a bad tree cannot produce good fruit. We cannot dwell in Jesus and produce destruction and ruin; we cannot dwell outside of Jesus and live in life.

What is the purpose of Ananias and Sapphira's story? It is an illustration of destruction due to the lack of completeness. They were not all in! Although they were Jews and embraced their historical heritage, they did not fully embrace the merger with Jesus. They experienced guilt over Jesus' crucifixion; they extended some form of repentance and sorrow. They knew the thrill of the early Church in ministry, miracles, and membership, but did not commit one hundred percent to the merger. We cannot live in both halves of the positive principle. We cannot live in ***"the wages of sin"*** and in ***"the gift of God."*** No one can ***"sit together in heavenly places in Christ"*** and dwell in self-centeredness. It is one or the other! We must get in or get out!

From the days of old until now, this is always the message. Joshua turned to the people of Israel and cried, ***"Serve the Lord! And if it seems evil to you to serve the Lord, choose for yourselves this day whom you will serve, whether the gods which your fathers served that were on the other side of the River, or the gods of the Amorites, in whose land you dwell. But as for me and my house, we will serve the Lord"*** (Joshua 24:14-15). There is no middle ground, no way to maintain both or take advantage of all. It is in or out; you are, or you are not. The positive production is an abandonment to Jesus.

Acts 5:6

REMOVAL

"And the young men arose and wrapped him up, carried him out, and buried him" (Acts 5:6).

Expositional preaching or study is natural for those who believe in the interaction of the Living Word and the Written Word. Cross Style is a commitment to the cross being the style of the Christian life, which we cannot have without death to self-centeredness. The interaction of the Living Word and the Written Word will continually reveal any residue of self-centeredness. The Living Word is the presence of Jesus residing in the believer. Every aspect of the believer's life comes under the influence of His presence. The believer begins to think, feel, and desire like Jesus. But this cannot happen unless Jesus speaks to us through the Written Word. The Scriptures are merely a written document unless the Living Word begins to communicate the Written Word to the heart of the believer. Then the Written Word becomes the whisperings of the Lover of our souls.

Therefore, we must involve ourselves in the Scriptures that God might reveal the truth. We dare not impose our theology or cultural persuasion on the Scriptures. We must allow the principles or concepts of the Written Word to shape us. For this to happen, we must abandon ourselves to what Jesus has to say to us. We must consistently guard against adjusting the Scriptures to our desires. It is easy to go beyond what the Scriptures say and impose our legalism, which is the struggle in the story of Ananias and Sapphira. There are so many details to the story that are not present. Luke gave other details that raise the question of "why?" Why did Luke put those details in the story? What was the concept he was trying to tell us?

Peter confronted Ananias with his embezzlement and lying. The truth struck Ananias in his heart, and he died. He did not repent of his sin; we must assume from the rest of the Scriptures that he did have that option. It does not say that God struck Ananias dead; we only know that death occurred. **"And the young men arose and wrapped him up, carried him out, and buried him"** (Acts 5:6). These same young men later were tasked with removing the dead body of his wife, Sapphira (Acts 5:10). Did Luke intend to communicate a spiritual concept to us through this study? Was it an insignificant detail of the story? Why did Luke include such a statement?

There is a difficulty with the statement's grammar. When we read it in the English language, it appears that Ananias died, and immediately the young men rushed to remove his body. They wrapped him in the appropriate cloth, carried him to the burial site, and buried him, which violates the customs for burial in every culture. No one notified or involved Sapphira in her husband's burial. The church assumed the responsibility of burying Ananias on their terms. One must wonder at the validity of this account.

The Greek presentation of the passage gives us a better understanding. There are two main verbs in our verse. The first *"wrapped up"* (systello), a combination of "sun" (together) and "stello" (to repress, withdraw oneself, contract, shrink, wrap together, envelop, wind in a garment or robe). As a rule, "systello" emphasizes the element of shrinking or diminishing.

Part One: The Agreed Resolve Continued

The second main verb is ***"buried"*** (thapto), having to do with the funeral rites. There are two remaining verbs, ***"arose"*** and ***"carried out"*** that are participles, verbs that act as adverbs giving content to the main verbs. "Anistemi" is the Greek word translated ***"arose,"*** used in the sense of rising up to take action, a combination of "ana," which means "again" and "histemi," meaning to stand. "Anistemi" is used consistently for "resurrection." Why did Luke include this statement? ***"And the young men arose and wrapped him up, carried him out, and buried him."***

The most startling issue of these four verbs is that they are all in the aorist tense. The verbs used in connection with the death and burial of Sapphira are also in the aorist tense (Acts 5:10). It is complicated to translate the aorist tense in the English language. We do not have anything equivalent to it, because it is a non-tense verb. It is a snapshot of the action of a moment. There was no indication when that moment happened, for it is not under the consideration of this tense. In the English translation, it appears that upon the death of Ananias, the young men immediately arose, carried him out, and buried him. Three hours later, his wife came in, not knowing her husband was dead and buried. But this is not the case indicated by the aorist tense. This tense allows for Ananias' and Sapphira's burial together at a later time. Luke does not try to relate the details of this burial to us, for it is not crucial to the truth and purpose of the passage.

If Luke was not giving the details of the burial of Ananias and Sapphira, what was his intent? Why did Luke include this statement? ***"And the young men arose and wrapped him up, carried him out, and buried him"*** (Acts 5:6). We want to be careful not to make more of the details than Luke intended. He did not focus on a historical account of the early church's actions. Yet, as in his Gospel account, he relates all of these stories and encounters. The reason is that the spiritual world always reveals itself on the stage of the physical. Is there a spiritual concept related to us in the physical details he gives? If Luke desired to describe the physical aspects, he would have given more to complete the burial information. He stated the activities in this verse in ways that were not necessary.

In a previous study, we discovered there is a war taking place. This war occurred in the spiritual realm, but the physical realm displayed its actions. Luke gave the story of Ananias and Sapphira as a negative illustration to those who are not "all in." Christianity cannot survive outside of completeness existing between God and man because both are required to give themselves entirely to the other. No one can question the completeness of God's giving. He displayed it clearly in the life and death of Jesus. **"But God demonstrated His own love toward us, in that while we were still sinners, Christ died for us"** (Romans 5:8). This total abandonment must take place in the life of man. Life is the result of completeness in the relationship, and death is the result of the lack of completeness. Relationship with Jesus cannot tolerate half-heartedness, which our passage clearly relates.

Answer
Factual

Our passage begins with the word **"And,"** translated from the Greek word "de." In some versions of the Bible, "de" is not translated. It is a continuative conjunction with the primary function being a contrast, which we must keep in mind in the meaning of our sentence. If Luke intended to link two equal ideas, he would have used the Greek word "kai." Therefore, in the context of Ananias' soul departing from him, Luke proposed the awareness of the presence of God. We acknowledge in Luke's statement that **"fear"** came upon everyone. We also assume the movement of God's presence in the convicting words of Peter

Part One: The Agreed Resolve Continued

to Ananias. The Holy Spirit confronted Ananias about his sin. He did not repent, yet something happened to his soul in the refusal of the opportunity. Death occurred. The clash of Light and darkness produced overwhelming consequences.

The clash of Light and darkness produced a consequence in Ananias' life. The young men rushed in to remove his dead body. What would be the natural continuation of the presence of death in the presence of life? What would you expect when darkness appears amid light? Death occurs but cannot remain. Death cannot be present amid life! God is not mad; He does not fly off in fits of rage. He is not that way. Do not underestimate the wonder of God's presence!

The Scriptures repeatedly remind us of the wonder of God's presence. John's Gospel records three chapters of Jesus' interaction with the disciples in the upper room before His crucifixion (John 14, 15, and 16). Jesus gave a final discourse to the disciples on the wonder of what is to come, the fullness of the Holy Spirit. He spoke in these terms, ***"At that day you will know that I am in My Father, and you in Me, and I in you"*** (John 14:20). This oneness with the Father is intimacy and merger. The merger between Jesus and man creates the new Kingdom person, a new creature. The disciples could not comprehend such a relationship from their old covenant status until they experienced the fullness of the Holy Spirit.

At the core of His discourse, Jesus gave a physical illustration, a parable of the merger between God and man. He told the parable of the True Vine (John 15:1-8), using the word ***"abide"*** seven times in the eight verses. Abiding is how a branch remains in the vine. The vine and branch are distinct and yet one. The branch shares the life of the vine, bears the fruit of the vine, and even looks like the vine; nevertheless, it remains a branch. According to Jesus, if anyone does not abide in the vine's life, immediate death occurs. The living vine cannot tolerate the death of the branch. The vinedresser removes, gathers, and burns the branch (John 15:6) without anger, meanness, or judgment. His action is "factual!" Death cannot abide in the presence of life!

Matthew wrote about several accounts of Jesus in the presence of demons. Jesus came into the country of Gergesenes (Matthew 8:28-34). Two demon-possessed men were living among the tombs. They dwelt amid death; in the presence of death, they were fierce, so that no one could pass that way. When Jesus approached them, they cried out, **"What have we to do with You, Jesus, You Son of God? Have you come here to torment us before the time"** (Matthew 8:29)? The Greek word "basanizo," translated "torment," refers to torture. The demons' existed in death (the tombs), and Life (Jesus) stepped into their presence. Life entering death is torture, and the two cannot abide together. Listen to the language of the demons. **"If You cast us out permit us to go away into the herd of swine"** (Matthew 8:31). The demons asked Jesus to allow them to escape His presence of Life by entering the swine. Jesus was not angry, mean, or judgmental when He sent the demons into the pigs. Life and death cannot abide together, which is the Bible's factual answer.

Aggressive
Forceful

"And the young men arose and wrapped him up, carried him out, and buried him" (Acts 5:6). This verse has an aggressive tone to it. The two main verbs are **"wrapped up"** and **"buried."** The first word in the Greek text is **"arose,"** a participle setting the tone for the two main verbs. The Greek word for **"arose"** is "anistemi," used in a variety of applications throughout the New Testament. The writers used "anistemi" consistently for "resurrection from the dead." "Anistemi" speaks of a sick person made well, someone lying down getting up, and another sitting now standing. The use of "anistemi" involves movement. Why did Luke give this additional information? He highlighted the aggressive work of death's removal from the presence of life. "Life and death cannot abide together" is not only a fact, but there is an aggressive element of the two repelling each other. Luke's introduction to this tone is crucial.

Returning to the parable of the True Vine (John 15:1-8), the intimacy between the vine and the branch is in sharing life. John used the word ***"abide"*** seven times in eight verses. When the branch does not abide in the life, death occurs. Jesus clarified this principle when He said, ***"If anyone does not abide in Me, he is cast out as a branch and is withered; and they gather them and throw them into the fire, and they are burned"*** (John 15:6). The Greek word translated ***"cast out"*** and ***"thrown"*** is "ballo," correctly translated except for the tone. "Ballo" used many times in the New Testament has the same tone, always impulsive and without hesitation. "Ballo" has no thought involved, no calculation with thoughtful action. Luke did not need to put this information in the details, but he emphasized the aggressive action of death's removal from the presence of life.

The participle ***"arose"*** modifies the main verb ***"wrapped up"*** (systello). "Systello" focuses on the idea of shrinking or diminishing though it can also refer to compression, crowding, or brevity. We see this in Light and darkness. The presence of Light diminishes and shrinks darkness. Light is an aggressive repellant to darkness. Light and darkness cannot abide together! Light does not punish darkness; light does not lose its temper; light does not judge. The nature of light aggressively repels darkness.

The old idea that "we must have a little sin, or we would have no fun at all" is ridiculous. The Christian's surrender must be a complete abandonment to Jesus, or he is not a Christian. There are no half-Christians, and no one becomes a Christian on a trial basis. We are either all in or all out.

Removal | Acts 5:6

Absolute
Filling

The final Greek word in the Greek text is "thapto," translated "buried." "Thapto" is not used often in the New Testament, but in our passage, burial is the removal of death. It bespeaks the final result of death and destruction. The Apostle Paul did a fantastic thing with this word. In some sense, he rescued the word from the negative and made it positive. He added a prefix to "thapto." In the Book of Romans, he speaks of "synthapto." The prefix of death is "with" or "together with" (syn). ***"Therefore we were buried with*** (synthapto) ***Him through baptism into death, that just as Christ was raised from the dead by the glory of the Father, even so we also should walk in newness of life"*** (Romans 6:4).

The wages of sin is death, and we have all sinned; therefore, all the consequences of death in its separation and destruction will be our experience. Death buried Ananias and Sapphira. The fact is life cannot tolerate death, and it is an aggressive separation. Life removes death and darkness, and death and darkness abide in destruction. But Paul proposed the merger of my sinful being with the righteousness of Christ's life. It is the mystery of the cross, beyond our wildest dreams. Jesus marched into the middle of my darkness and death; He set aside His light and life so He could embrace all that I am in darkness and death. If I merge completely with Him in death and darkness, all that transpired in Jesus' resurrection, I will know.

But we must carefully consider the critical element, which is together with Jesus. I must have complete abandonment and absolute surrender to Him. It only happens in "together with" Him. Outside of Jesus, I dwell in death alone. In my union with Him, His death and life become mine! His death and His presence are not mine without Him. In that sense, life and death

Part One: The Agreed Resolve Continued

are never mine because I am His! Again, Jesus calls us to come under His influence. We cannot partially surrender or commit. I must get in our get out! I choose to be His alone!

Acts 5:7

I DIDN'T KNOW

"Now it was about three hours later when his wife came in, not knowing what happened" (Acts 5:7).

The Wikipedia definition of "diptych" is "any object with two flat plates, which are a pair, often attached at a hinge. For example, the standard notebook and school exercise book of the ancient world was a diptych consisting of a pair of such plates that contained a recessed space filled with wax." In ancient days, builders used diptych art for altarpieces, a painting on two hinged wooden panels that could be closed. Luke describes this kind of dual picture painting when he tells the story of Ananias and Sapphira. He presents a parallelism, which enhances the narrative. The steps in Ananias' life were the same for Sapphira. As we walk through the story, we wonder if the end for each will be the same. The idea of the passage is underscored by doubling.

What is the idea of the passage? Christianity, by its essence, demands completeness. As Luke describes the members of the early Church, we see them as wholly abandoned to Jesus. Even when their loyalty to Jesus brings them persecution, they become even more determined. A relationship with Jesus cannot be

Part One: The Agreed Resolve Continued

part-time or casual. This relationship is so essential that Luke demonstrated it with a positive and a negative illustration. The positive example is Barnabas (Acts 4:36-37). Luke's negative illustration is about Ananias and Sapphira (Acts 5:1-11), which is eleven verses long. Within the negative example, Luke gives a diptych, making two stories one.

Ananias brought a portion of his land's selling price and gave it to the apostles. He proposed that it was the entire amount, but it was not. Sapphira agreed with this action (Acts 5:2). When Sapphira came to Peter three hours later, he asked her, **"Tell me whether you sold the land for so much"** (Acts 5:8)? She gave a positive response, which was in agreement with what Ananias had said. What Ananias did at the beginning of the story, Sapphira repeated. The next step in the story is Peter confronting Ananias' with his sin. Satan filled Ananias' heart, and he lied to the Holy Spirit (Acts 5:3). Later, Peter confronted Sapphira with her agreement with Ananias to test the Spirit of the Lord (Acts 5:9). The result for Ananias was not repentance, but death (Acts 5:5). Sapphira also did not repent, but fell down and breathed her last (Acts 5:10). The awareness of God's power swept through the early Church, and fear came upon all who heard Ananias' story (Acts 5:5). The sweeping fear repeated itself as the story continued with Sapphira (Acts 5:11).

This story is a diptych of truth painted in the lives of two people. If there is any doubt that Christianity demands total abandonment to Jesus, these two pictures settle it. Any thought of partial giving in our lives does not meet the criteria for the Christian experience. God is not egotistical, who cannot tolerate disloyalty, so His demands are not the basis of this story. The Scriptures present the Trinity God as compassionate, forgiving, and long-suffering. He desires what is best for us, not what is best for Him! However, the nature of merging with Him, forming a new creature, demands completeness. Any thought of using

God for self-advantage violates the core of my helplessness and is an expression of independence instead of dependence. Any self-centeredness expressed in physical activity nullifies intimacy with Jesus. You and I must be all in!

But what if I do not know? Sapphira did not know. ***"Now it was about three hours later when his wife came in, not knowing what happened"*** (Acts 5:7). At this point in the story, Sapphira did not know that her husband was dead. She was not confronted with her sin and had not experienced the full awareness of guilt before God. Her understanding of theology may have been limited. She followed the leadership of her husband and may not have known she was sinning.

However, the message of the passage is not about complete knowledge! The message is about the complete abandonment of the heart. Rules and laws may be in effect, but I may not understand or know all of them. My heart shrinks from the thought of hurting Jesus by anything I might do. My heart is His. Undoubtedly, there are actions in my life that are not as He desires, but I do not know what they are. My heart hungers and thirsts for righteousness; therefore, Jesus will teach me because my heart is complete. I do not have full knowledge; therefore, my decisions and judgments are not always right. But my heart longs for His destiny in my life. Jesus will produce growth in my life. I may not understand the circumstances in which I dwell, but I trust Him with all my heart. I cry for His will and not mine! The question "why" may approach my mind, but my heart is content in His provision. I focus my whole heart on Jesus!

The story of Ananias and Sapphira is a focus on the intent and motive of the human being. When Peter confronted Ananias, he confronted his heart (Acts 5:3). Peter explained that the problem was not the land because it belonged to Ananias and Sapphira. The issue was not the amount of money from the sale. In each case, they were free to do as they wanted with

Part One: The Agreed Resolve Continued

the land and the money. The problem was in their heart motive, for they allowed Satan to fill their hearts with his desires. They had not surrendered to Jesus, which divided their hearts. This partial surrender allowed rebellion, sin, and Satan to fill their hearts, which always leads to death. Jesus is Lord of all, or He is not Lord at all! The call of Christianity from beginning to end is a total abandonment of the heart.

No one needs to be embarrassed to propose such a call. It is not radical or too demanding. Our surrender to Jesus must match the worthiness of His Person. How can the value of redemption accept a cheap, half-hearted commitment? We are face to face with Jesus' total abandonment of Himself to us. How can God require anything less from us? The call of Christianity is not to the overall acceptance of theology. It is undoubtedly not an abandonment to a set of rules or activities or embracing an organizational structure. The call is not even to a particular career, such as a missionary or pastor. The request is to merge with the Person of Jesus. He must be Lord of my life. In Him, I find all the dreams of God for my life fulfilled. The actions of Ananias and Sapphira were a direct reflection of their lack of commitment to Jesus.

Therefore, the principal concept of our verse is simple. It is not what you do not know that matters; it is what you do know! It is not about all knowledge but complete heart commitment. Will you love Jesus with your whole heart? Despite all the things occurring around you of which you are not aware, will you love Him with your whole heart? The unknown will always be present; it cannot ultimately hurt you if you belong to Jesus. Does Jesus not have a plan and destiny for you? There is no unknown in His realm. God gives a renewed call to gather together all that you do know and abandon yourself to Jesus!

There is so much more to view in our verse.

Coming

Luke said, *"Now it was about three hours later when his wife came in, not knowing what happened"* (Acts 5:7). The Greek word "eiserchomai" is translated *"came in."* "Eiserchomai" presents the idea of "to enter" or "to come into." This main verb is in the indicative mood, meaning it is a simple statement of fact. Luke uses "eiserchomai" to say Sapphira entered into what she did not know. All of our lives have this picture. Every step we take places us in the realm of the unknown. If the unknown frightens us, we will live in constant fear, for we always dwell in and are surrounded by the unknown in our past, present, and future. The unknown will remain with us in eternity because we will never be omniscient. We were born in the unknown, and we will depart this world to face another unknown.

The reality of uncertainty is frightening. How can I find security and confidence as I face such a mystery? Security is only in the One who knows. There is no unknown in the dwelling place of our God! God has no unknown in His existence, and He knows all there is to know about my life!

"O Lord, You have searched me and known me.
You know my sitting down and my rising up;
You understand my thought afar off.
You comprehend my path and my lying down,
And are acquainted with all my ways" (Psalm 139:1-3).

"Your eyes saw my substance, being yet unformed.
And in Your book they all were written,
The days fashioned for me,
When as yet there were none of them" (Psalm 139:16).

Part One: The Agreed Resolve Continued

Perhaps the Trinity God does know every detail of all things, and for Him, there is no unknown, but how does that benefit me and bring security to my living? God is in love with you, and He molded you with His creative fingers. God has dreams, and He created you to fulfill those dreams. You are not merely a number in the census of the world. God chose you before the foundation of the world and destined you for His work before you were capable of doing it. Although I may face the unknown, there is no unknown for God. My security and confidence are in Him.

However, this requires your unconditional trust and surrender to Jesus. How can I trust Him for eternal salvation and not also trust Him for my financial security? I cannot depend on Jesus for the safety of heaven and not rely on Him for my earthly home. I have to abandon myself in every area of life to His controlling influence because He knows me. Suppose I control the known areas of my life that determine and direct the unknown areas. Jesus cannot be Lord over the unknown unless He is Lord over the known.

Trusting Jesus with our unknown is the concept of our passage. It is not what I do not know that matters; it is what I do know! Sapphira came into the unknown. She did not know her husband was dead, and that the young men had carried him out. Now the same thing happened to her. Her death did not occur because she did not know. It happened because of what she did know! She knew that she and her husband agreed to test the Holy Spirit (Acts 5:9). Since Sapphira did not come under the influence of the Holy Spirit in what she knew, there was no security in what she did not know. What we know is a call to total abandonment to Jesus!

Comprehension

What do you know? There are several Greek words

translated **"know."** Our favorite is "ginosko," a relational term, the most intimate of all relationships. "Epiginosko" is an expanded and strengthened version of "ginosko." "Gnostos" is the Greek word used to depict information or data. Then, there is the Greek word in our passage, "oida," which is the idea to perceive, one's perception or understanding. When you attempt to explain something to another person, and they say, "I see it," the Greek word "oida" applies.

Sapphira entered into a realm where she did not perceive or have any understanding of what was happening. She did not know her husband had physically died, the manner of his death, the confrontation of Peter, and the younger men's task of removing his body. But those facts only demonstrate an avalanche of spiritual realities. Her perception of the embezzlement was light and superficial. She and Ananias had merely hidden something from the apostles and the early Church. The sale price of their land was their business. She did not see the immense spiritual war between good and evil fighting on the stage of her life. She could not conceive the eternal consequences of what she did not know.

Paul said that God veils the Gospel to those who are perishing. He explained the source of this covering of their perception. Their **"minds the god of this age has blinded, who do not believe, lest the light of the gospel of the glory of Christ, who is the image of God, should shine on them"** (2 Corinthians 4:4). Although we know, there is always the unknown, and we regularly face the mystery, the reality of blindness and veiling speaks of what we could see but do not. Should Sapphira not have known? The strength of her Jewish background, the wonder of Christian experience, and the training of the apostles would all cry out. Sapphira should have known the spiritual reality of her sin. Did not the Holy Spirit faithfully speak to her and Ananias as they took steps to embezzle the funds? If Sapphira had followed what she knew, she would not have entered into what she did not know.

Part One: The Agreed Resolve Continued

Again, we have to face the concept of our passage. It is not what we do not know that matters; it is what we do know! If Sapphira had embraced what she did know, what she did not know would have been fine. What she knew about Jesus and her merger with Him could have saved her from all she did not know.

Childbirth

Luke described all that Sapphira did know as *"what had happened,"* the translation of the Greek word "ginomai." "Ginomai" portrays the idea of "coming into being" or "something being birthed." I have spoken to a variety of people who found themselves in undesirable situations. They looked at me with confusion and asked, "How did I get here?" They awakened to find themselves in life's circumstances and wondered what happened. They did not plan or expect the event, but they had birthed it!

Quiz a group of first graders about what they want to be when they grow up. None of them will report that their life's dream is to be an alcoholic, a child molester, or a murderer. Counsel a young couple who plan to marry, and they will not tell you they are getting married to fight and eventually divorce. How does that happen (ginomai)? None of the unwanted circumstances result from fate, happenchance, or luck. We birth them from what we know.

The state of security regarding the birthing of the unknown is in abandoning ourselves to what we do know. Ananias and Sapphira were Jews who knew the transforming power of Christ. They sat under the apostles teaching, experienced signs and wonders, and participated in the ministry of the early Church. How did they arrive at embezzlement? *"Satan has filled your heart to lie to the Holy Spirit and keep back part of the price of the land for yourself?"* Amid all they had experienced, they did not embrace Jesus in total abandonment. Therefore, what they knew was half-heartedness, compromise, and self-effort! What they knew birthed the embezzlement! What if they had entirely surrendered to Jesus? What if their abandonment to Jesus had been total? We can only imagine what God could have birthed in them.

We do not know what is going to be, but the birthing always comes out of what is. It is not what you do not know that matters; it is what you do know. We must know Jesus completely. ***"But if we walk in the light as He is in the light, we have fellowship with one another, and the blood of Jesus Christ His Son cleanses us from all sin"*** (1 John 1:7). God's call to us is to walk in all the light of His presence. What we know will quickly give birth to what we do not know. Ask Ananias and Sapphira!

Acts 5:8

A CRITICAL MOMENT

"And Peter answered her, 'Tell me whether you sold the land for so much?' She said, 'Yes, for so much.'" (Acts 5:8).

The Jews captured Jesus in the middle of the night and brought Him before Pilate at the crack of dawn. For Pilate, it was the most critical moment in the history of the world. Pilate responded as a judge. **"What accusation do you bring against this man"** (John 18:29)? The leaders of Israel did not have any evidence against Jesus that concerned Pilate. The Romans had only recently taken away the right for any nation to put anyone to death. Only the Romans could execute a person. Pilate urged the Jews to judge Jesus by their law, but that did not satisfy the Jews who wanted Jesus eliminated.

Pilate began a conversation with Jesus, asking, **"Are You King of the Jews"** (John 18:33)? Jesus tried to tell Pilate that indeed He was a King, but His kingdom was another world. If His kingdom were of this world, He would declare war, and His men would fight the Jews. So Pilate was correct, Jesus is King. Jesus answered, **"You say rightly that I am a king. For this cause I was born, and for this cause I have come into the world, that I should bear witness to the**

truth. Everyone who is of the truth hears My voice" (John 18:37). Pilates' response was significant. ***"What is truth"*** (John 18:38)?

I identify with Pilate's question! Many voices sound in my ear. We can pick and choose what religion we want. Even in the latest news in the country, there is "fake news." The reporters do not tell the truth, and what they do say is twisted to fit their agenda. Even the preachers of the Gospel do not speak with one voice. There are many denominations, each with their brand of truth. What am I supposed to believe? "What is truth?"

Most of us do the best we can. We operate out of truth from our viewpoint. We develop our philosophy, and if it is right for me, then it is truth. I decide between true and false, making me my final reference point for truth. In my younger years, I discovered the idea of "situational ethics." There is no absolute truth; the situations and the people involved determine their authenticity. The world view says premarital sex and adultery are right or wrong determined by the circumstances in which they happen. When a young couple loves each other, how can it be wrong? Indeed, not telling the truth is a gracious and benevolent thing to do in some circumstances. Telling you that your haircut is the worst may be the truth, but it is not kind. Therefore, is it right in light of kindness to say to you that I love your haircut? Is it an acceptable lie given the situation? Is there an absolute truth regardless of the circumstances?

Some have proposed they can offer a lie if it does not hurt anyone. Others think the truth may do more harm than good; therefore, it is in the best interest of everyone to lie. The person who smuggles Bibles into a restricted country, when questioned about possessing Bibles, says, "No." They tell a lie, but it is an acceptable lie because the result is good. Their situation demands a lie. But at the heart of it all, is there truth that we cannot violate? Is there that which is true regardless of the circumstances?

Part One: The Agreed Resolve Continued

Ananias and Sapphira sold a piece of property with the motive of helping the early Church in ministry. They both knew the selling price, and they agreed on how much of it they would give to the church. All of this was legitimate and truthful. The difficulty came in their agreement to lie about the amount received for the sale. They said that the amount they gave the church was the selling price, which was not the truth! But what was the harm? The early Church benefited from the money given, and Ananias and Sapphira had a little extra for personal use.

Lying was undoubtedly an issue for Peter. Listen to His words to Ananias. ***"Ananias, why has Satan filled your heart to lie to the Holy Spirit and keep back part of the price of the land for yourself? While it remained, was it not your own? And after it was sold, was it not in your own control? Why have you conceived this thing in your heart? You have not lied to men but to God"*** (Acts 5:3-4). Lying did matter to Peter. There is a definite reference for truth, and it is the Holy Spirit, the Spirit of Truth (John 14:17). Untruth violates the relationship with the One who is the truth! To live in deceit, you must live outside of Jesus.

But untruth not only is about God, but it is also about us. Falsehood is not a surface piece of dust on the human sleeve that we can quickly brush off. It is dirt in the heart of the person. The dust on the sleeve effects little of who we are, but the dirt in the heart determines our character. Untruth is not a cosmetic matter but is the foundational material of a person. Now in our passage, Peter questions Sapphira, ***"Tell me whether you sold the land for so much?"*** Sapphira answered, ***"Yes, for so much"*** (Acts 5:8). It was a moment of truth!

Truth matters every moment of our lives. However, there are some moments when it is critical. When Sapphira agreed with her husband to lie, she should have stood on truth. We do not know where she was for the three hours she was absent from her husband. She was living in the lie, but then, Peter confronted Sapphira with a critical moment for truth. Everything came together in that climactic moment. Could I impress upon you this reality? God is bringing you to a crucial moment of truth! He is now, at this moment, confronting you with His truth.

The Issue

The truth makes a critical moment. We often say there is my opinion, your opinion, and the way it is really. I am interested in living in "the way it is really," the truth. However, the reality is not perceiving correct data or information. Truth is more often than not beyond facts, for we can know all the facts and not know the truth. A person can diligently study the New Testament, glean all the facts about Jesus, and never embrace Him. Can we see the truth about Jesus and not know Him? On the other hand, we might not know all the facts about Him and still know Jesus, the Truth!

In the New Testament, the Greek word "aletheia" is translated "truth." The Scriptures seem to suggest three elements in the word's use. Truth is a picture of the CHARACTER of God. He is dependable, truthful, and upright in character. We understand from the Scriptures that we can trust God to keep His word. Paul wrote, ***"In hope of eternal life which God, who cannot lie, promised before time began"*** (Titus 1:2). According to the Book of Hebrews, God based His promises on His oath because He could not find anyone greater than Himself. ***"It is impossible for God to lie"*** (Hebrews 6:18).

Lying was the dilemma faced by Ananias and Sapphira. By their participation in the early Church, they claimed alignment with God's character. The fullness of the Holy Spirit, the essence of God's heart, supposedly filled them. But Peter said that Satan filled their hearts (Acts 5:3). They became an expression of Satan's character who ***"is a liar, and the father of it"*** (John 8:44).

Satan does not stand in the truth because there is no truth in Him. In the Sermon on the Mount, Jesus used six illustrations to contrast the old view with the new Kingdom reality. One of those illustrations deals with oaths. In the former view, telling the truth was only an obligation when they involved God. In the New Covenant, the character of God fills the believer; therefore, every word spoken by the believer includes God (Matthew 5:33-37), and there is never room for non-truth.

The second element of truth in the Scriptures is COMPLETENESS. Truth is real and complete as opposed to false and wanting. We are to see Christianity as the absolute truth (Ephesians 1:13). Jesus presented Himself as truth personified, saying, ***"I am the way, the truth, and the life"*** (John 14:6). What Jesus says is true because He is the truth! All the realities of the Trinity are visible in the Person of Jesus. He is not a partial revelation of truth, leaving more to come. No truth is wanting in Jesus. ***"For the law was given through Moses, but grace and truth came through Jesus"*** (John 1:17). Through the merger with Jesus, God promised, ***"when He, the Spirit of truth, has come, He will guide you into all truth"*** (John 16:13).

Now we come to the problem of Ananias and Sapphira. Jesus did not fill them; therefore, they did not speak the truth. The judgments of God are according to the truth (Romans 2:2). ***"But to those who are self-seeking and do not obey the truth, but obey unrighteousness"*** (Romans 2:8). God exposes the completeness of truth. Falseness cannot exist in His presence. Satan could fill their hearts with deception because Jesus did not fill them. Paul said, ***"Who hindered you from obeying the truth? This persuasion does not come from Him who calls you"*** (Galatians 5:7-8). Sapphira came to a critical moment of truth. The expression of her heart determined her destiny. She could know the truth, but would she be the vessel for its exposure?

The third element of truth in the Scriptures is CONCRETE. In this case, "alethinos" is usually an adjective, expressing the sense of something real as opposed to mere appearance or copy. The writer of the Book of Hebrews thundered into this use of "alethinos." For seven chapters, he presented his arguments. Now he summarizes all he said to give us the main point. ***"We have such a High Priest who is seated at the right hand of the throne of the Majesty in the heavens, a Minister of the sanctuary and of the true tabernacle which the Lord erected, and not man"*** (Hebrews 8:1-2). The tabernacle and the Levitical rituals are a copy or shadow of the real things (Hebrews 8:5). The Lord's Supper is a copy of the One who is the true bread (John 6:32, 35) and the true vine (John 15:1). Jesus is the eternal reality symbolized by the bread and wine.

Not being real was the issue faced by Ananias and Sapphira. Being Jews, they lived their lives in the copy or shadow, the Levitical rituals. Perhaps they found it easy to hide in the shadows, but now they had to step into the Light. Sapphira experienced a critical moment of truth. Would she try to remain in the shadows? Would she continue in deception? Regardless of her attempt, the Light exposed her. There is nothing but truth in the Light.

Satan may not fill our hearts to lie to the Holy Spirit, but the rejection of truth on any level is a rejection of authenticity on every level. Trying to solve a problem out of our strength and wisdom rejects the dependency Jesus demands of us in the merger. He will not let us deny the truth, ***"for without Me you can do nothing"*** (John 15:5). We come to a critical moment of truth! If we focus on materialism and worry about our future, we contradict the truth. ***"For your heavenly Father knows that you need all these things. But seek first the kingdom of God and His righteousness, and all these things shall***

Part One: The Agreed Resolve Continued

be added to you" (Matthew 6:32-33). Jesus always brings us to a critical moment of truth! Do not ever step out of the truth. Always be in Jesus!

The Intention

The intent of every critical moment is the past! Truth is not an attribute of the Trinity God but is the fiber of His character and essence. We do not have to argue to verify that truth fits His activities. God judges truthfully (Psalms 96:13), and He sends truth forth with His presence (Psalms 5:3). ***"For the law was given through Moses, but grace and truth came through Jesus Christ"*** (John 1:17). Jesus is the visible image of the invisible Trinity God, and His activities are a demonstration of truth. If we merge with Him in oneness, could anything less be expected of our actions as new creatures?

Ananias and Sapphira faced the problem of demonstrating truth. They deviated from God's character and the merger of His presence by deception. They had an attitude or spirit that manifested itself in the act of embezzlement. As the Spirit of Christ, the Truth, confronted Ananias and Sapphira, He required they return to their departure from His presence. They could not move beyond this departure. They couldn't ignore the past and move forward. Any further relationship with the Spirit of Truth must flow from the redemption of the departure. We cannot have a relationship with the Spirit of Truth without confrontation because He bases that relationship on truth, not falsehood.

The central issue of this moment is Truth! Jesus, the Truth, will confront the falsehood in our lives. Our hearts break at the experience of Ananias and Sapphira. Sapphira chose to remain in her deception (Acts 5:8). If she had only repented (given up a former thought to embrace a new thought), forgiveness could have been hers. She would have been set free by Truth. Jesus, the Light, would have embraced her in life (John 1:4).

Embracing the Truth, who is Jesus, is the call of God on our lives. We again face the message of completeness. All goodness, church support, or the authentic prayers of Ananias and Sapphira were to no avail. They deviated from Truth in one area, materialism; yet, all the assets of prior faithfulness did not compensate. ***"That God is light and in Him is no darkness at all"*** (1 John 1:5). The call is not to have perfect actions; the call is to have total openness to the Truth!

The Inheritance

The inheritance of every critical moment of truth is the future. Did Ananias and Sapphira think their deception would determine their fate? They agreed together to embezzle the funds from the sale of their property. In the deceit of hypocrisy, they proposed their complete commitment to Jesus in giving all while they selfishly held back. Did they think they would live in favor of the early Church and know the blessings of God's movement in others? Did they think God's blessings would flow in their lives while they benefited from deceit and embezzlement? They must have known the future is never determined by deception, but by the truth.

Suddenly Sapphira saw the truth as Ananias did, and her future was secured. Does this not scream at us that we must live in the truth? We cannot say that they were confused about what is truth and what is deception. Jesus is Truth! Again, Jesus calls us to abandon ourselves to Him. The Spirit of Jesus will guide you into all truth. He will continually reveal Himself to you and in you. There is no darkness in Jesus. He is the Light!

We do not find truth in facts, data, or the comprehension of information through education. We must have a relationship

Part One: The Agreed Resolve Continued

with the Person named Jesus. Facts and data focus on the discipline of learning, the achievement of knowledge, and the pursuit of degrees. Relationship with the One who is Truth focuses on intimacy, oneness, and merger. The relationship is the openness of life to the invasion of all that Jesus wants to be in you. Will you abandon yourself to Jesus? Will you allow Him to take you into intimacy to share His mind and heart, a place without deception?

Acts 5:9-10

AN AGREEMENT

> *"Then Peter said to her, 'How is that you have agreed together to test the Spirit of the Lord? Look, the feet of those who have buried your husband are at the door, and they will carry you out.' Then immediately she fell down at his feet and breathed her last. And the young men came in and found her dead, and carrying her out, buried her by her husband"*
> *(Acts 5:9-10).*

    The experience of Christianity dwells mostly in the realm of the abstract, creating difficulty for my masculinity. Sometimes I feel like I exist in only half of what God intended, which may be why God gave me a wife to help me in an area where I do not do well. After many years, I am willing to admit this problem, which is half the battle. Many men have issues with the church movement. The feminine approach to life that seems to shape the programs of the church repulses them. They see the church as a need of children and women, but it is not concrete enough for them.

    The use of feminine and masculine nouns is crucial in the original language of the Scriptures depicting the mystical element of Christianity. Rules, programs, and activities appeal to the concrete approach of the masculine. However, I find these are lifeless and routine without the feminine aspect. I was amazed to discover that everything I want in life appears as feminine in the Scriptures. Prayer, love, faith, and spiritual blessings are all in the feminine gender. Duty and obligation (masculine) begin to live when love and faith (feminine) are present.

With the feminine gender, things move beyond understanding. I can measure, gage, and fix things in the masculine, operating by the laws that I can manage. Masculine is factual and always the same. The steps to becoming a Christian are repentance and belief. If anyone does these two things, salvation is theirs. The problem is that repentance and belief are not concrete. Repentance says I am sorry for committing a list of sins. Belief is not merely stating the creed of the Bible because the Bible tells us that the devil believes. Therefore, no one can manufacture on their own mystical, feminine, or abstract elements involved in these steps.

Rules and programs never produced the Christian martyrs. People do not give their lives for the concrete. Christianity is a relationship with Jesus! However, even that language may be too weak to describe the intimacy involved. In the Old Testament, the relationship between God and man was a covenant. A covenant is an agreement enacted between two parties in which one or both make promises in advance, under oath, to perform or refrain from stipulated actions. This agreement is a concrete approach to relationships. However, in the New Testament, while we may refer to it as a covenant, it is far beyond the concrete (masculine). The New Testament covenant injects the element of the feminine. The union of God and man in oneness creates something new, the Kingdom person! The New Testament expresses it verbally in **"born again"** (John 3:3), **"born of the Spirit"** (John 3:8), **"children of God"** (John 1:12), or **"You, Father, are in Me, and I in You; that they also may be one in Us"** (John 17:21).

The mystery of the marriage relationship is evident in children! Marriage is a covenant relationship that is far beyond the performance of rules and or laws. Marriage dwells in emotions, attitudes, feelings, and the mystical expression of love. A person may see marriage as a concrete covenant that can be broken by divorce. The son or daughter, who is the physical expression of marriage unity, will never agree. Two people came together to form the child's life, and divorce rips that child apart. What does this do to them? Paul said, ***"This is a great mystery, but I speak concerning Christ and the church"*** (Ephesians 5:32).

You might think the actions of Ananias and Sapphira were harmless. After all, it was their money, and they were still generous to the church. Their story may be the view of the concrete, masculine approach. But this is not the opinion of the New Testament. Sin is not a Divine law that is broken and must receive an ascribed punishment. The Divine law does not come from God, removed from human relationship. He did not view human society and arbitrarily establish a law structure that allows us to exist together peacefully. When we break these laws, God already has a punishment assigned in advance. No! No! The Divine law is an expression of His Divine nature with which we have an intimate relationship. He fills us with His nature, we merge with His Spirit, and He creates a new creature in the fusion of our life with His. This oneness is not concrete, but abstract, on the highest level. Every sin is not the breaking of a law but a violation of His Person. We can see this in our passage.

Agreement

In our passage, ***"have agreed together"*** is a translation of the Greek word "symphoneo." "Smyphoneo" proposes the idea of being in accord or coming to an agreement. The undercurrent is the concept of linking, union, harmony, or oneness. "Symphoneo" is used six times in the New Testament, four times referring to a personal relationship. Jesus used the word to describe His presence interacting with the believers. The disciples rebuked Him when Jesus first predicted His death and resurrection (Matthew 16:22). The idea of redemption through bleeding, suffering, and dying seemed foreign to them. During their lives, the offering of sacrificial lambs for redemption was the practice. Yet, they argued with Jesus for six-days about the sacrifice of crucifixion (Matthew 17:1). Three of the disciples were at the Mount of Transfiguration as verification of redemption through suffering. Because of their argument, the other nine disciples found their ministry shut down (Matthew 17:14-20). Their disagreement with Jesus affected their relationships with each other. They argued over positions in the coming Kingdom (Matthew 18:1).

Jesus spoke to the disciples about "agreement (symphoneo)," beginning with the link that must happen between heaven and earth. He said, **"Assuredly, I say to you, whatever you bind on earth will be bound in heaven, and whatever you loose on earth will be loosed in heaven"** (Matthew 18:18). We must never think we can decide something in the physical and control the spiritual. Jesus proposed an agreement, link, harmony, and oneness between what is happening in the spiritual and physical realms. Jesus continued to verify the truth. **"Again I say to you that if two of you agree** (symphoneo) **on earth concerning anything that they ask, it will be done for them by My Father in heaven"** (Matthew 18:19). He began with the word **"again,"** repeating what He already said. He went on to describe the agreement as "symphoneo," which is the root word of our English word "symphony." Musical instruments come in all sizes, shapes, and varieties, stringed, brass, drums, and cymbals. An artistic masterpiece becomes a symphony when all the instruments come together. Jesus proposed a harmony or symphonic agreement between the spiritual and physical realms within the context of two or more believers.

What would be the result of such a symphony?" ***"For where two or three are gathered together in My name, I am there in the midst of them"*** (Matthew 18:20). The symphony of heaven and earth within the believers produces the presence of Jesus. Jesus is the revelation of complete harmony between heaven and earth, the link of oneness we know as Christianity. We dwell in a harmonious state when we merge with Jesus. Our lives give forth the music of the symphony!

We have to make it known that an agreement between the spiritual and physical realms is not optional. Our lives will and must reflect the spiritual and physical link. Peter confronted Sapphira with this agreement. He asked, ***"How is it that you have agreed together*** (smyphoneo) ***to test the Spirit of the Lord"*** (Acts 5:9)? The sin of Ananias and Sapphira was not a simple lie or the embezzlement of funds. The physical act of these sinful deeds revealed a harmony or link with Satan in the spiritual world (Acts 5:3). Had they at one time experienced the merger with the Holy Spirit? Had they given their lives to Christ in a symphonic harmony with His nature? Even if the answer to these questions is yes, a shift had taken place in their spiritual lives. They still had a part with the church movement and ministry, but something had happened in their link with Jesus.

The connection between the spiritual and the physical gives us a new view of sin! Christianity is not about God, who has arbitrarily established laws to govern society. The world says when a person disobeys a rule, God, the judge, inflicts the established punishment for the crime. There is no close link between the law, the sinner, and the punishment. However, Christianity proposes the opposite. There is a close relationship between the Trinity God and the law. The Old Testament law is a symphony flowing from God's nature. God did not arbitrarily establish the law to keep people within the boundaries of decency. The law is the pulse beat of God's heart. Therefore, sin is not the breaking of the law that does not matter in the future; it is a violation of the nature of God. Sin disrupts the symphony of physical and spiritual intimacy with God. Every sin is against God (Psalms 5:1-4).

If I lose my temper and physically harm a person, that is sin. Someone calls the police, and the police bring me before the judge. I broke the law of the land, but the judge has no involvement in my action. However, the judge, according to the law, sentences me to jail as punishment for my crime. Christianity is entirely different! If I lose my temper and harm someone, the judge before whom I stand is the one I injured. He bears the pain of my action; He suffers the consequences of my choice. Jesus experiences the full weight of my sin in Himself, so I do not suffer punishment. God forgives my sin and completely restores my link with Him, the one I violated. **"We implore you on Christ's behalf, be reconciled to God. For He made Him who knew no sin to be sin for us, that we might become the righteousness of God in Him"** (2 Corinthians 5:20-21). My sin destroyed the symphony between my life and God's heart, but God took the full weight of the punishment for the violation that He might bring me back into harmony with Him!

Peter asked Sapphira, **"How is it that you have agreed together to test the Spirit of the Lord"** (Acts 5:9). The statement refers to Ananias and Sapphira agreeing together to do this evil thing. But there is so much more. Their agreement was not a concrete covenant between two people to commit an act. There was an agreement of harmony with them and the spiritual forces of evil. What they did was not a lie or lack of generosity to the church. Ananias and Sapphira harmonized with evil in a war against the Holy Spirit. We must understand the sin in our lives in light of this war.

Assessment

According to Peter's statement, Ananias and Sapphira were in harmony with the evil of the spiritual world and attempted *"to test the Spirit of the Lord."* The Greek word "peirazo" translated *"to test,"* a morally neutral word. "Peirazo" is not bad or evil, and it is not good or beneficial. The testing takes on the character of the person who does the testing. If Satan does the testing, we call it "temptation." If God does the testing, we know it is a test to strengthen us in our relationship with Him.

In our passage, the verb "peirazo" is an infinitive, meaning connection with the main verb to give purpose. Ananias and Sapphira agreed together and linked with the spiritual evil to test the Spirit of the Lord. This link with evil is something of a contradiction; if Satan is involved, the act is a temptation to embrace evil. But, **"God cannot be tempted** (peirazo) **by evil, nor does He Himself tempt anyone"** (James 1:13). Therefore, it is foolish to instigate a situation in which we catch God in evil.

Satan's temptation of Jesus in the wilderness created the same situation (Matthew 4:1-11). After forty days of intense spiritual warfare, Jesus and Satan entered the climax of the battle. In the second of the last three temptations, Satan took Jesus to the pinnacle of the temple. The pinnacle of the temple is where the priest blows the horn to announce the time to offer the sacrificial lamb. Satan suggested to Jesus that He leap from the pinnacle and allow the angels to rescue Him. Such a spectacular deliverance would gain the attention of all Jerusalem and give Jesus immediate credence for ministry. Satan's temptation would bring quicker and easier deliverance than the cross. Jesus quoted to Satan this Scripture, **"You shall not tempt the Lord your God"** (Matthew 4:7; Deuteronomy 6:16).

Part One: The Agreed Resolve Continued

Both with Jesus and now Ananias and Sapphira, the issue was not a temptation to do an evil deed, but to compromise the boundaries. If God's will was to sell the property and give the proceeds to the church for ministry, could they accomplish this by not giving it all? What if we could redeem the world without suffering the crucifixion? Would that be acceptable? What difference would it make? Could we give less than all and still qualify? Will God accept partial giving within His will? The answer is, "NO." The consistent attitude of the Christian must always be total commitment. The deed may be flawed, but the manner of surrender requires completeness. Ananias and Sapphira linked with spiritual evil to reduce the boundaries of abandonment to Jesus. Anything less than complete and total surrender, and all in love, is not acceptable to Jesus! Any agreement that links us with spiritual evil manifests a half-heartedness that the Kingdom will not tolerate.

Attachment

Let us return to the original illustration of Ananias and Sapphira. We cannot agree with the evil of the spiritual world because it nullifies all that is Christian. If Christianity is a list of rules to keep, perhaps we can increase our commitment by keeping more rules. Therefore, statements like, "I am trying my best," "I am doing better than I was," or "I am improving" would apply. But Christianity is not rules to do, ceremonies to carry out, or meetings to attend. Christianity is a relationship with a Person, Jesus. The relationship is not casual but a merger. All that Jesus is merges with all that I am!

We must define sin by this relationship with Jesus. It is not about the act, a deed done, or not done. Sin is the inner motive and state of love within each person. Anything less than completely loving Jesus is not within the boundaries of Christian.

The early Church was passionate about Jesus. Everything we read about them in the Book of Acts projects completeness to their love for Christ. Being one with Jesus demands total availability. The musical drama He wants to produce from you requires a symphonic agreement with His Person.

Let me testify about Him! He captured me! After knowing Jesus in His greatness, I realize no one can be half-hearted about Him and really know Him. Everything else pales in light of who Jesus is! When Jesus brings what I have planned into His plan, what I have planned becomes insignificant. The pleasures of the world are empty and filled with death without His presence. Think of what Ananias and Sapphira sacrificed for a few dollars. They linked with spiritual evil and lost everything.

The Trinity God calls you to surrender completely to Jesus. Will you allow Him to tear down all the barriers and blockades that keep you from Him? Will you set aside every hindrance? Listen to the writer of the Book of Hebrews. **"Let us lay aside every weight, and the sin which so easily ensnares us, and let us run with endurance the race that is set before us, looking unto Jesus, the author and finisher of our faith, who for the joy that was set before Him endured the cross, despising the shame, and has sat down at the right hand of the throne of God"** (Hebrews 12:1-2).

Acts 5:10

BREATHING

"Then immediately she fell down at his feet and breathed her last. And the young men came in and found her dead, and carrying her out, buried her by her husband" (Acts 5:10).

We have had several discussions about the consequences of the lives of Ananias and Sapphira. Various commentaries say God struck them dead because of their disobedience. The reading in English could lead you to the same conclusion. The steps of the story are simple. Ananias and Sapphira contrived to sell their land and hold back a part of the selling price for themselves. That withholding was acceptable, except they said the funds they presented to Peter was the full selling price. In hypocrisy, they appeared to give it all. However, this progression views only the physical activity involved. In light of the world's sin, their actions do not seem that serious.

Luke gives us insight into the spiritual activities through Peter's questioning of Ananias. A raging spiritual war involved Satan and the Holy Spirit. The stakes were high; this couple faced life and death; the war determined their eternal destinies. When Peter confronted their sin, Ananias and Sapphira immediately died. First, Ananias was carried out by the young men, and three hours later, the same young men carried Sapphira out.

We must understand this story in the context of the New Testament as a whole. Listen to what Peter, who confronted Ananias and Sapphira, wrote in one of his epistles. ***"The Lord is not slack concerning His promise, as some count slackness, but is long-suffering toward us, not willing that any should perish but that all should come to repentance"*** (2 Peter 3:9). The heart of the mission statement of Jesus is ***"for He will save His people from their sins"*** (Matthew 1:21). Jesus Himself assured us that ***"God so loved the world that He gave His only begotten Son"*** (John 3:16). The intent of this love is ***"God did not send His Son into the world to condemn the world, but that the world through Him might be saved"*** (John 3:17). The evidence from the New Testament surrounds the confrontation of Ananias and Sapphira's sin. God did not stick them with death; He offered them life!

Because Jesus paid the penalty for this couple's sin, there was nothing to punish. As they arrived in the moment of confrontation, the forgiveness of God was already theirs, in place, and abundant. Already forgiven by God, they needed to respond to God's ever-present grace. God did not punish Ananias and Sapphira, but there were consequences for their sin. God was not to blame for these consequences; blame the devil; blame their lack of proper response, but do not blame God! We need to gain some understanding of what happened by looking at Sapphira's circumstances. Peter confronted Sapphira three hours after Ananias' death. He established their agreement (symphony) in the physical act of sin. They had linked with the evil spiritual world. Because of that link, the consequence Ananias experienced now came to Sapphira. ***"Then immediately she fell down at his feet and breathed her last"*** (Acts 5:10). There are three aspects of this verse we need to understand.

Part One: The Agreed Resolve Continued

Destruction

The destruction of ***"breathed her last"*** overcame Sapphira. Ananias and Sapphira lied about the sale price of their property, but that is not Luke's emphasis here. He says nothing about the loss of their reputation in the early Church community. Peter did not place Sapphira on probation with the possibility of reinstatement into full membership. The consequence of her sin comes from the core of her existence. It is a note of finality.

"Ekpsucho" is the Greek translation for ***"breathed her last."*** The prefix of this word is "ek," meaning "from" or "out of." The root word "psucho" means "to breathe." This compound word is used only three times in the New Testament, and two of these times are in our story. Death is involved in the meaning of the word, but there are six other Greek words used to describe death. "Thnesko" means "to die;" "apothnesko" means "to die off or out;" "koimaomai" means "to fall asleep;" "teleutao" and "appollumi" mean "to die or expire;" "apoginomai" means "to be away from." None of these words indicate death as the extinction of being, but each suggests a change in the state of existence. When a person dies, he goes from one state to another, but does not enter into extinction!

Out of all these Greek words for death, why does Luke choose to use the Greek word "ekpsucho?" Again, "ek" is a prefix to the root word "psucho," meaning "from" or "out of." "Psucho" is an interesting word, which means "to breathe, blow, refresh with cool air, or breathe naturally. "Psuche," the noun for "soul," is derived from the verb "psucho." In the passage voice, "psuchomai," means "to be cool, to grow cool or cold in a spiritual sense." Jesus told the disciples,

"And because lawlessness will abound, the love of many will grow cold (psuchomai)*"* (Matthew 24:12).

However, "psucho," translated as "soul," leads to confusion.

The New Testament uses this word as the principle of life that is present in human beings and animals (Revelation 8:9). It is life's energy that exists in every living being. God said, *"Also, to every beast of the earth, to every bird of the air, and to everything that creeps on the earth, in which there is life* (psucho)*, I have given every green herb for food"* (Genesis 1:30). Humanity is considered a dichotomy in the Old Testament. The material and the immaterial unite to form the human being. The material is the body or the "soma," and the immaterial is the "psucho." The creation story describes man as, *"And the Lord God formed man of the dust of the ground, and breathed into his nostrils the breath of life; and man became a living being* (psucho)*"* (Genesis 2:7). The breath of life God placed in humanity has two parts. There is the principle of living (psucho) and the spirit (pneuma). Even though animals may share "psucho" with humanity, it appears they do not have "pneuma." The "psucho" is the seat of the senses, desires, affections, appetites, passions, and the lower aspects of one's nature. The "pneuma" is the immaterial part of the personality that gives us the ability to communicate with God.

The Spirit of God fills the spirit of man (pneuma). In the merger, they become one! This new "spirit/Spirit" engulfs the "psucho" or principle of life and controls all desires, affections, passions, and appetites of the human being. This new creature is a living demonstration of God's heart, and the principle of that life (psucho) gives the expression of who God is! Not to be possessed with His Spirit, but filled with "self," makes the principle of life dominated by the spirit of man. The desires, affections, passions, appetites, become an expression of the self-centered person. If Jesus does not fill the "pneuma" of man, he is open to the infilling and influence of Satan, which always brings the consequence of destruction.

The Spirit of Jesus did not fill Ananias and Sapphira. Be assured this is not about one decision. The idea of keeping back part of the price for themselves expressed the progression of what happened in their spirits. The destruction occurred daily as they lived in hypocrisy in the fellowship of the early Church. Peter said that Satan filled their "pneuma" (spirit) to influence their "psucho" (principle of life) to lie. He highlighted the evil activity in their spiritual lives. Their spirit (pneuma) consistently destroyed their principle of life (psucho). Now, in this final scene, Sapphira's principle of life (her psucho) separated her body in death.

The message is clear! The principle of life (psucho) fills the body (soma), upon which the spirit (pneuma) acts. God intended the spirit of man to merge with the Spirit of God, enhancing, building, and constructing the principle of life (psucho). If you and I do not merge with Jesus, we live in destruction. We may not fall at the feet of Peter and die, but we continuously defeat and destroy ourselves and everything around us. The principle of life (psucho) decays within us. Jesus must fill us!

Dependency

Let me summarize the concept of the verse. The human being is a dichotomy in structure, consisting of the physical and spiritual. The physical aspect is the body, which is the flesh, the physical aspect of life. The inner being is the life energy consisting of the desires, affections, passions, and appetites. This internal life principle dominates and dictates the actions of the physical person. However, joining the internal life principle is the spirit of man, the aspect of man created by God, which He can fill with Himself, merged with Him. In this merger, the unique personality of the person takes on the heart of God. This spiritual aspect dictates the desires, affections, passions, and appetites of the person. In oneness with Jesus, the human being expresses the desires of God, has the mind of Christ and expresses God's heart through the principle of life merged with the Spirit of Jesus.

"But" is a tragic word. The man entered into sin! Instead of God filling the spirit of man, the man was on his own. The man's principle of life floundered with dependence on his spirit, void of God's Spirit. Questioning Ananias, Peter asked, ***"Ananias, why has Satan filled your heart to lie to the Holy Spirit and keep back part of the price of the land for yourself"*** (Acts 5:3)? The Greek word "nosphizo" translated, ***"keep back...for yourself,"*** means "to hold back or refuse to hand over." "Nosphizo," in the middle voice, "the subject of the verb, is affected by its action or acts upon itself." It shows a personal preference, is in the infinitive mood, which signifies purpose. The purpose of what Ananias and Sapphira did was selfish and for self-benefit. In the absence of God, the spirit of man took control.

Would we not suppose that God filled Ananias and Sapphira with His Spirit? They were involved in the early Church, and something radical had happened to them. But they had undoubtedly dethroned the Spirit of Jesus, and self took over the throne. Is this not the re-enactment of the first sin, Adam and Eve? The temptation of Satan was for them to become their god. Instead of the human spirit (pneuma) coming under the influence and authority of God, they lived independently and became their god. The actions revolved around a rebellious act of disobedience and independence.

Our passage leaves us with two conclusions, which are indisputable because of biblical truth and the consistent experience of humanity. First, the "core" of every sin is this same rebellious act. Man expresses an attitude of independence from the influence of God. All sins are equal in their severity; there are no small or insignificant sins. The core of both hate and murder is the self-centered control of the life principle, which affects my desires, appetites, and expressions of life. Ananias and

Sapphira retained money that was rightfully theirs but proposed they had given it all. Although their sin was not as shocking as some, their nature of rebellion produced the embezzlement, which was severe. The issue was not their deed, but the cause of the rebellion that did not allow the Spirit of God to control the principle of life.

A second conclusion is "consequence." The consequence of shifting from Jesus' Spirit to my spirit controlling my life principle is destruction. Luke used the Greek word "ekpsucho" to describe the deaths of Ananias and Sapphira. "Ekpuscho" is about the destruction of the principle of life (psucho) in the person. Although the destruction of Ananias and Sapphira was death, the result of every self-centered rulership over the principle of life (psucho) is destruction. Self-centered ruling always eliminates life. If we allow self-centeredness to dominate relationships, it will undermine the life and bring nothing but hate. When self rules the appetites, it focuses on the immediate pleasure and destroys the long-range destiny of the person. Nothing constructive ever comes from such expressions.

The principle of life (psucho) is dependent. Something or someone will control our desires, affections, passions, and appetites. Through the sacrificial redemption of Christ, God designed us to merge with the Spirit of Jesus, to live under His control and authority. If we are not dependent on Christ, we will depend on ourselves. We are not adequate for that position. We can only find life in Jesus; we find destruction in self!

Direction

The language Luke uses is significant for declaring spiritual truth. He said, ***"She fell down"*** (Acts 5:10), a translation of the Greek word "pipto." Luke said the same thing about Satan (Luke 10:18). Sapphira fell down into death, destruction, and ruin, all depicted in the imagery. Herein lies the cry of the Christian faith. Every person possesses the "psucho," the principle of life. The spirit ((pneuma), which sources the principle, determines the state of this principle. This spirit is the internal part of the person that can merge with God. When the spirit of man is sourced and merges with the Spirit of Jesus, the person lives in what the Bible calls "eternal life." ***"This is eternal life, that they may know You, the only true God, and Jesus Christ whom You have sent"*** (John 17:3).

In the church at Corinth, the people were confused about the resurrection from the dead. Many were concerned that their loved ones had died and missed the return of Jesus. Did this mean they would not be in heaven? In answering their questions, Paul focused them on Jesus. He said, ***"And so it is written, 'The first man Adam became a living being*** (psucho).*' **The last Adam became a life-giving*** (zoopoeio) ***Spirit*** (pneuma)***"*** (1 Corinthians 15:45). The first Adam became a living "psucho." God created him with the principle of life. But Jesus became a ***"life-giving*** (zoopoeio) ***Spirit*** (pneuma).*"* The mission of Jesus was to ultimately defeat sin and death's destructive power that His Spirit could merge with the human spirit and give eternal life. "Zoo" is the Greek word for ***"life."*** "Poieo" is translated ***"giving,"*** the Greek word consistently used for "trees bearing fruit." It is the picture of Jesus' Spirit merging with the spirit of man to source his body through the principle of life. Eternal life is the term for all Jesus accomplishes in this sourcing.

There is no "falling down" in this involvement. Paul said that death is swallowed up in victory because God removed the sting of death. The sting of death is sin (1 Corinthians 15:54-56). Ananias ***"fell down and breathed his last"*** (Acts 5:5), and Sapphira ***"fell down at his feet and breathed her last"*** (Acts 5:10). The question Peter asked remained unanswered by them. Why would they allow their self-centered spirits to source

Part One: The Agreed Resolve Continued

their principle of life (desires, affections, passions, and appetites) when they could have merged with the Spirit of Jesus? Why did they settle for temporary self-sourcing when God could have sourced them eternally? Why did they choose the downward spiral of death when they could have chosen to be up in Jesus? Why? Why? Why?

We must ask ourselves the same questions! We are in the midst of the spiritual war, which God fights on the stage of our lives. The central issue is the merger of Jesus' life and my life. He has made provision for us!

Acts 5:11
A FEARING CHURCH

"So great fear came upon all the church and upon all who heard these things" (Acts 5:11).

The Greek word "ekklesia" is translated ***"church"*** in our passage. "Ekklesia" is in the feminine gender, which highlights the abstract, mysterious nature of its existence. The believer's merger with Jesus is beyond comprehension, and the congregation of those believers is equally beyond knowing. The fact that we do not know everything does not mean we cannot know some things. The early Christian did not conceive of "ekklesia" primarily as an organization but as a theological entity. It was not a 501C3 registered with the Secretary of State receiving tax breaks. To be the church did not require a board, scheduled meetings, or a building.

"Ekklesia" appears only three times in the Gospel accounts, all in Matthew (Matthew 16:18, 18:17), reminding us of a positive development of its use. All three times, "ekklesia" comes from the lips of Jesus! The content and context in which Jesus uses this word in His teachings are essential. Jesus considered Himself and His mission at the core of the church's existence. He said, ***"And I also say to you that you are Peter, and***

Part One: The Agreed Resolve Continued

on this rock I will build My church, and the gates of Hades shall not prevail against it" (Matthew 16:18).

Jesus lived the last six months of His ministry with the disciples, moving His ministry focus from the "crowds" to the "disciples." He needed to prepare His disciples for what was coming. He removed his group from Palestine into Gentile territory, quizzing them about what they believed about Him. Peter responded with a bold statement declaring Jesus' Messiahship (Matthew 16:16), and in that context, Jesus called Peter the rock upon which He would build His church (Matthew 16:18). Jesus declared He was the Christ with a mission. He said He would build "ekklesia" His church, and nothing could stand in the way. However, the difficulty was the method of the building process. He would do it through "bleeding, suffering, and dying," the cross (Matthew 16:21). Jesus gave them the first of three predictions about His death and resurrection.

Jesus established the "ekklesia" of the church, and it exists in the context of the cross. Jesus called the disciples to embrace the style of the cross in their lives. The cross is the pattern of the church. ***"For whoever desires to save his life will lose it, but whoever loses his life for My sake will find it"*** (Matthew 16:25). The disciples argued with Jesus for at least six days about this style. After the Mount of Transfiguration (Matthew 17:1-8), training about John the Baptist (Matthew 17:9-13), and the inability to minister to a father and son (Matthew 17:14-22), the disciples involve Jesus in their argument over who is the greatest. They wanted Jesus to choose one of them for this position (Matthew 18:1). They did not comprehend or embrace the cross style, losing one's life.

Jesus patiently appealed to the disciples again. He told them the Parable of the Lost Sheep (Matthew 18:10-14), which focuses on the Father's heart! The Father is the Good Shepherd who cannot tolerate losing a single sheep, but through "bleeding, suffering, and dying, gives Himself to rescue that sheep. Then Jesus moved from teaching in parable form to practical life application (Matthew 18:15-20). As a person of the "ekklesia," we must go after the one who has strayed. We must link with one or two others to "bleed, suffer, and die," to win him back. ***"And if he refuses to hear them, tell it to the church*** (ekklesia). ***"But if he refuses even to hear the church*** (ekklesia)***, let him be to you like a heathen and a tax collector"*** (Matthew 18:17). The "ekklesia" must pour their lives out for the lost sheep. If he does not respond, he becomes like a heathen and tax collector, which means we double our efforts in "bleeding, suffering, and dying." Jesus did not come for those who are righteous but for sinners (Matthew 9:13).

Then Jesus paints a picture of the "ekklesia" (Matthew 18:18-20). This redemptive group represents on earth, all that is in heaven. As they link together on earth in oneness and reach into the unseen heavenly realm, a flow from heaven to earth happens. Jesus calls it a "symphony" of agreement and unity. When this happens, the face of God, His presence, appears! It is the "ekklesia," the church!

Now, for the first time in the Book of Acts, "ekklesia" appears (Acts 5:11). Although this is the first time Luke uses the word, he has described the early Church as the "ekklesia." They united in prayer and experienced heaven shaking the place where they assembled (Acts 4:31). God filled them with the Holy Spirit, and they spoke the Word of God in boldness. The presence of Jesus was felt throughout Jerusalem as they witnessed His resurrected presence. They poured their lives out for each other by having all things in common. ***"Neither did anyone say that any of the things he possessed was his own"*** (Acts 4:32).

Amid this symphonic unity between God and the early Church, Ananias and Sapphira broke the style of the cross by selfish living. They created disunity in the unity; in completeness,

Part One: The Agreed Resolve Continued

they fostered partiality; in truthfulness, they proposed dishonesty and hypocrisy. At the heart of selflessness, they projected selfishness. They tried to destroy the church!!

Relationship

The heart of the church (ekklesia) is the relationship. That is true now, but it was especially true in our passage when there were no church buildings. No one ever confused the involvement of a group of believers with a building. Therefore, the church is always a community, a group of connected believers, both the universal view and local presence. The community of believers and local gatherings across the world are appropriately called the church. Both are equally legitimate forms of the "ekklesia" created by God.

In secular Greek, "ekklesia" designated citizen assemblies. Paul used it twice to describe the people of Ephesus who gathered against Him. The Spirit of God was moving among the people, and the silversmiths who made the shrines of Diana caused a riot (Acts 19:32, 39). However, "ekklesia" took on its theological meaning as used consistently in the Septuagint (the Greek translation of the Old Testament). The Hebrew word "qahal," translated "ekklesia," describes the assembly or congregation of God's people (Deuteronomy 9:10).

Luke used descriptive phrases about the gathering of Jewish Christians in Jerusalem. He referred to believers (Acts 2:44; 4:32), their number (Acts 2:41; 4:4; 5:14), and their companions (Acts 4:23). In the early days of the Christian church, the believers called their meeting places "the synagogue" (James 2:2). But as the division between the Jews and Christians became permanent, the Jews went to their synagogues and the Christians to their churches (ekklesia). The Christians used this word to describe their corporate identity, claiming to be the true people of God, believing they were the rightful heirs of all God promised in salvation. The "ekklesia" became the new Israel (Romans 2:28-29; Galatians 6:16; 1 Peter 2:5, 9). The expression "ekklesia" conveyed the meaning that Christians, rather than Jews, were the true people of God!

The phrase, **"the church of God,"** begins to appear (1Corinthians 1:2; 10:32; 11:16, 22; 15:9; 2 Corinthians 1:1, and Galatians 1:13). The phrase **"of God"** is not added to "ekklesia" to give content to the word, but it becomes a fixed formula and is an integral part of the church (ekklesia). **"Of God"** is a declaration of relationship. Therefore, the description of the "ekklesia" as the body of Christ is profound. **"For as we have many members in one body, but all members do not have the same function, so we, being many, are one body in Christ, and individually members of one another"** (Romans 12:4-5).

In light of this unity, the sin of Ananias and Sapphira became monumental. What may appear to be an indiscretion concerning proper procedure became cancer in the body. Satan was involved in attacking the "ekklesia," the body of Christ. The oneness that caused the church to have all things in common, Satan wanted to destroy. Our passage contains the first time the word "ekklesia" appears in the Book of Acts (Acts 5:11), denoting the people of God gathered in a spiritual community. The church can only thrive as the people of God if it lives in the trust of all its members. The church thrives in the Spirit's power, with the unity of trust and the oneness of heart and mind.

The members of the body must be complete, surrendered, and abandoned to Jesus. Anything less than this creates death and destruction in the function of the body. The abandonment is to Jesus, not each other because without Him, we become a cult. In the passage (Acts 5:1-11), there is no message about how they hurt the body of Christ or hindered the mission of the church.

Part One: The Agreed Resolve Continued

The issue is how they lied to God. In violating their relationship with Jesus, they broke their relationship with the "ekklesia." Only in total abandonment to Jesus do we know the heart of God; in knowing the heart of God, we become the people of God, the body of Christ, the church! If I have difficulty with my fellow man, maybe I have not embraced God's heart. How does God feel about my fellowman? Am I not an extension of His hands, voice, and love?

Reverence

"So great fear came upon all the church and upon all who heard these things" (Acts 5:11). Luke records a similar statement at the death of Ananias (Acts 5:5). In a previous study, we discovered the Greek word "phobos," translated *"fear."* "Phobos" is the root word for "phobia" in English. In the Greek, its meaning ranges from terror to awe. The use of "phobos" is determined by the context. Although Luke mentions the church first, the news of Ananias and Sapphira's deaths must have spread throughout Jerusalem. The populous of Jerusalem held the early Church in awe and respect.

The awe and reverence toward God increased (if possible) within the church. The early Church experienced the threat of persecution and yet bound together in prayer and commitment to truth. *"And when they had prayed, the place where they were assembled together was shaken; and they were all filled with the Holy Spirit, and they spoke the word of God with boldness"* (Acts 4:31). Did not the filling of the Holy Spirit produce profound awesomeness (fear)? God did many signs and wonders through the apostles (Acts 5:12). Would this not have resulted in wonder at the greatness of God? We might think that the early Church had already reached the highest level of awe and reverence.

There is a definite indication that something new or deeper occurred through the deaths of Ananias and Sapphira. Luke includes this information twice in the story (Acts 5:5, 11). The awe and reverence the early Church experienced within the presence of God were great. But now, an additional fact is added to their reality. They become aware of the danger of being outside God's presence! It is thrilling to be in the boundaries of His presence. In His presence, we sense the awe of His protection, guidance, and mission. Security floods our lives, even when threatened. Awe and reverence increase as the Spirit of Jesus manifests His grace through our lives. But Ananias and Sapphira stepped out of that protection and immediately encountered the full consequences of their decision.

What do we do when left to our own resources? How do we feel when there is no answer in our abilities and reason? Outside the presence of Jesus, we are on our own! Another image of "ekklesia" in the Scriptures is the "Bride of Christ." Paul used the imagery of the "Bride of Christ" when teaching about marriage (Ephesians 5:22-33). **"For the husband is head of the wife, as also Christ is head of the church; and He is Savior of the body"** (Ephesians 5:23). Think of the safety and security in such a relationship! Now Ananias and Sapphira have severed that relationship. They virtually divorced themselves from their Husband (Jesus). They decided to provide for themselves, keeping back part of the price of their land. They entered into an illicit affair with Satan, and in hypocrisy, continued to claim Jesus as their husband. The explosion of their decision was catastrophic! They destroyed everything; there was no safety outside God's presence; no one survives without Him! Suddenly the early Church became aware of the danger.

Part One: The Agreed Resolve Continued

Revolution

What happened in the lives of Ananias and Sapphira affected their community. The early Church experienced a new awareness of completeness in Christ. They not only needed Jesus, but He required all of them. The Spirit of Jesus gave Himself completely; they needed to give themselves entirely to Him. Again, the severity of the issue was thrust upon them by the deaths of Ananias and Sapphira.

However, this also happened to **"all who heard these things."** Luke gives insight into some of the results in the next paragraph. The early Church was together on Solomon's Porch, the same place the leaders of Israel interrupted Peter's sermon to a large gathering. God had healed the lame beggar, which attracted many. The leaders of Israel had Peter and John arrested and put in jail, and the next day threatened them to never speak in the name of Jesus again. Now the early Church was in one accord in the same location. Luke wrote that **"none of the rest dared join them, but the people esteemed them highly"** (Acts 5:13). No one had come to this gathering to spectate or for entertainment. Everyone who was not in one accord with the believers was afraid to participate. They all understood the possessive nature of the fulness of the Spirit.

You would think that such a message and understanding would eliminate evangelism. Who wants to surrender to Jesus? Who wants to join a group of radical people in a commitment to Christ? But the next verse says, **"And believers were increasingly added to the Lord, multitudes of both men and women"** (Acts 5:14). Should this not shape our approach to evangelism?

We are often not confrontational in our approach to evangelism. We want to be "seeker-sensitive." We fear the confrontational approach of our message might offend. Peter did not share that view as he confronted Ananias and Sapphira. If we can only embrace the Gospel wholeheartedly, what do we gain in suggesting a lesser commitment? If Christianity requires complete surrender, what is the advantage of filling the church with those who are not Christians?

Perhaps our world is desperately searching for something or someone significant enough to command their total attention. Jesus is worthy of the full allegiance of all my time, energy, and life experience. Anything less than this is to demean and belittle all He is in redeeming the world. Reducing the value of Christ's sacrificial death makes Christianity a joke among the religions of the world. As narrow as it might seem, without embarrassment, Peter proposed, ***"Nor is there salvation in any other, for there is no other name under heaven given among men by which we must be saved"*** (Acts 4:12). Does this not challenge us to a full, absolute, and complete surrender to Jesus? Ananias and Sapphira proved it by their experience. The early Church embraced it as the reality of involvement with Jesus. The world around them understood the requirement and consequences of this challenge. Salvation through Jesus is still true today!

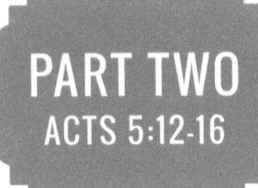

PART TWO
ACTS 5:12-16

ANOTHER REVIEW: ANOTHER SUMMARY

Acts 5:12-16

ANOTHER SUMMARY

"And through the hands of the apostles many signs and wonders were done among the people. And they were all with one accord in Solomon's Porch. Yet none of the rest dared join them, but the people esteemed them highly. And believers were increasingly added to the Lord, multitudes of both men and women, so that they brought the sick out into the streets and laid them on beds and couches, that at least the shadow of Peter passing by might fall on some of them. Also a multitude gathered from the surrounding cities to Jerusalem, bringing sick people and those who were tormented by unclean spirits, and they were all healed." (Acts 5:12-16).

There are crisis moments in the church. At the time of this writing, the Church is centralized in Jerusalem and is a Jewish congregation. After each crisis moment, Luke seems compelled to write a summary of the church's condition at that moment. He ceases to do this as the Church moves into a worldwide movement. In each summary, Luke suggests the critical elements of the Church. He does not highlight programming or structure, and he does not discuss membership rules. Luke underscores what makes this movement different from all other religions.

The first crisis moment is the event of Pentecost (Acts 2:1-4). Peter preached a sermon explaining the event (Acts 2:14-42).

Part Two: Another Review: Another Summary

This sermon resulted in the addition of three thousand individuals to the group of believers. Luke finds it necessary to share the general details of what was taking place within this group (Acts 2:43-47). He highlights the miracles, unity, financial support, fellowship, teaching, and growth taking place within the body of believers.

The second crisis moment is the threat of persecution (Acts 4:1-22). The power of Christ healed a lame beggar. This miracle would not have been any more significant than many others occurring through the church's ministry. However, the individual receiving the miracle is over forty years of age, which indicates that he begged at the temple's Gate Beautiful for a long time. His miracle became known by all who dwell in Jerusalem. Such a stir is created in the temple that it moves the Sadducees to action. Persecution begins in the early Church. The focus of the persecution is about Jesus. They are threatened never to mention the name of Jesus again. How will the early Christians respond to this threat? They pray and continue to proclaim His name boldly (Acts 4:31). God compelled Luke to declare the state of the Church amid such persecution.

His statements expressed an increase of intensity and enthusiasm in each area. In the first report, Luke simply said, ***"all who believed were together, and had all things in common"*** (Acts 2:44). He added to this statement that they sold their possessions and goods and gave them to anyone who had need (Acts 2:45). In the second summary, Luke intensified this by saying that ***"those who believed where of one heart and one soul; neither did anyone say that any of the things he possessed was his own"*** (Acts 4:32). In the first report, Luke said they had ***"favor with all the people. And the Lord added to the church daily those who were being saved"*** (Acts 2:47). Then he cried, ***"And with great power the apostles gave witness to the resurrection of the Lord Jesus. And great grace was upon them all"*** (Acts 4:33).

Another Summary | **Acts 5:12-16**

As we turn to the third report viewing the early Church amid persecution, the intensity increased again! Those who were not a part of the early Church hesitated to join because of the high level of commitment required. That requirement was evident due to the demise of Ananias and Sapphira. Luke portrays the ministry's evangelistic results as **"and believers were increasingly added to the Lord, multitudes of both men and women"** (Acts 5:14). The presence of God was so powerfully present in Peter that people wanted to get in his shadow (Acts 5:15). What happened within the early Church membership became the explanation for the events in the remainder of the chapter (Acts 5). Anger filled the high priest and Sadducees (Acts 5:17). The leaders of Israel placed the apostles in jail, but an angel of the Lord delivered them. They were captured again and beaten. But the chapter ends with, **"And daily in the temple, and in every house, they did not cease teaching and preaching Jesus as the Christ"** (Acts 5:42).

There are some common characteristics of all of the three reports as the early Church grew. They are "positive" reports. Amid persecution and threats, there are no negative statements, no doubts or dismay. In the context of Ananias and Sapphira's failure, the power of God is so great it overshadows every discouragement. Engrained into every report is "production." The church is viewed each time as abundantly growing. Despite persecution and the threat of death, Jesus won multitudes of men and women to Himself. The explanation for the success of the early Church is the "power" of God with no indication of self-centered fame or positional authority. What was the key to their success? Amid all the different personality types and needs, the potential for conflict is great. What is their secret?

Part Two: Another Review: Another Summary

Signs and Wonders

Miracles continually happened in their midst. Luke reported in the first view of the Church's state that ***"fear came upon every soul, and many wonders and signs were done through the apostles"*** (Acts 2:43). While in the second report, Luke did not mention signs and wonders; he indeed indicated them. ***"And with great power the apostles gave witness to the resurrection of the Lord Jesus"*** (Acts 4:33). This report's context is the expression in the heart of the Church's prayer after hearing of the threat of persecution. They wanted the same boldness and proclamation of His Word to take place through them by the strength of His hand ***"to heal, and that signs and wonders may be done through the name of Your holy Servant Jesus"*** (Acts 4:30). The third statement concerning the Church's condition begins with, ***"And through the hands of the apostles many signs and wonders were done among the people"*** (Acts 5:12). As the report continues, the cities outside of Jerusalem began to bring their sick and demon-possessed to Jerusalem to experience deliverance through Jesus (Acts 5:16). There is no doubt that "signs and wonders" were a consistent part of the early Church's successful ministry.

However, according to these biblical reports, there are crucial truths involving "signs and wonders" that we must understand. In each account, the apostles were the instruments through which these miracles took place. No one ever credited the members of the early Church with "signs and wonders." Out of the several thousand early Church members, God used only a few people as instruments of miracles, corresponding with Paul's teaching (1 Corinthians 12:27-31). We are the body of Christ. The members of the body do not all have the same function. No one discredits the gift of miracles as given by the Spirit of

Another Summary | Acts 5:12-16

Jesus. But do not envision that everyone in the early Church was doing miracles. It is easy to develop a feeling of spiritual superiority because God may select you to be the instrument. It is also easy to be defeated because God does not select to do through you something spectacular that others will applaud.

Understanding the essence of "signs and wonders" may be a benefit to us. The phrase ***"wonders and signs"*** is used some thirty times in the New Testament. These two words are typically used together. In the Book of Acts, ***"wonders and signs"*** appear four times and ***"signs and wonders"*** five times. These two words refer not to different miracles but different aspects of the same miracle. The idea of ***"wonders"*** is the miracle aspect, which is startling, imposing, or remarkable. Luke translated it from the Greek word "teras." It comes from the root word "tereo," which means "to keep, watch, connoting that which is apt to be observed and kept in the memory due to its extraordinary character." It is the overwhelming or shocking character of an event. It is entirely reasonable to assume that the early Church members were consistently astounding the populous of Jerusalem. But the astonishment or ***"wonders"*** went far beyond healing. They were shaking and invading the demonic realm of their city. Luke reported that there was such a powerful flow of spiritual influence through the early Church members that the city of Jerusalem was being amazed and changed.

The focus of ***"signs"*** is the spiritual end and purpose of the event. It is a translation of the Greek word "semeion," referring to a sign, mark, or token, and is a part of a miracle with a spiritual end and purpose. It leads to something out of and beyond itself. It is a giant finger pointing to God Himself. A miracle is valuable not so much for what it is as its indication of the grace and power of the Doer. It is to lead to something out of and beyond itself. The focus of a miracle is not on the miracle but on the One who produces the miracle.

Part Two: Another Review: Another Summary

"Astonishment" and "pointing beyond" are two vital aspects of every miracle. God was moving in the early Church to astonish Jerusalem's populous and point them back to Jesus. The Greek word translated as "miracle" is "dunamis." It expresses the movement or activity of the resource of God accomplishing the great happening. "Ischus" is a Greek word that focuses on the actual resource. God is great, mighty, and all-powerful. But this is "ischus" without any movement of the resource. However, when the power of God's resource in Jesus moves upon life, it is "dunamis." Jesus promised we would become avenues for the power of God (Acts 1:8).

The secret to the early Church's success was their total abandonment to the "ischus" of God in Christ, which allowed them to experience the "dunamis." The Sanhedrin warned them never to mention the name of Jesus again. But their surrender to the power of God would not allow this. There was an increase, **"And believers were increasingly added to the Lord, multitudes of both men and women"** (Acts 5:14). The wonder of Jesus was so powerfully present in their lives that multitudes desired to be close to Peter, as close as his shadow (Acts 5:15). The early Church's cry was not for miracles but for **"signs and wonders"** (Acts 4:30). They wanted their world to know the power of Christ moving among them. May it be so with us!

Singleness and Wholeness

Luke's emphasis on unity grew stronger in each report regarding the state of the early Church. In the first report, Luke gave two different references to their unity. **"Now all who believed were together, and had all things in common, and sold their possessions and goods, and divided them among all, as anyone had need"** (Acts 2:44-45).

Another Summary | Acts 5:12-16

He added, ***"So continuing daily with one accord in the temple, and breaking bread from house to house, they ate their food with gladness and simplicity of heart"*** (Acts 2:46). Luke strengthened this emphasis in the second report saying, ***"Now the multitude of those who believed were of one heart and one soul"*** (Acts 4:32). Also, in the unity of financial involvement, Luke said, ***"neither did anyone say that any of the things he possessed was his own, but they had all things in common"*** (Acts 4:32). In his third report, he said, ***"They were all with one accord in Solomon's Porch"*** (Acts 5:12). Increasing the statement of unity, Luke added, ***"Yet none of the rest dared join them, but the people esteemed them highly"*** (Acts 5:13). Their unity was so strong that no one was unwilling to join that unity connected with the early Church in light of the recent event concerning Ananias and Sapphira.

Luke used the Greek word "homothymadon," translated as ***"one accord,"*** to describe their unity in these reports. It is two words combined. "Homo" means "the same." "Thumadon" refers to the mind or the primary impulse that drives a person. It is the idea of "passion" or "heavy breathing." Everyone in Jerusalem understood and was aware of the passion the early Church members had for Jesus. Nothing else could have brought them together in such unity. People will unite over a cause, movement, or even philosophy but not for this long and with this intensity. When the city became aware of Ananias and Sapphira's death, they understood the commitment to this passion must be total. Anyone who did not share this same passion for Jesus did not join their number.

Luke again faces us with the total commitment to Jesus exhibited in the early Church, the standard for all Christians in their time. We must face the fact that the passion was intense, but the focus was upon a Person rather than a movement or theology. As people joined the early Church, they did not merely embrace a belief system. They dared not participate because they were homeless and needed financial help. No one was casual and joined because their parents raised them as Christians. Attendance to the fellowship was not a developed habit of activity. They converted to Christianity, and they burned for Jesus. He captured their lives through the fullness of His Spirit, and they could do nothing less. Regardless of the frightening message of Ananias and Sapphira's death, ***"believers were increasingly added to the Lord, multitudes of both men and women"*** (Acts 5:14). Perhaps it would be wise for us to take our spiritual temperature! Dare we propose anything less than "together with heavy breathing" (homothymadon)?

Spiritual World

In each of the three reports, Luke refers to the altering of their physical world. He began in the first report with a simple statement. ***"Then fear came upon every soul, and many wonders and signs were done through the apostles"*** (Acts 2:43). Luke also included the physical act of selling their possessions and goods to help each other (Acts 2:45). In the second report, while not mentioning wonders and signs, Luke declared ***"great power"*** and ***"great grace"*** occurred in the witness of the early Church and especially the apostles (Acts 4:33). Again, he highlighted selling lands and houses to meet others' physical needs (Acts 4:34). The third report begins with signs and wonders done through the apostles' hands (Acts 5:12), increasing until ***"a multitude gathered from the surrounding cities to Jerusalem, bringing sick people and those who were tormented by unclean spirits, and they were all healed"*** (Acts 5:16).

While the physical results of the early Church's ministry were impactive, it only gave evidence of the more excellent spiritual results. The invasion of demonic territory, the liberation from bondage, and the merging of the Spirit of Jesus with new believers brought about a furtherance of persecution. Luke moved into the spiritual reaction of the *"high priest... and those who were with him (which is the sect of the Sadducees)"* (Acts 5:17). Indignation filled their inner spiritual world, forcing them to the physical act of putting the apostles in jail.

The movement of the early Church was not about physically altering their culture or society. There was a significant spiritual war displaying itself in the physical reality of Jerusalem. The entire spiritual warfare focused on the person of Jesus! As the persecution unfolds in the early Church, the apostles are placed in jail only to be delivered by an angel of the Lord who opened the prison doors and brought them out (Acts 5:19). They obeyed the command of the angel who told them, *"Go, stand in the temple and speak to the people all the words of this life"* (Acts 5:20). Can you imagine the amazement of the officers who came to get the apostles from jail to interrogate them only to discover they were not in jail but in the temple preaching Jesus (Acts 5:22-25)? When the leaders brought them before the court, what was the issue? They did not discuss the jailbreak; they said, *"Did we not strictly command you not to teach in this name"* (Acts 5:28)? The name of Jesus so repulsed the leaders they did not even want to speak it themselves!

All that was happening in the physical world was because of what was happening in the spiritual world. The radical cause in both worlds was the person of Jesus! The early Church was calling for a complete and radical commitment to Jesus. There was no toleration for any deviation from His person, and no one dared join the church without total commitment to Him. It is the issue of this hour as well. Jesus is not one issue among many; He is the issue. He is not one answer among many; the single solution to the spiritual and physical world is Jesus. It is time to examine our alignment with Him.

Acts 5:12

YOUR HANDS

"And through the hands of the apostles many signs and wonders were done among the people. And they were all with one accord in Solomon's Porch" (Acts 5:12).

After Ananias and Sapphira's death, Luke describes the early Church's state, the third time for such a statement. As we discovered in our previous study, these summaries seemed to follow a crisis. The first summary (Acts 2:43-47) follows the Holy Spirit's outpouring, Pentecost Day. The second summary (Acts 4:32-35) occurs immediately after the beginning of persecution. The early Church is threatened never to speak of Jesus again (Acts 4:18). This third summary (Acts 5:12-16) follows a threat from within the church. Ananias and Sapphira have disobeyed God (Acts 5:1-11).

However, one might also understand that each summary of the early Church's state prepares us for the crisis that is to come. After the first summary (Acts 2:43-47), the lame beggar's healing miracle launches the early Church into persecution. The leaders of Israel threaten the early Church never to speak about Jesus. The second summary (Acts 4:32-35) prepares us for the internal turmoil caused by Ananias and Sapphira. The third summary (Acts 5:12-16) occurs before the apostles are imprisoned and brought to trial.

We discovered one of the reports' critical elements is ***"many signs and wonders were done among the people."*** No individual could or would want to argue against Divine healing. This third report relates the increase in miracles from just the people in Jerusalem to the surrounding cities (Acts 5:16). We must continuously see this in the context of the proper meaning of the phrase. ***"Signs and wonders"*** are two aspects of every miracle. The ***"wonder"*** is the astonishing element of the miracle. God was causing physical changes in the lives of people that were so dramatic as to be incredible, indicated in the third summary as Luke reports, ***"Yet none of the rest dared join them"*** (Acts 5:13). The miraculous happening among them caused some of the crowd to purposely not join the church out of fear. The ***"sign"*** distinctly relates that something is happening beyond the miracle, a mere finger pointing to something greater than itself.

The "common" purpose of every miracle is to point us back to the incredible power of God. We must not become mesmerized by the miracle. The greatness of God must capture us. Don't be miracle-centered but be Christ-centered! But there is not only a "common" purpose to every miracle but also a "concentrated" purpose. God never does a miracle without a purpose beyond the physical result of the miracle. The present miracle contains a great plan of God. We discovered this in the healing of the lame beggar (Acts 3:1-10). As the story unfolds into the next chapter, Luke never tells us his name because the miracle is not merely about him. This healing is the event that launches the persecution of the early Church. This miracle tipped the scales for the Sadducees. They could no longer tolerate the constant spread of the name of Jesus in Jerusalem.

But the early Church could not remain silent! In the face of the Sadducees' threat, the apostles repeatedly said, ***"We ought***

Part Two: Another Review: Another Summary

to obey God rather than men" (Acts 5:29, also seen in Acts 4:19). They could not cease to proclaim Jesus because of what they had witnessed and experienced. The increase in miracles became the platform upon which they proclaimed the Person of Jesus. It validated their message's authenticity, added fuel to the Sadducees' resistance, and increased the persecution's fury. The result was the scattering of the church from Jerusalem to evangelize the world.

Regarding ***"the many signs and wonders,"*** Luke clusters many notable factors in our passage.

Instrument

Luke was definite in saying the signs and wonders were done ***"through"*** the apostles' hands (Acts 5:12). ***"Through"*** is a translation of the Greek word "dia," which is a preposition of instrumentality beyond question. "Dia" refers to the instrument or intermediate cause through which an effect proceeds, meaning "through, by, or by means of." The apostles were the intermediate agents or causative agents through which or by which the signs and wonders took place. They were not the source of these miracles.

There is something about this reality that forms the core of Christianity. It is so central that any deviation from its existence destroys what can be called Christian. Indwelling the helpless person, the essence of God's person becomes the source of their life. We must investigate the many aspects of Christianity, such as forgiveness, holiness, faith, and love, a long list. We must view these aspects as something done to the individual, only experienced as God does these things through him. The Spirit of God indwells the individual's life, and he is an instrument of this Divine Person's activity! Some people may propose they are Christians because they received forgiveness from

God. But it is not a reception apart from His person. God did not deposit an item called "forgiveness" into their possession, but He embraced them in His fullness. Forgiveness is always relational and does not have substance apart from the intimacy of the relationship. Man cannot know forgiveness within the relationship between God and himself unless he is an instrument through which God expresses forgiveness. Jesus said, ***"For if you forgive men their trespasses, your heavenly Father will also forgive you. But if you do not forgive men their trespasses, neither will your Father forgive your trespasses"*** (Matthew 6:14-15). When we embrace the source of forgiveness, we become an instrument of this expression!

Some may propose they are Christians because they received the power of God. But it is not a reception apart from His person. The power of God is the person of God. It is always in a relationship with Him that we experience His power. However, we will not know this power from His presence unless we become an instrument of His mighty presence. Jesus promised man would ***"receive power when the Holy Spirit has come upon you"*** (Acts 1:8). We do not revel in the strength we possess, but we become an instrument of its expression to ***"Jerusalem, and in all Judea and Samaria, and to the ends of the earth"*** (Acts 1:8). All Christian qualities result from His person and can only be experienced in the expression of His personhood as we become an instrument.

Because the apostles possessed a "consciousness" of this truth, no arrogance was present. A crowd gathered at Solomon's Porch due to the news of the lame beggar's miracle. He was holding on to Peter as if Peter was responsible for the miracle. Focused on Peter, the crowds attributed this miracle to him. Peter was horrified and cried, ***"Men of Israel, why do you marvel at this? Or why look so intently at us, as though by our own power or godliness we made this man walk?"*** (Acts 3:12). He proceeded to proclaim Jesus, the One they had crucified, as the source of the miracle. Peter knew he was simply an instrument of Divine expression.

When brought before the Sanhedrin for interrogation, Peter gave voice to the resource within him. Israel's leaders wanted to know the power or the name in which the apostles had healed the lame beggar. Peter did not hesitate to say, ***"By the name of Jesus Christ of Nazareth, whom you crucified, whom God raised from the dead, by Him this man stands here before you whole"*** (Acts 4:10). Peter did not attempt to project himself into this miracle. He was aware and admitted he was simply an instrument of Divine expression!

This fact is what produced a "consistency" in their witness. Their proclamation was always the same and pointed to Jesus. They were consistently highlighting, praising, and honoring Jesus. Their focus was not on the miracles to create competition among them, and they did not control the miracles' source; they were instruments. The focus of the early Church's persecution was using the name of Jesus. The miracles, compassionate ministry, or the early Church's training sessions did not bother Israel's leaders. They hated the consistent proclamation of Jesus Christ. The early Church could have easily eliminated persecution and maintained their ministry if they simply downplayed Jesus. But they would and could not do so! They said, ***"For we cannot but speak the things which we have seen and heard"*** (Acts 4:20). Everything they had seen and heard was about Jesus! They had become instruments of His person!

For the early Church, there was a "completeness" about the person of Jesus. There was nothing beyond Him. They needed not to add any other facts or seek any other solution. Jesus completed the truth of their Old Testament and fulfilled the dreams of their lifetime. The Kingdom of God for which they had been waiting was in the Kingship of Jesus. There was nothing to add to Him. Christ completed all. No wonder Paul wrote, ***"For in Him dwells all the fullness of the Godhead***

bodily; and you are complete in Him, who is the head of all principality and power" (Colossians 2:9-10). Jesus fulfilled the search of a lifetime. They were complete in Him!

Individual Ownership

The overriding fact bringing stability to the apostles amid their persecution was the awareness that the ***"signs and wonders"*** were not theirs! They did not own the Source, but the Source owned them. Luke expressed this in the phrase ***"the hands of the apostles"*** (Acts 5:12). The Greek word "cheir" is translated as ***"hand."*** It is the object of the preposition ***"through"*** (dia), an instrument of action and power. Thus, to the hand is ascribed what strictly belongs to the person himself or his power. But the preposition ***"through"*** presents the hands as an instrument of something that does not belong to the apostles.

Luke refers back to the prayer of the early Church upon hearing of the persecution. Their prayer was not one of complaining or a cry for deliverance. They prayed for the Lord to give close attention to their persecution and grant them the ability to proclaim the name of Jesus in even greater measure. They desired to do this ***"by stretching out Your hand to heal, and that signs and wonders may be done through the name of Your holy Servant Jesus"*** (Acts 4:30). The early Church recognized that the ownership of the Source of all they were experiencing was in the Trinity God's hands. Now they were His hands bringing expression to all He desired. They were not in charge but were under His influence and control. He owned their hands!

At the beginning of this same prayer, they forcibly described the position of the Trinity God. They prayed, ***"Lord, You are God, who made heaven and earth and the sea, and all***

that is in them" (Acts 4:24). The phrase **"Lord, You are God"** is a translation of the Greek word "despotes," our English word "despot." God is a Tyrant! "Despot" is a negative term for us, but it was not for them. The Trinity God is in charge. They continued to describe how this Tyrant God herded all the world's nations together with their rulers. He permitted them to do what they wanted, which was precisely what He wanted them to do. They crucified Christ to redeem the world. Nothing is beyond the Trinity God's control. The early Church viewed the persecution they experienced as an extension of this same control and authority.

Therefore, they saw their hands as an extension of His hands. They did not own the signs and wonders. They were an instrument owned by the sovereign Trinity God. Because this truth became a reality in their lives, the upset of persecution did not disturb them. The security of their existence was unshaken. Great purpose permeated their lives. They saw themselves fulfilling God's planned destiny. Their lives were meaningful, not in self-importance, but Divine movement. They were the hands of God for their hour. The circumstances of their days could no longer dictate nor influence their response. They were His and His alone!

There was a totality about this awareness. The Trinity God did not have partial ownership. There were not some sections of their lives that were His but not others. The use of **"hands"** often refers in the Scriptures to the being. On the cross, Jesus cried, **"Father, into Your hands I commit My spirit"** (Luke 23:46), a reference to the person of the Father. If we apply this to our passage, Luke said that God was working through the being of the apostles. As described further in the passage, even Peter's shadow becomes an expression of God's power (Acts 5:15). Partial surrender has no place in the Christian experience.

Illustration

The apostles have become "instruments" for Divine movement. There is a direct link between their hands and Divine hands. It is an "individual ownership." The apostles, in total surrender, have become an avenue for Divine expression, an exciting element of our passage. Luke states that the apostles were a platform upon which signs and wonders ***"were done among the people."*** The Greek word translated ***"were done"*** is "ginomai." It highlights the phenomenon of something brought into existence. It is the concept of "birthing." The Trinity God was birthing ***"signs and wonders"*** through the apostles. But remember, these miracles were all designed to point to God Himself. God was using the apostles to birth an "illustration" or demonstration of Himself. He was revealing Himself through them!

God fulfilling Himself through His creation is the grand scheme and destiny of human life. We were not created to do our own thing or manifest our being. God uniquely designed us to demonstrate His nature, and anything less forms us into a cartoon character. Can you imagine a person created to be the visibility of an invisible God choosing to demonstrate the puniness of his own life? Why would we become the illustration of defeat when we could live in victory? Why would sin dominate our lives when we could possess holiness? Why would we live in hate and jealousy when perfect love could be our expression?

But Luke is clear that this demonstration did not happen in seclusion. It is not the monk hiding in a monastery. Others do not see God in our secret prayer room. Luke declares that the life of God was birthed ***"among the people"*** through the apostles. There are no secret Christians. Christianity is not a badge one wears; it is the very nature of God and the nature of man birthing a new creature. This new creature illustrates the nature of God seen in the culture and circumstances of humanity. Indeed, God reveals who He is through nature (Romans 1:20), and creation declares our God's greatness. But we cannot display the intimate details of God's being until people see them in the conflict and strife in my home. God must take on flesh and demonstrate Himself in the daily routine of my world. He did this in the person of Jesus. But now He is doing this through us.

The hands, mind, emotions, countenance, and even the shadow are all illustrations of the Spirit of Jesus. All Jesus was as the visible image of the invisible God (Colossians 1:15), we are! What a privilege! We are the hands of God for our generation.

Acts 5:12

ONE ACCORD

"And they were all with one accord in Solomon's Porch" (Acts 5:12).

Luke gives us a third "state of the Church" report (Acts 5:12-16). His consistent attempt is to highlight the unity among the believers in the worst of circumstances. In his first report, along with other statements of unity, Luke writes, ***"So continuing daily with one accord in the temple, and breaking bread from house to house, they ate their food with gladness and simplicity of heart"*** (Acts 2:46). Luke does not use the phrase ***"with one accord"*** in his second report but focuses on a commitment of belief that caused them to experience ***"one heart and one soul"*** (Acts 4:32). However, in this third report, he reverts to the statement of ***"with one accord"*** (Acts 5:12).

The Greek word translated ***"with one accord"*** is "homothymadon." Many other translations use "together," however, there is a deeper intent than the early Church members' physical location. "Homothymadon" means unanimous, of one mind and reaches into the inner heart and bespeaks a focus. Luke uses it in the political realm for the visible, inner unity of a group faced by a common duty or danger, not for common personal feelings or emotions but a cause more significant than the person. It is a focus!

The Book of Acts manifests a double kind of "homothymadon," oneness. "Homothymadon" applies to the members of the Church and their enemies. The cause of each is the same, Jesus Christ of Nazareth. The Church responds with faith and worship, while the leaders of Israel respond in hatred and rejection. The enemies of the Church unite as they reject the claims of Christ because they see their religious traditions and their commercial interests threatened. The Church's oneness is not based on sharing the same human or religious feelings and convictions but on the reality of Christ, who has brought together both Jews and Gentiles!

The oneness of "homothymadon" refers to the person of Jesus. The members of the early Church did not develop a new set of traditions or ceremonies. Although they expressed their oneness in action, that oneness was not because of uniformity of dress or religious rules. Neither was theology the cause of their oneness. Jesus had captured their lives. He was all they promoted, the irritation that caused the unity of rejection among Israel's leaders. While divided on many other issues, the early Church members came together in oneness concerning Jesus. Their heart's single issue was the threat that *"from now on they speak to no man in this name"* (Acts 4:17). The "homothymadon" of the early Church is the person of Jesus!

We might aid the clarification if we distinguish between *"with one accord"* (homothymadon) and *"unity"* (henotes). The Greek word "henotes" is used only twice in the New Testament. Paul encourages us to be worthy of the call of Christ on our lives by being patient, humble, and long-suffering, *"endeavoring to keep the unity of the Spirit in the bond of peace"* (Ephesians 4:3). We are to minister to each other *"till we all come to the unity of the faith and of the knowledge of the Son of God, to a perfect man, to the measure of*

the stature of the fullness of Christ" (Ephesians 4:13). "Henotes" is a form of the word "heis," meaning "one." Paul used "henotes" to describe the Church as the body of Christ. Christ is the head ***"from whom the whole body, joined and knit together by what every joint supplies, according to the effective working by which every part does its share"*** (Ephesians 4:16).

The heart of unity comes from the "Shema," the daily confession and creed of the Jew. It comes from ***"Hear O Israel: The Lord our God, the Lord is one"*** (Deuteronomy 6:4). Our Trinity God is united. There are no other gods; the so-called gods do not exist. We do not believe in three Gods but One because of their unity! The three merge in spiritual and mystical oneness, making them united. This unity does not exist in purpose or cause as in "homothymadon," only in spirit and heart. The nature of the Trinity is intertwined, causing them to be one.

The heart of Christianity is man's merger with the Trinity God. When believers unite with the Trinity, they express the unity of the Trinity. In the high priestly prayer, Jesus prayed for us. He said, ***"that they all may be one, as You, Father, are in Me, and I in You; that they also may be one in Us, that the world may believe that You sent Me. And the glory which You gave Me I have given them, that they may be one just as We are one: I in them, and You in Me; that they may be perfect in one, and that the world may know that You have sent Me and have loved them as You have loved Me"*** (John 17:21-23). This unity is far beyond cause, duty, or task. It is the uniting of natures, the intimacy of spirits, and the formation of a new creature!

While there is a distinction between ***"with one accord"*** (homothymadon) and ***"unity"*** (henotes), both present in the believer, one is not present without the other; both must exist to form the whole of the Christian person. Jesus said, ***"But you shall receive power when the Holy Spirit has come upon***

Part Two: Another Review: Another Summary

you, and you shall be witnesses to Me in Jerusalem, and in all Judea and Samaria, and to the end of the earth" (Acts 1:8). Cause and purpose connect with the indwelling of the Spirit of Jesus. But this cause is directly related to the merging of man's nature and God's nature. In unity with the heart of Christ, I begin to think with a redemptive perspective. God's desires become my desires. Therefore, while ***"with one accord"*** (homothymadon) and ***"unity"*** (henotes) are distinct, they are also united in oneness.

In each of the three statements of the early Church's condition, Luke hints at the oneness of heart and nature (unity), but he highlights the believer's ***"with one accord."*** The passion of Christ's heart drives them to redeem the world at any cost. Regardless of the persecution, they must impact their world with the message of Jesus. That cause overshadows all differences between them. The adverb ***"with one accord"*** is highlighted in the Book of Acts and occurs ten times, appearing in one other place in the New Testament (Romans 15:6). Luke primarily uses it in these summary statements expressing the heart of the early Church.

The State

Luke declared, ***"And they were..."*** (Acts 5:12), a translation of the Greek verb "eimi." It is a verb of existence, a state of existence. We can easily miss this state in light of the miracles at the hands of the apostles. The early Church's physical accomplishments were so strong in quality and quantity that they captured everyone's attention. The surrounding cities of Jerusalem brought their sick and those tormented by unclean spirits to the early Church (Acts 5:16), attracted by the physical activities of the Church. This attraction to the physical "doing" is always a danger in the Christian faith.

But the core secret to the early Church was not their physical activities but their state of existence. They were ***"with one accord"*** in a state of being captured by a cause, Jesus. The person of Jesus so engulfed these believers that they focused on Him. Everything else became non-essential and unimportant in comparison. Therefore, the essence of the Christian experience became this state, not any series of activities. The Christian faith's invitation is not to merely embrace new rules or activities for life but to embrace a spiritual state of intimacy with Jesus. This state is better experienced than described or only spoken.

The young man who truly falls head over heels in love with the young lady enters into a state of existence. There is an entire list of activities involved, but these activities do not merely describe it. He dwells in a state of "in love." All kinds of attitudes and feelings are beyond activities. There is a focused passion that seems to dominate his entire thought pattern. How does one describe the state in which he dwells? This state controls all of his activities, schedule, and purpose for life.

I have been trying to help someone who dwells in a state of depression. Psychiatry describes depression as a mental condition, an inner state of mind. It is a state characterized by feelings of severe despondency and dejection, typically also with feelings of inadequacy and guilt, often accompanied by lack of energy and disturbance of appetite and sleep. Therefore, depression is not a physical activity but an inner state! However, all of the physical characteristics are merely expressions of depression.

Luke describes the early Church as having an inner state, ***"with one accord"*** or captured by a cause. The Greek word "homothymadon," translated as ***"with one accord,"*** is a combination of two Greek words. The first word is the Greek word "homo," meaning "together" or "the same." The second Greek word, "thymadon," has to do with passion, as in heavy breathing. This combination of two words is expressive and signifies that they concentrated their minds, affections, desires, and wishes on one object. Every man had the same end in view. They had but one desire. There was no person uninterested, unconcerned, or lukewarm; all were in earnest. The early Church existed in a state that controlled all of its activities. It was a passionate state focused on Jesus!

The Scope

The Greek word commonly translated as ***"all"*** is "pas." However, in our text, Luke places a prefix on this word, "hapas," increasing the word's strength in the passage. The prefix "hama" can be translated "together," giving a double emphasis of the focus of "homothymadon," ***"with one accord."*** The early Church was united in a cause, Jesus. Every other endeavor simply did not matter in light of His person. They were so passionate about Him that even persecution did not detour their focus. Jesus brought them together and overshadowed all other issues that generally divide.

Luke tells us that everyone in this group of believers had this central passion for Jesus. He was the common element. There was diversity among these believers, but the great passion for Jesus made them a unit. In the future, they would select a group of seven men to oversee the daily distribution of goods to the widows (Acts 6:1-4), allowing the apostles to focus on prayer and the ministry of the word. There were various responsibilities and activities in ministry within the believers' group, but their one focus was Jesus. Their passion was not their particular responsibilities, such as youth, senior adults, or children; it was Jesus. Paul magnified this idea by calling the believers the body of Christ (1 Corinthians 12). He was clear that Christ is the head (Colossians 1:18). Each body member united and focused on and through the head, received their directions from the head, and responded only to the head. The early Church was together in one accord because of their passion for Jesus. He captured them!

If anyone wanted to join this group, they must be passionate about Jesus. There was no other driving force. Luke indicates this in the verse following our text. ***"Yet none of the rest dared join them, but the people esteemed them highly"*** (Acts 5:13). This verse requires a study on its own, but we must see it in the context of the early Church's focus upon Christ. No one joined the early Church because of their excellent suppers. No one was merely lonely and wanted the fellowship of others. No one was homeless and needed somewhere to sleep for the night. No one joined the Church for the miracles they could receive. The issue of the early Church was the person of Jesus. If a person did not want to embrace Jesus fully, they did not dare become a part of this group!

The early Church's passion for Jesus was not due to established and strict membership rules. Luke proclaimed the attitude of the early Church. The Church's passion exerted an inner pressure, which could not be tolerated by those not passionate about Jesus. They refused no one for membership who had this passion. The standard of intimacy and merger with Jesus was so strong no one attempted to join without it. That was especially true in light of the recent events in the lives of Ananias and Sapphira. This group of ***"all"*** was about Jesus!

The Solid

Luke ends his third summary with this opening statement, ***"And they were all with one accord in Solomon's Porch"*** (Acts 5:12). The Greek word translated ***"and"*** is "kai." It is a linking term joining two clauses together. This statement links with the emphasis on signs and wonders done among the people through the apostles. The signs and wonders pointed to the spiritual power moving through the apostles. The Spirit of Jesus' presence charged the atmosphere of the gathering. Luke gave further evidence to this by highlighting Peter's shadow. God's power was known and experienced through the touch of the apostles' hands and the extension of Peter's image among the people.

No one would want to discount the spiritual atmosphere dwelling among the people of God. The activity of God in the unseen world around us is a marvel. Christians believe that more is occurring in the unseen world than we can see in the seen world. However, Luke's emphasis is to continually make us aware of the activity of the mystical, spiritual presence of Christ demonstrated and experienced in the physical world in which we live. No one experienced the unseen Divine movement in a trance or vision; they experienced the unseen activity in the practical exchange among people in their physical existence.

Solomon's Porch was the location of all that happened. This colonnade was reportedly double-columned and spanned 49 feet. The columns were 38 feet tall monoliths of white marble and supported cedar-paneled ceilings. Nothing remains of Solomon's Porch except for the platform on which the builders founded it. Although we glory in God's power and greatness, people experienced a moment in history in this location. They shared that event in a physical place where hundreds of people filled with the Spirit of Jesus and passionate about Him assembled.

We cannot isolate the power of God's presence to high spiritual moments in the prayer closet; we must know and express it in the present moments of our physical lives. Luke consistently pressed this upon us as he described the movement of God through the early Church. The financial generosity expressed in physical care for each other is listed. The apostles demonstrated the miracle of His presence in physical healings and demon deliverances. The early Church was not a mystical, spiritual movement that abandoned the physical world around them.

The persecution by the leaders of Israel expressed this same dynamic truth. They recognized the name of Jesus was causing such physical change in their traditions and ceremonies that all would be lost if not stopped. They crucified Jesus because of the physical changes initiated by His spiritual teachings. It continued into the message of the apostles as they proclaimed His name. While we focus and are passionate about the person of Jesus, it must affect our physical actions and expressions.

There is an old story of a monk visited by God's presence during his prayer time in the chapel. Jesus was so real in those moments, the monk did not want to leave, but the hour to feed the poor was approaching. Should he stay in the presence of Jesus and abandon the needy of his world? The monk, with great regret, slipped out to minister to the poor. He rushed back as soon as he could to the place of prayer only to discover the presence of Jesus was more accurate than before. The monk expressed his surprise to Jesus and apologized for needing to leave to help others. Jesus quickly replied, "If you had stayed, I would have left!"

Acts 5:13

HIGH STANDARD

*"Yet none of the rest dared join them,
but the people esteemed them highly" (Acts 5:13).*

There is a hesitation to use the term "high" lest it suggests there is a lower acceptable standard. There is not! The standard offered in our passage is not determined by activities accomplished. The early Church members were not in one accord because they all acted the same but because they were united in their passion! Everyone was passionate about Jesus. He became the single focus of their lives. Their passion was not about theology, programming, or ministry style; it was about one Person. The resurrected Lord captured them. They did not proclaim anything or anyone else, as evidenced by the persecution from the leaders of Israel. Their persecution was because of their constant speaking about Jesus (Acts 4:18).

In this context, we come to our text. Many biblical scholars present this verse and the next as confusing. On the surface, they contradict each other, and the confusion is in explaining this contradiction. Our passage states that **"none of the rest"** dared to become a part of Solomon's Porch gathering (Acts 5:13). The next verse declares, **"And believers were increasingly**

added to the Lord, multitudes of both men and women" (Acts 5:14). Some scholars think the group called ***"none of the rest"*** is the Christian community of the early Church, and the group they did not have the courage to join (***"them"***) is the apostles. Because of the significant spiritual power operating through the apostles, the early Church's believers maintained their distance from them. That is highly unlikely given the description of the believers in chapter four. Others think that Israel's leaders removed themselves from the early Church while the populous of Jerusalem held them in high esteem. None of these explanations follow the true thrust of the passage.

The verse opens with a contrasting conjunction (de). The New King James translates it as ***"yet,"*** while some other translations do not even translate "de." The primary meaning and translation for "de" is the conjunction "but," establishing a contrast between the early Church's gathering at Solomon's Porch and this group that did not dare join with them. The group gathered at Solomon's Porch was ***"with one accord."*** We understand this as passion, being together with heavy breathing, focused on a cause or duty that captured the group. The focus is not on unity with the Spirit, although a merger with the heart of God must be present. Their unity focused on the Person of Jesus, the Cause. The early Church members are passionate about the resurrected Jesus!

Much of Jerusalem's populous admired the early Church members, but a group did not dare possess Jesus with this passion. They knew the story of Ananias and Sapphira, who joined but did not have this passion. Therefore, the high standard of being a Christian was beyond their desire of commitment, suggesting to us that there is not a lesser standard. But "the" standard for Christian experience is a heated passion for Jesus. He does not qualify as Christian if one has correct theology and doctrinal conviction but does not love Jesus with His whole heart, mind, and soul. If one serves in compassionate ministry and gives his

Part Two: Another Review: Another Summary

resources to help the poor but does not love Jesus with his entire being, he does not qualify. A heated, passionate, all-consuming love for Jesus is the standard!

One difficulty with this standard is in measurement. What is the measuring rod to gauge such love? What is the thermometer that tells me how "hot" I am for Jesus? Be assured; there is no way to measure this in the lives of others. When individuals determine the level of passion in others, they become critical and lose sight of their passion for Christ. However, if any person with a sincere heart wants to measure their passion for Christ in their own lives, it becomes very apparent.

In every other area of life, we admire an all-consuming passion. The athlete whose passion takes him to the Olympics receives applause with pride as he accepts the gold medal. He is not embarrassed by his all-consuming passion. The businessman who sacrifices everything for the sake of his business receives admiration for his success. His total commitment is recognized, and others attempt to be like him. Should anyone be embarrassed by the high standard demanded in being a Christian? There are no half attempts in the Christian experience. Would that our church would be so full of this passion for Jesus, everyone who lacked such passion would feel repelled. Each person taking the name "Christian" who lacks this all-consuming passion dilutes, lessens, erodes, and negates the essence of "Christian."

There is no confusion in this passage if we correctly understand ***"with one accord."*** Luke was not writing in confusion but with clarity and precision. He summarized the Christian church's standard presented to the community of Jerusalem. Yet, there were multitudes of men and women who gratefully embraced such a passion. Despite the frightening example of Ananias and Sapphira, many fully embraced Jesus. It is the testimony of the Church's history throughout the ages. The Church flourishes amid persecution without question about the standard in such an hour. When we deny all other allegiance, set aside all other means of safety, and eliminate all other dependencies, we see Jesus is enough! The message is, "Get in or get out." Jesus is not one resource among many; He is the only Resource!

Luke delivers this truth to us in the simple statement of our passage.

Exclusive Cliental

Luke begins this statement with the clarification of the group he describes. He entitles this group as ***"none of the rest."*** The Greek word "loipos," translated as ***"rest,"*** comes from the word "leipo," meaning "to leave or lack." It is an adjective describing this group. Another adjective describing this group is the Greek word "oudeis," translated ***"none,"*** and means "not even one." Luke draws a line between the ***"all"*** gathered with one passion at Solomon's Porch and this crowd. The passage suggests three groups of people. The early Church members are together with a passion for Jesus that overshadows everything else in their lives. ***"Multitudes"*** of other men and women join the early believers in this passion. Then, this third group did not dare to embrace such an all-consuming passion for Jesus. The line between these groups is very distinct.

In conclusion, in our passage, there may just be two groups. The ***"multitudes"*** joined the believers who have a passion for Christ dominating their lives. ***"None of the rest"*** will allow Jesus to possess them with this passion. "Not even one" person could become a believer without this passion. The passion for Jesus is the single definitive factor of the contrast. Luke is erecting a barrier. He tells us that no one will be in the category called "Christian" who will not let Christ consume their lives. There are no exceptions.

Part Two: Another Review: Another Summary

Luke does not indicate that there are degrees to passion. Some of the Christians are not more passionate about Jesus than others. The passion is total in each Christian, the ingredient that makes them Christian. To be a Christian and not burn with passion for Jesus would be an oxymoron. Such a contradiction would be a joke. It would be equivalent to referring to a living man who is not breathing, like experiencing water that is not wet. Ingrained in the fiber of being Christian is the burning passion for Jesus.

The moment any other passion dominates the person, Christianity is in jeopardy. The early Church understood this within the context of the experience of Ananias and Sapphira. They move from Jesus filling their heart to Satan filling them (Acts 5:3). Ananias and Sapphira could continue to do all the acts they did as Christians, participating in the services, sharing in the ministry, and giving their money. Still, the shift in their inner passion could not exist in the Christian community. The Christian life only survives in the atmosphere of intimacy, oneness, and merger with Jesus. That is the passion and single heart's desire of anyone called "Christian." The believers were first called this in Antioch (Acts 11:26). It was a derogatory label intending to "make fun" of their passion for Christ. Jesus was so dominant in their daily living and conversation; that passion distinguished the believers.

Thus, we are face to face again with Peter's conclusion. **"Nor is there salvation in any other, for there is no other name under heaven given among men by which we must be saved"** (Acts 4:12). The evil one working through the leaders of Israel attacked only one thing about the early Church. It was not a theological argument, style issue, nor activity objection. It was their passion for Jesus which compelled them to always speak His Name (Acts 4:18). The leaders of Israel could tolerate passion for everything but Jesus. It has not changed to this day. Our world will accept and even honor passion for athletics, business, education, achievement, stardom, and even religion in general, but not Jesus. But do not misunderstand the message. Luke proposes "not even one" person was a Christian who was not blazing with a passion for Jesus. The absence of such passion disqualified them as Christian. There was no other qualification!

Extreme Courage

Luke makes a solid effort to communicate this group's emotional and spiritual state called **"none of the rest."** He does so by telling us what this group lacked. He uses the Greek word "etomia," translated as ***dared.*** This word is the sentence's main verb; it is in the indicative mood, which presents a simple statement of fact. Luke placed this verb in the imperfect tense portraying action in process or state of being that occurred in the past with no assessment of the action's completion. It was not a momentary state but was the continual state determining their continual response to Christianity. The Greek word "etomla" comes from "tolmao," meaning "courage." "Tolmao" comes from "tlao," which means "to sustain, support, or endure."

There are two aspects involved in this response. One is the fear of what they must embrace. The degree of courage is measured by the state of the challenge faced. Their call was to a radical life change. They had focused their lives on themselves. They knew nothing but the law and their accomplishments of the righteousness determined by such rules. Their mindset was focused on ceremonies and feast days, giving them a sense of completeness. Now, the Person of Jesus was in their faces! Rules are concrete, removing the abstract element. A relationship with a person involves the enlistment of the total being. Entering into a passionate love relationship with Jesus takes me beyond a few life activity adjustments. In addition to this, planted in the courage in our passage is the context of fear. The persecution from the authorities in Jerusalem surrounds this summary. To become Christian meant to violate the trust and confidence of the leaders of Israel. It meant opening oneself for persecution. There is also the cloud of the death of Ananias and Sapphira.

Another aspect is the comfort of remaining in their present state. It takes courage to move from what I have always known and embrace a new thing. But there is a fundamental principle of truth. I must give up what has been to embrace what is to be! A person cannot hold on to both. It is incredible how we might consistently complain about our present situation but never have the courage to move beyond its boundaries. We become locked in the prison of our own making because we do not dare to move beyond it. We may not like it; we wish it were different. But it is all we know.

Embracing Jesus is the radical step of giving up what has been and embracing what is to be. It takes courage. However, God never asked you to do this on your own. The message of the Gospel declares that God's power reaches into our lives to enable us. We do not have to be bound by our fears and inabilities. We view the Christian experience and wonder how we can ever do it, so we never accomplish it. That fear traps us, for the call of passionate love for Christ is always beyond our ability. It demands courage enough to trust Him and Him alone! Perhaps, I should have more fear of being on my own than of being His! Perhaps, the foolishness of blinded deception is in feeling comfortable trusting myself instead of trusting Him!

Exceptional Cleaving

Luke is specific about the group ***"none of the rest"*** living in a state of fear. They did not dare to ***"join"*** the group that was passionate about Jesus. The English word ***"join"*** is hardly adequate to describe the intent of Luke. It suggests a link or connection with the Christian community. It might even mean becoming a Christian church member, for we know it is excellent for our children and community. *"Join"* promotes the idea of taking part in something. The early Church's physical activities become a part of our schedule, and we come into the company of the church members. The church becomes our place of fellowship, entertainment, and support. While all of these ideas may be present in what Luke proposes, they are not the heart!

The Greek word translated as *"join"* is "kollao," meaning "to glue together, to make cohere, or to cleave," not a word used with casual intent. For instance, the Pharisees test Jesus regarding divorce. Jesus quotes the Old Testament statement concerning marriage. **"For this reason a man shall leave his father and mother and be joined** (kollao) **to his wife and the two shall become one flesh"** (Matthew 19:5). The indication of the statement is much more than physical intimacy. There is something so mystical and spiritual about marriage that two people become one entity. Our English word *"join"* does not begin to include the depth of such a merger. Paul encouraged us to glorify God both in our body and spirit. He asked the question, **"Do you not know that your bodies are members of Christ?"** (1 Corinthians 6:15). He paralleled this thought with sexual intimacy by saying, **"Shall I then take the members of Christ and make them members of a harlot? Certainly not! Or do you not know that he who is joined** (kollao) **to a harlot is one body with her?" For 'the two,' He says, 'shall become one flesh.' But he who is joined** (kollao) **to the Lord is one spirit with Him"** (1 Corinthians 6:15-17). Think of the comparison that makes! The mystical and spiritual welding happening in marriage duplicates in intensity between the believer and Jesus.

Part Two: Another Review: Another Summary

Paul makes another attempt to describe the merger with God in becoming a new creation. ***"Therefore, if anyone is in Christ, he is a new creation; old things have passed away; behold, all things have become new"*** (2 Corinthians 5:17). All of the New Testament's imageries for oneness between God and man point to an intimate "joining" (kollao). It is beyond the description of words. We are the bride of Christ, sons of God, a new creation, the body of Christ, the branch connected to the vine, the wild branch grafted to the true vine, the house resting on the firm foundation, the clay in the potter's hands, or the soil containing the seed. All of the imageries yell at us concerning the mystical and spiritual joining of our lives with Jesus.

In our passage, many people were afraid to enter into close unity and oneness with Christ. This unity required an abandonment of the entire life, submerged and under the influence of Jesus. The severity of such oneness was fresh in their minds with the death of Ananias and Sapphira. Everyone understood to be Christian involved completeness in surrender. The standard has not changed. Jesus is worthy of our whole lives. Anything less is a degrading and belittling of who He is.

The verb "kollao" is always in the passive voice in the New Testament. In this case, it is what is called "a Divine passive." The One who is doing the action of the verb is God. Entering into the mystical and spiritual oneness with Jesus is not anything done on the human level. We cannot achieve it or even contribute to it. We can only posture ourselves in the proper spiritual place for the Divine action to occur in our lives. The full glory for such welding with Him will forever be His, emphasizing the totality of the abandonment present in this union. The privilege of such oneness with Him brought a passion for Jesus that could not waver. Do you dare join this group?

Acts 5:14
OTHERS - OTHERS - OTHERS

"And believers were increasingly added to the Lord, multitudes of both men and women" (Acts 5:14).

Evangelism is a consistent theme throughout the three summaries of the early Church in Jerusalem. Luke never indicates there was isolation or contentment within the Christian community. The early Church continually reached out to those around them, which directly contrasts with Jewish segregation. The strong emphasis on law isolated the Jews from the rest of their world. There were Gentile proselytes, but it was not because of the evangelistic efforts of the Jews. The law developed an exclusion from others who might bring defilement to them. However, the moment Jesus freed the early Church from the law, evangelism took place.

In the first summary, Luke highlights this fact. **"And the Lord added to the church daily those who were being saved"** (Acts 2:47). Although Luke does not directly say evangelism in the second summary, we can assume it. Luke said, **"And with great power the apostles gave witness to the resurrection of the Lord Jesus"** (Acts 4:33). The third summary increases the focus and highlights an increase in the results. These converted Jews moved from a religion based on laws to a relationship with Jesus raised from the dead. This shift demanded they embrace every person within their reach.

The law focused on performance rather than compassion. Its interest was in measuring how well one treats others rather than encompassing others' pain and guilt. Relationship with Jesus changes everything because we know Christ's heart. The fullness of the Spirit is a merger with the nature of Jesus. His presence infiltrates the mind, emotions, and will. It is impossible to have a passion for Jesus and not have a passion for others. Jesus clarified this in the Sermon on the Mount as He spoke of religion's four basic principles. The law demands charitable deeds but focuses on meeting the requirement, not the one in need (Matthew 6:2-4). Jesus calls us to such intimacy with Him that we express the Father's heart, always focused on others.

The grammar of our summary suggests a series of contrasts. Ananias and Sapphira's death contrasted with signs and wonders being done among the people by the apostles (Acts 5:12). Verse 12 begins with the Greek word "de," which has the primary meaning of "but." Ananias and Sapphira's self-focus brought death to their lives. When we surrender to Jesus, He changes our focus from self to others. We intervene, meeting their needs. Connected to God's movement through the apostles is the group of believers gathered under Solomon's Porch. Their chief characteristic was ***"all with one accord."*** We discovered this means that they were together with heavy breathing. Each one was passionate about the Cause, Jesus. Jesus consumed them!

Evangelism, church growth, or increasing their number was not what consumed them. Jesus was their cause! The Devil is deceptive and continually sets traps to shift our cause from Jesus. The issue is not about good or bad but Jesus. One might be entirely correct but be lost because He is not right "in Jesus." The early Church was passionate about winning the lost as a result of being passionate about Jesus. Evangelism is a byproduct of being in Jesus. If it does not flow from His heart, it is duty, obligation, or the product of a career. Pride quickly becomes the motive as we measure our success. Evangelism for the early Church directly resulted from their passion for Jesus; therefore, they genuinely desired to help people. Evangelism is the result of the heart of Christ indwelling the believer.

There is another contrast (Acts 5:13). The group gathered in Solomon's Porch had a passion for Jesus and is contrasted with this group who admired them but did not dare to allow Jesus to dominate their lives with such a passion. They realized that to join these Christians was to be welded or merged with Jesus. Jesus would not be a pleasant addition to an already established life. He would dominate and transform their lives with His passion. Although they admired those who had such courage, they did not. Keep in mind that this setting's context is the death of Ananias and Sapphira and Israel's leaders' persecution.

But there is good news! Luke gives an additional contrast. *"And* (but) ***believers were increasingly added to the Lord, multitudes of both men and women"*** (Acts 5:14). Christ captured them and became their passion. Luke expands this picture with his continued description (Acts 5:15-16). Physical miracles happened; the power of God moved through the lives of Peter and the apostles, evangelized the cities beyond Jerusalem, and rescued the demon possessed.

Flourishing
"increasingly"

In describing the early Church's evangelism, Luke injects the word *"increasingly"* (Acts 5:14), a translation of the Greek word "mallon," which means "flourishing." The English Standard Bible translates it, ***"more than ever."*** The evangelism of the early Church in Jerusalem moved to a new level. Luke continues to express this in the statement, **"*multitudes of both men and women*"** (Acts 5:14). The Greek word translated **"*multitudes*"** is "plethos." We must note that this Greek word is plural. Although this Greek word appears in various other places, this is the only place in the New Testament it is plural. Luke highlights the immense growth of the church. It is fair to say that the three summaries of the early Church's state reveal a continuing emphasis and increase in evangelism.

We should easily understand growth! Evangelism is not by addition but by multiplication. Although the word **"*added*"** is used in the passage, the emphasis is upon the hand of God taking each new believer and bringing them into fellowship with the heart of the Trinity. Therefore, we see multiplication in the method of evangelism. When one person wins another person to Christ, he doubles the evangelism force. There are now two people who are winning others to Jesus. As those two people each win another person, they expand the evangelism force to four. This multiplication takes place until everyone is affected by the person of Jesus. In seventy years, this group of Christians so infected their culture that the world recognized Christianity as the world religion.

Each believer's passion for Jesus should not surprise us. The inner heart of each one merged with Jesus and burned with love for Him. They could not keep silent about Him. When the leaders of Israel demanded they no longer speak about Jesus, Peter said, **"*Whether it is right in the sight of God to listen to you more than to God, you judge. For we cannot but speak the things which we have seen and heard*"** (Acts 4:19, 20). How could they not confront every person with Jesus when He was their life. To deny Jesus would be to deny their own existence. Evangelism was never a duty or requirement for membership; it was as natural to them as breathing is to anyone alive.

Others - Others - Others | **Acts 5:14**

The increase in the early Church was somewhat startling in light of the cultural environment surrounding them. The persecution, which began with the miracle of the lame beggar's healing at the Gate Beautiful, increased. The leaders of Israel once again placed the apostles in the common prison (Acts 5:18). God miraculously delivered them. When the officers came to the prison to bring them before the leaders, they were gone. They discovered them in the temple, teaching the people about Jesus. Stephen became the first martyr of the early Church. The persecution escalated under the leadership of Saul, but evangelism consistently increased. The passion for Christ within the believers was stronger than the persecuting spirit of their world.

Might we in the evangelical church find ourselves a bit embarrassed in light of this picture? There is no evil circumstance or resistance to the Gospel in our day that was not equally present in the early Church's culture. Our physical resources to spread the message of Jesus are more abundant than they had. The ability to reach the world with our passion for Christ is staggering. We experience the increasing supply of two thousand years of God's grace poured out. There is more depth and wisdom concerning the message at our disposal. If we fail in evangelism, our lack of passion for Jesus will be the reason. Let us be captured by Him again!

Focusing
"believers"

The terminology Luke chooses for those converted to Jesus is significant. In our passage, he writes, ***"And believers were increasingly added to the Lord, multitudes of both men and women"*** (Acts 5:14). The idea of "believe" or "faith" is not new to us. Luke identifies those who joined the number were as passionate about Jesus as people already saved. The apostles have not provided theological arguments to sway their thinking. It was not a doctrinal crash course that won them. Peter and the apostles proclaimed nothing but Jesus, the resurrected Lord. Their focus was not on the resurrection event; it was upon the Lord who was alive because God resurrected Him. They became believers because they found Jesus to be alive as He confronted their lives. These believers became passionate about the person of Jesus. "To believe" was not about a system but a person!

As stated repeatedly, we must see the reality of Jesus in light of this setting's culture and historical moment. Jesus was crucified, raised from the dead, and ascended to the right hand of the Father. Fifty days later, He poured out the Holy Spirit upon the believers. How long ago were the occasions for this group, Luke describes? Even if one demands it was two or three years, it was well within these people's memory span. When the apostles spoke of Jesus, they saw His face in their memory. They remembered shaking their fists in His face and screaming His name in blasphemy. He was not a belief system to them but a real person they had rejected.

Now in the Spirit of evangelism, Peter challenges them to reverse their involvement with Jesus. They crucified Him; they must "un-crucify" Him. They rejected Him; now they must embrace Him. They pushed Him aside as a false Messiah; now, they must bow to His Lordship. But how can they change all they have done? He is alive, and they have another chance. The memories of crucifying Him hounded them night and day; now they could make it right. They became ***"believers."*** With the same zeal with which they crucified Him, they must now merge with Him. As they wholeheartedly eliminated Him from their lives, now they will cherish His presence. They are passionate believers!

This picture is a reality for us. We have participated in Jesus' crucifixion. By our sin, we have defiled His name, rejected His presence, and refused the redemptive plan of God. In the spiritual realm and physical expression, we duplicated the actions of those in the Book of Acts. We are guilty! We depended on ourselves in our self-centered pride and rejected His guidance in our lives. Embracing Jesus is not about joining a church or adopting a particular theology. It is about Jesus falling in love with Jesus. As we have rejected Him with outstanding commitment, we must now embrace Him wholeheartedly. It is not a theological decision; it is a relational decision. Will I allow my life to be under His influence? Will I be a passionate believer?

Foundation
"were added"

We might say, "I want to love Jesus with my whole heart, but how do I do it?" As Peter completed his explanation of the Pentecost event, the crowd asked the same question. **"Men and brethren, what shall we do?"** (Acts 2:37). Peter's answer was, **"Repent, and let every one of you be baptized in the name of Jesus Christ for the remission of sins; and you shall receive the gift of the Holy Spirit"** (Acts 2:38). If you and I do not have the mindset of their culture, we will misinterpret Peter's instructions. He demanded "repentance!" It is the internal mind, will, and emotions of a person giving up a former thought to embrace a new thought. It is the inner being's willingness to reverse all previous opinions about Jesus and embrace Him fully. It is a state of availability to the real influence of Jesus within the life.

In their religious culture, the symbol of this was baptism. Submitting to baptism was submitting one's self to relinquishing self-control. No one can adequately baptize himself. The one baptized trusts the hands of the one baptizing. The candidate for baptism is no longer in charge of what will happen in his life. He is not responsible. Our passage strongly indicates this idea.

Part Two: Another Review: Another Summary

Luke says that believers *"were increasingly added to the Lord."* The Greek word "prostithemi," translated as *"were added,"* and the prefix "pros" means "to" or "besides." The basic word is "tithemi," meaning "to put" or "to set."

Significantly, this verb is in the imperfect tense, which means "an event in the past that continues into the present and has no view of ending." It is not a simple act or experience that they soon completed. It is a relational idea. Through the attitude of repentance, Jesus is allowed to take control of the believer's inner life and continually draw them into intimacy with Himself! It is not a visitation, a counseling session, or a mere touch. It is a merger, indwelling, or continual fusion of God's heart and the being of man!

Significantly, this verb is in the passive voice, which means "the verb's action is acting upon the subject." The subject is not responsible for the accomplishment or action of being *"added to the Lord."* The believer has simply placed himself in the position where Jesus could embrace him and continually draw him into intimacy. The believer cannot do this; the Divine provision is acting upon him. From the beginning to the end of the Gospel message, the Trinity God always instigated the action. He provided redemption through Jesus. Jesus has won me to His heart, embraced me with His presence, and is revealing His glory moment by moment. He is all in all! Jesus acts upon the believer!

Significantly, this verb is a movement term that means "a location change." The believer places himself at the disposal of the love of Jesus. In this state of surrender, Jesus embraces the believer and moves him from one location to another. This new location is *"to the Lord."* In the consistent language of the Apostle Paul, it is *"in Christ!"* The believer's place is within the boundaries of the person of Jesus. *"But God* (the Trinity God)*, who is rich in mercy, because of His great love with which He loved us, even when we were dead* *in trespasses, made us alive together with Christ (by grace you have been saved), and raised us up together, and made us sit together in the heavenly place in Christ Jesus"* (Ephesians 2:4-6). We have been merged with the Divine heart of God by the mercies and love of God. He acts upon our lives to bring us into oneness with Himself!

While you and I cannot do this, we decide whether or not to experience it. One cannot "try" this on a trial basis. It is "all or nothing." You and I are either "in or out." Would you allow Jesus to draw your life into an intimate love relationship with Jesus?

Acts 5:15

YOUR SHADOW

"So that they brought the sick out into the streets and laid them on beds and couches, that at least the shadow of Peter passing by might fall on them" (Acts 5:15).

There is a mystical element present in this paragraph (Acts 5:12-16), though it is somewhat dangerous to suggest that reality. I have always considered myself a mystic. According to the English dictionary, a mystic is "a person who seeks by contemplation and self-surrender to obtain unity with or absorption into the Deity or the absolute, or who believes in the spiritual apprehension of truths that are beyond the intellect." Of course, we must understand this within the boundaries of biblical truth. The wonder of merging with the Trinity God who desires to share His life with us is a mystical reality. An individual filled with God's essence and sharing His mind and heart is beyond the practical and is mystical!

In the opening verse of our paragraph, Luke presents the issue of ***"signs and wonders were done among the people"*** (Acts 5:12). It is mysticism within the realm of practical everyday life of Jerusalem's people. The apostles were the physical instruments of God's mystical presence,

Your Shadow | Acts 5:15

accomplishing beneficial physical results. The physical location of this mystical invasion was Solomon's Porch. The early Church gathered there ***"with one accord"*** (Acts 5:12), meaning they were passionate about the cause of Jesus! But it was not a dead Jesus who was a mere memory; it was Jesus alive in them, a mystical reality.

The presence of Jesus was so evident among them that ***"none of the rest dared join them"*** (Acts 5:13). A mystical presence of the Trinity God so powerfully permeated the atmosphere of this group of believers' that it repelled anyone who did not have the same spiritual hunger. How strange this must have been to the narrow, legalistic Jew who knew nothing but ceremonies and duty. It would have been as frightening for them as God descending on Mt Sinai in thunder and lightning was for the ancient Israelites. However, another group appears in our paragraph; they experience the mystical movement of the Spirit of Jesus and are ***"added to the Lord"*** (Acts 5:14). The mystical power of God relocated these Jews into a different and superior spiritual realm.

It follows this immense emphasis on the mystical element of spiritual atmosphere that Luke introduces us to the idea of people wanting to get into a position where ***"at least the shadow of Peter passing by might fall on some of them"*** (Acts 5:15). The tendency is to take this statement and remove it from the mystical and place it in the practical. When ***"they brought the sick out into the streets and laid them on beds and couches,"*** it was practical. But the moment we do not consider the practical in light of the mystical, confusion appears, and superstition dominates. Luke attempted to communicate the state of the early Church. They lived in the atmosphere of God's power, the mystical realm of the Spirit!

Significantly, Luke never recorded or indicated any miracles resulting from Peter's shadow. Peter's shadow did not have miracle power any more than Peter had miracle power. Jesus used Peter to heal the lame beggar (Acts 3). It was remarkable because of the man's age. He was over forty years of age and was known because he had been consistently begging at the temple gate for years. He reportedly held onto Peter and John as if they were responsible for his miracle (Acts 3:11). When the crowd gathered in Solomon's Porch, they were amazed at the healing of this man holding onto Peter. Peter was horrified at their response. He asked them, ***"Men of Israel, why do you marvel at this? Or why look so intently at us, as though by our own power or godliness we had made this man walk?"*** (Acts 3:12). They knew all the Old Testament stories that highlighted the deliverances of God! Why would it shock them that the same mystical power was working in this hour? Their focus should not be on the presence of a human being when God's divine, mystical presence was moving among them. It was not about a shadow but about the mystical power of God that was beyond understanding!

Sequence

A large amount of controversy surrounds this verse. It primarily relates to the opening words of the verse, **"so that,"** a translation of the Greek word "hoste," which indicates "for this reason." However, another Greek word not translated in our version, "kai," is a common conjunction meaning "and." The action of those who brought the sick into the streets is directly connected to what took place prior. But who is it that Luke links with this action? We must also note **"they brought,"** a translation of the Greek word "ekphero," which is an infinitive that depends on the main subject of the sentence. Who are **"they,"** and what caused them to bring the sick out into the streets?

Many Bible scholars in the past made verses twelve

through fourteen an insert section with parenthesis around it. That makes the paragraph read, *"And through the hands of the apostles many signs and wonders were done among the people . . . so that they brought the sick out, etc.,"* which is the Geneva Bible arrangement of the text copied by the King James Version. Other scholars dismiss the parenthesis and attach our verse to the end of verse thirteen, which reads, *"but the people esteemed them highly . . . so that they brought the sick out, etc."* However, there is no reason to accept either of these ideas. The natural sequence of the verses tells the correct story. Evangelism was increasing in the ministry of the early Church. Believers were added to the Lord, *"multitudes of both men and women"* (Acts 5:14). These were the people who brought the sick into the streets (Acts 5:15).

The increase in believers relates to the rise in miracles! It is not that miracles occurred; therefore, people became believers; but people became believers, and miracles took place. Miracles resulted from people abandoning themselves to Jesus. The miracle of salvation affected both the spiritual and physical life of the new believer. The Spirit of Jesus invading the life of an individual does something to the total being. While this does not establish the premise that salvation always involved total physical wholeness, it does indicate that salvation brings the entire being under the influence and purpose of Divine invasion. If this is not true, one might attempt to manipulate God for self-centered advantages. Demanding a miracle from God before abandoning one's life to Him does not establish a salvation relationship with Him. It certainly does not fit the picture of the early Church, whose members *"were all with one accord"* (Acts 5:12). They were with heavy breathing, extreme passion, and focused on Jesus, who enabled the miracles in their midst.

Part Two: Another Review: Another Summary

Superstition

In the Hebrew tradition, "shadow" never connotes a sinister or threatening phenomenon. It most often represents welcome shelter from the heat of the noonday sun (Judges 9:15; Job 7:2; 40:22; Isaiah 4:6; 32:2; 34:15; Hosea 4:13; Jonah 4:5+). "Shadow" can therefore signify protection (Isaiah 30:2+). The "shadow of Yahweh's wings" (Psalms 17:8; 36:7) and the "shadow of His hand" (Isaiah 49:2; 51:16) are metaphors for divine protection. While in a pagan world, "shadow" may involve superstition, there is no reason to come to the New Testament with such an understanding. The Jewish culture of Peter's day would not permit us to view superstitious people who believed Peter's shadow could do miracles.

There are two other passages in the New Testament that relate to this belief. Jesus accompanied Jairus to his house to minister to his daughter. A woman experiencing a physical condition for twelve years tried to get the attention of Jesus, but **"the multitudes thronged Him"** (Luke 8:42). In desperation, she came up behind Him and touched the border of His garment, and Jesus immediately healed her. She testified to the surrounding crowd that she intended to touch Jesus' garment, the only point of contact she could have because of the multitude. The purpose of the passage is not to relate healing through the power of the garment but through the person of Jesus.

Paul was an instrument of God for unusual miracles (Acts 19:11). Further stated, it reads, **"so that even handkerchiefs or aprons were brought from his body to the sick, and the diseases left them and the evil spirits went out of them"** (Acts 9:12). We must carefully note that this practice was not the consistent pattern of the early Church. There is no biblical record of any other like activity, and no one should base a pattern or doctrine on one verse in the Bible.

Luke explicitly highlights the power of God as the only source of the miracles. ***"Now God worked unusual miracles by the hands of Paul"*** (Acts 19:11). Luke focuses again on the person of God, not the magic of handkerchiefs.

The Scriptures are clear! Why would I stand in the shadow of a man when Jesus can fill me with Himself? Why would I desire the cloth that the apostle Paul touched and prayed over when I could go directly to the heart of God? Why would I want a guardian angel hovering over me when the Spirit of Jesus can fill me? We must stay focused! It is the trick of Satan to misdirect our attention. He may do it through addictions to drugs or drink; however, he will also use hobbies or other particular interests to distract us. It might even misdirect us in religious matters. It is easy to focus on methodology and programs rather than on Jesus. Satan loves it when we are theology-centered instead of Christ-centered.

The leaders of Israel persecuted the early Church for one reason, their focus on Jesus. The social good of the early Church did not concern these leaders. They did not care about the various gatherings of the early Church, their suppers, or their fellowship times. They did not even care about them teaching the doctrine of the resurrection. Their issue was always Jesus. The early Church must be silent about Jesus! Let us not get distracted by a "shadow ministry" or a "cloth ministry." Let us not turn to "magic" when we have the risen Lord!

Shadow

The Old Testament imagery of the shadow points to our Trinity God's protection. David prayed with confidence for our final salvation (Psalms 17). A factor in that confidence was the shadow of the great wings of Jehovah. He prayed,

Part Two: Another Review: Another Summary

> *"Show Your marvelous lovingkindness by Your right hand,*
> *O You who save those who trust in You*
> *From those who rise up against them.*
> *Keep me as the apple of Your eye;*
> *Hide me under the shadow of Your wings,*
> *From the wicked who oppress me,*
> *From deadly enemies who surround me"* (Psalms 17:7-9).

David considered the **"shadow of the Almighty"** not a place to escape for temporary safety but a permanent dwelling place.

> *"He who dwells in the secret place of the Most High*
> *Shall abide under the shadow of the Almighty.*
> *I will say of the Lord, 'He is my refuge and my fortress;*
> *My God, in Him I will trust'"* (Psalms 91:1).

The Greek words and word order in our passage are somewhat pointed. Not only does Luke use the idea of Peter's **"shadow"** (skia), but in addition, he includes the verb "episkiazo," translated **"might fall."** This word is used only five times in the New Testament. The other four times, scholars translated it **"overshadow."** These usages refer to the great and sovereign power or presence of God coming upon a person or people. For instance, the angel Gabriel confronted Mary. The purpose of his visit was to inform her of her position as **"highly favored."** Due to this position, she was told, **"You will conceive in your womb and bring forth a Son, and shall call His name Jesus"** (Luke 1:31). Significantly, Mary responded with total submission to this announcement with only one question, **"How can this be, since I do not know a man?"** (Luke 1:34). The answer was simple. **"The Holy Spirit will come upon you, and the power of the Highest will overshadow** (episkiazo) **you"** (Luke 1:35). While there is a mystery about what this might mean, it is clear that the power of God's resource presence engulfed Mary to the core of her physical and spiritual life. While we cannot understand or explain all that happened in this "overshadowing," we do not consider it magic but Divine embracing. The Divine presence merged with human flesh and brought an expanded revelation of who God created us to be!

Peter, James, and John experienced the same "overshadowing" on the Mount of Transfiguration. After six days of the disciples resisting the message of the cross, Jesus took three of the most influential to a prayer meeting on the mountain. He transformed before them, and Moses and Elijah visited them, representing the law and the prophets. According to Luke's Gospel, they spoke of His death as they encouraged Him to stay faithful to His calling. Peter decided to interrupt the heavenly conversation, expressing his desire to build three tabernacles in honor of this experience. "***While he was still speaking, behold, a bright cloud overshadowed*** (episkiazo) ***them; and suddenly a voice came out of the cloud, saying, 'This is My beloved Son, in whom I am well pleased. Hear Him!'***" (Matthew 17:5). Mark and Luke both recorded this same account in their Gospels (Mark 9:7; Luke 9:34).

The Holy Spirit overshadowed Mary; the presence of God overshadowed Jesus. This overshadowing speaks to the intimate involvement of the Trinity God in human life. The Trinity God designed the redemptive plan, and God's power accomplished it. But He decided to limit that power in a way to allow human participation. God would not redeem humanity without the involvement and cooperation of humankind. Mary knew the overshadowing of the Holy Spirit to have her humanity extended into the Redemptive Agent of the world. This Redemptive Agent knew the overshadowing of the sovereign God to establish such a redemption.

Part Two: Another Review: Another Summary

Now Peter, filled with the Spirit of Jesus, overshadowed those in Jerusalem, extending the presence of God in his shadow. Does this not cry out to us the biblical truth? We are to merge with the Divine nature. This merger will produce oneness, creating a new creature. Everything about this new creature is an extension of a helpless person filled with the Spirit of Jesus. This infilling saves us from the uncertainty of achieving holiness. We focus on intimacy with His person and allow Him to influence our lives. This intimacy arrests us from performance activities allowing God to use our lives, removing the fear of failure and giving us confidence in Him. He uses us when we do not know it. It is not our duty of conscious service that affects the lives of others but the unconscious flow of His presence.

Could I be the shadow of God for my world? This truth speaks the reality of our lives that we take for granted or do not even consider. Could God use these things to bring about healing? Could the power of His presence use me, and I am unaware? Could people find refuge in my presence because He is present?

Acts 5:16
CONFRONTATION

"Also a multitude gathered from the surrounding cities to Jerusalem, bringing sick people and those who were tormented by unclean spirits, and they were all healed" (Acts 5:16).

Everyone enjoys reading a novel where the story ends with resolve. Even though the conflict was severe, the final result is living peaceably ever after. Luke did not write the story of our passage (Acts 5:12-16) in that manner. Our passage takes the early Church and flings it into increased persecution. Accusations and imprisonment were immediate. The following pages portray the first martyrs of the early Church, which might leave you thinking things went from bad to worse. However, victory prevails in every scene. How did God consistently take what was bad and use it for His glory? That is the miracle of our story!

Luke presented the state of the early Church in Jerusalem (Acts 5:16), and our passage is the climax of the third summary. Through his summaries, Luke showed the progress and success of the early Church despite the hindrances around them. The persecution of the church arose from the miracle healing of the lame beggar (Acts 3). But persecution did not detour these believers! Some of their own, Ananias and Sapphira, betrayed the heart of total commitment to Jesus, a demonstration that clarified the level of relationship with Jesus required of all believers. The early Church members grasped this understanding as well as the Jerusalem community.

Now Luke felt compelled to give us another update to the condition of the early Church, presenting that condition with a series of contrasts. The English translations of this paragraph do not highlight this, but the original Greek language clarifies the contrasts. Of the five verses in our paragraph, four of them begin with the Greek word "de." This conjunction's primary meaning and translation are "but," suggesting a contrast or introduction of something new. Some of the contrasts are positive, and some have a negative focus.

The paragraph begins with a contrast (Acts 5:12), "passion" is the focus. The previous paragraph ends with the death of Ananias and Sapphira, which brought a new sense of fear and reverence both in the church and community. "But" the power of God continued to flow through the hands of the apostles, and there was great unity. The believers were **"with one accord in Solomon's Porch."** In previous studies, we discovered **"with one accord"** is a translation of "homothymadon." It means "together with heavy breathing," focusing the passion on a cause. Jesus was the cause! The disobedience and half-heartedness of Ananias and Sapphira, which resulted in their death, only intensified the commitment of the early Church members to Jesus. He was their "passion."

In the next verse, Luke shows the "passion" of the believers contrasted with the group that decided to "pass" (Acts 5:13). "**Yet** (But) **none of the rest dared join them, but the people esteemed them highly."** There was a group, when confronted with an all-consuming passion for Jesus, decided it was too demanding. The required commitment level was too high. Involvement with this Christian group meant they must risk persecution from the leaders of Israel and the consequences of not being total in their commitment. All in all, they did not dare to enter into such a relationship. They decided to "pass" on experiencing such a "passion."

However, the rejection of this group did not deter the early Church. "***And*** (But) ***believers were increasingly added to the Lord, multitudes of both men and women***" (Acts 5:14). The rejection of the Gospel by some has never stopped the evangelism of the church. In light of all the adverse circumstances, the early Church grew. Persecution, disobedience of Ananias and Sapphira, and the high standard of commitment rejected by some did not hinder multitudes of individuals abandoning themselves to Jesus. The "production" of new believers only increased. The "passion" of the early Church, while some would "pass" on being involved, continued a "production" of passion for Jesus in multitudes of others. Nothing could stop such a passion!

The "projection" of this "passion" began to impact those living outside Jerusalem. "(But) ***Also a multitude gathered from the surrounding cities to Jerusalem, bringing sick people and those who were tormented by unclean spirits, and they were all healed***" (Acts 5:16). The early Church remained within the boundaries of the city of Jerusalem. We have no record of anyone going beyond this city to minister or evangelize. However, God imparted His Spirit upon and through the believers and neighboring cities for the first time. The indication is that those of other towns came to Jerusalem and experienced the ministry of Jesus through the apostles. This visitation by others is the first step towards accomplishing the "Great Commission" given by Jesus to His disciples before His ascension (Matthew 28:16-20).

This evangelization is the conclusion of the third summary given by Luke concerning the state of the church. The summary, and especially this last statement, becomes the platform for the rest of the chapter and following. "Persecution" immediately follows; anger and jealousy filled the high priest and other leaders. "***Then*** (But) ***the high priest rose up, and all those who were with him (which is the sect of the Sadducees), and they were filled with indignation***" (Acts 5:17). They had severely warned the apostles never again to speak the name of Jesus. The early Church did not heed these threats. The early Church expanded, and their success in winning people to Jesus was apparent. This evangelism was an extreme irritation to the leaders of Israel, especially the Sadducees. The early Church consistently preached and taught Jesus, which violated the authority of these leaders. The abundance of miracles taking place undermined this same authority. These were undeniable in light of the number of witnesses in Jerusalem. There is jealousy in the hearts of the Sadducees over the success and popularity of the early Church. Those who came to the Sadducees for instruction and wisdom were now going to the apostles.

The Sadducees reacted by putting the apostles in the common jail. The rest of the chapter reveals the continual conflict and victories experienced amid persecution. Our verse establishes the platform for the content of the rest of the chapter, filled with victories through Divine intervention. The wisdom or cleverness of the apostles is not the focus, and Luke never mentions their talent and personalities. Jesus manifested His power continually as He protected His plan for winning the world! All of this is experienced and suggested in our verse.

Invasion

Multitudes from surrounding cities gathered in Jerusalem with great purpose. Their coming was the beginning of the early Church's evangelism outside Jerusalem. The apostles had not attempted to minister beyond the city, but now those beyond were coming to them. The physical and spiritual needs drove the people to come. Luke specifically focused on *"sick people and those who were tormented by unclean spirits"* (Acts 5:16).

Luke began with a presentation on *"a multitude,"* the sentence's main subject, and the verb is *"gathered."* Luke uses a participle phrase to give purpose to their gathering, "phero," translated, *"bringing."* This verb acts as an adverb providing content to the main verb, *"gathered,"* used 66 times in the New Testament, most of which express a sense of burden. The idea of burden is not always negative but positive and aggressive, implying action or motion and something of a load. The multitude of people made a purposeful effort to bring those in need to the power of Jesus. The Divine action was God's response to their direct intent and desperation.

Luke divides those brought by the multitudes into two groups. There were *"sick people,"* a translation of the Greek word "asthenema." "Asthenema" is most often a reference to a comprehensive understanding of weakness as that which is derived directly from the earthly-bodily existence of humankind. These were individuals who were in a state of weakness and could not physically bring themselves. Their physical condition is the definite emphasis of the word.

Luke focused on the spiritual aspect of the people the early Church members brought, *"those who were tormented,"* a translation of the Greek word "ochloumenous." "Ochloumenoux" comes from the Greek word, "ochleo," which means "disturb or trouble," and has the idea of a mob and the harassment from a crowd. It is only in the passive voice, which tells us the torture comes from something beyond themselves. It is the only time this word is used in the New Testament giving it distinct focus. Luke relates who is responsible for the torture and says it is *"by unclean spirits."* The Greek word "hupo," translated *"by,"* displays the instrument of the torture but must be understood in light of the primary meaning of the Greek word for "under." The *"unclean spirits"* tortured the people under their control.

Part Two: Another Review: Another Summary

The Divine power of God invaded demonic territory through the early Church. God freed lives under the control and authority of demonic spirits from such influence. The startling action revealed the wonder of Jesus' ministry. God entered into the flesh of humanity, marched into the territory of the devil, and claimed them as His own. Every miracle of Jesus was an invasion of what Satan secured for himself. In the healing of the paralytic, Jesus equated "forgiveness of sins" and "physical healing" (Matthew 9:1-8). The devil claimed ownership to **"all the kingdoms of the world and their glory"** (Matthew 4:8). He offered to give them to Jesus for His allegiance. God initially gave Adam these kingdoms (Genesis 1:26). But Adam yielded ownership and authority to Satan, which is the heart of "sin!" It is the issue of authority, influence, and sourcing.

God reclaiming the territory taken by Satan is the core of all redemptive ministry. We must never forget the battle is not against flesh and blood but against demonic forces (Ephesians 6:12). The early Church clung to Jesus. They found in Jesus the Divine resource overcoming all other powers. They understood any combination of authority mixed with the Divine resource brought destruction and death, Ananias and Sapphira. There was a totality about the early Church regarding Jesus. The ringing words of Peter highlighted their conviction, **"Nor is there salvation in any other, for there is no other name under heaven given among men by which we must be saved"** (Acts 4:12).

Introduction

While the early Church knew the enemy they were battling, they understood the platform upon which the enemy staged the battle. The physical is a demonstration of spiritual realities. The early Church did not consider every physical condition a direct result of demonic involvement. However, they viewed the difficulties of their physical existence as manifestations of spiritual involvement. The early Church saw the death of Ananias and Sapphira as much more than a physical cause of death. Did not the Jerusalem community understand their death as a physical result of spiritual disobedience acted out in the physical?

The persecution experienced by the early Church only highlights the spiritual displayed in the physical. The apostles were in the common prison; this physical situation directly resulted from their spiritual connection with Jesus shown in their physical world. The early Church could not separate their spiritual lives from their physical existence. The leaders of Israel threatened them to keep silent about Jesus. They were never physically to mention His name again (Acts 4:18). This threat suggests the early Church could continue to believe wholeheartedly in Jesus, but only if they could physically maintain silence. But Peter declared this was spiritually and physically impossible, **"For we cannot but speak the things which we have seen and heard"** (Acts 4:20). They had physically seen and physically experienced the spiritual reality of Jesus. Not allowing their physical expression to come under the influence of their spiritual experience would violate the wholeness of their being.

The New Testament writers assumed everyone understood this truth! James wrote, **"My brethren, count it all joy when you fall into various trials, knowing that the testing of your faith produces patience"** (James 1:2-3). The implication is that God allows the testing of our spiritual commitment with various physical trials or circumstances. We must demonstrate our spiritual faithfulness in the spiritual and in the physical realm with our physical response.

As is often recorded in the ministry of Jesus, Luke said, **"and they were all healed"** (Acts 5:16). The Greek word translated **"were healed"** is "therapeuo," the basis of our

Part Two: Another Review: Another Summary

word "therapeutic." The Divine power of God flowed through the apostles bringing spiritual change resulting in physical relief. Our spiritual condition has a direct bearing on our physical lives. God is interested in wholeness for the entire person. Would He not work in both the spiritual and physical areas of our lives?

Identification

Bible scholars identify these descriptive statements of the early Church's ministry as a direct parallel to the ministry of Jesus. Matthew records, *"**Great multitudes followed Him - from Galilee, and from Decapolis, Jerusalem, Judea, and beyond the Jordan**"* (Matthew 4:25). This remarkable popularity clustered around, *"**they brought to Him all sick people who were afflicted with various diseases and torments, and those who were demon-possessed, epileptics, and paralytics; and He healed them**"* (Matthew 4:24). Now the apostles witnessed the same experience. Crowds came from the countryside with relatives and friends who were ill. The influence of the early Church extended far beyond the city of Jerusalem.

The sameness of Jesus' ministry and the early Church's ministry is the Book of Acts' resounding theme. In the Gospel of Luke, God displayed the fullness of His Spirit in and through one Man. He was the first man to step into the New Covenant. Jesus proclaimed His actions as not of Himself. His life was a product of the fullness of God's Spirit merging with Him. Jesus did no miracles, ministry, or teaching until God filled Him with the Spirit (Luke 3:21-22). While we might view the life of Jesus and question being like Him, Luke brings us to the Book of Acts. It is the story of mean, nasty people just like us that God filled with the same Holy Spirit as Jesus. We see the same power, faithfulness, and intensity in them that we saw in Jesus!

The Resource that caused the life of Jesus recreated that life in the lives of the early Church in Jerusalem.

Many people resist this truth. This truth erases all our excuses. The abuse from the past, the lack of faithfulness among other Christians, the ungodly treatment from the church, and overwhelming circumstances of job and family have all been justifiable reasons for not being like the early Church. What if the same resource that lived within them could also live within us? Is it our personalities, talents, disciplines, or abilities that source us as Christians? What if all of that simply does not matter? Are all of those defeating experiences difficult for the power of God? Could the Spirit of Jesus victoriously source us through difficulties as God sourced Jesus within the crucifixion? So, where is our excuse for being less than what God has called us to be?

In the context of our passage, we know not everyone has the power to do miracles. Signs and wonders are not the means of measuring the fullness of the Spirit. We are the body of Christ (1 Corinthians 12). The Head designs the movement of the Spirit of Jesus through each member. The common factor within the early Church was **"they were all with one accord"** (Acts 5:12). They were together with heavy breathing and passion for Jesus. There was an undying love for Jesus within each believer that would not allow the promotion of any other. Jesus was their identity. They could speak of no other but Jesus; they lived Jesus; they shared Jesus; their cause was Jesus. All that Jesus is had come to indwell them, and Jesus empowered them by His Spirit.

PART THREE
ACTS 5:17-21

ADVERSITY REPEATED

Acts 5:17-21
ADVERSITY REPEATED

> *"Then the high priest rose up, and all those who were with him (which is the sect of the Sadducees), and they were filled with indignation, and laid their hands on the apostles and put them in the common prison. But at night an angel of the Lord opened the prison doors and brought them out, and said, "Go, stand in the temple and speak to the people all the words of this life.' And when they heard that, they entered the temple early in the morning and taught. But the high priest and those with him came and called the council together, with all the elders of the children of Israel, and sent to the prison to have them brought" (Acts 5:17-21).*

I hate change! Yet, the one inevitable fact of life is that nothing ever stays the same. God is really into change; it is an undeniable truth! While our focus of change is on physical things, His focus is on the spiritual. Change in the spiritual depth of our hearts brings desperately needed differences in the physical realm. However, we openly resist change in both the spiritual and the physical. How easy it is to establish our theological beliefs. Once established, we comfortably reside in its security and never think beyond its borders. While no one advocates an overthrow of Christian beliefs, have we gone to the depth of its understanding? Could we understand more clearly the truth and change in our physical application?

Part Three: Adversity Repeated

In the Gospel accounts, the Pharisees occupied the center stage, and their determination and structure became the platform upon which they committed themselves to the death of Jesus. Their traditions had been building for four hundred years. They applied the Scriptures through their personal bias forming a structure of "traditions of the elders" (Matthew 15:2). These traditions became the law of God for them. At the same time, according to Jesus, the fundamental commandments of God were left unattended (Matthew 15:3-6). Jesus ridiculed, dismissed, and broke their oral traditions. As His fame spread from the miracles, Jesus instigated a significant threat to this stable and secure tradition.

In a special called council, the Pharisees considered this crisis. They said, ***"If we let Him alone like this, everyone will believe in Him, and the Romans will come and take away both our place and nation"*** (John 11:48). Caiaphas was the high priest during this period. In the meeting, he proposed the solution, ***"You know nothing at all, nor do you consider that it is expedient for us that one man should die for the people, and not that the whole nation should perish"*** (John 11:49-50). John records that from that time, they plotted the death of Jesus (John 11:53). Jesus brought such change to the nation of Israel as established by the Pharisees that their traditions would not survive. They must crucify Jesus to eliminate change!

After the crucifixion of Jesus and the outpouring of the Holy Spirit, we face the early Church in the Book of Acts. The Pharisees fought and protected their traditions, and then they faded into the background. The Sadducees felt threatened in the days of the early Church in Jerusalem. Greatly disturbed, they had Peter and John dragged to jail after healing the lame beggar at the Gate Beautiful (Acts 4:1-2). They are the primary group in this second occurrence of persecution (Acts 5:17). The Sadducees were responsible for controlling and policing the temple, the dominant platform for the ministry and evangelism of the early Church in Jerusalem.

Adversity Repeated | **Acts 5:17-21**

The ministry of the early Church greatly upset the Sadducees on several levels. Theologically they were greatly disturbed *"that they taught the people and preached in Jesus the resurrection from the dead"* (Acts 4:2). One of the major disputes between the Pharisees and Sadducees was the belief in the resurrection of the dead. The Sadducees did not believe in life after death, angels, or spirits of any kind. They enjoyed a good argument with the Pharisees, but the apostles took the resurrection to a new level. The apostles accredited the resurrected Jesus with all the miracles done through them. Jesus working through the apostles was not a mere argument but a convincing demonstration gaining significant momentum as the miracles increased.

However, the Sadducees were not just disturbed by a doctrine or its practice; it was the effect it would have on their materialism. If you do not believe in life after death, angels, or spirits, the only thing left is the advantage gained in this present world. Their personal comfort found in materialism was the focus of their lives. It was for this reason they compromised with Rome. The only way to maintain the financial level they preferred was to link with Rome to benefit commerce. The early Church created a stir in Jerusalem; it was sure to reach the ears of Rome and affect their financial agreements. With this understanding, we come to our passage.

Repeated

The situation in our passage repeats what occurred in the previous chapter. The lame beggar's dramatic healing caused a significant stir in the temple. A large crowd gathered around Peter, John, and the healed beggar in Solomon's Porch (Acts 3:11). This transformed beggar radically demonstrated his healing, *"leaping up, stood and walked and entered*

Part Three: Adversity Repeated

the temple with them - walking, leaping, and praising God. And all the people saw him walking and praising God" (Acts 3:8-9). Realizing the healed man and the crowd attributed the miracle to the apostles, Peter addressed the crowd. He gave graphic details concerning the crowd's involvement in the crucifixion of Jesus. He equally highlighted and presented the resurrection of Christ as the restoration of all God dreamed for Israel!

The message of the resurrection, not in theory but in practical reality, was more than the Sadducees could tolerate. The priests and the temple captain rushed in to capture Peter, John, and the healed beggar and thrust them into jail to hold them for the court meeting the following day. They interrogated these apostles only to hear more about the resurrected Jesus. Fearing the people, the Sadducees could do nothing but threaten the apostles with a single demand, which highlights their desperate concern. ***"So they called them and commanded them not to speak at all nor teach in the name of Jesus"*** (Acts 4:18). The answer of Peter and John was quite clear, ***"Whether it is right in the sight of God to listen to you more than to God, you judge. For we cannot but speak the things which we have seen and heard"*** (Acts 4:19-20).

Upon their release, the apostles shared all this beginning persecution with the early Church in Jerusalem. The early Church prayed for boldness that they might continue in the same manner to proclaim the name of Jesus (Acts 4:29-30). Despite the early Church's fear over the deception and death of Ananias and Sapphira, their evangelism began to reach outside Jerusalem. The resurrected Jesus became visible through their lives and changed those in the communities around Jerusalem (Acts 5:16). As evangelism increased, so did the concerns of the Sadducees. A duplicate scene now takes place between the Sadducees and the early Church. The difference was in the marked intensity and increase of the persecution.

Adversity Repeated | Acts 5:17-21

We find one increase in the "response of the Sadducees." On the first occasion, the Sadducees were ***"greatly disturbed"*** (Acts 4:2). It is a translation of the Greek word "diaponeo," which presents as being worried. The combination of "dia," meaning "through," and "poneo," meaning "to labor, toil, or pain," form the word. The presence of Jesus, risen from the dead, was painful, discomforting, and highly stressful for the Sadducees. Now, in this second response, the Sadducees possessed more intense concern. ***"They were filled with indignation"*** (Acts 5:17). Other translations use the word "jealousy." It is a translation of the Greek word "zelos." It means "to be hot, fervent, zeal," used in a good sense in the Scriptures (John 2:17; Romans 10:2; 2 Corinthians 7:7), but more often in an evil sense. Envy, jealousy, and anger express this word (Acts 13:45; Romans 13:13; 1 Corinthians 3:3).

The "representation of the apostles" is also increased in the second narrative. In the first session, Peter and John are the focus of attention. They were directly related to the miracle as they approached the temple (Acts 3:1). A crowd surrounded Peter and John at Solomon's Porch, where Peter addressed the crowd (Acts 4:11-12). Just the two apostles were taken into custody and placed in prison. In this second scene of persecution, the focus expanded to include all twelve apostles (Acts 5:18).

The story shifts in the manner of the apostle's "release from jail." Peter and John were required to spend the night in custody (Acts 4:3). Bible scholars believe this was not a public jail with criminals but a private holding jail used only by the Sanhedrin. They put the apostles into what was commonly called ***"the common prison"*** (Acts 5:18). Many translations use the word "public" prison. The Greek word "demosios" is based on the root word "demos," which means "people," a prison used by and for the people. The apostles would have been thrown together with criminals guilty of various crimes.

In the first scene, they released the two apostles the

following day for interrogation. But notice that during the interrogation, the Holy Spirit filled Peter (Acts 4:8). The Spirit of Jesus so filled the answer given by Peter that the members of the Sanhedrin recognized Him (Acts 4:13). But in this second scene, the presence of Jesus is even more blaring. Not only is Peter continuing to be filled with the Spirit of Jesus, but the angel of His Presence boldly intervenes in their release from prison. The Scriptures give no details of how the angel accomplished this without attracting the guards' attention. However, the passage provides the purpose of the angel's instructions to the apostles. They are to return immediately to the temple, the place of witness, and proclaim to the people ***"all the words of this life"*** (Acts 5:20).

This repeat is a solid clue to the heart and passion of God. It repeatedly appears in the Book of Acts. The redemptive heart of God does not give up on us. He is constantly manipulating the scene of our lives to bring a witness to us even amid our rejection. Carefully view the intense witness of Jesus brought to the leadership of Israel again and again. These leaders cannot escape the radical truth of His presence. The Pharisees pleaded and received from Pilate the right to secure the tomb containing the dead body of Jesus (Matthew 27:65). The Roman guard and the seals gave them security only to be disrupted by the guards reporting the story of bright lights, an angel, and a missing body. This witness was not from a radical Christian but pagan Roman guards (Matthew 28:11). Would they consider the witness? They commanded and paid the guards to lie, relating that the disciples stole the dead body. They would not embrace the resurrection of Jesus.

The early Church's powerful ministry was constantly reaching the Sanhedrin's ears in Jerusalem. Through the beggar's healing miracle, God established another setting where He gave a powerful witness to these men. They refused once again to embrace the truth. The church's ministry increased until the leadership could no longer ignore it. God once again established a setting for another strongly related witness. An angel delivered the apostles from jail, and they preached the message again.

Your life and mine have this same sequence! It is the message of prevenient grace. God simply will not let us go. He invents situations, directs people into place, and blares His message into our lives. What kind of God is it that He keeps loving and reaching toward us despite our stubbornness and rebellion? How do you measure the love of God who emptied Himself of all the advantages of being God to become one with us? Is God not speaking to you again and giving you a renewed opportunity?

Restated

In the first scene, Peter and John proclaim the message of Jesus in Solomon's Porch. A large crowd gathered to see the well-known healed beggar. Their message was powerful and penetrating, only to be interrupted by the leaders of Israel. The message caused many to believe, **"and the number of the men came to be about five thousand"** (Acts 4:4). Although this interruption seems a tragedy, it set the stage for Peter to address the Sanhedrin. Without Jesus, whom they crucified (Acts 4:8), the leaders of Israel would continually ignore the message of the Gospel.

In the second scene, a particular ministry occasion is not interrupted, but the Sadducees have all the apostles thrown into the common prison. This interruption will again set the stage for Peter and the other apostles to proclaim to the leaders of Israel the message of Jesus (Acts 5:29-32). God creates an extraordinary impact through an angel of the Lord delivering the apostles from jail. The apostles do not act like ordinary prisoners who have escaped and do not run or hide. The purpose

Part Three: Adversity Repeated

of their deliverance was for the proclamation! God ordered them to preach again ***"all the words of this life"*** (Acts 5:20).

There is no indication that God intervened in the apostles' lives for their safety! The intervention of the angel only increased the hostility of the Sadducees. If the apostles' safety were the focus, they would have escaped from jail and gone into hiding. The sole purpose seems to be the declaration of the redemptive heart of God! In the first scene, the message is interrupted only to reoccur as the Sanhedrin demands an explanation of the miracle. The message is focused on Jesus and is so bold the leaders of Israel recognize it (Acts 4:13). In this second scene, the message is interrupted only to present a platform upon which an angel can appear. The miraculous deliverance of the apostles from jail and their renewed presence to proclaim the truth delivers a message to the Sanhedrin that is more than words. The apostles will again appear before the Sanhedrin and proclaim Jesus (Acts 5:29-32).

Could this be the purpose of God's involvement in your life? The core of His merger with you is not your safety, comfort, or enjoyment but the declaration of His life. Could the adversities of your days be how God makes Himself known to those around you? The Book of Acts does not promote happiness as an appeal for commitment to Jesus! Peace in our physical environment is not a slogan for the movement of the early Church. The risen Lord captured them; their loyalty and commitment are to Him and not the pressure of men (4:19-20).

Response

In the first scene, the leaders of Israel hear the message, threaten the apostles, and release them. They desperately wanted to punish them but could not because of the people (Acts 4:21). They could not dismiss the reality of the miracle, for everyone

Adversity Repeated | Acts 5:17-21

in Jerusalem glorified God for what the miracles did. Fear of the people controlled the leaders, and their power and influence among the people was their priority. There was no repentance! In the second scene, they return to the same pattern, hold the same council, and interrogate the same way. As they ignored the marvelous miracle found in the life of the lame beggar in the first scene, now they ignore the deliverance of the apostles from jail by an angel of the Lord. There is no openness, searching, desire for truth, or hunger for reality.

There is nothing more damning for our spiritual lives than to be closed in our spirits. It does not seem to matter what the apostles say, how God demonstrates Himself, or what spiritual power overshadows them; they will not respond. It is to this same group Jesus began to tell parables. His disciples wanted to know the reason for such a change in His ministry. Jesus said, ***"Therefore I speak to them in parables, because seeing they do not see, and hearing they do not hear, nor do they understand"*** (Matthew 13:13). It is a rejection of truth in the inner heart.

This same reality faces us. The Trinity God repeatedly reveals Himself to us and will not stop! His revelation is always at His own expense and comfort. The revelation of truth does not come cheap. The heart of redemption is a cross! Will we hunger and thirst for righteousness?

Acts 5:17

POSITIVE OR NEGATIVE

"Then the high priest rose up, and all those who were with him (which is the sect of the Sadducees), and they were filled with indignation" (Acts 5:17).

Is the glass half-full or half-empty? From my perspective, it is half-full! Jesus is the reason for my positive mindset. Saturation in His presence and His Word trains the fibers of the mind to take a positive approach. The Scriptures' prophetic writings are not about prophecy but a positive picture of the outcome of all things. We are winning the war. The characters of the New Testament Church in the Book of Acts demonstrate this victory. Their viewpoint is one of incredible joy in every circumstance, each an opportunity to proclaim Him! They live in an atmosphere of confidence and faith in His greatness.

This positive attitude rests solidly on the sovereignty of God. Luke clearly explains this in the first hint of persecution. When Jesus healed the lame beggar through the apostles, the Sadducees brought Peter and John before the Sanhedrin. There is no depression, anxiety, or whining expressed in this scene. The leaders are astonished at the way the apostles respond to their interrogation. **"Now when they saw the boldness of Peter**

and John, and perceived that they were uneducated and untrained men, they marveled" (Acts 4:13). The members of the Sanhedrin could find no legitimate reason for the positive outlook of the apostles. After the Sanhedrin threatened the apostles' lives, they immediately reported the threats to the early Church. The Christians gave verbal expression to their inner confidence. Luke writes, ***"So when they heard that, they raised their voice to God with one accord and said: 'Lord, You are God, who made heaven and earth and the sea, and all that is in them'"*** (Acts 4:24). The Greek word used in this passage addresses God as a Tyrant. It is not a negative expression but shows extreme confidence in One, who is in charge. He is so completely in control that regardless of the circumstances, He always accomplishes His will! Their prayer is not for deliverance from the persecution but for boldness to continue proclaiming Jesus, irrespective of the circumstances. They know the glass is half-full, and Jesus is their Resource!

Even the betrayal of Ananias and Sapphira does not deter their confidence. The threat is not only from without, but now it has occurred from within. The sovereignty of God is adequate even in the deception of those joining them. They do not see the actions of this couple as a threat to them but as done to God, the sovereign God. Peter repeatedly told them, ***"You have not lied to men but to God"*** (Acts 5:4), the foundation for their positive approach. They are "in Christ!" All things are occurring to Jesus, who is faithful. They understood the fullness of the Holy Spirit as the saturation of their lives with Him. They merged with the Trinity God, who freely gave Himself to them. No persecution, hatred, anger, or evil circumstance would confront their lives that He was not covering them in His greatness.

On the second occasion before the Sanhedrin, the threat against them went to a new level. The Sanhedrin was no threat to them, considering Jesus! But listen to their positive report: "***We ought to obey God rather than men. The God of our*** *fathers raised up Jesus whom you murdered by hanging on a tree"* (Acts 5:29-30). While the Sanhedrin degraded Jesus, the Trinity God exalted Him to the right hand to be Prince and Savior! God is present; therefore, the evil in their plot did not defeat Him. Would it not be true for them as well?

The person who is one with Jesus views every circumstance through Jesus' eyes. ***"And we know that all things work together for good to those who love God, to those who are the called according to His purpose"*** (Romans 8:28). The glass is always half-full! How can we lose, for in losing, we win? The greatness of Jesus in the lives of the apostles brought an undefeatable attitude of faith. A mental exercise of positive thinking was not their secret. It was their intimate relationship with Jesus. He was their confidence. Only that which could defeat Jesus can defeat them, for they are His!

In contrast to the positive apostles, there are the negative Sadducees. ***"Then the high priest rose up, and all those who were with him (which is the sect of the Sadducees), and they were filled with indignation"*** (Acts 5:17). The Greek word "de" translated as ***"then"*** is the usual translation for the contrasting conjunction "but." Luke contrasts the feelings and expressions of the Sadducees with the preceding paragraph, the third summary of the success of the early Church. The zeal of the early Church increased even with the threat of the Sanhedrin and the betrayal of Ananias and Sapphira. They continued to proclaim Jesus in the temple, adding multitudes of men and women to the church. Even those in the surrounding cities began to come to Jerusalem to experience the power of God. The glass is more than half-full!

"BUT" the high priest and the Sadducees were filled with negativity. The glass is more than half-empty. They feel powerless amid all their political and social power. The evangelism of the early Church is out of their control and authority so insecurity dominates them. They live in fear of the people and their political support. The temple crowds are enamored with this new Christian movement. It must stop, but how do they eliminate it?

Details of the Negative

"filled with indignation"

In my Bible translation, the reaction of the Sadducees is ***"indignation."*** An English dictionary describes this as "anger or annoyance provoked by what is perceived as unfair treatment." Other common words expressing the same idea are "resentment, umbrage, affront, disgruntlement, displeasure, anger, outrage, annoyance, irritation, exasperation, vexation, offense, and pique." What a state in which to dwell! This behavior reminds us of a four-year-old who had his toy taken from him. He lives in a fit of rage or indignation over the unfairness. His entire life is captured by the turmoil of this upset, lashing out against everyone around him. The "indignation" is not merely one element in his life; it has conquered and permeated every aspect of his being. This one attitude dominates him.

The Greek word "zelos" is translated as ***"indignation."*** "Zelos" comes from the root word "zeo," which means "to be hot, fervent." When used in a good sense, "zelos" is translated as "zeal" (John 2:17; Romans 10:2; 2 Corinthians 7:7, 11; 11:2; Colossians 4:13). However, more often in the New Testament, it is used in an evil sense, meaning "envy, jealousy, anger" (Acts 5:17; 13:45; Romans 13:13; 1 Corinthians 3:3; Galatians 5:20; Philippians 3:6; Hebrews 10:27). Aristotle, the philosopher, reported that anyone in a state of "zelos" in the evil sense always "grieves." His grief is not because another has good, but that he does not have good and seeks to supply the deficiency in himself.

However, "zelos" often degenerates into jealousy, as is the case with the Sadducees. They make war on the good seen in

Part Three: Adversity Repeated

another, thus attempting to trouble that good and diminish it. Some English translations translate "zelos" or ***"indignation"*** with the English word "jealousy." The Sadducees are not rejoicing over the miracles occurring through the apostles in the name of Jesus, and the demonstration of God's power does not cause them to rejoice. Their inward state is anger, indignation, jealousy, and resentment.

Paul speaks of ***"the fruit of the Spirit,"*** the inner state of a person sourced by the Spirit of Jesus! It is singular, which means it is only one fruit. The list is ***"love, joy, peace, long-suffering, kindness, goodness, faithfulness, gentleness, self-control"*** (Galatians 5:22-23). Notice "jealousy or indignation" is not on the list. This attitude is not a product of the Spirit of God! However, something within the person produces such an attitude. Paul gives another list, ***"the works of the flesh."*** They are ***"adultery, fornication, uncleanness, lewdness, idolatry, sorcery, hatred, contentions, jealousies, outbursts of wrath, selfish ambitions, dissensions, heresies, envy, murders, drunkenness, revelries, and the like; of which I tell you beforehand, just as I also told you in time past, that those who practice such things will not inherit the kingdom of God"*** (Galatians 5:19-21). In the middle of ***"the works of the flesh"*** is "zelos," translated ***"jealousies."***

The conclusion is straightforward. The Sadducees are not sourced by the Spirit of Jesus but by their selfish flesh! The mighty works of Jesus' Spirit manifested in the early Church's evangelism are contrasted with the evil spirit of the Sadducees. Is this not the spiritual war we all face? Politics, fairness, or power is not the issue. These are mere platforms upon which the negative view of self-sourcing appears. The resurrected Lord does not possess and indwell the inner lives of the Sadducees. They are jealous of the popularity and success of the apostles. After all, they do not have the education, background, or heritage to play this successful role. They are from Galilee following a crucified criminal from Nazareth, from which nothing good has ever come (John 1:46).

Everyone must take the attitudes and actions of their lives and compare them to the lists of *"the fruit of the Spirit"* or *"the works of the flesh."* I must be intimate with Jesus so that I express His heart through my life. I want to be a product of His mind, from the inner core of my life to the exterior actions of my physical living. I want to be sourced by Him!

Depth of the Negative

Is this reaction of *"indignation"* or "jealousy" in the lives of the Sadducees a superficial expression? How often do we hear it say, "That is not how I am! I really am a good person!" Is this just a passing moment that I will soon forget? Luke gives us insight into the depth of the critical, negative spirit. He begins by stating the reaction of the high priest. Luke speaks of him in the first scene of persecution (Acts 4:6). He refers to Annas as the high priest who served this position for years but had officially relinquished it to his son-in-law, Caiaphas. Annas remained the dominant authority behind all the decisions of the priesthood.

"Then the high priest rose up" is Luke's description (Acts 5:17). The Greek word "anistemi" is translated as *"rose up."* The aorist tense is a snapshot of the action and does not focus on when it occurred. Luke is not relating a moment in which the high priest *"rose up"* but describes a state in which he dwells. The high priest's attitude of jealousy is continually driving all his actions. This Greek word, "anistemi," is "ana," which means "again," and "histemi," which means "to stand." The prefix "ana" refers to repeating the attitude of the high priest. "Anistemi" is used in various contexts, such as healing, awakening, and resurrection. In each case, the undercurrent of the word is to cause something; those lying down in sleep are

Part Three: Adversity Repeated

awakened to stand; those who are dead are resurrected back to life. Luke points to the severe inner reaction of the high priest ***"and all those who were with him."*** Deep within them, their motivation is to act against the disciples.

Luke concludes his statement in our passage with ***"and they were filled with indignation"*** (Acts 5:17). He describes what is taking place deep within them as ***"filled,"*** a translation of the Greek word "pimplemi." We studied this word carefully in Luke's account of the Day of Pentecost. The disciples were ***"filled"*** with the Holy Spirit on this day. Luke begins his description with the Holy Spirit filling the disciples (pleroo) (Acts 2:2). But notice that it is not the same Greek word. He continues to describe their filling with "pimplemi" (Acts 2:4). In using these two different Greek words, he emphasizes the filling of a container and the idea of saturation. John tells us that at the crucifixion of Jesus, they ***"filled"*** (pimplemi) a sponge offering Jesus a drink. After Pentecost, this is the Greek word Luke continually used for the filling of the Spirit within the disciples (Acts 4:8, 31; 9:17; 13:9). It highlights the picture of something already within the container saturating and permeating the whole.

Luke paints this picture of the high priest and the Sadducees. The inner depth of their self-centeredness ***"rose up"*** and ***"filled"*** them. This moment of ***"indignation"*** or jealousy was not an accidental moment, a result of dire circumstances, or a passing reaction. It was a spiritual state within them that rose to the surface. It dominated their lives continually and was an expression of who they were. It is easy to blame the circumstances or others for how we respond. But could it be that the way we react in those moments is the way we are? We do not calculate the action but respond from the depth of our inner being. It is an expression of our hearts. The Sadducees revealed their real hearts in these moments.

Are we willing to learn from them? Will we view our lives through the lens of what fills us to discover our true state? The apostles challenged the Sadducees with the fullness of Christ. The resurrected Lord wants to fill them and us. The risen Lord has manipulated the scene, bringing the Sadducees to a moment of clarity and change in their lives.

Desperation of the Negative

We see their desperation in the extent the Sadducees were willing to go to satisfy this inward saturation of ***"indignation"*** or "jealousy." God manifests His power in Christ again and again. God heaped the physical manifestations of His resurrection upon them. The healing of the lame beggar, which initiated this persecution, was so blaring they could not deny it. They admitted, ***"For, indeed, that a notable miracle has been done through them is evident to all who dwell in Jerusalem, and we cannot deny it"*** (Acts 4:16). These miracles increased until multitudes from the cities surrounding Jerusalem came to experience the power of God. Luke records, ***"and they were all healed"*** (Acts 5:16). The Sadducees become deeply conscious that wisdom and insight expressed through the apostles is beyond mere education and training (Acts 4:13).

In our passage, the high priest and the Sadducees threw the apostles into the common prison (Acts 5:18). The council gathered the following day and brought them out of jail for interrogation. Those sent to get the apostles reported that they were not in the common prison. The guards were there, and the doors were secure, but the apostles were gone. The apostles were down at the temple proclaiming Jesus again! An angel of the Lord had delivered them in the night hour. BUT the high priest and the Sadducees ignored this miracle of deliverance. God reversed everything they attempted to do, and they would not acknowledge it. How is that possible?

Part Three: Adversity Repeated

One might ask, "What would it take to convince and convert the Sadducees to Jesus?" How many miracles would it take? How strongly would God have to speak to them? How often would God need to intervene in their plans? That is history and long ago. But God is still doing this in our lives. His intervention is just as miraculous and definite as in days of the past. We must not make the same mistake they did! We must stare into the deep inner state of self-centeredness that adjusts everything around it for its benefit. In acknowledgment of this state, we must embrace Jesus, who has come to us. The openness of our hearts is all He requires for His grace to be applied. We cannot change ourselves, but we can confess our needs! Jesus is risen and is adequate to change us!

Acts 5:18

SHUT UP

"And laid their hands on the apostles and put them in the common prison" (Acts 5:18).

Deception is a terrible thing obscuring reality, which results in wrong decisions and dire consequences. An incorrect view always results in destruction. The enemy greatly deceived the leaders of Israel, causing them to embrace a long-standing choice of deception. In its basic form, deception means "to be led astray." Immediately this assumes two fundamental ideas. Someone wants to lead you astray. Deception is not an accident; no one slips into deception without distinct intention. Thousands of voices sound in our ears every day, trying to allure us into deception, which will benefit them. The Bible shares that there is only one deceiver, the Devil! Jesus said to the leaders of Israel, **"You are of your father the devil, and the desires of your father you want to do. He was a murderer from the beginning, and does not stand in the truth, because there is no truth in him. When he speaks a lie, he speaks from his own resources, for he is a liar and the father of it"** (John 8:44). Many times, Jesus referred to the devil as the father, the source of all lies, for he speaks from his resource, which contains nothing but lies. He is the deceiver!

Part Three: Adversity Repeated

There is a second element to deception. While it is true someone wants to lead us astray, we must be willing to be led! We do not accidentally end up in the wrong; we make a choice. The choice to embrace deception is not blind or unintentional. We choose it because it is easier than truth; it caters to our selfish desires. We voluntarily participate in the deception. It is a picture of the leaders of Israel in our passage. They embraced the deception so entirely that it had become truth for them. Their deception justified all their decisions and actions as they placed the apostles in the common prison.

Deception scares me! What if the devil is deceiving me? How can I be assured that I have no deception in my life? What is the great deterrent to deception? For years I thought the truth would eliminate all possibility of deception. But it does not seem to be so in our passage. No one has been exposed to the truth as much and as clearly as these leaders. Jesus, the visible image of the invisible Father, walked their streets. They heard truth after truth from His lips. How often He wanted to guide them into the reality of truth (Matthew 23:37). The apostles demonstrated the truth of Jesus in their preaching and miracles in the temple. They interrogated Peter and John and received a clear statement of truth (Acts 4:8-12). The visible demonstration of truth, such as the lame beggar's healing, was undeniable (Acts 4:16). If truth is the great deterrent to deception, why were these leaders deceived?

BUT the great deterrent to deception is not truth; it is "seeking." Seeking is about openness and positive response. Seeking is about a willingness to change. Seeking breaks down all self-covering barriers and allows truth to do its work. The truth may be present, but there is nothing but deception if seeking is not active. God has made promises to those who will seek. Listen to the Scriptures.

"When You said, 'Seek My face,'
My heart said to You, 'Your face, Lord, I will seek'"
(Psalm 27:8).

"Seek the Lord while He may be found,
Call upon Him while He is near" (Isaiah 55:6).

"And you will seek Me and find Me,
when you search for Me with all your heart"
(Jeremiah 29:13).

"But seek first the Kingdom of God and His righteousness, and all these things shall be added to you" (Matthew 6:33).

"Ask, and it will be given to you; seek and you will find; knock, and it will be opened to you" (Matthew 7:7).

Our paragraph begins with the strength of their deception. The high priest and the Sadducees were aggressive in their deception, and their jealousy drove them to extreme resistance to all truth. They were ***"filled"*** with such barriers to the truth that nothing the apostles did or said could penetrate. They are not seeking! The expression of this lack of seeking is ***"and laid hands on the apostles and put them in the common prison"*** (Acts 5:18). Deception always gives rise to physical responses. Their deception could no longer ignore nor tolerate the activities of the apostles. Let us look at the following aspects of the response to their deception.

Shut Down

Deception absolutely must "shut down" any truth that might change it. Its only defense is to reject, block, and eliminate all truth that contradicts the physical action of our passage. The physical action of the high priest and Sadducees corresponds with their inner spirits. If the apostles hoped that these leaders would at least consider the truth of Jesus, there is the reality of the common prison. They rejected Jesus inwardly and shut down the proclamation of this truth, the healing miracles of this truth, and the growth of the early Church.

At the beginning of this paragraph, Luke uses extensive language to describe this action! That language describes the aggressive inner emotions of these leaders. The high priest *"rose up,"* and they were all *"filled"* with indignation (Acts 5:17). Now we see the physical actions to that heated emotional response to truth. Deception will not tolerate exposure. Luke said, *"and laid* (epiballo) *their* (tas) *hands* (xeipas) *on* (epi) *the apostles"* (Acts 5:18). Another translation simply states, *"they arrested the apostles."* However, this statement does not express the intensity or aggressive action involved. "Epiballo" is translated as *"laid."* The prefix is "epi," which is repeated for further emphasis. The root word is "ballo," meaning "cast or throw." This word describes the devil's suggestion to Jesus on the pinnacle of the temple: *"if You are the Son of God, throw* (ballo) *Yourself down"* (Matthew 4:6). "Ballo" is used in the New Testament to describe an impulsive action. Luke may not mean that these leaders placed their physical hands on the apostles, but the emphasis is there. The double use of "epi," meaning "upon," indeed focuses on their rejection. They cannot stand Jesus, who they recognize working through the apostles (Acts 4:13). In addition, Luke said that they *"put"* (tithemi) the apostles in the common prison, focusing on their intent. They shut down the threat of their deception.

Seeking is not in any of their actions. Seeking is not a part of their attitude, which dictates their actions. Regardless of the numerous revelations from Jesus, they determined to "shut down" any indication of revelation that would change their comfortable traditions. There are no measures beyond this! This attitude marks the drawing of the line across which God has decided not to invade. All the resources of the Trinity God placed in Jesus for the believer are suddenly held at bay. Paul described them as ones *"who are perishing, whose minds the god of this age has blinded, who do not believe, lest the light of the gospel of the glory of Christ, who is the image of God, should shine on them"* (2 Corinthians 4:3-4). Jesus told the disciples, *"Let them alone. They are blind leaders of the blind. And if the blind leads the blind, both will fall into a ditch"* (Matthew 15:14).

A cry comes from the heart of God for you and me to seek! Do not protect; do not guard. Will we be open to the revelation that brings us to His heart? This kind of openness opposes self-will and self-protection. At the heart of seeking is yielding all that does not come from Him. Seeking demands change in our lives, sometimes radical change. I am a seeker! It is right to seek!

Shut Up

The leaders of Israel wanted to "shut down" the entire Christian movement. They placed the apostles in the common prison, silencing their message. Their threat was singular on the first occasion of interrogating Peter and John. The only request they made of the two apostles was *"not to speak at all nor teach in the name of Jesus"* (Acts 4:18). Before making such a request, they discussed the issue among themselves, *"saying, 'What shall we do to these men? For, indeed, that a notable miracle has been done through them is evident to all who dwell in Jerusalem, and we cannot deny it. But so that it spreads no further among the people, let us severely threaten them, that from now on they speak to no man in this name"* (Acts 4:16-17). The Sadducees' threat was not regarding the philosophy of the resurrection. They were not concerned over the fellowship gatherings among the early Christians, and they certainly did not refute the miracles that were taking place. The only factor was the proclamation of Jesus!

This second time, they placed all the apostles in prison, intending to interrogate them the next day. They expressed a singular concern. *"Did we not strictly command you not to teach in this name? And look, you have filled Jerusalem with your doctrine, and intend to bring this Man's blood on us"* (Acts 5:28). *"When they had called for the apostles and beaten them, they commanded that they should not speak in the name of Jesus, and let them go"* (Acts 5:40). They were not against miracles, compassionate ministries, religious gatherings, or philosophical arguments. The only thing they could not tolerate was Jesus! They wanted to shut up His voice!

There is a parallel passage to this that is very intriguing. Herod the Great was ruler over all of Judea during the time of Christ's birth. At his death, his three sons received the divided territory. Herod, the tetrarch, ruled over the area where John the Baptist was preaching. Herod had an affair with Herodias, his brother Philip's wife. John the Baptist denounced this affair publicly and exhorted Herod to correct his evil ways. Luke makes an interesting comment about Herod's response to these accusations. *"And for all the evils which Herod had done, also added this, above all, that he shut John up in prison"* (Luke 3:19-20). The malicious activities of Herod are too numerous to list or describe publicly. Luke uses the phrase *"added this, above all"* to describe the singular action of placing John in prison. Why would this be viewed as above all the other things? It was because Herod silenced the voice of God in his life!

When God's voice is silent, we cannot know the truth. There is no revelation of reality, and conviction cannot come to the inner heart if God does not speak. The only blockade to our destructive ways is God's voice. His voice is the only chance we have for life change. God must speak! What could be worse than the rebellious act of shutting up the voice of God? Herod did this to his defeat and ruin. The leaders of Israel shut up the voice of God in their lives, which brought them to destruction.

Is it not a warning to each of us? God distinctly calls you to Himself. You have heard His plea for your life. Paul tells us that it has come through the visible world of nature all around us, but more specifically, it has come from the inner heart of our being (Romans 1:19). God has attached Himself to your inner soul so that He might speak to you. Have you been listening? Paul said, ***"So then faith comes by hearing, and hearing by the word of God"*** (Romans 10:17). Herod told the preacher to "shut up" by placing him in prison. The leaders of Israel would not hear the word either, for they put the apostles in prison. Carefully consider the prison in which you have placed the avenue of God's message to your life. We silenced the Divine message! Perhaps we cease coming to church and no longer saturate in His Word.

It is incredible how the Scriptures highlight the emphasis on "hearing." Jesus' explanation for changing His preaching style to parables focused on "hearing." He said, ***"Therefore I speak to them in parables, because seeing they do not see, and hearing they do not hear, nor do they understand"*** (Matthew 13:13). The author quotes the Old Testament passages to his brethren as a warning in the Book of Hebrews. They should not be like their forefathers, who refused to listen.

> *"Therefore, as the Holy Spirit says:*
> *'Today, if you will hear His voice,*
> *Do not harden your hearts as in the rebellion'"*
> *(Hebrews 3:7-8).*

We must seek! We must listen!

Part Three: Adversity Repeated

Shut Out

The focus of the apostles' proclamation was the temple. The early Church clustered in Jerusalem, and as Jews, they continued the temple activities they had always observed. All the temple observances naturally pointed to Jesus; the early Church observed the fulfillment of those ceremonies in Jesus. The popular place for the early Christian assemblies in the temple was at Solomon's Porch (Acts 3:11; 5:12). By his confession before his conversion, Paul was constantly capturing Christians in the synagogues to beat and imprison them. The Jerusalem temple and the synagogues outside Jerusalem were the centers of revelation for truth and the presence of God.

In our passage, Israel's leaders have again removed God's voice. They removed Jesus from the heart of their religion, the temple. Jesus returned to Jerusalem, ministered in the temple, and tipped the scales for His crucifixion. The leaders of Israel could not tolerate Jesus in the temple. In our passage, the leaders of Israel removed the apostles from speaking in the temple by placing them in jail. They discovered the apostles were not in prison but were back in the temple proclaiming Jesus.

Paul declared, ***"Do you not know that you are the temple of God and that the Spirit of God dwells in you? If anyone defiles the temple of God, God will destroy him. For the temple of God is holy, which temple you are"*** (1 Corinthians 3:16-17). The plan of the evil one has not changed. He must "shut down," "shut up," and "shut out" the Living Word from the inner heart of your being. The one thing he has never been able to tolerate, for it always defeats him, is openness, seeking, and responding at the inner core of our lives. Not seeking is the reality for someone who has never been a Christian, and it is true for the one who has been a Christian for much of their life. The need is the same in all of us; we must listen, seek, and respond.

We live in a period of great distraction. A thousand voices scream at us, and it is easy for the one voice we must hear to be silenced. The allurements are everywhere to distract our attention from the One who has truth for our lives. Jesus spoke to the crowds of disciples the great truth they needed to grasp. John records that ***"many of His disciples went back and walked with Him no more"*** (John 6:66). Jesus turned to His twelve disciples and asked them what they intended to do. Simon Peter answered, ***"Lord, to whom shall we go? You have the words of eternal life"*** (John 6:68).

Is it not true for you and me? Where else shall we go? Where else shall we look? To whom shall we listen? There is no truth outside of Jesus. Do not "shut Him down." Outside of Jesus, there is no voice of truth speaking to us. Do not "shut Him up." There is no place He is speaking outside of your inner heart. Do not "shut Him out."

Acts 5:19

A CONTRAST

"But at night an angel of the Lord opened the prison doors and brought them out, and said" (Acts 5:19).

Luke is a historian. This "volume two," known as the Book of Acts, depicts the beginning formation of the early Church. In "volume one," known as the Gospel of Luke, we discover the details of the life of Christ. He is one Man operating under the control of the Holy Spirit. His ministry did not begin until God filled Him with the Spirit. He is the first person to enter a merger with the nature of God. Luke does not attempt to camouflage the physical display of the spiritual war on the stage of Christ's life. Jesus lived in the fullness of the Spirit, and God fulfilled His plan in creating redemption for the world!

"Volume two" has all the same characteristics. The spiritual conflict continues to rage under the direction of the King of the Kingdom. With all its hatred for the movement of God, the world unleashed itself upon the early Church. Luke gives us all the physical consequences of such a war. This historical account is vital to understanding how God established the Church. How did we get from the life of Jesus to the established church, as seen in the epistles? Luke gives us this information. But he constantly contrasts this physical history with insight into the spiritual, unseen world. All the physical events are a direct result of this spiritual war.

We will focus our study on a paragraph (Acts 5:17-21). The structure of this paragraph is a series of contrasts. Ironically, the Jews, the leaders of the religious world, represent the evil demonic world. It is not the pagans of the Roman Empire with their multiple gods but the nation to which God especially gave birth. The Jews have the Scriptures and a history filled with the instructions of the prophets. The aggressive barrier against the church follows religious rules and scheduled prayer. However, the focus of the contrast is not on these things but on the person, Jesus. The contrast is between those who embrace Jesus and those who do not!

The first contrast in the paragraph is a "Contrast of Circumstances" (Acts 5:17). Luke gives a third summary concerning the expansion and ministry of the early Church (Acts 5:12-16). Persecution started as the early Church experienced the first threats against them (Acts 4:13-22), but they did not stop the proclamation of the name of Jesus. Through the Spirit of Jesus, the apostles were changing lives and performing miracles. The threats against the church seemed to bring a more profound commitment and dependency on Jesus, exposing those who were not fully committed (Acts 5:1-11). The consequences of insecurity became known to everyone. Yet, the church was expanding beyond the borders of Jerusalem into surrounding cities (Acts 5:12-16).

After highlighting the tremendous success of the early Church, Luke writes, ***"Then"*** (Acts 5:17). It is a translation of the Greek word "de." The principal translation of "de" is "but," for it is a contrasting conjunction. But ***"the high priest rose up"*** filled with indignation. He was leading a sect of the Sadducees. They could not capture all the members of the early Church; they concentrated on the apostles. They placed them

Part Three: Adversity Repeated

in a common prison, waiting for the next day's interrogation. The early Church grew and experienced the power of God. The people embraced the Gospel as it changed their lives. The leaders of Israel found their control over the people eroding. If it continues, their status with Rome will shift; they will find their commerce agreements threatened; their financial security will weaken.

Luke quickly moves to a second contrast, "Contrast of Concealed" (Acts 5:19). The Sadducees adjusted their beliefs about God to match their fleshly desires. They did not embrace any of the unseen, spiritual world and ignored the unseen world of spirits and angels. They utterly denied the resurrection of the dead, giving rise to physical materialism, which dominated their lives. "***But***" an angel of the Lord, whom the Sadducees determined did not exist, opened the doors of the common prison, and released the apostles. The unseen world made itself known realistically! Such revelation did not seem to matter to the Sadducees. It is not recorded anywhere in the story where they acknowledged or discussed such a visitation.

Luke closes our paragraph with a third contrast, "Contrast of Concrete" (Acts 5:21). "***But***" the high priest and Sadducees returned to their customary procedures. They called the council and sent soldiers to the prison to bring the apostles for interrogation. Of course, they did not find the apostles, for they were at the temple proclaiming the name of Jesus. The resurrected Lord demonstrated Himself repeatedly, but the leaders of Israel continued to walk as if they were blind. The unseen world became visible often, but these leaders were indifferent to its existence.

We must highlight the middle contrast. It reveals some great truths discovered in the other contrasts but vividly presents them in "Contrast of Concealed." They did put the apostles in the common prison, "BUT." ***"But at night an angel of the Lord opened the prison doors and brought them out,*** *and said, 'Go, stand in the temple and speak to the people all the words of this life'"* (Acts 5:19-20).

Contrast of Circumstances

The first two verses of our paragraph are filled with the spiritual response of the leaders of Israel, moving them to physical activity. Remember to note the increase in the evil state of their spiritual lives, easily depicted through their physical actions. ***"Then the high priest rose up"*** is Luke's attempt to relate this increase. The high priest could no longer tolerate the ministry of the apostles, and his concern over their influence became so great that it demanded aggressive action on his part. The increase in miracles and the growth of the early Church in numbers proposed a significant problem. What had been a few disciples of a dead Jesus became an advancing army of believers threatening Israel's stability. The high priest was in the most elevated leadership position and must assume this role in stopping the Christian movement.

Luke adds the fact that ***"they were filled with indignation."*** He used ***"filled"*** to relate the permeating emotion that dominated the ***"sect of the Sadducees."*** The word "zelos," translated as ***"indignation,"*** further strengthens the emotional increase. "Zelos" comes from the noun "zeo," which means "to be hot or fervent." In a good sense, it means "to be zealous." Again, we receive a picture of the extended emotional upset that the leaders of Israel experienced regarding the ministry of the early Church. Their physical expression is one of aggression. They gathered all the apostles and placed them in ***"the common prison."*** They acted immediately, even though it was evening. They cannot interrogate or decide until the council meets the following day, but they must do something immediately.

Part Three: Adversity Repeated

"BUT. "God is not caught napping. While the irritation of the leaders of Israel is increasing, God's concern and involvement remain the same. His plan, which He announced in the first Messianic promise (Genesis 3:15), has not wavered. His zeal has not decreased; His love is the same. In contrast to the leaders of Israel, panic is not in the heart of God. ***"Jesus Christ is the same yesterday, today, and forever"*** (Hebrews 13:8). We would do well to contemplate the consistent, unwavering, and steadfast love of Jesus. The Sadducees do not believe in angels, but an angel of the Lord appears and brings deliverance to the apostles.

Previously, God used Peter and John to heal a lame beggar at the Gate Beautiful of the temple. He is over forty years of age and has been begging most of his life. Jesus intervenes and gives complete healing to the whole man (Acts 3:6). Great crowds gathered at Solomon's Porch to rejoice in the miracle. The healed beggar holds on to Peter as if he is responsible for the miracle. The crowd was amazed at the power of God demonstrated through Peter. Luke wrote, ***"When Peter saw it, he responded to the people"*** (Acts 3:12). Peter was surprised that they thought he did the healing. ***"Men of Israel, why do you marvel at this? Or why look so intently at us, as though by our own power or godliness we had made this man walk?"*** (Acts 3:12). Then he points to ***"The God of Abraham, Isaac, and Jacob, the God of our fathers"*** (Acts 3:13). Had they forgotten all the miracles and Divine interventions God did through the history of Israel? He delivered them from Egyptian slavery, provided for them in the wilderness, miraculously delivered them in battle, and supplied the promised land. Has God changed? Is His provision for the needs of a lame beggar larger than all God has already done? Why would they marvel?

Have you not heard, "Jesus never fails!" Does He not always intervene on our behalf? Has He not always provided according to His will? God's intervention on behalf of the apostles amid the evil plotting of the Sadducees is just one more incident among the many scenes of past days! God has not grown weak; He has not wavered in His love. You and I must live in this confidence! Where do anxiety and worry fit into this wonder? What situation allows for panic? Is He not the same? If you state that this is a record from ancient days of long ago, I will encourage you to speak to the saints of our day. They sing the songs *"Great is Your Faithfulness"* and *"Jesus Never Fails."* They live in a state of rejoicing and praise over His great love. The fickle fate of the world has no hold on them, for "the steadfast love of the Lord never fails."

Contrast of Continuity

The dictionary definition of "continuity" is "continuousness, uninterruptedness, flow, progression." While we highlighted continuity in the above study, we must see the long view of God's planning. There is an unbroken and consistent existence or operation of the Divine plan from the world's creation to this moment. The plan of God dwells in a state of stability without disruption. There is a connection or line of development in all God's dealings and desires for humanity with no sharp breaks. Our God is sovereign. Paul declares, ***"In Him, also we have obtained an inheritance, being predestined according to the purpose of Him who works all things according to the counsel of His will"*** (Ephesians 1:11). Let these statements shape your thinking. ***"Oh, the depth of the riches both of the wisdom and knowledge of God! How unsearchable are His judgments and His ways past finding out! For who has known the mind of the Lord? Or who has become His counselor? Or who has first given to Him and it shall be repaid to him?"*** (Romans 11:33-35).

Part Three: Adversity Repeated

This continuity was the foundation of the confidence of the apostles. God has had a sovereign plan from the world's creation until now. All these thousands of years, it has not wavered or failed. Even the crucifixion of Jesus was not a setback for the plans of God. Here is what the apostles said, *"For truly against Your holy Servant Jesus, whom You anointed, both Herod and Pontius Pilate, with the Gentiles and the people of Israel, were gathered together to do whatever Your hand and Your purpose determined before to be done"* (Acts 4:27-28). When the first phase of persecution came to the early Church, they did not waver because God does not waver. They cried, *"Now, Lord, look on their threats, and grant to Your servants that with all boldness they may speak Your word, by stretching out Your hand to heal, and that signs and wonders may be done through the name of Your holy Servant Jesus"* (Acts 4:29-30).

Whatever you and I are going through is puny considering God's sovereignty. We find excellent safety being in the middle of His plan. Listen to Paul, *"We give no offense in anything, that our ministry may not be blamed. But in all things we commend ourselves as ministers of God: in much patience, in tribulations, in needs, in distresses, in stripes, in imprisonments, in tumults, in labors, in sleeplessness, in fastings; by purity, by knowledge, by longsuffering, by kindness, by the Holy Spirit, by sincere love, by the word of truth, by the power of God, by the armor of righteousness on the right hand and on the left, by honor and dishonor, by evil report and good report; as deceivers, and yet true; as unknown, and yet well known; as dying, and behold we live; as chastened, and yet not killed; as sorrowful, yet always rejoicing; as poor, yet making many rich; as having nothing, and yet possessing all things"* (2 Corinthians 6:3-10).

Whatever may seem uncertain in our world, contrast

that with the unwavering sovereign plan of God. You must get into His plan. He has planned for you and destined an excellent purpose for your life. The uniqueness of who you are parallels the distinct purpose He dreamed for you. The difficulties experienced in the plan only help to fulfill the plan. Each moment of suffering is a step in accomplishing God's dream. In the Great Commission, at the close of the Book of Matthew, the resurrected Jesus met with His disciples. He sent them on a mission to win the entire world. He proceeded with this commissioning by declaring, **"All authority has been given to Me in heaven and on earth"** (Matthew 28:18). The Greek word "exousia" is translated as **"authority."** It means "the right to decide." The Trinity God gave Jesus the right to decide concerning our lives as we fulfill His call. Nothing can come to our lives except that we must knock on His door and receive His permission. Live in surrender and confidence!

Contrast of Content

The Sadducees saw an immediate problem with the early Church. The growth and influence of the church threatened their authority and jeopardized their lifestyle. The perspective of the Sadducees could not see beyond the immediate threat of the church. Their self-centeredness encompassed them, and they responded the same with each confrontation. The same attitude brought about the same physical action, and they were predictable.

What would need to happen to change their response to Jesus? Would their response change if an angel appeared, released the apostles from jail, and they did not hide but appeared again in the temple teaching Jesus? The apostles raised a lame beggar to complete wholeness, and it was an undeniable miracle in the name of Jesus. Would this alter their opinion? God moved, and they responded each time with the exact content of rejection!

Part Three: Adversity Repeated

Consistency appears in the response of the apostles. They use the same language in their response to the Sanhedrin during the first encounter and again in this second encounter (Acts 4:19; 5:29). The boldness expressed in the first interrogation appears in the second one. As they obeyed the leadership of the Spirit in response to the first threats of the Sanhedrin, they obeyed the angel and faithfully proclaimed Jesus in the temple.

Are we not all establishing significant patterns in our lives that continually shape our response to the circumstances of our lives? The negative individual tends to be negative in every circumstance, while the positive person will follow their pattern of positivity. The contrast between the leaders of Israel and the apostles may give us insight into the patterns we want to develop in our lives. Could God be challenging us to establish a new pattern? It will never be easier to change the response pattern than at this moment. The more time we spend in a pattern, the deeper the grip it has on us. The pattern is so set in the Sadducees that it appears unchangeable. Yet, the power of God moved all around them and challenged them repeatedly to change. Jesus is doing the same in our lives! We must respond to Him!

Acts 5:20

PARABLE OF PENTECOST

"Go, stand in the temple and speak to the people all the words of this life" (Acts 5:20).

I have always wanted to be a biblical preacher. This statement may mean different things to different people, for all preachers profess they preach the Bible. However, biblical preaching focuses on exposition, meaning to expose the text. A preacher can accomplish expository preaching by presenting a narrative or story from the Scriptures. The message may present a topic, or the focus may rest on a particular text. All methods are legitimate if they are expositional.

No preacher can impose his thoughts or opinions upon the Scriptures, and we must remain within the boundaries of the passage and the author's intent. A fundamental of biblical preaching is the realization that the Scriptures are in layers. The narrative gives the circumstances of the event, but what do they mean? Why would the author provide those details? The preacher must answer these questions with the application of the truth.

The Sanhedrin threatened the early Church regarding their declaration of Jesus had risen from the dead and told them

Part Three: Adversity Repeated

never to speak to anyone regarding Jesus. These threats did not deter the early Church. An increase in the proclamation of His name produced an increase in miracles and members joining the church. The high priest, with the Sadducees, captured all the apostles and placed them in the common prison. But God fully displayed His blessing as an angel of the Lord and released the apostles from jail. The angel quickly stated the purpose of the rescue, saying, ***"Go, stand in the temple and speak to the people all the words of this life"*** (Acts 5:20). Luke does not mention the deliverance from jail in the rest of the narrative. The leaders of Israel completely ignore this mystical deliverance. The apostles obey the angel and are in the temple the following day. They are arrested again and brought before the Sanhedrin for interrogation.

What is the great truth of this passage? Why does Luke record the instructions of the angel? How does this apply to our lives? The book's purpose is the guiding force behind interpreting every passage. Luke proposed that the power of God working in one Man, Jesus, as seen in Volume One, the Gospel according to Luke, is now available and filling many people. He highlighted this in Peter's explanation of Pentecost as he quoted the prophet, Joel,

"And it shall come to pass in the last days, says God, That I will pour out of My Spirit on all flesh" *(Acts 2:17).*

The New Covenant is fully operational through Jesus. Everything happening in Jesus is now within us because the same Spirit empowers us. It is easy to understand the Spirit of God moving through Jesus, but now we see a group of mean, nasty people just like us whom the same Spirit has filled. It is an invitation for everyone to allow God to fill them with the Spirit of Jesus! They merged with God, and their lives demonstrated the power of God.

Parable of Pentecost | **Acts 5:20**

Our passage is another "lived out" example of Pentecost, and it is the Garden of Gethsemane experience of Jesus lived out in the disciples' lives. In the face of physical pain and death, will they allow God to accomplish their destiny and redemptive plan through them? They become living proof of the power of God working in and through helpless humanity! The angel's instructions to the apostles are virtually the throbbing heartbeat of the Spirit's fullness, and it is the call for every Spirit-filled helpless individual.

GO
"poreuesthe"

"Poreuesthe" is the main verb the angel speaks to the released apostles (Acts 5:20). It is in the imperative mood, which makes it a command! It is in the present tense, portraying the idea of continual action. Immersed within the merger of Jesus' Spirit is a mission. The destiny intended to create every unique individual is a valuable piece of the mission. Paul pictured it as a body that fulfills the head's dreams and desires. He especially related this to the diversity of functions within spiritual gifts. ***"There are diversities of gifts, but the same Spirit. There are differences of ministries, but the same Lord. And there are diversities of activities, but it is the same God who works all in all. But the manifestation of the Spirit is given to each one for the profit of all"*** (1 Corinthians 12:4-7).

Luke never presents Pentecost with an emphasis on comfort and happiness. Jesus is the unmarred, unblemished picture of the merger with the Spirit of God! Jesus never said that "happiness" is the atmosphere of the fulness of the Spirit, but He consistently spoke of "joy." He explained the Kingdom to us in parable form. A farmer discovered a treasure and joyfully sold all he had to

Part Three: Adversity Repeated

obtain it (Matthew 13:44). In "The Parable of the Talents," the master said, *"Well done, good and faithful servant; you were faithful over a few things, I will make you ruler over many things. Enter into the joy of your lord"* (Matthew 25:21). John used three chapters in his Gospel to record Jesus' assurance of the coming Holy Spirit. Jesus said, *"These things I have spoken to you, that My joy may remain in you, and that your joy may be full"* (John 15:11).

This concept of joy disagrees with the prevailing modern understanding of happiness. Joy is not an involuntary or internal "emotion" fluctuating with the circumstances around us. Joy's focus is a value-centered intimacy with the heart of Jesus that discovers purpose and meaning to life. It is a state of existence in the merger with Jesus' Spirit that spills forth in mission. Jesus effectively displayed "joy." In the Book of Hebrews, the writer encourages us to *"run with endurance the race that is set before us, looking unto Jesus, the author and finisher of our faith, who for the joy that was set before Him endured the cross, despising the shame"* (Hebrews 12:1-2). Merge with Jesus; let intimacy with Him become the atmosphere determining your life's focus until the circumstances of your life no longer control your emotions.

Speaking to His disciples, Jesus described the fullness of the Spirit in the mission context. Just before His ascension, He gave His parting instructions. *"But you shall receive power when the Holy Spirit has come upon you; and you shall be witnesses to Me in Jerusalem, and in all Judea and Samaria, and to the end of the earth"* (Acts 1:8). During the persecution the angel does not tell them to flee for their safety, but the deliverance reveals the mission undergirding Pentecost. The angel restates the purpose of Pentecost and sends them back to the temple to proclaim *"the words of this life"* (Acts 5:20).

The joy of the mission captured Peter and the other apostles. In merging with Jesus, they had His mind and heart.

When the officers came to the temple and escorted them before the council, they responded in the same manner with the exact words as in the first interrogation. They cried, **"We ought to obey God rather than men. The God of our fathers raised up Jesus whom you murdered by hanging on a tree. Him God has exalted to His right hand to be Prince and Savior, to give repentance to Israel and forgiveness of sins. And we are His witnesses to these things, and so also is the Holy Spirit whom God has given to those who obey Him"** (Acts 5:29-32). Peter aligned his life with Jesus even if it meant joining Jesus in suffering. The mission of redemption dominated their witness and aligned with the Holy Spirit God gave them!

Stand
"stathentes"

The verb "stathentes" is a participle, which acts as an adjective. It is in the nominative form and gives content to the understood subject of the command. "Stathentes" means "to place or set." The emphasis in its use is often more on the attitude than actual physical activity. The angel is not concerned with the apostles' position when they appear in the temple to speak to the people. Is it the instruction to stand rather than sit while preaching? Is the focus of Pentecost a methodology or cultural norm? The verb describes the spiritual posture of the filled believer, further highlighted by the fact it is in the "aorist tense." The angel is not pinpointing a time when this should take place. It is a snapshot of the verb's action. The impact of this thought is that we will live in a state of "standing!" It is who we are naturally in the fullness of the Spirit!

The empowerment of a person for placement in a mission is at the heart of the fullness of the Holy Spirit. Paul described

Part Three: Adversity Repeated

himself as an ambassador or official representative, sent by a King, accredited, and empowered as a diplomat. Paul was a picture of the Kingdom merger! He was a helpless individual with no power; however, the King of the Kingdom invaded and fused Paul with His nature. The authority and power that resides within the King's nature fills and unites with the helplessness of the believer. Paul asked the Ephesian Church to pray for him. His request was, ***"and for me, that utterance may be given to me, that I may open my mouth boldly to make known the mystery of the gospel, for which I am an ambassador in chains; that in it I may speak boldly, as I ought to speak"*** (Ephesians 6:19-20). Notice he uses the word "boldly" twice! He wants to boldly ***"stand"*** in the mission for which God placed him.

Paul gave the same message to the church in Corinth. He presented himself to them as an ambassador for Christ who was to ***"stand"*** before them. He said, ***"Now then, we are ambassadors for Christ, as though God were pleading through us; we implore you on Christ's behalf, be reconciled to God"*** (2 Corinthians 5:20). Is this not the picture of the New Covenant filling of the Spirit of Christ? Are we not helpless individuals who merge with the Spirit of Jesus? God does not send us to carry out a mission for Him! He unites with us. Jesus makes us a new creature in Him, and He places or sets us in a place of boldness as a redemptive force for our world. We are to ***"Go*** and ***"stand."***

Speak
"laleo"

"Speak" is the main verb linked with ***"Go"*** in the imperative mood, emphasizing the angel's command to the apostles. The angel commands them to ***"Go"*** and to ***"speak."***

Both commands are in the present tense, emphasizing the continual action of the verbs. The emphasis on "standing" is linked both with **"Go"** and **"speak." "Speak"** is in the active voice emphasizing that we are to respond with our voice. "Laleo" does not focus on the content of the speaking but on the act of speaking. The angel of the Lord continued in the message focusing on what was to be said. "Laleo" is used to describe the mute individual who is demon-possessed. Upon deliverance, he speaks (laleo). The point is not the content of his message but the act of his speaking (Mark 7:37).

The speech demonstrated the merger of Jesus' Spirit with the believer, and Luke emphasized that repeatedly. During the Pentecost event, **"they were all filled with the Holy Spirit and began to speak** (laleo) **with other tongues, as the Spirit gave them utterance"** (Acts 2:4). What impressed the crowd was not their message but the act of speaking in languages the believers did not know! Look again at Jesus' insight into what will happen when God fills the disciples with the Holy Spirit: **"But you shall receive power when the Holy Spirit has come upon you; and you shall be witnesses** (martys) **to Me"** (Acts 1:8). The content of this word is a person who has information or knowledge of something; he can reveal that information, bring light to, or confirm something. The word "martys" quickly evolved into one who gives their life for this speaking.

The believer's life becomes the mouthpiece for speaking the wonder of Jesus. It is not a doctrinal statement but a penetrating act that causes those who hear to realize **"that they had been with Jesus"** (Acts 4:13). According to Jesus, our speaking is the fruit that the tree of our life bears. It spills forth from the nature of who we are in Him! **"How can you, being evil, speak** (laleo) **good things? For out of the abundance of the heart the mouth speaks** (laleo)**"** (Matthew 12:34). In the following verse, Jesus changes his language to refer to the speaking as **"good things"** or **"evil things."** The heart becomes the *"good treasure"* or the *"evil treasure"* (Matthew 12:35). Then Jesus returns to the action of speaking (laleo) as He focuses on *"every idle word"* and *"the day of judgment"* (Matthew 12:36). This language causes the issue of our speaking (laleo) to be very serious!

Luke highlights all the elements of Pentecost in this scene of persecution. The unseen spiritual world invades the circumstances of men's lives. An angel of the Lord rescues the apostles from the common prison, an invasion with a distinct purpose. The primary concern is not the safety or comfort of the apostles but the mission of redemption coming from the heart of God. The angel commanded the apostles to *"Go"* back into the midst of the conflict and *"speak."* With great confidence and boldness, they are the demonstration of God's redemptive power. They *"stand."*

Words
"rhema"

The Greek word "rhema," translated as *"words,"* is a direct object in the accusative case. All the action of speaking is to focus on the content of "rhema." John calls Jesus *"the Word"* (John 1:1). However, this is a translation of the Greek word "logos." These two words are distinctly related to each other. "Logos" is the expression of the thought, while "rhema" is the thought itself or the subject of the thought. If God is the subject to be discussed (rhema), Jesus is the expression of this subject (logos).

The angel gave specific instructions that the apostles were to proclaim *"this life"* in the temple. God spoke through the prophet Jeremiah, saying, *"Behold, the days are coming, says the Lord, when I will make a new covenant with the house of Israel and with the house of Judah"* (Jeremiah 31:31). In describing this New Covenant, He said,

"But this is the covenant that I will make with the house of Israel after those days, says the Lord: I will put my law in their minds, and write it on their hearts; and I will be their God, and they shall be My people" (Jeremiah 31:33). That is a description of Pentecost! They express the wonder of Jesus, the heart of the New Covenant that the Trinity God dreamed of throughout the Old Testament.

Jesus was the first Kingdom person! He was the visible image of the invisible God, and His speaking was not just in preaching, teaching, and miracles. He went about the cities and the villages of His day and was the living expression of the attitude and heart of God (Matthew 9:35). The "rhema" of the Old Testament became the "Logos" of the New Testament. God gave the same Spirit indwelling Jesus to the apostles and believers, and they were to return to the temple and be the expression of the "rhema."

The high priest and Sadducees specified "rhema" as Jesus! They do not want Jesus proclaimed. When they captured the apostles in the temple and brought them before the Sanhedrin, they accused them, ***"Did we not strictly command you not to teach in this name? And look, you have filled Jerusalem with your doctrine, and intend to bring this Man's blood on us"*** (Acts 5:28). The apostles focused on Jesus. His resurrected Person was present in all they did. They did not just do miracles or hold services. They did not just help the poor or needy. They were constantly proclaiming Jesus both in word and deed. He was their "rhema."

The angel's message has not changed. God wants to deliver you and me, but it will not be for safety or comfort. There is a message to proclaim that goes beyond words and is not limited to Sunday morning. We cannot isolate the message to certain relationships or segment it to an organization. We are to ***"Go"*** and ***"stand"*** in the heart of our world. We are to ***"speak"*** with great boldness the "rhema," which is Jesus. There is no other subject or cause, and Jesus is our single message!

Acts 5:20

WORDS OF LIFE

*"Go, stand in the temple and speak to the people
all the words of this life" (Acts 5:20).*

We all have discouraging moments and often wish for a Christian status that eliminates such experiences. Can you imagine a life without obstacles or hindrances? Many believe heaven will be free of calamities, while this earthly life is not. The disciples felt the leaders of Israel's resistance throughout Jesus' three years of ministry, ending in His crucifixion. God completely reversed their discouragement with His resurrection of Christ, a glorious moment. They experienced forty days of living with the resurrected Lord, helping them assimilate the meaning of it all (Acts 1:3). They were disappointed when He ascended, and they were alone again with nothing but promises that it would be better. But God reversed that disappointment with the indwelling presence of Jesus. Pentecost was beyond comprehension!

The early Church multiplied following Pentecost but soon came under the fire of persecution. The leaders of Israel threatened Peter and John. The early Church shared in those threats (Acts 4:23). But God soon overrode these dark moments with renewed outpourings of the Holy Spirit. Ministry roared on with great victory (Acts 4:31). But defeat and loss were not over as Ananias and Sapphira tore the heart of the early Church with their sin and death (Acts 5:1-11). But even this discouragement seemed to bring determination and commitment to others, and evangelism continued in even greater ways (Acts 5:16). But then it happened again; the leaders of Israel captured the apostles and placed them in the common prison (Acts 5:17-18). Will it never end?

But God is so faithful; an angel of the Lord delivered them, but it was not what you think. God's deliverance was not for safety or comfort but to thrust them back into the battle. ***"Go, stand in the temple and speak to the people all the words of this life,"*** the angel commanded (Acts 5:20). In the dark hour of persecution, in a miserable prison, the angel told them that they were on the right track. They were doing what they needed to be doing. Do not quit! They must fulfill the single purpose of Christian communicators filled with the heart of God. Can you imagine what confirmation the angel's words were to the apostles? They were on target! Their message was their unswerving emphasis on Jesus and the abundant life in Him, and they must not change. God changed their world as they proclaimed His life. They were set free from prison, so they returned to speaking ***"all the words of this life."***

It is helpful to read the various Scripture translations regarding ***"all the words of this life."*** The New International Version says, ***"tell the people the full message of this new life."*** The Amplified Bible says, ***"declare to the people the whole doctrine concerning this Life (the eternal life which Christ revealed)."*** The English Standard Version states, ***"speak to the people all the words of this Life."*** The common emphasis of all the translations is on both the proclamation's speaking and content. The idea of preaching and teaching expresses the scope of ***"speak to the people."***

Part Three: Adversity Repeated

The Greek word translated as *"speak"* is "laleo," which focuses specifically on the action of the speaking and not the content. It emphasizes the issue of speech contrasted with speechlessness and highlights the proclamation through speech. While our example through daily living is valuable, we must, of necessity, give a verbal explanation of the activity. The ministry of the apostles was filled with marvelous miracles, but the critical issue in the cause of those miracles is Jesus! We must note that it is always the resurrected Jesus!

Jesus is Life

The angel commanded the apostles to return to the temple and boldly proclaim *"all the words of this life."* The writer uses the noun *"life"* to summarize the apostle's proclamation. The Greek word is "zoe." In general, it refers to physical life and existence instead of death and nonexistence, which relates to the difficulty the Sadducees had with the apostles' message. They strictly confined their belief in "life" to their present physical existence, and their personal life focus was on the comfort and materialistic ease of the present.

In the first persecution scene, the Holy Spirit moved on Peter. Peter's message to the Sanhedrin answered their question. *"By what power or by what name have you done this"* (Acts 4:7)? They were interested in knowing the source of the miracle involving the lame beggar. Peter proclaimed Jesus Christ of Nazareth, saying, *"Whom you crucified, whom God raised from the dead, by Him this man stands here before you whole"* (Acts 4:10). Jesus was the explanation for all the miracles gaining attention (Acts 5:16). But His miracles were not the issue; the problem was the early Church demonstrating Jesus's life (Acts 4:18; 5:28)! The apostles were preaching and teaching *"words of this life,"* and it is Jesus!

Peter's sermon to the crowd gathered at the healing of the lame beggar proclaimed Jesus as **"the Prince of life"** (Acts 3:15). "Archegon" is the Greek word translated as **"Prince."** It is a combination of "arche," beginning or rule, and "ago," to lead. Jesus is the originator, founder, leader, chief, first, and prince of life as distinguished from simply being the cause. A person may cause something without being a beginner. In describing Himself to the church of the Laodiceans, Jesus said, **"These things says the Amen, the Faithful and True Witness, the Beginning of the creation of God"** (Revelation 3:14). **"Beginning"** is a translation of "arche" and excludes Jesus from Himself being a product of that beginning. Jesus is **"Life."**

Often, we use the word **"life"** as a synonym for Jesus Himself. **"In Him was life, and the life was the light of men"** (John 1:4). Jesus confronted those who wanted to stone the woman caught in adultery. The accusers dropped their stones and spared the woman with mercy and forgiveness. Jesus encouraged her to live her life without sin. He turned to the crowd still present and said, **"I am the light of the world. He who follows Me shall not walk in darkness, but have the light of life"** (John 8:12).

At the beginning of his first epistle, John declared the essence of his message in his first words, **"That which was from the beginning, which we have heard, which we have seen with our eyes, which we have looked upon, and our hands have handled"** (1 John 1:1). Who is this Jesus with whom we are involved? He is **"the Word of Life"** (1 John 1:1)!

No one could speak of these things without referring to the great "I Am" statements of Jesus. During the last six months of Jesus' ministry, He tried to explain the coming crucifixion and resurrection to His disciples. In their misunderstanding and sorrow, He declared, **"I am the way, the truth, and**

the life (John 14:6). During the great sorrow over the death of Lazarus, Jesus declared, ***"I am the resurrection and the life"*** (John 11:25).

Self-interest motivated the crowd's attraction to Jesus, and they wanted and needed healing miracles in their lives. The free meals He offered appealed to them, and they challenged Jesus to feed them all the time. After all, God did that in the Old Testament with the manna from heaven. The manna of the old days was a symbol of the true bread, which should come from the Father. The crowds cried, ***"Lord, give us this bread always. And Jesus said to them, 'I am the bread of life'"*** (John 6:34-35).

God was assuring the apostles that they were speaking correctly. The angel commanded them to return to the temple, not to run for safety. They must proclaim the true message. Jesus is Life! Life is not what one possesses and can lose; life is the essence of who Jesus is. Let us know that if anyone discovers real life, they discover Jesus. Life experienced is Jesus experienced. Life and Jesus are equal! The apostles framed it in the language of "resurrection." It is not surprising that they experienced His crucifixion and His amazing resurrection. Everything in their lives happened because Jesus was alive in them.

Jesus is Our Life

We must realize that Jesus is our Life! Life is all that we experience within the boundaries of His indwelling presence. We derive life from the One who is Life. Carefully consider Paul's declaration. ***"Therefore, if anyone is in Christ, he is a new creation; old things have passed away; behold, all things have become new"*** (2 Corinthians 5:17). Link this reality with ***"Christ in you, the hope of glory"*** (Colossians 1:27). I am in Him, and He is in me; it is the formula that equals life! We must understand that He does not give us life apart from Himself. Outside of Him, there is no life. This relationship with Life is unlike any other description. There are many attempts in the Scriptures to illustrate it, but they all fall short of the depth and wonder of Life. Being a child of God, the imagery of father and son is a strong illustration in the Scriptures. But the actual birthing of the son in the physical sense is not comparable to the birthing in the spiritual. The Father does not give me His DNA; He is my DNA. He does not contribute to my genetics, but He is my genetics. He does not tell me what is on His mind; He gives me His mind. His and my nature become united in a merger beyond description. He is my Life!

The wonder of intimacy found between the bride and bridegroom is excellent imagery. How does one describe the "one flesh" experienced in the relationship of marriage? But intimacy with Jesus, who is Life, is beyond this description. Paul displays this connection: **"For the husband is head of the wife, as also Christ is head of the church; and He is the Savior of the body"** (Ephesians 5:23). But Jesus is not the head in the sense of direction or decision making. He is the blood that flows through the entire system of our lives, giving us all the elements we need for life. He is the stimulus for the continued beating of the heart and the movement of every muscle. Remove Him, and the body dies.

The angel's instructions are commanding and specific. He commanded the apostles to ***"Go"*** and ***"speak."*** These are the two main verbs in the imperative mood, giving action to the statement. They were also encouraged to ***"stand,"*** a verb in participle form, providing content to these verbs. The apostles' actions were bold and direct. The statement's direct object, accusative, receives the action of the two main verbs as ***"in the temple."*** The apparent intent is that the disciples would not retreat to safety and hide but would boldly return to the place of ministry from which the leaders of Israel took them. The temple was the platform for evangelism from the outset of Pentecost.

The temple begins to take on importance throughout the Holy Spirit's infilling description. God established the tabernacle. It contained all that God is and all He was doing in the lives of the children of Israel as they traveled throughout the wilderness. Celebrations of the feast days, lighting of candles, worship experiences, and sacrificial offerings for sin were all centered in the tabernacle. David brought this symbolism into a permanent fixture in Jerusalem's temple. Was there any blessing of God not connected to the temple? Even the Jewish synagogue in the local communities across Palestine were merely symbols of the temple in Jerusalem.

Consider the words of Paul. ***"Do you not know that you are the temple of God and that the Spirit of God dwells in you? If anyone defiles the temple of God, God will destroy him. For the temple of God is holy, which temple you are"*** (1 Corinthians 3:16-17). Was this merely a passing observation from Paul? ***"Or do you not know that your body is the temple of the Holy Spirit who is in you, whom you have from God, and you are not your own"*** (1 Corinthian 6:19). In the spiritual sense, are we to be released from the bondage and prison of sin to boldly stand in to speak the Life of Christ to our world? Notice that it is a complete speaking of Life! We are to stand in the temple of our lives and speak ***"all the words of this life!"*** Whatever and Whomever the Spirit of Jesus is within the structure of our temple, we are to make known to the people in our world, holding back nothing. Our talent or education must not hide His life. People must see and know through us!

Jesus is Life Communicated

Now we come to the communication of this Life! Can God fill us with *"Life,"* and we not communicate it? Communication is not data, information, or theology; we are to share Jesus! It is not a challenge to sharpen your communication skills, and it is not about personality types or whether we are extroverts or introverts. People must see Jesus! Biblical knowledge for arguing specific theological perspectives is not the issue. The revelation of Jesus must take place!

Do we need to be trained or educated to accomplish this life communication? If this is true, the members of the Sanhedrin would have vehemently said that Peter and John do not qualify. ***"Now when they saw the boldness of Peter and John, and perceived that they were uneducated and untrained men, they marveled. And they realized that they had been with Jesus"*** (Acts 4:13). Is it a matter of skill or talent? Luke never mentioned this in the evangelistic efforts of the early Church. The focus of expressing this Life is that Jesus, the Life, must fill us! We cannot see Jesus if He is not present; if He is present, we will see Him!

In our passage, the angel commanded the apostles to ***"Go, stand in the temple and speak to the people all the words of this life"*** (Acts 5:20). The angel emphasized the action of speaking words. The Greek word "laleo" focuses on speaking rather than the content. There are undoubtedly many methods by which you can communicate Jesus through your life. Attitudes give a vivid expression of Christ's heart. Often actions speak louder than words. Often our actions speak so loudly that others cannot hear what we say. The focus of a person's life gives vivid revelation of what is important to them. While all of these are methods of revealing Jesus in everyone's life, there comes a time when we must speak words. We must

Part Three: Adversity Repeated

proclaim Him. The messages in the Book of Acts centered on Jesus being alive and acting in the speaker's life. That was the dilemma of Peter and John when the leaders of Israel told them never to talk about Jesus again. Their answer was, ***"Whether it is right in the sight of God to listen to you more than to God, you judge. For we cannot but speak the things which we have seen and heard"*** (Acts 4:19-20). Denying what they learned through education was not the problem. They experienced the resurrected Jesus in their lives. There was no way to deny this or keep from speaking of it. Jesus affected every aspect of their lives. They operated within the merger of His presence. How could their lives not dispense the essence of His presence to their world? To deny Him would be to deny themselves. They had to declare His name!

You and I are the ***"words of this life."*** We are one with Him and the expression of His presence. What an opportunity Jesus gives us in the unity of His presence!

Acts 5:21

FUTILITY

"And when they heard that, they entered the temple early in the morning and taught. But the high priest and those with him came and called the council together, with all the elders of the children of Israel, and sent to the prison to have them brought" (Acts 5:21).

The unfolding story of Moses' life is marvelous. His futile attempts to run and hide from the call of God on his life reveal the sinful nature of the human heart. Why are we resistant to the will of God? Are we so irrational that we can win against God's sovereign wisdom? The overwhelming miracles in Moses' childhood should have given him the confidence to succeed in God's plan. But he sourced himself through his anger and fled in failure to the wilderness. He was now an eighty-year-old failure-tending sheep.

Does Moses think God is defeated? A bush on fire but not being consumed captured his attention. The voice of God commanded a return to Egypt and a confrontation with Pharaoh. Is God not sovereign? Will He not accomplish His plan? He will establish a nation through which He will birth the Messiah. Evil will not triumph! Moses returned to Egypt to represent the sovereign God, who made demands. Our sovereign

Part Three: Adversity Repeated

God has a plan that He must fulfill. Can we expect to rebel and win against Him?

Moses stood before Pharaoh, speaking the command God gave him, **"Let My people go, that they may serve Me"** (Exodus 8:1). But each time Pharaoh refused to yield to God's sovereignty, God hardened his heart. Do you see how futile such rebellion is? How can you succeed against a sovereign God? Ten plagues took place! Each of them was a confrontation of a sovereign God with the puny gods of Egypt. In the first plague, God turned the Nile River into blood; the fish died, and the river stank (Exodus 7:14-25). For seven days, the water supply of Egypt flowed with blood. How can you rebel against the sovereign God? Do you think you can conquer? But God hardened Pharaoh's heart to show His miracles to the people, and he did not heed the voice of God.

The second plague focused on frogs (Exodus 8:1-15). The Nile River brought forth multitudes of frogs; they filled the kneading bowls, the ovens, and the people's houses. The third plague was all the land of Egypt becoming lice (Exodus 8:16-19). In the fourth plague, God corrupted the land of Egypt with swarms of flies (Exodus 8:21-24), filling the houses and saturating the land. The fifth plague brought severe pestilence on the cattle of the field, the horses, donkeys, camels, oxen, and sheep (Exodus 9:1-7). All the livestock of Egypt died! But each time, God hardened Pharaoh's heart, and Pharaoh refused the will of the sovereign God. What is your will, Pharaoh? Can you go to war with the sovereign God and expect to survive?

In the sixth plague, on the command of God, Moses took ashes from a furnace and scattered them toward heaven in the presence of Pharaoh (Exodus 9:8-12). It caused boils that broke out on man and beast throughout Egypt. But Pharaoh did not listen! The seventh plague brought hail to the land of Egypt (Exodus 9:13-33). Thunder, hail, and fire darted to the ground; its heaviness was like none the land of Egypt had ever seen since becoming a nation. The eighth plague was locusts covering the face of the earth, darkening the land (Exodus 10:12-15). The ninth plague was darkness over the land of Egypt that every Egyptian felt (Exodus 10:21-29). The darkness was so thick that they did not see one another, and no one left his place for three days. But Pharaoh would not listen to the voice of God! Pharaoh threatened the life of Moses. Did Pharaoh think that he could conquer a sovereign God? Was he not filled with stupidity in the depth of his soul rebelling against such a God?

Then, the ultimate plague came in full reality and force in the land of Egypt! God ushered in the death of every firstborn of man and beast (Exodus 11). Can you hear the cries of the people of Egypt, for there was not a house where there was not one dead? Pharaoh finally changed his mind. They urged the people of God to leave their land. Did Pharaoh finally learn his lesson? No! He changed his mind again! He took six hundred choice chariots with captains over every one of them to pursue the children of Israel. What will it take to convince Pharaoh that God is sovereign? The Egyptians went after the Israelites into the midst of the sea, all Pharaoh's horses, chariots, and horsemen. But our sovereign God troubled the army of the Egyptians. Their chariot wheels fell off, so they drove with difficulty. Moses stretched his hand over the parted sea, and the sea returned to its full depth swallowing the Egyptians fleeing into it (Exodus 14). When will you learn that you cannot rebel against a sovereign God and win?

Hundreds of years later, the Sovereign God captured twelve apostles. He revealed Himself in Jesus! These apostles experienced the unfailing power of Jesus, bringing victory into their lives. He was so powerful that they called Him a "Tyrant" (Acts 4:24). No one could stop Him. His plan of redemption for His world could not be altered or hindered. Every obstacle in His path became a mere stepping stone for His success. These twelve apostles were staking their lives on Him! Because of their faithfulness, they were thrown into a common prison by the high priest and Sadducees. ***"BUT at night an angel of the Lord opened the prison doors and brought them out"*** (Acts 5:19). However, it was not for their escape to safety. The angel's instruction was not to flee for their lives, escape to another country, or hide lest the leaders of Israel capture them again. He said, ***"Go, stand in the temple and speak to the people all the words of this life"*** (Acts 5:20). The command meant they were to return to the temple and do the very thing for which the leaders of Israel had captured them. But this was only a problem if God was not sovereign! Is it safe to be His?

How do these apostles respond? ***"And when they heard that, they entered the temple early in the morning and taught"*** (Acts 5:21), which only makes sense if God is sovereign. Does He have a plan into which He has called us? Are we safe to live in submission to Him regardless of the circumstances? Rebelling against His Divine will would be ridiculous! Being the source of our own lives, operating out of our strength, and designing our destiny brings only chaos and destruction. The only sensible decision to make is to submit to Jesus! Would we dare become the Pharaoh of our existence and exert our wills? Could we expect anything less than the wheels of our chariots to fall off and we drown in the sea?

However, note the response of the high priest and the Sadducees who were with him! ***"BUT the high priest and those with him came and called the council together, with all the elders of the children of Israel, and sent to the prison to have them brought"*** (Acts 5:21). Are they worse than the Pharaoh of Egypt? In many ways, the answer is "Yes!"

Foolishness

The religious training of the Old Testament belongs to the children of Israel. They celebrated year after year the feast days, which told the stories of the great deliverance by the hand of their sovereign God. They memorized the stories of the foolishness of Israel's enemies who attempted to rebel against their God. They quoted the Scriptures that displayed their sovereign God working through the most foolish efforts of feeble men, giving them victory. The Old Testament screams the greatness of God and the foolishness of those who tried to thwart His Divine plan. How could they miss it now?

The Old Testament was filled with the victories of their sovereign God and a constant display of their ancestors' foolishness who did not hide in His greatness. Note carefully the admonition coming from one of their own. "***For who, having heard, rebelled? Indeed, was it not all who came out of Egypt, led by Moses? Now with whom was He angry forty years? Was it not with those who sinned, whose corpses fell in the wilderness? And to whom did He swear that they would not enter His rest, but to those who did not obey***" (Hebrews 3:16-18). Those who experienced the strength of God displayed in the plagues marched out of bondage with the Egyptian's wealth and received the promises of God. Though God gave them the promised land, they were foolish and rebelled against the sovereign One who delivered them. The high priest and those with him followed in their forefather's footsteps. What does our sovereign God need to do to convince you? How can He win your heart?

Jesus pleaded with this group, who eventually crucified Him. He called them "hypocrites" seven times in His last preached message. He described their foolishness, their blindness, their straining out a gnat and swallowing a camel, their cleansing of the outside, and their total disregard for the inward condition and pretense (Matthew 23). They should know better! They became witnesses against themselves by testifying that they were the sons of those who murdered the prophets. Jesus wept over them as He cried, *"O Jerusalem, Jerusalem, the one who kills the prophets and stones those who are sent to her! How often I wanted to gather your children together, as a hen gathers her chicks under her wings, but you were not willing"* (Matthew 23:37)!

It is a cry of Jesus' desperate heart for you and me. We are equally foolish and have heard this repeatedly! An angel of the Lord intervenes, yet we call for the council. We send for the prisoners who our sovereign God has already delivered. Do we think for one moment we can rebel against the will of God for our lives and survive the damnation our rebellion births? What are we thinking? Should we not fall at His feet, risk our existence in obedience, and return to where He placed us? We must push aside the foolishness of our stupidity to embrace His wisdom. He has never failed; we cannot win on our own. *"Where is the wise? Where is the scribe? Where is the disputer of this age? Has not God made foolish the wisdom of this world? For since, in the wisdom of God, the world through wisdom did not know God, it pleased God through the foolishness of the message preached to save those who believe"* (1 Corinthians 1:20-21). Listen to the statement above all statements. *"Because the foolishness of God is wiser than men, and the weakness of God is stronger than men"* (1 Corinthians 1:25).

Are *"the high priest and those with him"* worse than the Pharaoh of Egypt? In many ways, the answer is "Yes!"

Fullness of Self

The egotism of Pharaoh is so blaring; all must recognize it. He demanded worship of his image and considered himself to be a god. Power and authority over all of Egypt supported arrogance and pride. Was it not incredibly insulting for a peasant man, a Hebrew failure from the desert, to confront him and make demands in the name of some God about whom he knew nothing? Was not God gracious in bringing revelation to the heart of Pharaoh? Indeed, all the transactions and demonstrations were understandably a God-granted revelation to Pharaoh.

But the leaders of Israel already had a multitude of instructions and demonstrations. Their high priest and the members of the Sanhedrin screamed about their knowledge and supposed understanding of God's purposed movement. Such defiance and rebellion against the arrival of the Messiah for which they have waited for centuries are unthinkable. God moved; He resurrected Jesus; miracles occurred, and the message spread in Jerusalem. But the high priest and those with him continued in their pattern of self-importance. They called the council to determine what they had already decided. They sent officers to the common prison to bring the apostles. They became aware of the apostles' deliverance and their continued preaching and teaching in the temple. But these leaders ignored the Divine intervention, continued with their council, and maintained their control. They would not acknowledge any authority or power beyond themselves!

Have you and I not experienced the same pattern in our personal lives? God moves with Divine love and repeatedly intervenes during our self-inflicted plans. They are plans that create destruction and ruin for us and those around us. When confronted with His truth, we turn inward to our council and agree with our decided egotism. God has veiled the Gospel to us, and our self-centeredness has blinded us (2 Corinthians 4:4). But, be assured, ***"it is the God who commanded light to shine out of darkness, who has shone in our hearts to give the light of the knowledge of the glory of God in the face of Jesus Christ"*** (2 Corinthians 4:6). Our God will continue to send angels to deliver. He will consistently return His messengers to the temple to continue preaching and teaching. He will turn our self-dominated councils into testimonies of His love and truth! We will not be able to miss it. The redemptive heart of the Trinity God can do no other!

Are ***"the high priest and those with him"*** worse than the Pharaoh of Egypt? In many ways, the answer is "Yes!"

Futility

Pharaoh refused to yield to God's call on His life throughout the ten plagues. But the high priest and those calling the council had the intervention for a lifetime and beyond. The land upon which they stood was given to them by God. The glory of God's presence filled the temple where they worshipped (1 Kings 8:11). From the character of God flowed the laws on which He had constructed their nation. Their hope for the future came from God's heart, His plan for their lives!

What hope do they have in rebelling against Him? It is futile! Outside of His dreams for them are destruction and ruin. Do they have any hope of victory against the God who planted them as a nation to bring the reality of Jesus? To rebel against Him was to rebel against the flow God created within their histories. They cannot win! Yet, they strut on in their arrogance, exerting their wills and demanding their rights. They crucified Jesus, but God raised Him from the dead. They demanded the apostles' not to mention the name of Jesus again, but His praise filled all of Jerusalem. They did not believe in angels, but an angel delivered the apostles from the common prison. They fought to protect their nation and temple, but destruction will come to Jerusalem. They cannot win fighting against God!

Paul described the foolishness of our arrogance demonstrated in demanding our way. Our self-centered pride wars against everything that God placed within our natures. We cannot oversee our lives, yet we insist on our wills. We fight against the same patterns established by God in the universe (Romans 1:19, 20). **"Professing to be wise, they became fools"** (Romans 1:22). Should the word **"they"** become "I"? How can an individual succeed if he exchanges the truth of God for a lie? Do we not receive in ourselves the penalty of our foolishness (Romans 1:27)? What chance do we have? It is futile!

But God has not abandoned us! He sends an angel to free His messengers from the common prison. The angel does not instruct us to flee or hide the truth but proclaims the truth once again! He gives us another chance; will we hear His voice? Jesus confronts our lives; will we surrender to Him? The revelation comes like a blinding light; will we see the truth?

Acts 5:21

CONSISTENCY

"And when they heard that, they entered the temple early in the morning and taught. But the high priest and those with him came and called the council together, with all the elders of the children of Israel, and sent to the prison to have them brought" (Acts 5:21).

There is something admirable about "faithfulness," defined in the dictionary as "loyal, constant, and steadfast." Regarding employment, it is an employee who has decades of faithful service. In marriage, it is a spouse who never betrays their marriage partner. Regarding an object, it is a reliable instrument one can count on. Faithfulness has to do with being true to the facts or the origin of something. In religion, it means never wavering from one's belief. Other words substituted for "faithfulness" are "loyalty, consistency, truth, devoted, true-blue, unswerving, staunch, steadfast, dedicated, committed, trustworthy, dependable, or reliable."

The epitome of all faithfulness is the character of God! Often, we quote the passage, **"Jesus Christ is the same yesterday, today, and forever"** (Hebrews 13:8). It is a recognition of the unchanging nature of God! **"For He is the living God, and steadfast forever; His kingdom is the one which shall** *not be destroyed, And His dominion shall endure to the end"* (Daniel 6:26). His Word is secure. The psalmist cried, *"Your testimonies, which You have commanded, are righteous and very faithful"* (Psalms 119:138). Paul told Timothy, *"If we are faithless, He remains faithful; He cannot deny Himself"* (2 Timothy 2:13). God is not capable of being unfaithful because of who He is.

We are constantly admonished in the Scripture to be faithful. *"Continue in the faith, grounded and steadfast, and are not moved away from the hope of the gospel which you heard"* (Colossians 1:23). Faithfulness is not a decision or a discipline we impose upon ourselves. It is a fruit of the Spirit: *"But the fruit of the Spirit is love, joy, peace, longsuffering, kindness, goodness, faithfulness"* (Galatians 5:22). While in our self-centeredness, we may express an unwillingness to change regarding certain things essential to "self," the faithfulness produced by the Spirit is vastly different. There is a difference between faithfulness and stubbornness. Self-centeredness produces stubbornness; Spirit-centeredness produces faithfulness.

In His humanity, men acknowledged Jesus' "faithfulness." Jesus is the faithful high priest who expresses His steadfastness, and the Trinity gives him the destiny for His saving work of humanity (Hebrews 2:17; 3:2-6). In the Book of the Revelation, Jesus is called the "Faithful Witness" or absolutely the "Faithful and True" (Revelation 1:5; 3:14; 19:11). This characteristic of God is in Jesus and contrasted with human changeableness. When the heavens open, Jesus will appear as a victorious warrior whose name is faithful and true. He is the One in whom the attribute of faithfulness has its highest realization and of whom it is so characteristic as to become the name of our exalted Lord.

Incredibly, the Scriptures connect God's faithfulness to His gracious promise of salvation. He is unwavering in His commitment. *"He has delivered us from the power of*

Part Three: Adversity Repeated

darkness and conveyed us into the kingdom of the Son of His love" (Colossians 1:13). God is wholly focused on redemption. It is the dominant theme of His existence, which elevates Him to Lord in my life. He is worthy because of His faithfulness! As He draws us into His nature, we know "faithfulness" as we focus on Him. How can we understand the martyrs except through their "faithfulness?" ***"Others were tortured, not accepting deliverance, that they might obtain a better resurrection. Still others had trial of mockings and scourgings, yes, and of chains and imprisonment. They were stoned, they were sawn in two, were tempted, were slain with the sword. They wandered about in sheepskins and goatskins, being destitute, afflicted, tormented - of whom the world was not worthy. They wandered in deserts and mountains, in dens and caves of the earth"*** (Hebrews 11:35-38). They could do this because they were faithful. Jesus became so great in their lives that He overshadowed every circumstance! The apostles and the members of the Sanhedrin were faithful, but the contrast of their faith was in the object of their faithfulness.

The Concept

The two main verbs in the beginning sentence are ***"entered"*** and ***"taught"*** (Acts 5:21). The verb translated ***"entered"*** is in the indicative mood indicating a simple statement of fact. Argument or debate is not in the apostles' response, nor is the angel allowing such. Without hesitation, the apostles step back into the situation that previously got them imprisoned. In most translations, the Greek verb ***"taught"*** means "began to teach." The verb appears in the imperfect tense, where the writer portrays an action in the process or a state of being that occurred in the past, not assessing the action's completion. The apostles did not start something new but returned to the temple to do the same thing they had done all along!

They responded to the first scene of persecution by praying, ***"Now, Lord, look on their threats, and grant to Your servants that with all boldness they may speak Your word"*** (Acts 4:29). God abundantly answered their prayer. ***"They were all filled with the Holy Spirit, and they spoke the word of God with boldness"*** (Acts 4:31). The apostles remained faithful and continued to teach in the name of Jesus even though Peter and John were placed in prison and threatened. Now, during heightened threats and the imprisonment of all the apostles, they remained faithful. This faithfulness is especially significant, considering they could have fled to safety after the angel released them from jail. Is it not inevitable that the Sadducees will capture them again because they returned to the temple to teach? But they do not hesitate!

We must understand their faithfulness was not to a career, tradition, or fame. That was not the last time Peter was placed in jail and delivered by an angel. Herod the King put him in prison and chained him between two guards. The church prayed, and ***"the Lord sent His angel"*** (Acts 12:11). Peter did not return to the synagogue to teach; instead, he went into Caesarea and stayed there (Acts 12:19). Whether Peter stayed or went did not determine his faithfulness; his response to God's instructions determined his faithfulness. The apostles were faithful to the exact instructions of the angel.

Faithfulness is the core of the merger with Jesus. In merging with His life, we live out His mind and heart. Legalistic obedience to the angel's commands did not project the apostles' actions. The Spirit of Jesus filled, saturated, permeated them, and the mind of Christ became their mind. Their hearts and His heart became one. In this oneness, they became new creatures who Jesus is and who they are! Obedience to the angel's instruction is a spontaneous response from these new creatures.

Part Three: Adversity Repeated

This apostles' faithfulness contrasts with the response of **"the high priest and those with him."** Once again, Luke introduces a startling contrast, **"But"** (Acts 5:21b). The apostles go to the temple to teach, while the high priest and Sadducees go to the hall of the supreme court, the Sanhedrin. Luke writes, **"But the high priest and those with him came"** (Acts 5:21). The main verb is not **"came** (paraginomai)."** It is a participle giving content to the action of the main verb. Luke continues by stating that they **"called the council together,"** which is the main verb (synkaleo) (Matthew 5:21).

An identical approach is presented to us by Luke in the first scene of persecution. After interrogating Peter and John, the members of the Sanhedrin find themselves in a dilemma. **"And seeing the man who had been healed standing with them, they could say nothing against it"** (Acts 4:14). Everyone in Jerusalem was also speaking about this notable miracle. There was no way to deny it! What was the response of the members of the Sanhedrin? **"But when they had commanded them** (Peter and John) **to go aside out of the council, they conferred among themselves"** (Acts 4:15).

In each case, the Spirit of Jesus filled the apostles. The focus of God's heart is always outward! The apostles' concern was the healing of the lame beggar, as was the crowd gathered at Solomon's Porch and even the leaders of Israel. They must win all of Jerusalem to Jesus, and the multitudes needed a Divine touch. The reason for the second imprisonment of the apostles was this outward focus. Even though an angel of the Lord delivered them from prison, their focus did not change. They did not care about their safety or comfort. The angel sent them back to the temple to proclaim the message. Their focus was on others.

But the leaders of Israel were focused on themselves, turning inward to confer with themselves and not seeking beyond themselves. That was their constant pattern. They would not seek beyond themselves, which always turned them back to the same conclusion. The Trinity God injected their lives with new and fresh revelation, revealing the fallacy of their spiritual rejection; an angel of the Lord crossed their path again, but they turned inward and rejected such a thought. Jesus spoke this same truth concerning the Devil (John 8:44). Satan is a liar and the father of all lies. Why does he continually lie? It is because his pile of information and resource is nothing but lies. He always goes to his pile; therefore, he always lies. His only chance for change is to go beyond his inner personal pile.

We must apply this concept to our lives! We must seek beyond ourselves. The prevenient grace of God continually bombards us with new and fresh revelations of Himself, and He wants to guide us into all truth (John 16:13). But to be guided, we must not turn into ourselves. We must be willing to listen, respond, and embrace, which will require a life-giving change. Constantly conferring with ourselves brings nothing but destruction and death!

The Content

Faithfulness always has content or a focus, the object to which an individual is faithful. The content becomes the driving force that keeps a person's life within the boundaries of faithfulness. Once we lose interest in the object, our faithfulness ceases to exist. Jesus is the singular object of the apostles' faithfulness! In a previous study, we discussed the content of their proclamation, ***"all the words of this life"*** (Acts 5:20). It is not a focus on "life in general," "our life," or "eternal life." It focuses on the "resurrected Life," the resurrected Jesus! Only one focus is significant enough to compel the apostles to return to the temple, assuring their capture again. Jesus raised from the dead is their compulsion!

Part Three: Adversity Repeated

Luke highlighted the early Church's faithfulness from the beginning of the Book of Acts until this story. They stayed in Jerusalem because the resurrected Lord remained with them for forty days (Acts 1:3). This seminar discussing the content of the Kingdom of God only cemented their focus and faithfulness. Before His ascension, Jesus assured them He would come to them in a new and realistic filling (Acts 1:5). In the few days they remained in Jerusalem, they experienced the Spirit of Jesus indwelling them (Acts 2:1-4). How could they proclaim anything else except the resurrected Lord living within them? Peter's sermon on the Day of Pentecost, explaining the event, was focused on Jesus. After the healing of the lame beggar, Peter again pointed exclusively to Jesus. His concern was for everyone to focus on Jesus (Acts 3:12). When interrogated by the members of the Sanhedrin, his sole explanation for the miracle was Jesus (Acts 4:8-12). This focus was verified by those threatening the early Church. The Sanhedrin demanded that the apostles never speak the name of Jesus again (Acts 4:17). Their concern was not miracles, church gatherings, or compassionate ministry. It was the constant and unrelenting focus on Jesus! In response, the cry of the early Church was that they might speak His name with the same boldness regardless of the threats (Acts 4:29-30).

The events in our passage occur only because of the early Church's faithfulness to Jesus. If the apostles had removed Jesus from the center, the Sanhedrin would not have imprisoned them. There would have been no angelic appearance. Indeed, they would not return to the temple with the blazing message of **"this life."** Their focus was the resurrected Jesus! Nothing or no one can capture our focus until circumstances do not matter. Only Jesus is worthy of eliminating all other concerns in our hearts, and He sets the standard for all Christians everywhere and through all generations. The person of Jesus must capture us! Mere theology will divide us; legalism will condemn us;

miracles will focus us back on ourselves, causing competition; gifts of the Spirit will cause spiritual superiority. While all these elements may have their place, they must not be our focus. Jesus alone is worthy of our focus.

Jesus is not an object on which we focus, and He is not an organization with rules for doing good things in the community or a belief system that I firmly believe in. The apostles' focus is directly due to their intimacy and oneness with Jesus. They experienced Him in His resurrection appearances, and He has filled them with His Spirit. Their linkage with His person is the content of their focus.

The faithfulness of the Sanhedrin's members focuses on "self." "Self" is not an object of their gaze or an organization of which they are members. "Self" is not a belief system to which they adhere. The Sadducees were so linked with themselves that they focused every decision on "what is to our advantage?" Self-centeredness permeates every decision, overshadows every activity, and dictates every thought. Their intimate relationship with themselves is the center of their faithfulness. In contrast, the apostles' intimacy with Jesus dominates their attention while self dominates the Sadducees.

The Clerical

Whether we focus on Jesus or self, practical results are equally predictable. Those who focus on Jesus cannot help but glorify Him. That is the crucial issue between the apostles and the Sadducees. The apostles are not merely speaking about Jesus but glorifying Him, dwelling in a state of praise for Jesus. All the miracles are activities glorifying His name. They express the transformation of their lives and live in the atmosphere of glorifying His name. Their speech naturally contains nothing but glory for the name of Jesus. The Greek word for "glory"

Part Three: Adversity Repeated

is "doxa." It has to do with perspective, what one values, or what one sees necessary. Jesus so captured the apostles' lives that He was their supreme value. He was more valuable than their own lives.

The practical results of faithfulness to "self" are equally possessive. Self-focus demands the elimination of everything that challenges its authority. In the spiritual realm, the greatest threat to self-sovereignty is Jesus. Jesus is Lord; He threatens every other lordship! All must bow under His authority. In every facet of life, Jesus confronts the self because His nature demands total surrender. Jesus does not need to fight for the position of Lord; He does not need to persuade others of His value. It is inherent within His nature. Light does not need to prove its superiority over darkness. Light does not fight against darkness. Light simply appears, and darkness is gone. Darkness must bow to the authority of Light!

The Sadducees could not simply ignore Jesus. Of necessity, they must crucify Him. They cannot overlook the Jesus who filled the apostles, and they had to stop them! The presence of Jesus confronted the self-centeredness of the Sadducees, where every aspect of their lives cried out against Jesus. As they participated in crucifying Jesus in days gone by, they must now eliminate Him in the present. We must understand that Jesus is so superior He continually confronts us. The Sadducees were constantly battling to eliminate Jesus from their lives, and Jesus simply would not stop His pursuit of them. It is who He is!

Every one of us experiences the challenge of our faithfulness. Focus on ourselves produces faithfulness to self, and focus on Jesus produces faithfulness to Him. We dwell on one focus or the other.

PART FOUR
ACTS 5:22-32

APOSTLE'S RESTATEMENT: THE UNEXPLAINABLE

Acts 5:22-32

THE UNEXPLAINABLE

"But when the officers came and did not find them in the prison, they returned and reported, saying, 'Indeed we found the prison shut securely, and the guards standing outside before the doors; but when we opened them, we found no one inside!' Now when the high priest, the captain of the temple, and the chief priests heard these things, they wondered what the outcome would be. So one came and told them, saying, 'Look, the men whom you put in prison are standing in the temple and teaching the people!' Then the captain went with the officers and brought them without violence, for they feared the people, lest they should be stoned. And when they had brought them, they set them before the council. And the high priest asked them, saying, 'Did we not strictly command you not to teach in this name? And look, you have filled Jerusalem with your doctrine, and intend to bring this Man's blood on us!' But Peter and the other disciples answered and said: 'We ought to obey God rather than men. The God of our fathers raised up Jesus whom you murdered by hanging on a tree. Him God exalted to His right hand to be Prince and Savior, to give repentance to Israel and forgiveness of sins. And we are His witnesses to these things, and so also is the Holy Spirit whom God has given to those who obey Him." (Acts 5:22-32).

The details are familiar as we begin our investigation into this new paragraph. Another encounter between the Sanhedrin

Part Four: Apostle's Restatement: The Unexplainable

and the apostles is a repeat of Peter and John's first imprisonment and interrogation (Acts 4:1-22). The Holy Spirit and Luke considered giving the same information regarding actions and outcomes essential. What is the primary teaching of the passage? How must we apply this knowledge to our lives?

We are dividing the material of this passage into five sections.

The Assembly
Acts 5:21

Although this verse is not in our paragraph, it establishes the context of the material's action. The Sanhedrin ordered that the apostles be confined to the common prison until morning. When morning arrived, the Sanhedrin came together to settle this matter and sent for the apostles.

The Absence
Acts 5:22-32

Our paragraph begins with the Sanhedrin discovering that the apostles are absent from the common prison. The officers sent to retrieve the apostles reported the security of the prison and the presence of the guards standing outside. However, when they went inside to get the apostles, they were gone. No one seemed to know how they escaped. At the peak of perplexity, they received the information that the apostles were in the temple preaching Jesus!

The Arrest
Acts 5:26

The temple captain decided to supervise the second arrest of the apostles himself. The apostles were so popular they could have resisted, but the people might have stoned the officers in protest. The apostles went quietly with the guards.

The Accusation
Acts 5:27-28

When the apostles stood before the Sanhedrin, these leaders accused them of disobedience. Their first interrogation was focused on the consistent teaching and preaching about Jesus. Nothing else mattered to the Sanhedrin except the person of Jesus. The Sanhedrin commanded the apostles to never again mention the name of Jesus. Notice in our passage that the Sanhedrin avoided mentioning Jesus' name in their accusation.

The Answer
Acts 5:29-32

The apostles respond with the same answer they offered at their first interrogation. What are they to do? Will they obey God or man? God made the apostles and the Holy Spirit witnesses to the life of Jesus, and they simply cannot keep still about Him!

We must evaluate this paragraph through the lens of the persecution narrative. God is moving; the consistency of that movement becomes apparent through the repetition of persecution. The faithfulness of the apostles in obedience to the angel's instruction highlights their consistent focus on Jesus. In the second interrogation before the Sanhedrin, the apostles repeat the same declaration as in their first interrogation. Everyone can see God's movement and the Apostles' faithfulness in the setting of the Jewish religion. The high priest and the Sadducees' practical religious, political, and financial worlds were welded together, and they viewed Jesus as a threat to all three worlds. Luke displayed the mystical movement of God in the rigid physical practices and traditions of men!

Part Four: Apostle's Restatement: The Unexplainable

Faith
Religious Practices

The high priest called *"the council together, with all the elders of the children of Israel"* (Acts 5:21). *"Now when the high priest, the captain of the temple, and the chief priests heard these things, they wondered what the outcome would be"* (Acts 5:24). Those fulfilling the priestly role were at the heart of all the decisions made in this scene. The high priest's primary function was to administrate and direct the sacrificial system of Israel. He alone was allowed to go behind the veil of the Holy of Holies on the Day of Atonement (Leviticus 16:2). He dealt with the sin offerings. He brought the blood into the temple's sanctuary (Leviticus 4:3-21). All the sacrificial activities inside the temple were either with his direct involvement or under his supervision.

The sacrificial system of Israel was their means of atonement and communication with God. The primary purpose of the high priest was to serve as a representative and mediator between the people and God. As a representative of the people of God, the high priest was the enforcer of the covenant. Everyone had to observe the duties of the temple and the law of Moses. In this role, the high priest directed the people's hearts toward God. He had the privilege of bringing all the needs of the people before God.

The high priest represented the people to God and represented God to the people. While he was not a prophet, his responsibility was more significant than a prophet's in many ways. He was the consistent, daily influence for righteousness and the voice of the covenant for God to the people of Israel. The people did not bring their sacrifices directly to God but to the high priest. Therefore, special regulations were applied to the high priest above other priests. He must be free from every bodily defect (Leviticus 21:16-23), and his dress, appearance, and activities affected his role. He must marry only a virgin of Israel, not a widow, a divorced woman, or a profane one (Leviticus 21:14).

God moved amid these religious leaders. The high priest, above all others, should have a deep awareness of the Divine movement. There was a foreshadowing and throbbing hope of a more perfect high priesthood throughout the Old Testament. No one understood this, as did the writer of the Book of Hebrews. No one would choose for himself the responsibility of being a mediator between God and man. God must appoint him (Hebrews 5:4). Does the high priest in our passage not recognize he has served his time? God erected a new High Priest on a higher level. Jesus is the God-Man who can fulfill the duties as no other priest in Israel's past. He knows us, for He was tempted in all points as we are, yet without sin (Hebrews 4:15). The high priest in our passage enters the Holy of Holies every year with the blood of a bull. But Jesus, our High Priest, offered His blood only once (Hebrews 9:28). He did not enter the Holy of Holies made with hands but appears in the presence of God for us (Hebrews 9:24). In Jesus, we see all of the duties, responsibilities, and symbolic foreshadowing of the office of the Old Testament high priest fulfilled.

The high priest in our passage rose up and was filled with indignation (Acts 5:17). God was moving. Jesus fulfilled all the old religious structures and made the once-for-all sacrifice known as the Day of Atonement. Through the indwelling Spirit of Jesus, man has direct access to the throne of God. God placed in Jesus' hands control over the people's religious practices. Jesus is our High Priest! What the high priest in our passage could not accomplish, Jesus fulfilled. ***"Also there were many priests, because they were prevented by death from continuing. But He, because He continues forever, has an unchangeable priesthood. Therefore He is also able*** *to save to the uttermost those who come to God through Him, since He always lives to make intercession for them"* (Hebrews 7:23-25). Our High Priest is holy, harmless, undefiled, and separated from sinners. He has become higher than the heavens (Hebrews 7:26). He does not need to offer up daily sacrifices for the sins of the people, for He did this once and for all (Hebrews 7:27).

God moved during Israel's religious practices, and the leaders rebelled against it vigorously. They recognized that God's movement centered on Jesus, fulfilling their spiritual practices, and Jesus was bigger than their religion.

Jesus fulfilled their sacrificial system's requirements, for He is the Sacrifice. *"Not with the blood of goats and calves, but with His own blood He entered the Most Holy Place once for all, having obtained eternal redemption"* (Hebrews 9:12).

Jesus fulfilled and replaced their priesthood, for He is the eternal High Priest! *"We have such a High Priest, who is seated at the right hand of the throne of the Majesty in the heavens, a Minister of the sanctuary and of the true tabernacle which the Lord erected, and not man"* (Hebrews 8:1-2).

God replaced the *"first covenant,"* which was the foundation of their religion, with a *"better covenant"* (Hebrews 8:6). This reality was a fulfillment of prophecy: *"Behold, the days are coming, says the Lord, when I will make a new covenant with the house of Israel and with the house of Judah"* (Jeremiah 31:31). *"In that He says, 'A new covenant,' He has made the first obsolete. Now what is becoming obsolete and growing old is ready to vanish away"* (Hebrews 8:13).

The Jews focused on the physical structure of the temple, which gave them a sense of security in God's presence. Now God replaced their false sense of security with something better. *"But*

Christ came as High Priest of the good things to come, with the greater and more perfect tabernacle not made with hands, that is, not of this creation" (Hebrews 9:11). The physical tabernacle was a mere symbol for the present time. It was ***"concerned only with foods and drinks, various washings, and fleshly ordinances imposed until the time of reformation"*** (Hebrews 9:10).

God overrode and replaced the religious world of the high priest and the Sadducees with Jesus. Christ fulfilled all they held dear and counted as their salvation. Will they release it and cling to Jesus? Will they give themselves in dedication to Him as to the old structure? Our passage declares that they refused. Today's issue is not them but us! We have established our religious traditions and patterns and created rituals that give us satisfaction and a sense of righteousness. We have our organizations, and we build our buildings. We feel secure in them. Does what we have established provide us with security? Jesus moves again to break up all the old covenants and traditions so we might only see Him!

Flesh
Physical Practices

The movement of God radically affected the physical lives of everyone, the apostles and leaders of Israel. The wealthy Sadducees firmly focused on comfort and security found in materialism. They were the aristocratic and conservative priestly party that clung to their ancient traditions and resisted every new idea the domination of Rome demanded. The movement of God through the apostles brought such popularity to the movement that the status quo felt threatened. If this movement continued, it would threaten the compromises and alliances made with Rome for financial gain.

Part Four: Apostle's Restatement: The Unexplainable

In our passage, the high priest and the Sadducees ignored the radical shift happening in the physical circumstances through the angel of the Lord. Upon hearing of the apostles' deliverance, they sent the captain down to the temple as if nothing had occurred. They would correct any change in the apostles' physical circumstances to maintain control. But God had different plans. While His ultimate goal was spiritual, not physical, the design of His creation is that the spiritual world will display itself in physical realities. God did not move in the unseen world without radical changes in physical circumstances. The intense battle the Sadducees faced was the impossible attempt to maintain their comfortable circumstances within the movement of God. It was a futile attempt!

This battle was a repeat of what happened at the crucifixion of Jesus. The Sadducees joined the Pharisees in demanding the death of Jesus. The moment Jesus *"yielded up His spirit,"* God radically affected the physical world. The temple's veil ripped in two from top to bottom, the earth quaked, the rocks split, and the graves of many of the saints opened (Matthew 27:51-52). What was the response of the leadership of Israel? They did not repent or recognize any movement of God in their midst. They repaired the damage to the temple and restored physical order to their world. But you and I know that their physical world has ended. In a few short years, Jerusalem was destroyed, and the nation of Israel ceased to exist.

Likewise, the apostles experienced radical changes in their physical world. From the moment they encountered Jesus, He dramatically altered their physical lives. Peter went from the ordinary life of fishing to dangerously standing before the Sanhedrin. All of the apostles moved from some sense of security to being thrown in jail and beaten by the leaders of Israel (Acts 5:40). They went from being obscure individuals to worldwide evangelists. Uneducated men became writers of the New Testament, and we still read their writings today.

Do we dare think that will not be true with us? Our merger with Jesus will affect our religious world, and our physical circumstances will not remain the same. Paul warned us of this effect. *"**There is therefore now no condemnation to those who are in Christ Jesus, who do not walk according to the flesh, but according to the Spirit**"* (Romans 8:1). *"**For if you live according to the flesh you will die; but if by the Spirit you put to death the deeds of the body, you will live**"* (Romans 8:13). Our commitment to Jesus is not only in spirit but in flesh!

Foundation
Witness Practices

That brings us to the heart of the issue, which is Jesus! Our spiritual and physical lives become *"**His witnesses**"* (Acts 5:32). The focus of our merger with Him is not emotional healing or physical comfort, and it is not about protection from unfavorable circumstances or prosperity and good health. All our circumstances bend themselves for the accomplishment of a single purpose, *"**His Witnesses,**"* the same single driving passion of the *"**Holy Spirit whom God has given to those who obey Him**"* (Acts 5:32).

Jesus gave practical instructions to His disciples in the upper room before His crucifixion. *"**But when the Helper comes, whom I shall send to you from the Father, the Spirit of truth who proceeds from the Father, He will testify of Me. And you also will bear witness, because you have been with Me from the beginning**"* (John 15:26, 27). Jesus stated the apostles' truth in our passage (Acts 5:32). Jesus continued, *"**However, when He, the Spirit of truth, has come, He will guide you into all truth; for He will not speak on His own authority, but whatever He hears**

Part Four: Apostle's Restatement: The Unexplainable

He will speak; and He will tell you things to come. He will glorify Me, for He will take of what is Mine and declare it to you" (John 16:13-14).

Since the Holy Spirit's driving passion is to give witness to Jesus, and the Holy Spirit fills us, would we not conclude this will also be our passion? If God moves within our lives, we can expect a radical upset in religious practices and traditions. We can expect God to alter our physical lives to achieve His will. Most certainly, our lives will have one single passion - Jesus!

Acts 5:22

DIVINE PROTECTION

"But when the officers came and did not find them in the prison, they returned and reported" (Acts 5:22).

Luke emphasized the apostles' imprisonment in several ways, consistently referring to it in the narrative. In the first persecution, he mentioned the arrest and detention of the apostles only once, excusing their placement in prison because of the lateness of the day (Acts 4:3). He downplayed the Sanhedrin, sending for the two apostles, saying, **"They set them in the midst"** (Acts 4:7). Luke fixated on the apostles' interrogation and their continual focus on Jesus, making the imprisonment minor.

In Luke's second view of the continued persecution, he focused more on the apostle's imprisonment. The Sanhedrin had the apostles arrested and put in the **"common prison"** (Acts 5:18). Their arrest set the stage for Divine intervention, which opened the **"prison"** doors (Acts 5:19). While the apostles obeyed the angel of the Lord's instruction, the council sent officers to the **"prison"** to bring them for the interrogation (Acts 5:21). However, when the officers arrived at the **"prison,"** finding the apostles gone, they returned to the council with

Part Four: Apostle's Restatement: The Unexplainable

their report (Acts 5:22). The officers described the ***"prison"*** as secure, with the guards standing before the doors as if nothing was disturbed. This report thoroughly perplexed the council. Then someone else reported, ***"Look, the men whom you put in prison are standing in the temple and teaching the people"*** (Acts 5:25)! In this second phase of persecution, Luke referred to the apostles' imprisonment six times.

Luke uses three Greek words to describe imprisonment to support his focus. This second persecution begins with a description of the emotional upset and jealousy motiving the high priest and the Sadducees (Acts 5:17), resulting in the orders to place the apostles ***"in the common prison"*** (Acts 5:18). The Greek word ***"prison"*** is "teresis," used three times in the New Testament. Luke used "teresis" in the first persecution scene. ***"And they laid hands on them, and put them in custody*** (teresis) ***until the next day, for it was already evening"*** (Acts 4:3). Paul also used this Greek term to challenge us. Whatever state we are in when God calls us, we should be content to live in that state. The one thing that should characterize our living is ***"keeping*** (teresis) ***the commandments of God"*** (1 Corinthians 7:19). Paul said that this is what matters. The Greek word "teresis" comes from the Greek noun "tereo," meaning "to keep watch," and describes a place of "keeping." It means "attention, vigilance, watch, observation, preservation, care, or custody." "Teresis" appears in the New Testament three times (Acts 4:3; 5:18; 1 Corinthians 7:19).

As Luke describes the activities surrounding the apostle's prison experience, he changes Greek words. "Phuake" is the Greek word he uses to introduce this word in describing the angel of the Lord's action, ***"opened the prison*** (phuake) ***doors"*** (Acts 5:19). He reflected on Israel's council being called together with the elders of the children of Israel. The purpose of their gathering was to interrogate the apostles. ***"But when*** *the officers came and did not find them in the prison* (phuake), *they returned and reported"* (Acts 5:22). *"Look, the men whom you put in prison* (phuake) *are standing in the temple and teaching the people"* (Acts 5:25). "Phuake" refers to a place where someone is watched, guarded, or kept in custody, such as a prison." The word appears three times in this account (Acts 5:19, 22, 25).

Luke used the Greek word "phuake" forty-seven times in the New Testament in both positive and negative surroundings. The shepherds played a role in the celebration of Christ's birth. Luke wrote, *"Now there were in the same country shepherds living out in the fields, keeping watch* (phuake) *over their flock by night"* (Luke 2:8). During the ministry of Jesus, He went to the mountains to pray and sent the disciples in a boat to Bethsaida. The boat was in a storm in the middle of the Sea of Galilee in the evening. Mark wrote, *"Now about the fourth watch* (phuake) *of the night He came to them, walking on the sea, and would have passed them by"* (Mark 6:48).

John wrote in the Book of Revelation concerning the end of the ages. He tells of an angel coming down from heaven with great authority. A light shone from the angel's presence, and glory illuminated the entire earth. He cried with a mighty voice, *"Babylon the great is fallen, is fallen, and has become a dwelling place of demons, a prison* (phuake) *for every foul spirit, and a cage* (phuake) *for every unclean and hated bird"* (Revelation 18:2)! He continued to explain the mission of another angel who had the key to the bottomless pit. Satan is bound in this pit for one thousand years while the saints reign with Christ. However, *"when the thousand years have expired, Satan will be released from his prison* (phuake)*"* (Revelation 20:7). Peter gives us mystical insight into the death and burial of Jesus. He said that Jesus, through the power of the Holy Spirit, *"went and preached to the spirits in prison* (phuake)*, who formerly were disobedient, when once the Divine longsuffering waited in the days of Noah, while the ark was being prepared"* (1 Peter 3:19-20).

"Phuake" is the most frequently used Greek word for ***"prison."*** Many of the Scripture references concerning Herod Antipas' imprisonment of John the Baptist used this Greek word (Matthew 14:3,10). Luke uses "phuake" five times to describe Peter's third arrest and imprisonment (Acts 12:4, 5, 6, 10, 17). Herod the King killed James with a sword and saw that it pleased the Jews; therefore, he captured Peter and imprisoned him (phuake). "Phuake" is often used in settings with established boundaries. We see this clearly in ***"the fourth watch** (phuake) **of the night"*** *(*Mark 6:48) and the shepherds ***"keeping watch*** (phuake) ***over their flock by night"*** (Luke 2:8).

These Greek words, "teresis" and "phuake," can be interchanged as we do many English words. However, "teresis" is focused on "watching." "Phuake" focuses on the place where someone or something is watched. When Paul refers to ***"keeping*** (teresis) ***the commandments of God,"*** it would not be proper to use "phuake" (1 Corinthians 7:19). We must guard the translation principle, which requires we always maintain the primary meaning of the Greek word.

The third Greek word Luke used in this second persecution is "desmoterion." When the high priest and those with him called the council together, with all the elders of the children of Israel, they ***"sent to the prison*** (desmoterion) ***to have them brought"*** (Acts 5:21). Luke repeats this word in the report of those who retrieve the apostles. In their message to the Sanhedrin, they said, ***"Indeed we found the prison*** (desmoterion) ***shut securely, and the guards standing outside before the doors; but when we opened them, we found no one inside"*** (Acts 5:23)! This Greek word comes from the noun "desmoo," meaning "to bind." In this context, it refers to a place of bondage.

There are two other places in the New Testament where the writers use "desmoterion." Matthew writes, *"And when John had heard in prison* (desmoterion) *about the works of Christ, he sent two of his disciples and said to Him, 'Are You the Coming One, or do we look for another'"* (Matthew 11:2-3)? This word's last place is the Philippian jailer's salvation story. The magistrates put Paul and Silas in prison due to the complaint of the slave girl's owner, and Paul was the instrument of her deliverance from a demonic spirit. The magistrates put Paul and Silas in the inner prison with their feet in the stocks, but these men prayed and sang hymns to God. *"Suddenly there was a great earthquake, so that the foundations of the prison* (desmoterion) *were shaken; and immediately all the doors were opened and everyone's chains were loosed"* (Acts 16:26).

One of the strong contrasts in our passage is the bondage inflicted by the demonic forces and the freedom found in our resurrected Lord. One could make a strong case for this contrast in the Book of Acts. We see the Divine miracles occurring through the apostles. In the context of our passage, the ministry spread to surrounding cities. *"Also a multitude gathered from the surrounding cities to Jerusalem, bringing sick people and those who were tormented by unclean spirits, and they were all healed"* (Acts 5:16). The resurrected Lord, through the apostles, marched into a demonic-dominated territory and liberated those held in bondage.

We see the same contrast in the message delivered by the apostles compared to the message of the high priest and Sadducees. Consistently in their message, the apostles propose "the resurrected Jesus!" Their emphasis suggests liberation from the bondage of death. They proclaimed the purpose of Jesus' death, resurrection, and ascension *"to give repentance to Israel and forgiveness of sins"* (Acts 5:31), a message of liberation from the bondage of guilt and defeat. While the high

Part Four: Apostle's Restatement: The Unexplainable

priest and Sadducees deny any such freedom from death in the resurrection of Jesus, they acknowledge the message that Jesus brought nothing but guilt into their lives (Acts 5:28).

This contrast is not limited merely to the spiritual realm, but the physical demonstrates it. The apostles' imprisonment becomes a constant threat and occurrence throughout the Book of Acts. Establishing domination and control over the physical lives of the apostles is the entrapment of bondage. The leaders of Israel consistently threatened the apostles, and the Apostle Paul experienced the same. But God always overrides all such bondage, and He is creative in His liberation.

Luke gives us three Greek words in the second phase of the early Church's persecution. Let me remind you again that the primary meaning of each word must be maintained within the setting of its use. "Teresis" focuses primarily on "watching or guarding." "Phuake" focuses on "where someone or something is watched." "Desmoterion" focuses on "binding or bondage." Let's investigate the use of these three words in the context of our passage.

Behold
"teresis"

Luke introduces the contrast between bondage and freedom with the Greek term "teresis." This term focuses on the watching or guarding element. The leaders of Israel carefully watched the apostles and the early Church. The release of the apostles from this second phase of imprisonment was to watch them. Gamaliel, a highly respected teacher, appealed to the Sanhedrin. He recalled several people who started movements that merely dissipated on their own. Gamaliel recommended watching this apostle group and seeing what happens (Acts 5:33-42). Is there any doubt that the devil and his demonic forces are watching us? In the spiritual warfare of the hour, we are stalked! The devil notices every step we take toward Christ and records it.

Peter warns us about our adversary: ***"Be sober, be vigilant; because your adversary the devil walks about like a roaring lion, seeking whom he may devour. Resist him, steadfast in the faith, knowing that the same sufferings are experienced by your brotherhood in the world"*** (1 Peter 5:8-9). The devil is stalking you. He watches you for any sign of weakness, every vulnerable part of your life, that he might bring you into bondage. You are under surveillance by the demonic forces who desire to imprison you. These warnings are not to scare you but to alert you. Peter gives us this message following the admonition to ***"humble yourselves under the mighty hand of God, that He may exalt you in due time, casting all your care upon Him, for He cares for you"*** (1 Peter 5:6-7). Our awareness of such stalking should increase our dependency on Jesus.

James gives us the same warning and instruction. ***"Therefore submit to God. Resist the devil, and he will flee from you. Draw near to God, and He will draw near to you"*** (James 4:7-8). Both Peter and James insist that we must ***"resist."*** How do we do that? I do not focus on the devil and his "watching" but must ***"submit to God."*** The answer is in the liberating person of Jesus! The answer is not focusing on the devil but focusing on Jesus. Allow the same awareness of the devil's stalking to bring you into intimacy with Jesus. He is our only protection; in Him, we find liberty.

Bondage
"desmoterion"

The Greek word "desmoterion" brings us to the devil's entrapment level. Bondage is the focus of this word. Is the devil not stocking you to get you under his control? In our passage and throughout the New Testament, the contrast is the devil's bondage and Jesus' freedom. Listen to the words of Paul. **"Stand fast therefore in the liberty by which Christ has made us free, and do not be entangled again with a yoke of bondage"** (Galatians 5:1). Paul referred to the law of the Old Covenant that established the boundaries of bondage, which Christ fulfilled and gave us liberty. Paul contrasted the two covenants: **"the one from Mount Sinai which gives birth to bondage,"** however, the other is from the heart of God, **"Jerusalem,"** which gives us freedom (Galatians 4:24-26).

The apostles propose an amazing problem for the high priest and Sadducees in their freedom in our passage. The authority of this council does not control them. When the officers sent to retrieve the apostles from prison, they returned to report, **"Indeed we found the prison** (desmoterion) **shut securely, and the guards standing outside before the doors; but when we opened them, we found no one inside"** (Acts 5:23)! The Sanhedrin could not contain the apostles within the boundaries of their control. Jesus described it in the illustration of putting new wine into old wineskins (Matthew 9:17). Putting the new wine in the old wineskins will expand and break the bond! Prison cannot hold the new wine of the Spirit in bondage!

The devil is stalking us, carefully watching for an opportunity to bring us within the boundaries of his established control. The leaders of Israel could not set boundaries to contain the apostles. They could not master the apostles with the threat of death and could not be controlled by their need to survive. The leaders of Israel could not master the apostles with the fear of suffering; after beating them, **"they departed from the presence of the council, rejoicing that they were counted worthy to suffer shame for His name"** (Acts 5:41). The apostles lived

Divine Protection | Acts 5:22

within the boundaries of the Person of Jesus! They were bound to Him alone, free from all other controls.

Base
"phuake"

In the final Greek word, "phuake," Luke used to focus not on watching or stalking a person, putting boundaries of bondage around him, but concentrated on the prison bondage. "Phuake" is used 47 times in the New Testament, referring to where someone or something is watched, guarded, or kept in custody, such as a prison. Luke used this word to describe the occupation of the shepherds who were *"living out in the fields, keeping watch* (phuake) *over their flock by night"* (Luke 2:8). Mark used "phuake" to describe a time. *"Now about the fourth watch* (phuake) *of the night He came to them, walking on the sea, and would have passed them by"* (Mark 6:48). The typical use of the New Testament word refers to prison, as seen in our passage. The officers sent to retrieve the apostles *"did not find them in the prison* (phuake)*"* (Acts 5:22). The explanation was given earlier by Luke: *"But at night an angel of the Lord opened the prison* (phuake) *doors and brought them out"* (Acts 5:19). When the officers returned to the leaders of Israel, they reported, *"Look, the men whom you put in prison* (phuake) *are standing in the temple and teaching the people"* (Acts 5:25)!

As quoted above, John used the word "phuake" in Revelation. *"And he cried mightily with a strong voice, saying, 'Babylon the great is fallen, is fallen, and has become a dwelling place of the demons, a prison* (phuake) *for every foul spirit, and a cage* (phuake) *for every unclean and hated bird'"* (Revelation 18:2). John continued, *"Now when the thousand years have expired, Satan will*

Part Four: Apostle's Restatement: The Unexplainable

be released from his prison (phuake)*"* (Revelation 20:7). Peter used "phuake" to describe Jesus preaching during His burial time, "***by whom also He went and preached to the spirits in prison*** (phuake)*"* (1 Peter 3:19).

We can legitimately say that the devil's purpose is to stalk us, bring us into bondage, and imprison us in hell. However, there is a present-tense reality to His imprisonment. There are a dozen forms of the future prison in our present day. Many experience emotional captivity, physical incarceration, mental internment, abusive detention, religious imprisonment, and so on. Many feel trapped with no hope of release. BUT the devil is a liar! It appears the door is locked, BUT it is not. You and I are free to walk out of our apparent bondage. Jesus invaded every place of bondage and made a way out; He is the Way (John 14:6). Let us proclaim it long and loud, "There is freedom in Christ!"

Acts 5:23
SEEKING / FINDING

"saying, 'Indeed we found the prison shut securely, and the guards standing outside before the doors; but when we opened them, we found no one inside!'" (Acts 5:23).

    The drama of our passage is relatively simple. The high priest and the Sadducees with him are filled with indignation (Acts 5:17). They are greatly disturbed by the impact of the early Church, specifically, the constant use of Jesus' name. In glorifying Jesus, they feel the apostles are condemning their leadership. They said it as if they **"intend to bring this Man's blood on us"** (Acts 5:28). These leaders imprisoned Peter and John for the second time and included all of the apostles, placing them in the **"common prison"** (Acts 5:18). Gathering the following day with all the elders of Israel, they sent officers to bring the prisoners before the council.

    The officers had a single task to retrieve the apostles from the prison and bring them to the council. However, they discovered the apostles were not there when they arrived at the prison. Luke carefully describes the officers' reaction and reports to the Sanhedrin. **"But when the officers came and did not find** (heurisko) **them in the prison, they returned** *and reported, saying, 'Indeed we found* (heurisko) **the prison shut securely, and the guards standing outside before the doors; but when we opened them, we found** (heurisko) **no one inside'"** (Acts 5:22-23)!

"Heurisko" is a Greek word translated as *"find"* or *"found."* It is used by Luke three times in our passage, once to describe the officer's mission given by the Sanhedrin and twice in their report to Sanhedrin. The core idea of "heurisko" is "to discover" or "to perceive or learn by experience." The complementary word is "seek," the context of finding. "Seek" and "find" repeatedly appear in the Scriptures. A unique experience of finding without seeking is possible. However, even when "seeking" is hidden, it bleeds into the reality of finding. The tenet farmer was not seeking a treasure as he was plowing but discovered wealth beyond his imagination (Matthew 13:44). But one leaves the story wondering if seeking something better for his family wasn't the motivation for plowing the field. Jesus clarifies this seeking in the next verse relating to the Parable of the Pearl of Great Price (Matthew 13:45-46). He describes the kingdom of heaven as a merchant seeking beautiful pearls and finding one pearl of great price!

Perhaps, in reality, there is no occasion when one finds what he has not sought. While we may not find what we seek, we are always seeking. The officers brought the high priest, council, and all the elders of Israel fully into the presence of a miracle of God. These leaders heard of miracle after miracle accomplished by the name of Jesus. They experienced the miracle of the lame beggar, which they declared as **"a notable miracle has been done through them is evident to all who dwell in Jerusalem, and we cannot deny it"** (Acts 4:16). Now they unwillingly participate in a miracle of God. They placed the apostles in prison and thought they were still there, yet they were not there but at the temple, continuing to preach in Jesus' name. Is there a hidden seeking in these arrogant leaders that continually brings them to a reality they do not want to embrace? Could it be that they are not satisfied with what they have become? Is God not trying to bring them to a new place of finding?

Do we not desire to go beyond where we are? Our most basic seeking expresses the deep longing of our soul. Do we not have a hidden selfish desire to seek a better job, car, or home? The craving of my inner heart is beyond the mere physical things of life. Through prevenient grace, God draws me into the miracle of finding! I then can discover Christ! It is amazing! Even despite their resistance, the leaders of Israel were always finding Jesus. Much to their dismay, the apostles confronted them with Jesus in every seeking action.

Movement Term

"Zeteo" is the common Greek word translated as "seek," used 117 times in the New Testament and 83 times in the Gospel accounts. This verb means "to seek," "search for," "investigate," "study," "consider," or "strive for something," used in the sense of seeking worldly and sacred things. The prefix "ana," meaning "up," is added twice to intensify the seeking. "Anazeteo" means "to seek carefully or diligently" and always relates to seeking human beings (Luke 2:44-45; Acts 11:25). In a few passages, the prefix "ek" is added, "ekzeteo," signifying "to seek out," "after," or "to search for." In thirteen passages in the New Testament, the prefix "epi" is added, "epizeteo," giving direction to the seeking with the idea of "toward." It is used for seeking after or demanding and desiring.

None of these words are in our passage, but they apply. The high priest, members of the council, and all the elders of the children of Israel are definitely "epizeteo" concerning the apostles. They focus on this group of men leading the

Part Four: Apostle's Restatement: The Unexplainable

Christian community in proclaiming Jesus' name. The apostles are "ekzeteo," evidenced by sending the officers to bring them to the council. The intensive "anazeteo" applies to the search expanding to the temple where the apostles teach. The leaders of Israel's indignation expresses their emotion and intensity, and Luke emphasizes that indignation is why they put the apostles in prison at the beginning of our story (Acts 5:17).

This information about seeking should convince us that seeking comes with personal involvement. Determination and direct intent, motivated by inner desire, move a person to seek. Luke highlights this personal involvement in his story revealing the leaders of Israel's drive to end the apostles' actions. In the first persecution scene, their capture of Peter and John directly relates to the priests, the captain of the temple, and the Sadducees. They are *"greatly disturbed that they taught the people and preached in Jesus the resurrection from the dead"* (Acts 4:2). Their fear of the people of Jerusalem was their only limitation (Acts 5:21). In the second phase of persecution, their "indignation" that the apostles continued to preach in Jesus' name motivated them (Acts 5:17). There is some indication in the Scriptures that people may become so dominated by the evil that they no longer have the capacity to seek the truth. For instance, Jesus started His ministry by preaching close to John the Baptist on the Jordan River in Judea. When Herod imprisoned John, Jesus shifted His focus from Judea to Galilee. He spent most of His earthy ministry *"in the regions of Zebulun and Naphtali"* (Matthew 4:13), a fulfillment of prophecy quoted by Matthew (Matthew 4:15-16). Matthew's description of the population of this area is most intriguing, and he quoted the prophet Isaiah (9:2).

"The people who sat in darkness have seen a great light.
And upon those who sat in the region and shadow of death
Light has dawned" (Matthew 4:16).

The emphasis of his statement is significant. The grammar gives us insight into truth. The Greek word "laos," translated as *people,* is in the nominative case. The Greek word "kathemai," translated as *sat,* is a participle (a verb used as a noun), also in the nominative. Therefore, the sentence's subject is "the act of the people setting." Matthew highlights the "setting people." The phrase *in darkness* is a locative dative indicating where this occurred. The people of the region of Galilee were surrounded and immersed in darkness.

"The people who walked in darkness" (Isaiah 9:2) is a quotation from the Hebrew language of the Old Testament. It seems Matthew changed the word *walked* to *sat* to intensify their condition. Sitting in darkness suggests the conquering force of the darkness. The Greek word "kathemai," translated as *sat,* is the same Greek word used to reference Jesus seated at the Father's right hand. It suggests the image of a person or item of great authority sitting in a place of great authority. It is in the middle voice indicating "personal preference." The suggested image is that the darkness has so encompassed the people that it has conquered them, and they embrace it as their chosen desire.

Is this the inner state of the leaders of Israel? Perhaps they have lost their ability to seek, yet God is seeking them! Jesus fulfilled the prophecy, for He is the light who has come to them. Our passage proves this truth. Perhaps the leaders of Israel are no longer capable of seeking truth, but the One who is Truth seeks them! The resurrected Lord manipulated their circumstances; light came again to their lives. The angel of the Lord delivered the apostles from the imprisonment imposed by the high priest and Sadducees. The message resounds in the temple again in the freshness of the resurrected Lord's power.

I can make you a promise based on the Scriptures! There is nowhere you can go that Jesus cannot find you (Psalms 139:7-12). Perhaps we do not seek Him as we ought, and the intensity of our search may not be as strong as the act of finding demands.

Part Four: Apostle's Restatement: The Unexplainable

But regardless of where we are, our resurrected Jesus seeks us. He consistently moves into the heart of our existence. He will find you!

Motive Term

No one seeks without reason. There is always a driving motive at the heart of seeking and finding. One must ask the question: "What do you want?" Let it be the driving force that causes you to seek when you discover that! The council in our passage is far too short-sighted. The high priest and the Sadducees limited their desires to eliminate the name of Jesus. In both of the interrogations of the apostles, their only demand was **"not to teach in this name"** (Acts 5:28). There is no concern regarding miracles, assemblies, or compassionate ministry. Instead of seeking to eliminate the proclamation of His name, they should participate in acclaiming it.

When Jesus rode the donkey into Jerusalem on Palm Sunday, the crowds began to rejoice and praise God. They witnessed the mighty works of God accomplished through Jesus. The chant of praise was so strong it resounded throughout Jerusalem, upsetting some Pharisees. They called out to Jesus, requesting Him to rebuke the crowd for their outburst of praise. Jesus said, **"I tell you that if these should keep silent, the stones would immediately cry out"** (Luke 19:40). The leaders of Israel did not realize the necessary depth of proclaiming Jesus' name.

In the creation story, the Trinity God formed man from the dust of the ground and breathed the breath of life into him. The climax of this act of God is the statement, **"and man became a living being"** (Genesis 2:7). The Hebrew word "nepes," translated as **"living,"** gives content to the heart of humanity. This term focuses on "desire" or "appetite" and is closely related to the meaning "throat." In the Old Testament, "nepes" denotes simple hunger (Hosea 9:4; Deuteronomy 23:24-25). Solomon gave an interesting proverb regarding man's appetite, saying that the appetite (nepes) of the worker works for him. His mouth drives him on (Proverbs 16:23). The Holy Spirit used this Hebrew word to describe God's creation of man's heart. Man is an "appetite," one huge craving. He has an inner hunger and desire that continually motivates and drives him. This craving is for intimacy with Jesus. The Trinity God placed everything I crave in Jesus. All I need is Jesus!

Once again, Jesus confronts the leaders of Israel with what they crave. He proclaims the message not with mere words but in the power of His resurrected presence. The Gospel accounts tell how Jesus' ministry shook their world with His message and miracles. He again confronts them with the same message and presence in His resurrection. What they crave is in this name, and they want it silenced.

You and I are "living cravings!" Every satisfaction other than Jesus only relieves us from our soul's deep craving. Could we go to the depth of our lives and discover what we want? It is Jesus!

Mandate Term

The boundaries of "hepes" frame our being. The throat, appetite, and craving demand we seek, a command continually yelling in our ears. But we must understand that it is not God ushering the command. "Seeking: is not one of the many commandments that God gives us. The commandment comes from the core of our beings, the nature of our existence. We cannot help ourselves and are a living "craving!"

We see the "living craving" in our passage. You will quickly discover this truth if you start on the surface and follow

Part Four: Apostle's Restatement: The Unexplainable

the desires. The officers go to the prison to get the apostles, commanded by the council. They cannot accomplish their task because the apostles are no longer there. They return to the council to report the missing apostles with no excuses. They were seeking but could not find the apostles! Then someone came and told them, ***"Look, the men whom you put in prison are standing in the temple and teaching the people!"*** (Acts 5:25). Again, the officers seek to bring the apostles before the council because the council commanded them. Why is the council seeking the apostles? Their seeking is directly related to Jesus, the name the apostles proclaimed. The council is seeking Jesus one way or the other!

Jesus proclaimed this repeatedly, seeking in story form. The Parable of the Hidden Treasure is the story of a poor tenant farmer seeking to plow his field for the sake of a coming crop. But is that what he was seeking? Is there, not something hidden beneath the surface of his life and the soil he is plowing that he wants? It is the hidden treasure (Matthew 13:44). The Parable of the Pearl of Great Price is a story of a merchant who buys and sells pearls to turn a profit. But is that what he is seeking? He may deal with many pearls in his life, but the cry of his being is for the one great pearl (Matthew 13:45).

The leaders of Israel need to clarify what they seek; they seek Jesus. Luke expressed it in the word ***"indignation"*** (Acts 5:17), a translation of the Greek word "zelou" focused on "jealousy." "Zelou" gives the sense of "a greedy or prideful longing for something that belongs to another." The leaders of Israel want what they see in the disciples, which is the message of the Book of Acts. It is the reality of the resurrected Jesus indwelling and merging with humanity. A person only has one craving: that Jesus fills them, and they are intimate and merged with Him.

When one person is filled, intimate, and merged with Jesus, his life stimulates and increases the craving in the hearts of others. Why did the leaders of Israel find the apostles an irritation? It was because the apostles demonstrated the intimacy God created within the leaders of Israel. The presence of Jesus within the apostles continually pointed to the deep desires of the leaders. That is the very heart of "witnessing!" It is who we are in Him!

Acts 5:23

SECURITY

"saying, 'Indeed we found the prison shut securely, and the guards standing outside before the doors; but when we opened them, we found no one inside!'" (Acts 5:23).

Security is the driving desire at the core of every human being. Security calms fears, relieves tensions, and establishes joy. Without security, a person experiences stress, anxiety, and terror. Security in each individual varies; the list can be long and a combination of many things. It only takes one thing on the list to be insecure for a person to feel insecure. The single factor between security and insecurity seems to be "self." "Self-confidence" is the underlying culprit. Self-security depends on good health, education, mental sureness, personal relationships, and financial well-being.

Luke highlights security in our passage when he speaks about the Israel leaders' ability to control and dominate the apostles. The officers were sent to bring the apostles before the council returned with this report. **"Indeed we found the prison shut securely** (asphaleia)**, and the guards standing outside before the doors"** (Acts 5:23). The Greek word "asphaleia" means "safe, secure, firm, security, or safety." This exact Greek word is only used three times in the New Testament (Luke 1:4; Acts 5:23; 1 Thessalonians 5:3); however, the word group occurs fifteen times. It signifies the certainty or stability of something (Hebrews 6:19) or the guarding or safekeeping of a person or thing (Acts 5:23). In a figurative sense, it refers to objective truth (Acts 21:34; 22:30; 25:26). Paul used the watchwords of **"peace and security"** (1 Thessalonians 5:3). He emphasized the security of the believers as he wrote to them (Philippians 3:1). Peter summoned the Jewish listeners to **"know assuredly"** (asphalos) **that God has made this Jesus, whom you crucified, both Lord and Christ"** (Acts 2:36). That is secure knowledge based on the preceding proof from the Scriptures (Acts 2:34-35).

Luke highlights the security issue, as seen in the importance of this Greek word and the prepositional phrase in which it is placed. Many translations combined this prepositional phrase into a single word, **"securely."** A literal translation of the phrase would be "in (en) all (pas) security (asphaleia)." That increases the intensity of the idea of security in the passage. The Greek word "en" means certainty and security in its emphasis upon "fixed or remaining." It expresses the primary meaning of "rest," standing between "into" (eis) and "from" (ek). Each suggests a motion or change of location, while "in" emphasizes "remaining in place." The Greek word "pas" is translated as "all." It includes the idea of oneness, totality, or the whole. In our passage, "all" modifies **"securely,"** not **"prison."** Again, the officers' report signified the completeness of the security they found.

Hearing of the apostles' escape, the leaders of Israel became insecure, a distinct point Luke highlights. The high priest, the temple captain, and the chief priests **"wondered what the outcome would be"** (Acts 5:24). An additional word in the Greek language included in other translations of the Scriptures is **"they were greatly perplexed"** (diapareo). This verb is in

Part Four: Apostle's Restatement: The Unexplainable

the imperfect tense, portraying an action in process or a state of being that occurred in the past without assessing the action's completion. "Diapareo" is contracted from "dia," meaning "through," and "apareo," which means "to be perplexed." The leaders were thoroughly perplexed, meaning they hesitated greatly. They were in doubt and quickly forgot when another officer reported that the apostles were in the temple, teaching the people (Acts 5:25). What is Luke trying to explain with this strong emphasis on security?

False Security

One purpose of this consistent reference to security is to highlight the false security of the leaders. They founded their security on their power and demonstrated it in their control over the circumstances of themselves and others. While the Romans conquered all of Palestine, the Sadducees felt secure in the arrangements they had established with them. The high priest, Sadducees, and Pharisees could continue their governmental structure, the Sanhedrin. They oversaw the temple activities with minor adjustments, and Jewish life continued as usual.

The Sanhedrin had their "system" in place; it was their security. The high priest officiated over this system. It was his responsibility to see that the Jewish system was enforced and the people completed the duties of the temple and the Law of Moses. He oversaw the regular handling of sacrifices and offerings and was in charge of the temple and its finances. The Sanhedrin, located in Jerusalem, was the supreme judicial council of Judaism with 71 members and was the court that figured prominently in the passion narrative during Jesus' trial. This judicial court was now investigating and persecuting the apostles and the growing Christian church.

Such a system as the Sanhedrin must guard and protect

itself for survival. Daily life, religious structure, and financial stability were secure within that system, and a vital part was the oral interpretation of the law. The Pharisees felt confident in this interpretation. Jesus threatened that security, not only with His teaching but with His lifestyle. He consistently revealed the hypocrisy of the Pharisees' belief structure. In their minds, they had no choice but to crucify Jesus. ***"Now it was Caiaphas who advised the Jews that it was expedient that one man should die for the people"*** (John 18:14). One Man must not be allowed to upset the system or their security.

You would think Jesus' death would bring a renewed sense of security to the leaders in Jerusalem. But the resurrection disturbed the heart of their system. They could tolerate resurrection as a discussion in a theological classroom, but the resurrected Jesus working miracles through His apostles and altering life experiences was too radical for the system. They could not abide the growth of the early Church and the constant proclamation of Jesus' name. Jesus completely transformed a lame beggar in the temple and sent shockwaves throughout the system of Judaism (Acts 3). Now multitudes of people came from all around Jerusalem to experience the power of God from the resurrected Jesus (Acts 5:16). The presence of Jesus in the apostles' lives brought condemnation to the system responsible for His crucifixion.

The Jews found their security in their system. But what about us? Have we not established our own systems? We must be keenly aware Jesus threatens our system. Can Jesus plant Himself amid our system without bringing upheaval? When He arrives, everything unaligned with His nature begins to rebel. Can the status quo be maintained when He is present? Life naturally develops a structure in which to live. We establish patterns; our relationships demand a system. The issue is not whether our system is right or wrong; the problem is when that becomes our security instead of Jesus! When we rely on our established structure instead of His Person, we worship the creature instead of the Creator.

Samuel, the prophet, was old, and his sons were wicked. The elders of Israel came to Samuel demanding ***"a king to judge us like all the nations"*** (1 Samuel 8:5). Their demand disturbed Samuel, and he prayed to the Lord. God told Samuel, ***"Heed the voice of the people in all that they say to you; for they have not rejected you, but they have rejected Me, that I should not reign over them"*** (1 Samuel 8:7). The people of Israel did not find their security in God. Israel knew the world around them found security in their established system, and they wanted such a system. Through the prophet Samuel, God warned Israel of their foolishness. Their approach would demand sacrifice and would ultimately provide false security. God's care is proper security, and we find safety in only Him!

Can you see this pattern in your life? We work night and day building our systems like a great wall of protection. Then a crisis comes, and we discover the crumbling decay of our security. Listen to the admonishment of Jesus. ***"For what profit is it to a man if he gains the whole world, and loses his own soul? Or what will a man give in exchange for his soul"*** (Matthew 16:26)? Jesus addressed this issue in the Parable of the Rich Fool (Luke 12:16-21). A farmer's ground produced so many crops that he constructed new and bigger barns to hold them. He said, ***"Soul, you have many goods laid up for many years; take your ease; eat, drink, and be merry"*** (Luke 12:19). That night, God required his soul. We trust Jesus for our eternal destiny but do not want to trust Him for our finances. We depend on Him to save us but do not want to rely on Him for our daily living. We want Him to deliver us in the moment of tragedy but do not allow Him to reign in all circumstances. We have substituted ourselves for His sovereign greatness! Our systems are false securities!

Fixed Security

Luke contrasts the false security of the leaders of Israel with the firm security of the apostles. The guards stood outside the secured prison, yet an angel of the Lord miraculously removed the apostles. Upon arrival, the officers could not find the prisoners. The Sadducees did not know their security was insecure. Not believing in the angelic hosts, they did not calculate an intervention of Divine power! They saw this Divine movement of God in miracle after miracle they could not deny. Yet it was simply not a part of their system.

In both interrogations, the apostles answered the demands of the Sanhedrin the same. The leaders of Israel wanted the apostles to obey their security system. Each time the apostles responded, **"We ought to obey God rather than men"** (Acts 5:29; see Acts 4:19). Their security system was contained in a Person! The Trinity God raised Jesus, whom the leaders of Israel murdered by hanging Him on a tree (Acts 5:30). This same Jesus sits at the right hand of God as Prince and Savior (Acts 5:31). The apostles' security system was not a manufactured structure to control circumstances. They trusted only in the resurrected Jesus!

The testimony of Peter and John in the first interrogation caused the leaders of Israel to marvel (Acts 4:13). They quoted the Old Testament Psalms. **"This is the stone which was rejected by you builders, which has become the chief cornerstone"** (Acts 4:11; see Psalms 118:22). Jesus is the security of the building. Everything in the system must rest on Him! Then Peter said, **"Nor is there salvation in any other, for there is no other name under heaven given among men by which we must be saved"** (Acts 4:12). Our safety is secure in this single Person! Outside of Jesus, there is no security.

The apostles were not alone in finding their security in

Part Four: Apostle's Restatement: The Unexplainable

Jesus; the early Church aligned themselves with this reality. As the persecution came to the members of the early Church, they immediately went to prayer. Their prayer began with, **"Lord, You are God"** (Acts 4:24), a translation of the Greek word "despotes." Our security is in the sovereign Lord **"who made heaven and earth and the sea, and all that is in them"** (Acts 4:24). They quoted David from the Old Testament, who pictured the world's systems as "snorting horses" (Acts 4:25-26; see Psalms 2:-2). The kings of the earth strutted around as if they were secure in their self-made systems, only to find themselves fulfilling the design and purpose of God (Acts 4:27-28). Our security is in Him!

Luke described the attitude of the early Church following Pentecost. **"Neither did anyone say that any of the things he possessed was his own"** (Acts 4:32). Incredible generosity permeated the activities of the early Church. No one lacked anything (Acts 4:34) due to their security in Jesus. When anyone among them violated this trust, they did not survive. Ananias and Sapphira lied to the Holy Spirit and the church, and their lie was rooted in the false security of their system rather than Jesus. The news of their death spread everywhere. Everyone understood to join the early Church meant placing your trust in Jesus, your only security. Some individuals did not dare join the church because of this spiritual reality (Acts 4:13).

The leaders of Israel focused their security on their religious, political, and financial systems, only to find them insecure. The apostles focused their security on Jesus and found He never failed them. In our days of uncertainty, we face a clear decision. We live in anxiety, tension, and worry. Our financial security is threatened; our life system is undermined. Is it an awakening for us as it was for the leaders of Israel? There is no security outside of Jesus!

Forever Security

Eternal security was bleeding into the actions and attitudes of the apostles. They never raised the issue of their retirement security, and they never discussed it within the continued ministry in future years. They did not seem to be concerned about building religious structures. No one maneuvered for authority positions, and their attitudes were nonchalant and casual regarding these issues. Their only concern was maintaining their trust and security in Jesus during their persecution. They prayed, *"Now, Lord, look on their threats, and grant to Your servants that with all boldness they may speak Your word, by stretching out Your hand to heal, and that signs and wonders may be done through the name of Your holy Servant Jesus"* (Acts 4:29-30). Did you notice the number of times the pronoun *"Your"* appears? *"Your servants," "Your word," "Your hand,"* and *"Your holy Servant Jesus"* give expression to their concern. Their trust was in the sovereign Lord, their security, and this trust would never be broken!

The early Church placed their present, future, and eternal lives in the hands of Jesus, which was the reason they could so easily risk their lives. Luke raises this issue in the final paragraph of this chapter (Acts 5:33-42). The leaders of Israel were furious over the apostles' steadfast commitment to Jesus, and they plotted to kill them. However, Gamaliel, a teacher of the law, reasoned with them. He based his appeal on the sovereignty of God, citing several examples of individuals who found popularity among groups of people. These groups quickly scattered and came to nothing. Gamaliel argued if this Christian group is of God, we cannot overthrow it, but if it is of man, it will die on its own. Is he not admitting lasting security is only within the power of our sovereign God?

Part Four: Apostle's Restatement: The Unexplainable

History records that Rome overthrew the Jewish nation, which had placed its security in its system. In just a few short years, Rome destroyed Jerusalem, and Israel ceased to be a nation. The Jewish system came to an end. However, Christianity thrived and quickly became the religion of the world. It is a message resounding throughout the ages. The only permanent and everlasting security is in Jesus. All other securities are temporary and will soon disband. Jesus is not merely the answer for the immediate but the future. He does not grow old or is out of date. With its new ways and styles, the modern culture cannot push Him aside as noneffective for this time. Jesus was the heart of the matter for the apostles in the past, and He is crucial to security in modern times.

This story of the early Church is a call for a total focus on Jesus. There is no safety outside His person, and we are only secure in Him.

Acts 5:24

WHAT'S GOING ON?

"Now when the high priest, the captain of the temple, and the chief priests heard these things, they wondered what the outcome would be"
(Acts 5:24).

We must understand the growth of the early Church in the context of the unfolding story. The early Church infiltrated the temple, becoming the platform for evangelism. Pentecost took place in the temple. Peter preached a sermon of explanation for this event in the temple, highlighting Jesus and **"about three thousand souls were added to them"** (Acts 2:41). **"And the Lord added to the church daily those who were being saved"** (Acts 2:47). The impactive event of the lame beggar's healing and conversion happened at the Gate Beautiful at the temple. Again Peter explained and proclaimed Jesus. Despite being interrupted by the priests, the captain of the temple, and the Sadducees, **"many of those who heard the word believed; and the number of the men came to be about five thousand"** (Acts 4:4).

The miracle of the lame beggar launched the first phase of persecution when the leaders of Israel imprisoned Peter and John. After the leaders threatened Peter and John never

Part Four: Apostle's Restatement: The Unexplainable

to speak the name of Jesus again, they released the apostles. When the early Church heard the report, they responded with prayer. They experienced a fresh renewing of the Holy Spirit (Acts 4:31). The apostles' message took on a new boldness as they ministered at Solomon's Porch in the temple. People came from the surrounding cities and witnessed abundant miracles (Acts 5:16).

The people's response triggered a second phase of persecution as the Sanhedrin imprisoned all twelve apostles. The Sanhedrin had faced many difficulties but always maintained certainty and control over their authority. Zealots have always been a threat to the stability of the status quo. Theudas instigated a rebellion (Acts 5:36), joined by about four hundred men, but the Sanhedrin maintained control. They killed Theudas, and nothing came from the rebellion. Judas of Galilee and his followers also started a rebellion during the census (Acts 5:37). The leaders quickly conquered him, and he perished. The leaders of Israel were confident that things would be no different with this new Christian movement. After all, they had crucified Jesus, their leader, and indeed the lie of His resurrection would not survive.

The big obstacle for the Sanhedrin was the twelve apostles. If the leaders could silence the apostles, that would eliminate the movement. In this second phase of persecution, not just Peter and John experienced the wrath of the leaders of Israel, but all the apostles did. They had the apostles placed in the common prison, where they experienced discomfort and the threats of other prisoners (Acts 5:18). When the Sanhedrin called the council together the next day, they sent for the imprisoned apostles. The officers they sent hurriedly returned and reported the apostles were not in prison. The prison was secure, and the guards were outside the doors; they did not report any disruption. There was no evidence of a prison escape.

The focus of our passage (Acts 5:24) is the effect of this

report on the leaders of Israel. The mindset of the high priest, the captain of the temple, and the chief priests is highlighted beyond a usual statement. Luke uses phrases and grammar to ensure we do not miss the uncertainty within them. These leaders are unaware that the apostles are at the temple teaching the people (Acts 5:25), and they do not know the angel of the Lord's involvement in the deliverance of the apostles. This news shook their confidence and risked their authority for a brief time.

Luke's language in this passage is extreme because he wants us to know how worried and uncertain the leaders of Israel have become. He does it in three different ways. First, he used the Greek word "diaporeo," coming from "dia," meaning "through," and "aporeo," meaning "to be perplexed." "Diaporeo" has a strong emphasis, meaning "thoroughly perplexed," "in much doubt," or "hesitate greatly." The King James and the New King James versions do not translate this Greek word, but the English Standard Version translates it as **"they were greatly perplexed,"** the same statement used for the Jews of the Dispersion. When the Holy Spirit filled the believers, those witnessing the outpouring were **"all amazed and perplexed saying to one another, 'Whatever could this mean?'"** (Acts 2:12).

Secondly, Luke used the Greek conditional particle "an," typically not translated in English translations. Using this Greek word in the text proposes a stamp of uncertainty, a mere possibility, and indicates a dependence on circumstances. Thus, it designates the content of the clause in which it occurs as conditional. Our passage, "an," strengthens the mental and emotional state of the Jewish leaders, and they wondered what would be the result of the apostles' disappearance from the prison.

Luke notes that these leaders **"wondered"** or were uncertain in a third way. Their perplexity was focused on **"what the outcome would be,"** a translation of the Greek word

Part Four: Apostle's Restatement: The Unexplainable

"ginomai," a verb occurring in all books of the New Testament except Jude. It is one of the most commonly used words in the Scriptures, and in a literal sense, it means "to become, originate, or come into existence." The uncertainty for the leaders of Israel is that they did not know the future. The disappearance of the apostles produced many questions. Where did they go? What were they going to do? Remember, the questions they asked concerning the future were in the context of the miracles and the influence that flowed through the apostles. Although the leaders did not believe the apostles, they recognized the unusual activities and results that happened through them.

Luke contrasts the uncertainty in the leaders of Israel with the stability and certainty in the hearts of the early Church. In both interrogations, the apostles did not hesitate. They expressed absolute steadfastness in their experience with Jesus. They said, ***"For we cannot but speak the things which we have seen and heard"*** (Acts 4:20; see Acts 5:29). In the first interrogation, Peter and John were asked, ***"By what power or by what name have you done this?"*** (Acts 4:7). The Sanhedrin was amazed by the boldness and clarity of Peter's answer. ***"Now when they saw the boldness of Peter and John, and perceived that they were uneducated and untrained men, they marveled"*** (Acts 4:13). When the threats of the Sanhedrin reached the early Church, they prayed, and ***"the place where they were assembled together was shaken; and they were all filled with the Holy Spirit, and they spoke the word of God with boldness"*** (Acts 4:31). After the second interrogation, the Sanhedrin threatened and beat the apostles. ***"So they departed from the presence of the council, rejoicing that they were counted worthy to suffer shame for His name. And daily in the temple, and in every house, they did not cease teaching and preaching Jesus as the Christ"*** (Acts 5:41 - 42). There was no uncertainty among the apostles or the early Church, only in the leaders of Israel. Let us look at three differences between the Sanhedrin and the early Church.

Mystery of the Supernatural
Divine Person

The Jewish nation relied heavily on its heritage. It was the responsibility of the leaders of Israel, especially the priests, to maintain and foster this heritage among the people. The Pharisees dedicated themselves to the law. The scribes gave themselves to the correct interpretation of the Scriptures among the people. The Sadducees embraced the Old Testament law given by Moses, revolving around their God, Jehovah. Did they not sing in their courts the praises of their God?

> *"And the heavens will praise Your wonders, O Lord;*
> *Your faithfulness also in the assembly of the saints.*
> *For who in the heavens can be compared to the Lord?*
> *Who among the sons of the mighty*
> *can be likened to the Lord?*
> *God is greatly to be feared in the assembly of the saints,*
> *And to be held in reverence by all those around Him.*
> *O Lord God of hosts*
> *Who is mighty like You, O Lord?" (Psalms 89:5-8).*

How does uncertainty reign in one's heart if this is your God?

All of the Jewish feast days were celebrations of the great deliverance of Israel by Jehovah. The ten plagues in Egypt brought their deliverance from slavery. God delivered their firstborn from death through the lamb's blood in the last plague. Have they not celebrated the Feast of the Passover every year? Were they not brought through the Red Sea on dry ground while

Part Four: Apostle's Restatement: The Unexplainable

the soldiers on the chariots of Egypt drowned? God fed them with manna from the sky and gave them water from the rock. Fifty days after their deliverance from Egypt, they gathered at Mt. Sinai. Jehovah God established them as a nation; they were His people, and He was their God. They fought and won many battles through the instructions and deliverance of their God. They did not buy or earn the promised land; God gave it to them. How can uncertainty dominate your thoughts if this is your God?

In every Israelite home, the first words spoken every morning came as a question. They asked, "Will this be the day?" They were focused on the promise of the Anointed One, the Messiah. God was coming through the Messiah to bring deliverance to them. The prophets of old proclaimed this message without hesitation. Every page of their Scriptures declared His coming, and He was referred to as "the Coming One" (Matthew 11:3). They expected a forerunner to the Messiah. Did not John the Baptist come in the style and manner of Elijah? Did not a great revival break out in Judah, changing the hearts of Israel? How could the leaders of Israel not see the hand of their God working on their behalf?

BUT they did not recognize their Jehovah God when He came! They crucified Him! However, in the manner of the Old Testament, God graciously gave them repeated chances. The Trinity God raised Jesus from the dead; the Spirit of Jesus descended upon believers in the temple. In two distinct encounters, the apostles powerfully proclaimed the message of Jesus to all of Jerusalem. The leaders of Israel witnessed miracles they could not deny. What else could convince them? Now they experienced a great struggle of uncertainty. The apostles had disappeared from the common prison. What will happen next?

Could all worry, uncertainty or anxiety be connected to not knowing Jesus? Knowing Him is not about knowledge or data; it does not bring certainty to the soul. When we abandon ourselves to Him, we know intimacy beyond mental knowledge.

The leaders of Israel embraced a system of religion but not the God of their religion. They would not have dwelt in uncertainty if they had known Him personally, embraced Him properly, and merged with Him spiritually. They did not know Jesus!

The same is true for us! We have the same Scriptures they had and have experienced abundant miracles. Jesus reveals Himself to us repeatedly. Merging with His loving heart can bring nothing but peace and comfort. The future may be uncertain, but Jesus is Lord of all uncertainties. He does not need to prove His life; His power is beyond questioning. We must embrace His person!

Mystery of the Spiritual
Divine Plan

The leaders of Israel did not know or understand their God of the Old Testament; therefore, they did not grasp His plan! They may have understood the facts or data of the plan; because they did not know Him, they misinterpreted those plans. They knew the fact of the coming Messiah, but they could not grasp the content or heart of that Messiah. The fact that God called them to be His people was well known, but they did not know Him and misunderstood their role. The plan of God was much more than mere activities or physical accomplishments, and it engulfed the spiritual world, which they ignored.

The apostles' physical absence from the secure common prison upset the leaders of Israel's physical certainties. What was the next physical activity in which they should participate? In the context of their perception, their concern was *"what the outcome would be."* God sent the angel of the Lord to change their physical circumstances, but they had no comprehension of the spiritual world; they only saw the physical. The spiritual realm surrounded them and was pressing into their physical world; it was a platform for spiritual activity. However, they ignored the existence of this spiritual world. They cleaned the outside of the cup but allowed extortion and self-indulgence to dominate the inside spiritual (Matthew 23:25). The picture of white-washed tombs could characterize their lives. They appeared beautiful outwardly, but on the inside spiritual realm, they were full of dead men's bones and all uncleanness (Matthew 23:27). They did not know their own God and did not know His plan.

We face the same danger in our lives. We may know many religious facts, observe religious traditions, and follow established laws, but we do not know His plan. His plan is much more than physical activities; it expresses His inner heart. Jesus told this same group that they searched the Scriptures because they believed the Scriptures gave them eternal life. They did not know their God; therefore, they did not see Jesus in the Scriptures. They were not willing to come to Jesus so that they might have life because they did not know God's plan or know Him (John 5:39-40).

Physical security does not dissolve our deep uncertainties, but we overcome them through the wonder of His presence and understanding of His plan. We do not solve our financial uncertainties with more money but with the security of His presence. Anger management techniques do not solve our anger, but we have no anger when we know His heart and embrace His perspective. We do not eliminate stressful times by removing physical circumstances, but in the merger of His person, He bathes us in His peace.

Mystery of the Scheme
Divine Purpose

Because the leaders of Israel did not know their God, they did not understand His plan. Because they did not understand

His plan, so they did not know His purpose. In our passage, these leaders were uncertain regarding the physical outcome of the apostles' disappearance. Their effort to control the apostles was to protect and preserve their existing religious traditions. They projected that the apostles' teaching **"*filled Jerusalem with your doctrine, and intend to bring this Man's blood on us*"** (Acts 5:28). They had no comprehension of the Divine purpose!

Peter proposed the Divine purpose to the Sanhedrin in explaining the lame beggar's healing miracle. He said, **"*You are sons of the prophets, and of the covenant which God made with our fathers, saying to Abraham, 'And in your seed all the families of the earth shall be blessed.' To you first, God, having raised up His Servant Jesus, sent Him to bless you, in turning away every one of you from your iniquities*"** (Acts 3:25-26). The leaders of Israel fought against this purpose with their entire beings. Jesus came to them first so Israel could spiritually be the nation used by God. Then, they would be the avenue through which God would redeem the world. They missed the plan of God; therefore, they missed their purpose within the plan. It was all because they did not know their God!

No wonder their lives were shaken to the core. Great uncertainty gripped them because God was destroying their perception of life. They did not know their own God; therefore, they missed the plan of God and did not know His purpose within the plan. You and I must not start with understanding the plan of God or embracing the purpose of such a plan. We must begin by merging with Him; we must know Him. Could the root of every uncertainty in my life be that I do not know Him well enough? Is this not my single need? All anxiety comes from not embracing and knowing His heart. All worry is rooted in the lack of His presence. I need Him!

Acts 5:25

GOD'S PLACEMENT

"So one came and told them, saying, 'Look, the men whom you put in prison are standing in the temple and teaching the people!'" (Acts 5:25).

In our passage, a nameless individual makes a strange declaration to the high priest, the captain of the temple, and the chief priests. The early Church has continued to grow, proclaiming Jesus accompanied by many miracles. The ministry of the ever-increasing Jerusalem Church was impacting the cities outside Jerusalem (Acts 5:16). The leaders of Israel instituted a second phase of persecution by putting the twelve apostles in the common prison. An angel of the Lord came at night, opened the prison doors, and brought them out. The angel did not do this to free them but that they might return to the temple and proclaim Jesus (Acts 5:20).

An exciting twist happens in the story. You might think an angel's appearance would have stirred all of Jerusalem. Strangely enough, no one but the apostles seemed to know about the angel. The Sanhedrin called the council together in the morning and sent officers to bring the apostles for interrogation. The officers returned to say, **"Indeed we found the prison shut securely, and the guards standing outside before**

the doors; but when we opened them, we found no one inside" (Acts 5:23)! This report brought overwhelming uncertainty to the leaders of Israel. Where were the apostles? What were the apostles going to do? Perhaps the leaders placed their hateful attitudes upon the apostles, thinking they might physically attack them. Were they in danger?

The leaders of Israel's insecurity quickly dissipated with the latest report. Luke used the Greek word "paraginomai,' translated as "came," to highlight the unnamed person's coming and his announcement. The prefix "para" means "to, at, and;" "ginomai" refers to the origin or come into being, and always gives the sense of arrival. "Apaggello" is translated as, ***"told;"*** the prefix "apo" means "from," and "aggello" means "angel, messenger, or pastor." Neither of these words is typical for the average scene of someone coming along and giving information. This individual burns with a message and runs to the council to deliver important news. You can imagine the message's urgency driven by the surprise that the apostles supposedly in jail were not!

The messenger exclaimed, ***"Look, the men whom you put in prison are standing in the temple and teaching the people"*** (Acts 5:25)! That became the foundation for the critical wordage Luke used to display contrast. It begins with ***"Look,"*** an exclamation word that can stand alone and calls attention to something external or exterior to oneself. Immediately, the messenger states the council's action, ***"the men you put in prison."*** Then he contrasts it with what God has done, ***"the men... are standing in the temple and teaching the people."***

The Greek word translated as ***"you put"*** is "tithemi," used one hundred times in the New Testament, and the majority of times translated as "lay or laid." The ongoing story in our chapter (Acts 5) uses this word five times, translated as "laid, conceived, put" (Acts 5:2, 4, 15, 18, 25). The Greek word translated as ***"are standing"*** is "histemi," used 157 times in the New Testament. In our chapter, Luke used "histemi" four times; three times, he used it as "stand or standing" (Acts 5:20, 23, 25), and the fourth time translated it as "set" (Acts 5:27). Both "tithemi" and "histemi" are similar in that they indicate the occupation of a location. However, "histemi" means something beyond occupying space. It varies, and we must see it in the context of its use, but with empowerment connected. Often it expresses stalwart or being strong, contrasted with "pipto," which refers to "falling down, fall to pieces, collapse, or falter."

In the context of our passage, the council placed the apostles in the common prison, but God empowered them to stand in the temple. The council imprisoned them, but God freed them. The council was silenced by placing, but God declared by standing. Man's orders may put someone in a specific location, but the order of an angel empowers someone to stand in the face of opposition. The council ***"put"*** (tithemi), a verb in the middle voice, means to set or place on one's behalf or by one's order. The imprisonment was an expression of the council's self-will motivated by selfishness. The majority of Jerusalem's people were not concerned. The council ***"feared the people"*** (Acts 5:26). Their self-protection a focus on themselves motivated their action. But the ***"standing"*** of the apostles is a verb in the active voice, which means no guards came to overpower them. The angel of the Lord told them where to go and what to do (Acts 5:20). In the fullness of the Spirit, God empowered them to overcome self-protection and fear and to stand in the face of persecution.

The council's action to put the apostles in prison is in the aorist tense, indicating the council's focus was on their activity with no consideration of the time. It was simply a snapshot of the action. However, the empowering of the Spirit of Jesus within the apostles caused them to stand in the perfect tense. Here, the verb tense describes the completed action occurring in the past but producing a state of being or a result in the present.

The emphasis is not on the past action but on the present "state of affairs" resulting from the past action. In connection with the perfect tense of "histemi," the verb *"are"* is present, a translation of the Greek word "eimi," which refers to a state of being. What the apostles did was not merely an activity the Sanhedrin could stop but a state of being that would continue regardless of imprisonment. They will proclaim the message!

The movement of God is not like the movement of man. Humanity can place or put laws, activities, or organizations in place, but only God can empower people, the message of the Book of Acts. The Spirit of Jesus came to merge with the spirit of the person. In the merger, God creates a new creature that lives beyond doing or existing in a location but is empowered to stand. The "standing" itself is an expression of the teaching power of God!

Value
Appraisal

Usually, the location of an object directly expresses its value. A family photo album stored in the closet rather than displayed in the living room suggests its value. You might consider your presence unimportant if your assigned seat is in the back corner. The location of the tabernacle in the Israelite camp told of its importance (Numbers 2 & 3); it was in the center of the camp, not a distance away. Leaving Egypt, the Israelites were scattered with no fixed order, but after building the tabernacle, their tribal rank determined the fixed order around the tabernacle. A cloud rested upon the tabernacle, dark by day and fiery red by night (Exodus 40:38). When the cloud moved, the Israelites knew that was the signal to move forward (Exodus 40:36-37). The location of God's dwelling place told all Israelites that Jehovah was the most valuable asset in their lives.

Part Four: Apostle's Restatement: The Unexplainable

Wise men from the East traveled for two years seeking to locate the newborn King. After discovering He was a Jewish-born King, they went to Jerusalem. Herod, the king, took them to the chief priests and scribes, who revealed His location through prophecy. As they departed for that location, ***"and behold, the star which they had seen in the East went before them, till it came and stood*** (histemi) ***over where the young Child was"*** (Matthew 2:9). The star's location indicated the end of the search, the fulfillment of the wise men's dream.

Stephen, an elder of the early Church, preached to the Hellenistic Jews, giving their history and recounting the constant rebellion of their forefathers. He proclaimed the change of God's location from the temple made with hands to the hearts of the believers. But as did their forefathers, they rejected the truth and angrily ground their teeth at him. ***"But he, being full of the Holy Spirit, gazed into heaven and saw the glory of God, and Jesus standing*** (histemi) ***at the right hand of God"*** (Acts 7:55). God was declaring the value of both Stephen and his message.

In the Book of Revelation, Jesus declares His location to every person. ***"Behold, I stand*** (histemi) ***at the door and knock. If anyone hears My voice and opens the door, I will come in to him and dine with him, and he with Me"*** (Revelation 3:20). Doesn't His location at the entrance of your life declare how valuable you are to Him? Jesus does not expect you to come to Him; He comes to you! He does not come to groups or multitudes; He comes to you! Jesus does not come asking for help; He comes to help! How much He values you is determined by His location.

In our passage, Luke contrasts two sets of values. How did the council value the apostles? They put the apostles in the common prison. The apostles were of no importance to the leaders of Israel. If they could remove them, the Jewish society would prosper. The positive effect of the miracles, compassionate ministries, and religious enthusiasm became hostile to the leaders because the apostles promoted Jesus. In the leaders' minds, the apostles had no valuable contribution; therefore, they had placed them in prison. I have personally experienced this repeatedly in the lives of jail inmates. They are removed from society and devalued from all worth, often eliminated by their families. They are a liability rather than an asset; they have no value or self-worth. The occasions of attempted suicide are too many to discuss. The leaders of Israel boldly proclaimed this to the apostles by putting them in the common prison.

But God sent an angel to stand the apostles in the temple before Jerusalem. He made a bold declaration of their extreme value and worth. God needed the apostles' teaching in the temple. Will the evangelization of the world happen without them? Will the New Testament be written without the participation of many of them? Are there not hundreds of lives that will be lost without the proclamation and leadership of these men? When the leaders of Israel interrogated the apostles, the apostles declared their value in Jesus. They proclaimed Jesus crucified and risen from the dead! The Trinity God exalted Jesus to their right hand to be Prince and Savior (Acts 5:31). Jesus' location declares His value to the Trinity God! This location communicated value to all of Israel, for He was in this location to extend repentance and forgiveness of sins to all of Israel. Located within the apostles, the Holy Spirit made both the apostles and Himself witnesses in this valuable location (Acts 5:32)!

May I loudly declare your value to God, indicated by your location? *"**Even when we were dead in trespasses, made us alive together with Christ (by grace you have been saved), and raised us up together, and made us sit together in the heavenly places in Christ Jesus"*** (Ephesians 2:5, 6). Will you stay at the location He has placed you?

Part Four: Apostle's Restatement: The Unexplainable

Victory
Authority

The report from the officers said, ***"the men... are standing*** (histemi) ***in the temple and teaching the people!"*** Luke contrasted that with the description of ***"the men whom you put*** (tithemi) ***in prison."*** The Greek word "tithemi" was used for the actions of God throughout the Scriptures. A fourth of the time, God is the subject, and "tithemi" is used in the Old Testament Greek translation. The order for creation was set (tithemi) by Him. He set (tithemi) the stars (Genesis 1:17), just as He gathered (tithemi) the primal waters and oceans into their boundaries (Psalms 33:7). In the New Testament, God set up (tithemi) the word of reconciliation for us (2 Corinthians 5:19). God has not destined (tithemi) us for wrath but rather to obtain salvation (1 Thessalonians 5:9). There are many references to the authority and power of God establishing things.

The Greek word "histemi" portrays placement in a location and carries additional emphasis. In 157 times, the writers use "histemi" in the New Testament, and its translation is "stood" or "standing," conveying the idea of strength or power, often with an undercurrent of "being empowered." That is true in the context of our passage. The apostles did not merely appear in the temple or were placed there by God. God filled them with the Spirit of Jesus, commanded them by the angel of the Lord, and delivered them by His power.

The "power of man" placed the apostles in jail, but the "power of God" stood them in the place of witness. The value of the apostles is in the victory of obedience and their response to God's power working through them. His power comes to man in dependency! We must understand the closing of this paragraph in this context. The apostles are not only ***"His witnesses"*** but also ***"the Holy Spirit whom God has given to those*** *who obey Him"* (Acts 5:32). The apostles stood in the plan and destiny of God. Indeed, God has and can use the rebellious heart of man to bring about His will (Acts 4:27, 28), but what could He do with us if we would respond to His authority?

Viewpoint
Advantage

The Scriptures consistently propose the action of God with extreme purpose. God never acts without purpose, and He does not operate accidentally or on a whim because it feels good. Every movement of God is to accomplish His purpose and is always singular in reality; REDEMPTION! Even the Old Testament actions of God, when interpreted through the eyes of the New Testament perspective, we must consider redemptive. Although the Scriptures propose God acting out of *"His good pleasure,"* it is always in the context of redemption (Luke 12:32; Ephesians 1:5, 9; Philippians 2:13; 2 Thessalonians 1:11).

This passage is to aid our understanding. The apostles *"whom you put in prison"* were placed there without purpose. One might argue the council had a negative intention in the imprisonment, and they held them for future interrogation, to silence their message, or to cause fear in their hearts. But in our passage, there is no recorded purpose. However, God's placement of the apostles was *"standing in the temple and teaching the people."* The deliverance of the apostles from prison was not for their safety. God was not simply demonstrating His superior power over the council's decision. The purpose of God was the continued proclamation of His revelation of Jesus!

Do you struggle with God's purpose for your life? Does He have a singular and consistent purpose for each of us? God always wants to proclaim Jesus through us. We will be the platform for Jesus' revelation of who He is! Listen to this declaration from Paul. ***"In Him also we have obtained an inheritance, being predestined according to the purpose of Him who works all things according to the counsel of His will, that we who first trusted in Christ should be to the praise of His glory"*** (Ephesians 1:11-12). All God does in and for us is that our lives should be ***"the praise of His glory."*** He wants us to stand by His power, released from the imprisonments of our making, to stand in the temples of our world to be the revelation of Jesus! We must focus all our energy on Jesus. We must embrace Him in every minute of our day. Every song we sing, and the message we preach must echo His name. Proclaiming the name of Jesus is the purpose of our lives.

Acts 5:26

FEARLESS

"Then the captain went with the officers and brought them without violence, for they feared the people, lest they should be stoned" (Acts 5:26).

The New Testament Scriptures admonish us 75 times not to be afraid, a common struggle of the human heart. Luke revealed the fear in the high priest, the captain of the temple, and the chief priests. The captain of the officers' action resulted from his fear. In our verse, **"*captain*"** is the subject of the sentence, the main verb is **"*brought,*"** and the direct object is **"*them.*"** The Greek word "gar," translated as **"*for,*"** points to the cause or reason for the verb's action. The leaders of Israel were afraid of the people!

The leaders of Israel reacted to the news that the apostles were not in prison. **"*Now when the high priest, the captain of the temple, and the chief priests heard these things, they wondered what the outcome would be*"** (Acts 5:24). In a previous study, we related the depth of uncertainty that rages within the leaders of Israel. While Luke does not mention the word "fear," it certainly has the same characteristics. The English Standard Version translates the last phrase of Luke's description

Part Four: Apostle's Restatement: The Unexplainable

as ***"they were greatly perplexed."*** It is a translation of the Greek word "diaporeo," which comes from "dia," meaning "through," and aporeo," meaning "to be perplexed." They were "thoroughly perplexed," "much in doubt," or "hesitated greatly."

Luke further emphasized their perplexing response by using the Greek conditional particle "an," which is not usually translated into English. "An" proposes a stamp of great uncertainty. Our verse, "an," strengthens these Jewish leaders' mental and emotional state. They wondered what the result of the apostles' disappearance from prison would mean. They were afraid! Where had the apostles gone? What were they going to do?

We must see the fear in the context of those who were afraid. What was the status of the fearful? Luke describes the local Jerusalem temple officers and Israel's religious and political leaders. These leaders were not merely governing the city of Jerusalem as great as that might be. The entire nation of Israel was under their jurisdiction. 35 Pharisees and 35 Sadducees made up the council of the Sanhedrin. The high priest was the additional member who decided if the body was tied. The captain of the temple was second in rank to the high priest himself and was responsible for order on the temple grounds. All officers under his direction were members of the priesthood. They were massive in number and organization, for they oversaw a daily average of 25,000 visitors coming to the temple for prayer and worship.

Fear of being stoned by the worshippers at the temple possessed these influential leaders. That is surprising because of their status and authority. Were they not in charge? Did they not decide the fate of every person coming into the temple? Did they not have many officers to protect them and fulfill their wishes? How could they possibly be afraid? The Greek word for fear is "phobeo," where we get our English word, "phobia," a verb in the imperfect tense. "Phobia" means fear was not a momentary state, but they kept fearing. The writers used this Greek word for every degree of fear imagined. Fearing God, which is reverence and respect for being terrorized by circumstances, is in the definition of this word. We can only calculate the extent of fear by the context. The mystery of the apostles' disappearance from prison had captured the leaders. Discovering the apostles did not flee but continued to do what the Sanhedrin had commanded them not to do caused anxiety in these leaders. Why were the apostles fearless? Did they have some kind of secret power? The captain of the temple decided not to send his officers to arrest the apostles, but he went to supervise. The motivation for this decision was *"for they feared the people."*

Luke contrasts the fear of the leaders of Israel with the apostles who have no position in governing Israel. Many of them are fishermen without education and lack the manners and skills of the upper-class people in Jerusalem. They are from Galilee and entirely out of their element in Jerusalem. Galilee is on the northern border of Palestine, removed from Jerusalem by 100 miles. Galilee is on a trade route that consistently invites ungodly gentile foreigners into their cities with sinful beliefs and practices. The synagogues of the Galilean towns tend not to be as orthodox as the temple in Jerusalem.

The uneducated and unorthodox apostles are fearless. The leaders of Israel rightly stated the reason for the second imprisonment and interrogation. **"Did we not strictly command you not to teach in this name"** (Acts 5:28)? You would think the first imprisonment and interrogation would have been sufficient. That did not stop the apostles, but they increased their witness. The leaders of Israel said, **"And look, you have filled Jerusalem with your doctrine, and intend to bring this Man's blood on us"** (Acts 5:28)! How can we explain this fearlessness?

When threatened the second time by the leaders of Israel, the apostles replied, **"We ought to obey God rather than men"** (Acts 5:29). As before, they said they were not going

Part Four: Apostle's Restatement: The Unexplainable

to heed any threat from these leaders. When the officials demonstrated their authority by beating the apostles, ***"they departed from the presence of the council, rejoicing that they were counted worthy to suffer shame for His name"*** (Acts 5:41). The apostles did not retreat into hiding! The beatings they experienced were fuel on the fire of their blazing witness. ***"And daily in the temple, and in every house, they did not cease teaching and preaching Jesus as the Christ"*** (Acts 5:42). How can we explain this fearlessness?

However, you must be aware that this is not always true! On their way to the Mount of Olives, Jesus shared they would all stumble because of Him that night. Peter was furious with the suggestion of such betrayal. He cried, ***"Even if all are made to stumble because of You, I will never be made to stumble"*** (Matthew 26:33). Jesus continued telling Peter that he would deny Him three times that morning. Peter exploded in protest, ***"Even if I have to die with You, I will not deny You"*** (Matthew 26:35)! Peter may have meant well, but the words of Jesus would prove true. He was even afraid of a servant girl (Matthew 26:69-70). Peter was not alone in such gripping and controlling fear. At the close of the great betrayal scene in the Garden of Gethsemane, ***"all the disciples forsook Him and fled"*** (Matthew 26:56).

What happened to the disciples that brought them to a new level of courage and faithfulness? Did they acquire new knowledge from a seminar or book study? Was it a lecture from Jesus that shamed them into courage? Was it the recent popularity they received from the ordinary people of Jerusalem? It was PENTECOST! Luke recounts all historical stories to highlight and focus on the indwelling, merging, and intimacy with the Spirit of the resurrected Lord within the believer. The nature of God and man merged to form a new creature. The apostles began to think like Jesus, feel like Jesus, and express the life of Jesus. It was beyond fear!

Absoluteness
Sovereignty

The apostles experienced the absolute power of God against the background of personal weakness and failure. They embraced God's sovereign power through the resurrected Jesus. The most influential people of their world plotted and crucified Jesus, yet the sovereignty of God did not allow their plan to defeat Jesus. The Trinity God raised Jesus from death! The apostles encountered the presence of the resurrected Jesus for forty days (Acts 1:3). The *"infallible proofs"* convinced them so that nothing caused them to fear. Pentecost, the indwelling Spirit of Jesus, sealed the proofs. For many months they knew the power of God moving through them to push back the demonic forces. Miracle after miracle took place among them. If the physical Jesus they knew in three years of ministry was real, if the resurrected Jesus they experienced for forty days was real, if the indwelling Jesus experienced in the intimate merger was real, they could know no fear.

Knowing the sovereign God and having no fear became the consistent message to Jerusalem and each other. In Luke's four-verse explanation of Pentecost, he described it as *"a sound from heaven"* (Acts 2:2). The Greek word translated as *"sound"* is "echos," and is where we get our English word "echo." *"Heaven"* is not a location but a reference to "transcendent." What happened to the believers at Pentecost was an echo of the sovereign, transcendent Person of God invading the flesh of humanity. Peter explained what was occurring to the people in a sermon. The sovereign Spirit of God indwelling Jesus had now merged with the believers (Acts 2:22). God's sovereignty is so beyond the power of humanity that even the lawless hands of men who crucified Jesus were overcome by the *"determined purpose and foreknowledge of God"* (Acts 2:23). Their arrogance and rebellion accomplished the plan of God. The sovereign Life of God that raised Jesus from the dead is greater than even death (Acts 2:24). Peter preached, ***"Therefore let all the house of Israel know assuredly that God has made this Jesus, whom you crucified, both Lord and Christ"*** (Acts 2:36). Therefore, we have nothing to fear!

The lame beggar's healing stirred the temple, and the crowd around him experienced the praise coming from his life. Peter realized they attributed the miracle to him as though by his power or godliness, he had made the man walk (Acts 3:12). Peter explained the source of the miracle was the power of the resurrected Jesus. He described Him as the Prince of Life whom they killed, ***"whom God raised from the dead, of which we are witnesses"*** (Acts 3:15). The weakness of humanity became the platform to display the sovereign power of God! When the Sanhedrin interrogated Peter about this miracle, he proclaimed, "Jesus!" ***"Nor is there salvation in any other; for there is no other name under heaven given among men by which we must be saved"*** (Acts 4:12). What God did in Jesus removes all fear!

The Sanhedrin could not deny the miracle but would not embrace their guilt in rejecting Jesus. They threatened Peter and John never to speak the name of Jesus again and released them. When they returned to the early Church and shared the threat, the church cried out in prayer: ***"Lord, You are God, who made heaven and earth and the sea and all that is in them"*** (Acts 4:24). ***"Lord, You are God"*** is translated from the Greek word "despotes." God is a despot, tyrant, dictator, and absolute ruler; He is sovereign! In explaining His sovereignty, they declared that God herded together the kings, rulers, Gentiles, and Israelites, permitting them to do whatever they desired. They crucified Jesus, precisely what His hand and purpose determined before to be done (Acts 4:28). Therefore, there is no need to fear because our God is in charge!

In both threat-filled interrogations, Peter said, ***"We ought to obey God rather than men"*** (Acts 4:19; 5:29). How could we be afraid in light of Jesus being crucified and raised from the dead? The Trinity exalted Jesus to the right hand of God to be the Prince and Savior. We are witnesses of these things, and we know the forgiveness of sins. We live in the merger with the Spirit of Jesus God has given to us (Acts 5:30-32), the truth that engulfed the apostles' lives. This reality permeated every sermon, every witness, and every miracle. Fear has no place in this picture!

What was true for them is true for us! The Spirit of God that lived in Jesus came to live in the apostles and now lives in us! We merge with our sovereign God, who is accomplishing His plan. Paul proposed that this gives us knowledge beyond fear. ***"And we know that all things work together for good to those who love God, to those who are the called according to His purpose"*** (Romans 8:28). God's sovereignty is complete, not partial; it knows no limits, circumstances never overcome, and it defies the wisdom of humanity! We have no fear in the loving embrace of our merger with the Sovereign Jesus!

Abandonment
Surrender

The sovereignty of God is an irrefutable truth. The members of the Sanhedrin would not have denied it. Generations of Jews repeatedly told the stories of Israel's deliverance by the hand of Jehovah. While they may have consented to God's sovereignty, they did not abandon themselves to Him. At night, an angel released the apostles to deliver the message again, but the Sanhedrin would not hear. Fear permeated their lives. The apostles believed in the sovereignty of God, and He delivered them from all fear! What made the difference? It was their abandonment of their lives to Jesus!

Part Four: Apostle's Restatement: The Unexplainable

The high priest, captain of the temple, and the chief priests had abandoned themselves to a system of religion. They strictly observed the rituals of their sacrifices and lived within the confines of their accepted laws. They followed the hours of prayer and memorized their Scriptures. They surrendered to their religious system, but fear reigned in their lives. The apostles have abandoned their lives to a Person. Jesus captured them! He is not a belief system, a set of rules, or an institution to maintain, and the sovereignty of God moved from theory or philosophy to the living Christ. The Pharisees believed in the resurrection from the dead; the Sadducees did not believe in the resurrection, leading to theological debates. But now, they were confronted by the resurrected Jesus, not the concept of the resurrection. The resurrection is IN Jesus (Acts 4:2).

Jesus was the focus of the Sanhedrin's threats given to the apostles. If Jesus was a theological belief, the Sanhedrin could have debated the issue and argued by exploring additional concepts if He was a philosopher. What would they do with this Person? They might crucify Him again, but they tried that once, and God raised Him from the dead! They try to silence His name, but those who embrace Him will not stop proclaiming Him! They might substitute another focus, but there is nothing that equals Him! What will they do with Jesus? They must abandon themselves to Him or encounter all the consequences of rejection!

We have the same issue. It is much easier to abandon ourselves to the established practices of traditional religion that become comfortable habits. As with the Pharisees and Sadducees, we can adjust the traditions to fit our desires, making us the god of our made-up religion. We have virtually abandoned ourselves to ourselves! In abandonment to Jesus, we lose control. "Ceasing resistance to an enemy or opponent and submitting to their authority" is the definition of surrender. While abandonment proposes the reality of "giving up completely," it has nothing to do with an enemy or adversary. It goes beyond an act or moment in life to "a course of action, a practice, or a way of thinking."

Jesus does not demand the surrender of our lives as One who is sovereign, and He is not a tyrant in the sense of an enemy or opponent. Indeed, Jesus is transcendent, far above us, and passionate love drives Him. Holiness is His nature; therefore, He never thinks about Himself but only about us. His plan and destiny for our lives will only be for our good. The apostles have not surrendered to Jesus; they have abandoned themselves to Him. He is their "course of action, a practice, or a way of thinking." They can do nothing else! What about you?

Activity
Substance

Let us forever acknowledge the sovereignty of Jesus, to whom we must abandon ourselves, is not only in the heavenly realm! His transcendency does exist in the spiritual, unseen world. Paul declared the mighty power of the Trinity God as ***"what is the exceeding greatness of His power toward us who believe, according to the working of His mighty power which He worked in Christ when He raised Him from the dead and seated Him at His right hand in the heavenly places, far above all principality and power and might and dominion, and every name that is named, not only in this age but also in that which is to come"*** (Ephesians 1:19-21). Although God's authority exerts itself in the unseen world, it invades the physical realm of life, and it raised Jesus from the dead.

The wonder of the physical becomes the platform on which the majesty of our sovereign

Christ expresses His life. While members of the Sanhedrin were fearful for their lives, the indwelling sovereign Jesus released

Part Four: Apostle's Restatement: The Unexplainable

"those who through fear of death were all their lifetime subject to bondage" (Hebrews 2:15). The council feared the people lest they might stone them (Acts 5:26). How does this compare to the apostles whom the Sanhedrin threatened with death as they plotted to kill them (Acts 5:33)? They did not waver in their commitment to proclaim Jesus (Acts 5:29-32). After they were beaten and released, ***"they departed from the presence of the council, rejoicing that they were counted worthy to suffer shame for His name"*** (Acts 5:41).

Abandonment to Jesus must reveal itself in my everyday activities and govern my physical responses to all circumstances. Jesus must be the Lord of all physical activities, which are always beyond my control. What was true for the apostles will be true for me. We are in a spiritual battle; abandonment to Jesus brings about physical discomfort and struggle. I must end my griping and complaining to experience the joy of suffering shame for His name. I cannot accomplish this state of joy, and I cannot discipline myself to embrace it. I must abandon myself to His sovereignty to know His provisions. Will you join me in such abandonment?

Acts 5:27

EXPOSED

"And when they had brought them, they set them before the council. And the high priest asked them" (Acts 5:27).

Our previous studies highlighted Luke's amazing presentation of two persecution scenes (Acts 4:5-22; Acts 5:17-40). The reason for the first and second scenes of persecution was the same, with the content of the interrogations being identical. However, the intensity of the second phase seems more robust than the first, easily explained by the increase in miracles, the boldness of preaching Jesus in the resurrection, and the disciples' disregard for the instructions given at the first interrogation. Luke indicates the motivation of the high priest, and Sadducees is not a theological difference concerning the resurrection but a fit of jealousy (Acts 5:17).

After a deeper investigation, we discover a difference in Luke's approach to the second phase of persecution. In the first phase, He moved from **"they laid hands on them, and put them in custody"** (Acts 4:3) to the interrogation itself. The Sanhedrin asked a simple question (Acts 4:7); Peter startled them with his answer (Acts 4:8-12); Luke recorded the response of the leaders to Peter's statement (Acts 4:13-22). In both phases of

Part Four: Apostle's Restatement: The Unexplainable

persecution, Luke gives insight into the private discussion of the leaders, separate from the apostles. Both times the leaders are uncertain of what to do because they fear the people (Acts 4:21; Acts 5:26), and Luke highlights the movement of God in both phases (Acts 4:8; Acts 5:19).

In writing about the second phase of persecution, Luke adds an element of contrast. In the first phase, Luke moves us from one scene, statement, or confrontation with various conjunctions. We can see the unfolding of a continuous story. However, in this second scene, he consistently uses the Greek conjunction "de!" This Greek conjunction is a particle standing after one or two words in a clause, strictly adversative but more frequently denoting transition or conversion. It introduces something else, whether opposed to what precedes or simply continuative or explanatory. Generally, it has the meaning of the conjunctions but, and, or also. Out of the eleven verses in the paragraph we are studying, Luke used the Greek conjunction "de" seven times to introduce the next step in the story (Acts 5:22, 24, 25, 27, 29, 33, 34). We cannot ignore the constant repetition of this word.

Luke used the Greek word "de" to introduce additional aspects of the persecution and interrogation, denoting transition and further information. Could he suggest a distinct contrast between the leaders of Israel and the apostles? The motivation of the apostles was very different from the high priest and Sadducees; their experiences related to Jesus were radically different. The apostles experienced Jesus in His resurrection appearances for forty days and the infilling of His resurrection Person at Pentecost. The Sanhedrin knew nothing about this reality. Admittedly the education level of the leaders of Israel was far superior to the apostles, and the position, political power, and financial status of the Sadducees were far above the status of the apostles. The spirit of the Sanhedrin was one of distaste, dislike, scorn, fear, and hatred; the apostles seemed to dwell in love consistently! What a contrast!

Although Luke used the Greek conjunction "de" to suggest continuation and additional information, the nature of the story itself indicates this contrast. The conflict raging between the two groups supports a radical difference. Luke reveals the true nature of the high priest, captain of the temple, and the Sadducees against the backdrop of the character and ministry of the apostles. Three strong emphases in our passage portray the contrast of the council with the apostles (Acts 5:27).

Core
"When they had brought"

The council assembled the following day, sending officers to the prison to bring the apostles (Acts 5:21). While all was secure at the prison, the officers reported that they could not find the apostles (Acts 5:22-23), creating quite a stir among the council (Acts 5:24). Where were the apostles, and what were they planning? The council's emotions changed from concern and fear to anger when someone reported the apostles were in the temple teaching about Jesus (Acts 5:25). They again sent the officers to secure the apostles. However, they were concerned that the temple would be crowded with people. How would this crowd react to another arrest of the apostles? The captain of the temple decided to go himself to ensure there was no violence.

Luke then writes, **"When they had brought,"** a translation of the Greek word "agagontes." The primary Greek word is "ago," not the main verb, but is part of a particle phrase giving content to the main verb. The main verb is **"set"** (histemi), which is modified by **"brought."** Luke provides us with a sense of the attitude and motive of the leaders toward the apostles by describing how they conducted them from the temple to the council meeting. "Ago" is used sixty-seven times in the New Testament, and its basic meaning is "to lead." However,

Part Four: Apostle's Restatement: The Unexplainable

twenty-four of those uses display a forced leading, such as in our passage. Often it is under the influence of a legal command, which surrounds it with "arrest," "drag away," or "capture."

Luke establishes the tone or style of the Sanhedrin's actions. The leaders demonstrated the same spirit when they heard the apostles' explanations concerning their continued ministry. ***"When they heard this, they were furious and plotted to kill them"*** (Acts 5:33). What is present inwardly in the leaders of Israel that causes them to react this way? Why are they jealous? Amid their political position and power, why are they afraid of the crowd? They feel threatened by these uneducated apostles from Galilee! That is evident by their reaction to the first announcement of the apostles' absence from prison (Acts 5:24). The apostles escaped jail by mysterious means. What might they do to them?

The apostles' motivation was the exact opposite! They were not filled with hate but love. They do not desire to kill or destroy but to save and restore. They do not seek the security of position but safety in submission to God. Physical comfort is not their desire, for they rejoiced ***"that they were counted worthy to suffer shame for His name"*** (Acts 5:41). The contrast is not simply in outward actions but inner spirit. The inner nature of the high priest and Sadducees was not the same as the inner nature of the apostles! The Spirit of Jesus filled the apostles! They not only personally experienced the resurrected Jesus, but they were also united with His Spirit. When Luke described Pentecost, he said, ***"And they were all filled with the Holy Spirit"*** (Acts 2:4). ***"Filled"*** is a translation of the Greek word "pimplemi," used for filling a sponge (Matthew 27:48; John 19:29). It depicts a person filled with something, to be wholly imbued, affected, influenced with or by something. The Spirit of Jesus merged with the apostles, and His nature became their expression. As Jesus is the visible image of the invisible Father, so the apostles were filled with the same Spirit.

The leaders of Israel (agagontes) arrest, drag away or capture the apostles, ***"guide"*** (hodegeo). In Jesus' last intimate conversations with His apostles, He explained "hodegeo" to them. There were many things that He wanted to share with them, but they were not experienced enough to grasp the content. His confidence in them was in the Holy Spirit, ***"the Spirit of truth." "He will guide*** (hodegeo) ***you into all truth"*** (John 16:13). ***"He will glorify Me, for He will take of what is Mine and declare it to you. All things that the Father has are Mine. Therefore I said that He will take of Mine and declare it to you"*** (John 16:14-15). The Trinity God shared everything in God's nature with the apostles through the Spirit of Jesus. Jesus moved with compassion for the multitudes through the apostles (Matthew 9:36). Jesus willingly embraced a cross and rejoiced in suffering at the hands of the Sanhedrin through the apostles (Acts 5:41). The apostles became an expression of the nature of Jesus!

John wrote about the heart of Jesus. ***"Behold, I stand at the door and knock. If anyone hears My voice and opens the door, I will come in to him and dine with him, and he with Me"*** (Revelation 3:20). That is why the crowds gathered from the surrounding cities of Jerusalem (Acts 5:16). While the members of the Sanhedrin were "arresting, dragging away, or capturing," the apostles, in the Spirit of Jesus, were knocking, inviting, and uplifting! The leaders were filled with self-centeredness, self-sufficiency, and pride, while the apostles were filled with Jesus. It is the only answer to the radical difference between the two groups.

Who do I want to be like? That is the radical decision of our lifetime. It has nothing to do with religious activities. The leaders of Israel scored top marks in that area. They kept prayer, sacrifices, feast days, and fasting schedules. They held their heads high above all others regarding the laws of the Old Testament. Where did they miss it? The missed "Jesus!" Jesus, the

Part Four: Apostle's Restatement: The Unexplainable

fulfillment of the plan of Jehovah, stepped into their world, and they crucified Him, something of which Peter reminded the Jews. In the interrogation of the first persecution, Peter said, **"Let it be known to you all, and to all the people of Israel, that by the name of Jesus Christ of Nazareth, whom you crucified, whom God raised from the dead, by Him this man stands here before you whole"** (Acts 4:10). In the second persecution, the leaders condemned themselves by saying, **"And look, you have filled Jerusalem with your doctrine, and intend to bring this Man's blood on us"** (Acts 5:28)! What will I do with Jesus? Will I be filled with Him? Will He be the core of my existence; will I merge with Him; will I allow His nature to source my being?

Commission
"They set"

The officers went to the prison to secure the prisoners and transport them to an appearance before the council (Acts 5:22). They reported the startling news. **"Indeed we found the prison shut securely, and the guards standing outside before the doors; but when we opened them, we found no one inside"** (Acts 5:23)! That frightened the high priest, the captain of the temple, and the chief priests because they had no idea what the apostles might do (Acts 5:24). But the solution quickly came to them when they discovered the apostles were at the temple teaching the people (Acts 5:25).

The council did not attempt to discover how the prisoners escaped. They did not inquire why the prisoners were teaching the people in the temple. Indeed, the apostles understood they would be captured again. The council simply ignored all of those facts! But Luke gives us insight. The angel of the Lord delivered the apostles (Acts 5:19). The angel opened the prison doors, and the prisoners departed without the guards' awareness. The angel commissions them to ***"Go, stand in the temple and speak to the people all the words of this life"*** (Acts 5:20). The angel did not release them for safety but for ministry, not self-protection, but the proclamation of the message of Jesus! God did not move in their lives for their comfort but for the redemption of their world.

Luke contrasts the release of the apostles with the intent of the council. The identical Greek verb Luke used for the angel's command to the apostles he used for the council's action. The angel said, ***"Go, stand*** (histemi) ***in the temple and speak to the people all the words of the life"*** (Acts 5:20). The council captured the apostles, and ***"they set*** (histemi) ***them before the council"*** (Acts 5:27). Luke uses the same Greek word but with different intent and motive. Proclamation of the name of Jesus, regardless of comfort or safety, was the angel's intent; silencing the declaration of Jesus' name enforced by punishment was the council's intent.

The same is always true in our world. Every Divine intervention in our lives is to proclaim His name. But this was the intention of the Trinity God from the beginning of the Book of Genesis. The prophets had one message: ***"But those things which God foretold by the mouth of all His prophets, that the Christ would suffer, He has thus fulfilled"*** (Acts 3:18). Now the apostles proclaim the same message. The upset within the heart of the council was not about the miracles, the assemblies, or even the idea of Jesus' resurrection. They could not tolerate the name of Jesus. We discover the power of the Trinity God in the person of Jesus. In Jesus, we find forgiveness and victory over sin. In Jesus, God fulfills His plan for our lives. There is no other subject to discuss. The apostles were set before the people in the temple to proclaim Jesus; they were set before the council to be accused.

Part Four: Apostle's Restatement: The Unexplainable

Content
"Questioned"

Luke ends our passage with the statement, *"And the high priest asked them"* (Acts 5:27). The Greek word "eperotesen" is translated as *"asked them."* This phrase in other Biblical versions is translated as "the high priest questioned them" and "the high priest began his examination." This verb means to attempt a legal or semi-legal procedure to know the truth about a matter by interrogation. It means to put a question to someone, and here it refers to a judge questioning someone when making an investigation.

Again Luke strongly contrasts the apostles with the council. See how the council states their guilt. *"And look, you have filled Jerusalem with your doctrine, and intend to bring this Man's blood on us"* (Acts 5:28)! Their core issue is the constant proclamation of Jesus' name. The apostles' continually proclaiming the name of Jesus highlights their guilt. If Jesus was raised from the dead through the power of Jehovah, they were guilty of rejecting the plan of God for Israel. Each time the apostles proclaimed Jesus, they questioned and examined (eperotesen) these leaders. The message of Jesus continually demanded the council think again and re-examine their involvement in His death.

Luke contrasts the guilt and constant pressure of the council with the apostles' attitude. In both interrogations, the apostles expressed no sense of guilt. However, they were as guilty of Jesus' crucifixion as these leaders were! The apostles pledged to go to the death with Him but did not. They all scattered in fear and left Him to die alone. They all were betrayers equal to Judas. Yet, the proclamation of His name did not produce guilt and shame in the apostles as it did with the leaders of Israel. The apostles experienced what they were consistently challenging the leaders to share. ***"Repent therefore and be converted, that your sins may be blotted out, so that times of refreshing may come from the presence of the Lord"*** (Acts 3:19). They embraced the resurrected Jesus through Pentecost and would not waver. Guilt was no longer their state, but God filled them with such great confidence that they could not but speak His name!

Do we not all stand in the place of need? Through the proclamation of His name, He has pronounced us all guilty. Have we not all crucified Him afresh (Hebrews 6:6)? Have we not allowed barriers of tradition and self-protection to reject the full embrace of who He is? Through our self-promotion, we have dethroned Him to the position of our errand boy. We desire angels to deliver us, but we do not want to go to the temple to proclaim the name of Jesus. We crave our safety and comfort. We are all at the crossroads of this scene. Will we be proclaimers of His name with victory in His presence or rejectors of His reality with the message of accusation?

Acts 5:28

UNEXPECTED TESTIMONY

"saying, 'Did we not strictly command you not to teach in this name? And look, you have filled Jerusalem with your doctrine, and intend to bring this Man's blood on us'" (Acts 5:28)!

One of the most startling revelations of the Scriptures is the extent to which God will reveal Himself! We can see this in the amazing instruments of His revelation. Jesus concluded the proclamation of the Sermon on the Mount (Matthew 5, 6, 7). The crowd listening, including His disciples, did not understand the depth of God's nature revealed (Matthew 7:28). Jesus took the truth of the Sermon on the Mount proclaimed in preaching to the physical activities of the streets. The first encounter recorded by Matthew is between Jesus and a leper (Matthew 8:1-4). We could understand the testimony of a successful businessman or a famous movie star, but of what value is the testimony of the worst, lowest, and most rejected individual in society? Yet, this healed leper presents the love of God as unrestricted. Such love can reach the most defiled! Who would allow a leper to give voice to who you are? God did!

The second encounter in Matthew's Gospel is between Jesus and a Roman centurion (Matthew 8:5-13). This revelation is hardly an improvement over the leper. The centurion was a defiled Gentile, symbolizing all the evil in the Roman world. Everyone hated him for his barbaric methods and despised him for his pagan gods. Yet, Jesus embraced him as a man of great faith: **"Assuredly, I say to you, I have not found such great faith, not even in Israel"** (Matthew 8:10). The Roman centurion was the worst of the gentile world, so who would choose such a barbarian to be the face of proper faith? God did!

Several disciples were fishermen with many years of experience on the Sea of Galilee. They found themselves in a great tempest where the waves covered the boat (Matthew 8:23-27). The panic in the disciples' hearts pointed to the storm's fury. They pleaded with Jesus to save them, but He was asleep in the boat. Jesus arose and rebuked the winds and the sea, bringing a great calm. The disciples marveled, **"Who can this be, that even the winds and the sea obey Him"** (Matthew 8:27)? Who can use even nature to declare their revelation? God can!

Jesus and His disciples landed in the country of the Gergesenes, descendants of the Israelite tribe of Gad (Matthew 8:28-34). The storm caused their boat to veer from its destination. The Gadites had compromised their connection to Israel when they began raising pigs. Two demon-possessed men came out of the tombs to attack the disciples. They cried, **"What have we to do with You, Jesus, You Son of God? Have You come here to torment us before the time"** (Matthew 8:29)? The demons could not resist the power of God flowing through Jesus. He commanded the demons out of the men and into the pigs. Who is so great that even His worst enemies in the spiritual realm must express His greatness? God is!

Throughout his Gospel account, Matthew highlights every facet of natural and spiritual life-giving testimony of the greatness of Jesus! Sickness and disease testify to His power, for He healed them all (Matthew 12:15). The prophecies of the Old Testament were fulfilled in His person (Matthew 5:17). The

Part Four: Apostle's Restatement: The Unexplainable

Sabbath submitted to His authority and declared His greatness (Matthew 12:8). God called Moses and Elijah, the Law and the prophets, to return to the physical realm to testify to His purpose (Matthew 17:3). Even the rich, in their rejection of His call, gave testimony to His wisdom and went away sorrowfully (Matthew 19:22). God shamed the wisdom of the world contained in the leaders of Israel to admit His truth (Matthew 22:46). Even a rooster participated as the voice of God to a wayward disciple (Matthew 26:74). Indeed Paul was correct in saying, ***"that at the name of Jesus every knee shall bow, of those in heaven, and of those on earth, and of those under the earth, and that every tongue should confess that Jesus Christ is Lord, to the glory of God the Father"*** (Philippians 2:10-11).

The revelation of God continued during the ministry of the early Church! "Lots cast" declared the will of God (Acts 1:26). Galilean tongues proclaimed ***"the wonderful works of God"*** in fifteen languages they did not know (Acts 2:11). People usually protected their physical possessions, but in the early Church, ***"neither did anyone say that any of the things he possessed was his own"*** (Acts 4:32). In their death, a hypocritical married couple declared the reality of God's truth (Acts 5:1-11). Imprisoned apostles were back at the temple teaching about Jesus (Acts 5:25). The high priest, desperate to silence the proclamation of Jesus, declared, ***"Did we not strictly command you not to teach in this name? And look, you have filled Jerusalem with your doctrine, and intend to bring this Man's blood on us"*** (Acts 5:28)! The unbelieving leadership of Israel knew the presence of Jesus was filling Jerusalem. Their guilty hearts admitted that demonic deliverances and physical healings were happening!

The Arrogance

The high priest's statement begins with an interesting combination of words. ***"Did we not strictly command"*** is translated from the Greek phrase "parangelia parengeilamen." The first Greek word (parangelia) is in the noun form. The second Greek word (parengeilamen) comes from the word "parangello," the verb form. Notice they are the same word. The noun form means "a command, proclamation, or charge," strictly used for commands received from a superior and transmitted to others. This noun form is used only five times in the New Testament (Acts 5:28; 16:24; 1 Thessalonians 4:2; 1 Timothy 1:5; 1:18). The verb form of this word means "the act of commanding, declaring, to advance an order." It is used thirty-two times in the New Testament as "we command you." However, the noun and verb form combination is used only in our passage!

Combining a noun and a verb from the same root word produces a Semitic idiom. Such a construction is emphatic and intensifies the basic meaning of the terms. We see this particular combination of words used in our passage in literature outside the New Testament related to an official summons to court or an order from a court. ***"Did we not strictly command you"*** is a statement of absolute authority. The high priest refers to the first phase of persecution. The council interrogated Peter and John. They **"commanded** (parangello) **them not to speak at all nor teach in the name of Jesus"** (Acts 4:18). The high priest was not merely reminding the apostles of their order but emphatically stressing the authority and superiority of the court. It is unthinkable that the apostles would not submit to the command of the high priest and council!

There is an unwavering arrogance from the high priest, which only validates the reality of the Gospel! Why does the ***"multitude gathered from the surrounding cities to***

Part Four: Apostle's Restatement: The Unexplainable

Jerusalem" become unbearable to the council? The healing of all those *"sick people and those who were tormented by unclean spirits"* radically irritated them. How could a small group of twelve uneducated, untrained men from Galilee be a threat to the high priest? The very presence of the resurrected Jesus completely overwhelmed the arrogance of the leaders of Israel. They must rise and give testimony to the validity of His resurrected presence. Are they not admitting the power of His presence, *"For, indeed, that a notable miracle has been done through them is evident to all who dwell in Jerusalem, and we cannot deny it"* (Acts 4:16). The extreme demands and commands of the council validate the reality of God's movement in Jerusalem.

The leaders of Israel gave the same validation to the resistance to Jesus' name. In the first phase of persecution, the recorded threat of the Sanhedrin to Peter and John did not use the word Jesus. They said, *"What shall we do to these men? For, indeed, that a notable miracle has been done through them is evident to all who dwell in Jerusalem, and we cannot deny it. But so that it spreads no further among the people, let us severely threaten them, that from now on they speak to no man in this name* (Jesus)*"* (Acts 4:16-17). The interrogation was intense and more emphatic in the second phase of persecution. The high priest refused to use the actual name of Jesus. He said, *"Did we not strictly command you not to teach in this name* (Jesus)*? And look, you have filled Jerusalem with your doctrine* (Jesus)*, and intend to bring this Man's blood* (Jesus) *on us"* (Acts 5:28)!

The Talmud is a collection of rabbinic Jewish texts that record the oral tradition of the early rabbis. It is the primary source for studying Judaism during Jesus' and the apostles' lifetimes. The Talmud reflects the hesitation of the high priest to mention the actual name of Jesus, and it even calls Him "so and so!" The population of Jerusalem widely used the name of Jesus, which was undoubtedly true before His crucifixion. Matthew records that His fame was not only in Galilee but ***"Decapolis, Jerusalem, Judea, and beyond the Jordan"*** (Matthew 4:25). If the leaders of Israel thought they could silence His name after His crucifixion, they were wrong. Not only did His resurrection appearances create consistent proclamation of His name, but Pentecost empowered the witness to His name. Jesus told the apostles, ***"But you shall receive power when the Holy Spirit has come upon you; and you shall be witnesses to Me in Jerusalem, and in all Judea and Samaria, and to the end of the earth"*** (Acts 1:8). The high priest gave testimony to this reality. He said, ***"And look, you have filled Jerusalem with your doctrine"*** (Acts 5:28). The council understood the content of the apostles' doctrine was Jesus! The power of His name represented the power of His presence everywhere in Jerusalem. The rebellion of the Sanhedrin against the name of Jesus only verified the strength and power of His presence. Why was His name so offensive to them? Why did they feel threatened by the name of Jesus? Is it not true in our own lives? The more we protest His convicting presence, the more we testify to the reality of who He is! We do not use the name of Buddha, Muhammad, or Allah in vain, only Jesus. Every time we do, we validate the reality of His claim on our lives!

The Achievement

The high priest acclaimed the accomplishment of the apostles and the early Church. He said, ***"And look, you have filled Jerusalem with your doctrine"*** (Acts 5:28). The verb ***"have filled,"*** translated from the Greek word "pleroo," is one of the Greek words used for the "filling" of the Holy Spirit

Part Four: Apostle's Restatement: The Unexplainable

at Pentecost. ***"And suddenly there came a sound from heaven, as of a rushing mighty wind, and it filled*** (pleroo) ***the whole house where they were sitting"*** (Acts 2:2). Luke refers to the filling of the Holy Spirit through the imagery of ***"sound"*** and ***"divided tongues."*** The Greek verb means "to fill, supply abundantly with something, impart richly, or to imbue." The high priest confessed that the message of Jesus' saving power raised from the dead had touched every individual in Jerusalem.

The Greek verb is in the indicative mood, meaning it is a simple statement of fact. It was even admitted by those violently against the spread of this name. The verb is in the perfect tense. The high priest used it to describe a completed verbal action that occurred in the past but produced a state of being or a result that exists in the present. The emphasis on the perfect is not the past action but the present "state of affairs" resulting from the past action. This verb is in the active voice. The high priest accredited the apostles with this "state of affairs." The apostles, with the early Church, were empowered and merged with the Spirit of Jesus; they were focused entirely on the resurrected Jesus, and their message touched every individual in Jerusalem.

According to the high priest, that which permeated all of Jerusalem is ***"your doctrine."*** The Greek word translated as ***"doctrine"*** is "didache." The New Testament translates "didache" as "teaching." Often it is not a single aspect of the proclamation but indicates the summary of the entire teaching. The high priest accused the apostles of having a single focus: Jesus. Luke verifies their insight from the council's command to the apostles: ***"So they called them and commanded them not to speak at all nor teach in the name of Jesus"*** (Acts 4:18). The issue is not the doctrine of the resurrection. The Pharisees believed there was a resurrection from the dead, but the Sadducees did not, and they continually argued and debated it. The issue was not miracles. Who could regret the improvement in the lives of needy people? They did not question the compassionate ministry of the early Church. The upsetting factor was the person of Jesus!

Again, we understand the approach of the high priest only validates the reality of Jesus' power. The high priest testified on behalf of Jesus. Despite all the authority, position, and prestige residing in the high priest and his fellow priests, they could not stop the person of Jesus from captivating all of Jerusalem. The resurrected Jesus, whom they crucified, filled and moved in the lives of believers, and the leaders of Israel could not silence them. The Trinity testified on behalf of Jesus through a most unlikely source.

The Acceptance

A startling element of the high priest's testimony concerns Jesus' death shifting to the plural. The high priest moved the involvement from his participation to that of his fellow priests. He said the apostles' intention was ***"to bring this Man's blood on us."*** ***"Us"*** is a translation of the first-person plural of "ego." Is there any question about the involvement of the leaders of Israel in the crucifixion of Jesus? Had it not been a few months or perhaps a year? Could they possibly deny standing before Pilate on that dreadful day? Pilate did everything he could to shift the decision concerning Jesus to someone else. He transferred Jesus to Herod, only to have Herod return Jesus to him. He presented Barabbas as an alternative to releasing Jesus. Who in their right mind would want the release of Barabbas back onto the streets of their city? Had not this leadership group demanded the crucifixion of Jesus and the release of Barabbas?

They blackmailed Pilate until he had no choice but to accept their demands. In desperation, he performed the symbolic act before them all. A bowl of water placed before him allowed him

Part Four: Apostle's Restatement: The Unexplainable

to wash his hands as he cried, ***"I am innocent of the blood of this just Person. You see to it"*** (Matthew 27:24). How could the high priest deny his leadership in Jesus' crucifixion as he cried out, ***"His blood be on us and on our children"*** (Matthew 27:25)? While they might be unable to deny their responsibility in His death, will they embrace their guilt?

Every sermon or exhortation recorded before this second phase of persecution presents the reality of their guilt. The Jews were not just responsible for crucifying Jesus but guilty of rebelling against God's will, of doing the wrong thing! Peter's sermon on Pentecost day declared, ***"You have taken by lawless hands, have crucified, and put to death"*** (Acts 2:23). Peter immediately recounts how God corrected their sin and rebellion by raising Jesus from the dead. When the manifestation of Jesus' power stirred Jerusalem through the miracle of the lame beggar, Peter again proclaimed their guilt. He cried, ***"But you denied the Holy One and the Just, and asked for a murderer to be granted to you, and killed the Prince of life, whom God raised from the dead, of which we are witnesses"*** (Acts 3:14-15).

During the interrogation of the first phase of persecution, Peter explained the miracle experienced by the lame beggar. He plainly said, ***"Let it be known to you all, and to all the people of Israel, that by the name of Jesus Christ of Nazareth, whom you crucified, whom God raised from the dead, by Him this man stands here before you whole"*** (Acts 4:10). However, we must understand that the apostles were not looking for someone to blame. They were as guilty as the leaders of Israel in embracing their self-centered will. Did they not deny Him? Not one of them died with Jesus. The apostles pleaded to assume the guilt, repentance of the heart, and receive forgiveness. They experienced such forgiveness, and God filled them with His presence. This forgiveness and infilling caused the apostles to saturate Jerusalem with His name!

It is our intent as well. We do not come as one to judge or condemn. We come to embrace you and kneel together in great confession. Have we not sinned? Are we not guilty? It is not that we have just done wrong things. We **"have tasted the good word of God and the powers of the age to come** (Hebrews 6:5). We have crucified Him again and put Him to open shame. His crucifixion is not a past deed that we can blame on the high priest and his fellow priests; we daily participate in crucifying Jesus in the spiritual realm of our lives. As the apostles touched the high priest with the message, the message also touches us. As God confronted the high priest with his guilt, He confronts us with our guilt. As Jesus again reaches out to the high priest, He is reaching out to us. Let us embrace Him together.

Acts 5:29

COMPELLED

*"But Peter and the other apostles answered and said:
'We ought to obey God rather than men'" (Acts 5:29).*

We sometimes feel confused with the various translations of the Scriptures. Why did the writers include some things in the texts while eliminating others? Often, they preserve the fundamental truth of the passage, yet they miss the depth of insight. In our passage, after the angel released the apostles from prison, the leaders of Israel captured them again, threatened them, and asked the apostles to clarify their actions. Why did the apostles continue to speak about Jesus? The apostles **"answered and said"** (Acts 5:29). Several translations leave out the **"and said."** The Greek text says, **"Apokrinomai** (answered) **de** (but) **Petros** (Peter) **kai** (and) **oi** (the) **apostolos** (apostles) **eipon** (said).**"** The sentence begins with **"answered,"** and the reference to **"said"** is attached to the end of the phrase. The Greeks often place the most critical issue at the beginning of their sentence.

You will often read **"answered and said"** in the New Testament; in 163 verses, we can find it 349 times, only in the Gospels and the Book of Acts, which are narratives. This typical Greek expression appears redundant in English. If a person *"answered,"* we know they *"said."* There is no need to state it twice. However, in the Greek language, "eipon," translated as *"said,"* means "speak or to tell." *"Answered"* downplays the importance of the word *"*eipon." "Apokrinomai," translated as *"answered," is* a combination of "apo," meaning "from," and "krino," meaning "to operate, discern, judge, or evaluate." This word indicates a movement from confusion or uncertainty into a state of reason and evaluation.

Jesus experienced spiritual war with Satan in the wilderness temptation for forty days. Matthew gives three examples of the conflict. In the physical realm, Jesus ate nothing for forty days. When the awareness of hunger struck Him, He must have felt overwhelmed. The Devil immediately suggested, *"If you are the Son of God, command that these stones become bread"* (Matthew 4:3). Jesus must have found it difficult to be objective. What could be evil about eating? Eating is not sinful; miracles are not wrong; it is proper to meet the physical needs of one's life. Is this not a good suggestion? Jesus must have turned to the Devil and instructed him to wait momentarily. Jesus moved into the heart of the Father to discern, evaluate, and judge the situation. Matthew records, *"He answered and said"* (Matthew 4:4). When Jesus returned from the embrace of the Father, He knew what to do. He made His decision from the heart of the Father!

Did the apostles know what to do in this similar situation? Their emotions must have screamed for personal safety. They needed to win the favor of the leaders of Israel to convert the Jews to Jesus. If the apostles continued their present ministry, the high priest and the Sadducees would eliminate them, and they would have no ministry. Would it not have been better to compromise that they might continue? How should they respond? They *"answered and said!"* They returned to the fullness of the Spirit of Jesus within them to know His mind and heart. That is the pattern of the Spirit-filled life!

Part Four: Apostle's Restatement: The Unexplainable

Understanding that this was not merely the apostles' response in a crisis hour is essential. The fullness of the Spirit within them was their consistent state of existence. It is somewhat misleading to indicate they ran back to the fullness of Christ's Spirit. He was their dwelling place, their constant state. In their helplessness, they had merged with Jesus. He did not give them life; He was their life. He did not advise them as a counselor; He was their thought process. He did not instruct them concerning actions to accomplish; He was the power by which they moved, the muscle of their activity. In the intimacy of His embrace, they knew His heart! They lived in a conscious dependency on Jesus. The apostles were not going to give any answer that did not come from the heart of God. The apostles had merged with Jesus!

The difficulty for the high priest and the Sadducees was Jesus' constant confrontation. During His earthly ministry, He was a continual irritation to them. By His very nature, He violated and exposed their religious practices. They could not survive as they were with Jesus present. Think of how difficult it was for them now! In crucifying Him, they set the stage for God to elevate His life and nature into the spiritual lives of others. His resurrection, ascension, and outpouring of His Spirit brought the possibility of a merger with God. Suddenly the Holy Spirit was not filling one Man but hundreds and thousands. The Life of Jesus was not a demonstration in the flesh of a single individual, but Jesus filled the multitudes. The life of Jesus bombarded the high priest and Sadducees at every turn.

The apostles told the high priest and Sadducees precisely what Jesus said to them. ***"We ought to obey God rather than men"*** (Acts 5:29). Jesus said, ***"My Father has been working until now, and I have been working"*** (John 5:17). Are not the Father's works Jesus' works? He continued, ***"Most assuredly, I say to you, the Son can do nothing of Himself, but what He sees the Father do; for whatever He does, the Son also does in like manner"*** (John 5:19).

The inner condition of Jesus' life is now the inner condition of the apostles' lives. They dwell in a state of merger with the Father, who continually supplies the flow of life through them. They will not depend on the leaders in the Sanhedrin, the Jewish system, for their life's support. Jesus is their life!

Abandonment
"obey"

In a grand sense, the word **"*obey*"** is misleading in our passage. In our culture, obedience centers on "doing what you are told." We learn to obey the laws of the land. The authorities impose the law structure on us; we must perform the proper level of obedience to fulfill those demands. "Doing what they were told" was not the apostles' response to the high priest, although it was the Old Testament view of obedience. God was on Mount Sinai or in the temple, giving forth religious regulations for the people of Israel. They must discipline themselves to come under the domination of those requirements. In the New Testament, God moved into the inner being of the individual. He does not merely change locations but alters the method of interaction with the individual. God does not demand specific requirements but merges with the human being. He does not communicate to the person what he must do; God does it through and with the person. That person does not merely surrender to God's desires but abandons Himself to the person of God!

The Greek word "peitharcheo" means **"*obey*"** in our passage. It combines two Greek words: "peitho" and "arche." "Peitho" means to persuade, and "arche" means to rule or begin as the first. The Greek word in our passage is only used four times in the New Testament (Acts 5:29; 5:32; 27:21; Titus 3:1). "Peitharcheo" presents the idea of being persuaded by and is more significant than merely surrendering to an authority.

Part Four: Apostle's Restatement: The Unexplainable

Surrender is often "a gun in one's back," forcing or manipulating obedience. The Spirit of Jesus persuaded the apostles who have become one with Him. The mind convinces them of Christ, and they have abandoned themselves to merge with the Spirit of Jesus within them.

This concept was presented to the Sanhedrin by Peter and John in the first phase of persecution. Their response to the threats of the leaders of Israel was, **"Whether it is right in the sight of God to listen to you more than to God, you judge"** (Acts 4:19). The focus of their answer was on the Greek word "akouo," which means **"to listen."** In this context, it means more than merely hearing words; it refers to coming under God's influence, allowing Him to determine our lives and blend our thought processes and heart with His desires. In the merger with the Spirit of Jesus, the apostles began to think like Jesus, feel like Jesus, and desire what He desired, the new creature the leaders of Israel faced in Jesus but crucified. Then the life of Christ expanded to thousands of individuals.

Paul used this same idea in admonishing children regarding their parents. **"Children, obey** (hupakouo) **your parents in the Lord, for this is right"** (Ephesians 6:1). He is not instructing a surrender to every command the parent makes for the child. He calls for the child to come under the influence and authority of the parent. The Greek word translated as **"obey"** is "hupakouo." It combines the prefix "hupo" and "akouo." "Hupo" means "under," and "akouo" means to hear. The child is not simply to listen to the parent but to come under the parent's expression. After all, doesn't the child have the biological nature of the parent within him? Doesn't the parent's DNA flow through the child's physical structure? If this is true of the parent separate from the child, how much more will it be true for the child filled with the One who gives him life?

We do not just surrender to Jesus; we abandon to Him! In the merging of His nature and our nature, we are giving expression to His life. In the first interrogation, the leaders of Israel revealed their concerns. ***"But so that it spreads no further among the people, let us severely threaten them, that from now on they speak to no man in this name"*** (Acts 4:17). How can a person who is merged with and abandoned to Jesus cease to give expression to His nature and person? If He is my DNA and His nature shapes me, how can I not look like Him? It is not about the ceremony but the intimacy of life! It is not about memorized speeches, but the uniting with Him in living expression!!

Absoluteness
"ought"

There is a parallel between the apostles' responses in the first and second interrogations. In the second interrogation, the apostles said, ***"We ought*** (dei) ***to obey God rather than men"*** (Acts 5:29). In the first interrogation, they said, ***"For we cannot*** (dynamai) ***but speak the things which we have seen and heard"*** (Acts 4:20). The Greek word "dei" is often translated "must." There are five different uses of the word in the New Testament determined by its context, each expressing an absolute necessity that may be the nature of the case presented. The circumstances or conduct of others may bring about what is necessary to acquire an end or conclusion. If based on the law or commandments, it may involve the counsel and decree of God. These could logically be the driving force of the apostles' statement.

We should note that the undercurrent of all five uses is the last one, the counsel and decree of God. The apostles reveal the Divine power of God working in their lives. This Divine power reveals Jesus through life and speech, which we cannot alter. It is not a product of the apostles' discipline or education; they have not manufactured it. The early Church movement was

Part Four: Apostle's Restatement: The Unexplainable

not a new business venture that a group of enterprising apostles started. They did not produce the crucifixion, the resurrection, the ascension, or Pentecost! The expression through their lives concerning Jesus is a product of God moving in and through them. The apostles express, "What choice do we have? Expressing the life of Jesus is who we are, and the sovereignty of God backs that up!" "Dei" designates an unconditional necessity, an expression of an absolute, unquestioned, and deterministic character.

The first interrogation conveyed this same emphasis. While the apostles did not use the Greek word "dei," they did use the Greek word "dynamai," a word focused on the power that gives one the ability to do. The apostles did not deny the right of choice or eliminate free will. The reality of God raising Jesus from the dead and infilling their lives is so overwhelming that there is no way to question it. How can they pretend they did not interact with Him for forty days during His resurrection? How can they dismiss Pentecost and the abiding presence of Jesus merged with their lives? How can they view all God did in the early Church as if it does not matter? How could they live in a lie or a life of denial when they clearly see?

Is it not true for us? We must not be like the Pharisees who demand a sign when Jesus demonstrated the power of God in so many convincing ways (Matthew 16:1-4). God must fill us with His Spirit, merged with His nature, until Christianity is no longer duty, self-discipline, or ceremony. Christianity must go from the meager level of "have to" to the level of "want to." Obedience must move from "commandments of God" to "passion of our hearts;" because He is our heart! It must be what we cannot help but be! Anything less than this makes Christianity another religion, another set of life-forming obligations. The Divine hand of God is moving within our lives to produce the life of Jesus through us. We cannot turn on or off; it is what we have become in Him!

Abundance
"rather"

The apostles used language that leaves no room for question. They said, ***"We ought to obey God rather*** (mallon) ***than*** (e) ***men"*** (Acts 5:29). ***"Rather"*** is the translation of the Greek word "mallon," meaning "even more, more than ever, or rather." It establishes a comparison; the statement's context determines the comparison's strength. In the apostles' minds, ***"men"*** are not on the same level as ***"God."*** The apostles gave an absolute comparison, strengthened because it is the second time they have used this comparison under the threat of persecution. In the first interrogation, they answered, ***"Whether it is right in the sight of God to listen to you more*** (mallon) ***than*** (e) ***to God, you judge"*** (Acts 4:19). The apostles gave the decision back to the leaders of Israel in the context of the comparison. Is God sovereign? Does His command take precedence over the orders of men? Should your life come under the authority of men's or God's desires?

The apostles state their argument of "reason." In the context of the Jewish faith, there is no other reasonable conclusion, and this reason is the proclamation of the Old Testament.

> *"All the inhabitants of the earth are reputed as nothing;*
> *He does according to His will in the army of heaven*
> *And among the inhabitants of the earth.*
> *No one can restrain His hand*
> *Or say to Him, 'What have you done?'" (Daniel 4:35).*

Should you and I listen only to Him?

The argument of "reward" is present in the statement of the apostles. On the one hand, would not the consequences be destructive not to come under God's authority? Gamaliel, ***"a***

Part Four: Apostle's Restatement: The Unexplainable

teacher of the law held in respect by all the people," appealed to the council. His argument was, *"And now I say to you, keep away from these men and let them alone; for if this plan or this work is of men, it will come to nothing; but if it is of God, you cannot overthrow it - lest you even be found to fight against God"* (Acts 5:38-39). Rebellion against the voice of God is absolute foolishness!

The argument of "reference" is present in the statement of the apostles. The necessity of obedience to God rather than obedience to men is in what they have already experienced. *"**The God of our fathers raised up Jesus whom you murdered by hanging on a tree**"* (Acts 5:30). The resurrection of Jesus from the dead is enough to convince any individual! But the Trinity God dramatically continued. *"**Him God has exalted to His right hand to be Prince and Savior, to give repentance to Israel and forgiveness of sin**"* (Acts 5:31). In the exaltation of Jesus, we find reconciliation to the heart of God despite our rebellion. He poured out His embracing Spirit upon us! The Holy Spirit witnesses all God is doing in and through Jesus. God has given this witness to those who *"**obey**"* Him (Acts 5:32). Should this not command our total allegiance? How could we not be His?

Acts 5:30

A PROPER ANSWER

"The God of our fathers raised up Jesus whom you murdered by hanging on a tree" (Acts 5:30).

Can you imagine the overwhelming pressure the apostles experienced? The Sadducees threw them into an unfamiliar, religious, political arena, and seventy of the most powerful men of Israel interrogated them. Their interrogators are men who control life and death by their decisions. Even Pilate, the representative of the ruling presence of Rome, catered to these leaders. This interrogation was not the apostles' first time before the council! They cannot plead ignorance. The council already said, ***"Did we not strictly command you not to teach in this name? And look, you have filled Jerusalem with your doctrine, and intend to bring this Man's blood on us"*** (Acts 5:28)! Admittedly, the apostles were in direct disobedience to this supreme ruling body. They did not casually infringe on the orders of the Sanhedrin. They boldly, without hesitation, intentionally, and continually disobeyed the direct command of these leaders. Within the apostles' disobedient proclamation of Jesus, they consistently criticized the council for their involvement in Jesus' crucifixion.

Part Four: Apostle's Restatement: The Unexplainable

All reason and logic should guide the apostles to apologize for their disobedience with a spirit of repentance. They will be most fortunate if the council gives them another chance. How many times will the angel of the Lord intervene and deliver them? What difference would the deliverances make if the intent was not safety or escape but continued proclamation? Shouldn't the apostles at least build a bridge between them and the council to maintain order? But such reason and logic are from the self-centered view of the council. Something more incredible than the self-focus of the sinful heart of humanity is taking place within the apostles' lives. The sovereign wonder of the person of Jesus has captured them! Jesus gives them a perspective beyond the temporal. This view determines their response, ***"We ought to obey God rather than men"*** (Acts 5:29).

The second interrogation is a repeat for Peter and John. The council confronted them with the bold command never to speak the name of Jesus again. They answered, ***"Whether it is right in the sight of God to listen to you more than to God, you judge. For we cannot but speak the things which we have seen and heard"*** (Acts 4:19-20). The issue in each answer focused on the superior influence. Is the self-focus reason for man's desire going to dictate and control, or is the sovereignty of God's will? All the apostles' preaching directly threatens the establishment of the council's tradition. The conflict is so realistic that both cannot survive.

All the council members would readily agree that a person must listen to God. In the first interrogation, Peter gave the decision back to the council. He said, ***"You judge."*** The religious teaching of Judaism demanded the acknowledgment of Jehovah God's authority! The issue of debate was not about listening to God but about what God was saying. The last recorded event of this chapter in Acts verifies the need to know what God is saying. Before the Sanhedrin makes any decision concerning the apostles, Gamaliel, ***"a teacher of the law***

held in respect by all the people" (Acts 5:34), addressed the council. His appeal included several illustrations of people who started movements contrary to their present Jewish tradition, with all of them dying on their own. Gamaliel's final appeal was simple, ***"And now I say to you, keep away from these men and let them alone; for if this plan or this work is of men, it will come to nothing; but if it is of God, you cannot overthrow it - lest you even be found to fight against God"*** (Acts 5:38-39).

This passage is a display of the conflict that is present in our personal lives. How can I know what God is saying? No one wants to rebel against God, who is sovereign, but His message is confused. Our traditions, a mixture of teachings, my self-centeredness, and circumstances all twist the message of God. Many voices propose God's pure message, contradicting each other and producing confusion. Why doesn't God clarify His message? He has!!!

God is distinctly speaking. He is not whispering or sharing riddles. He is not telling parables, leaving the subject open for discussion. The Trinity God blares His message directly to us. His speech is Jesus! ***"In the beginning was the Word"*** (John 1:1). The Word that the Trinity God desires to communicate to us is Jesus. The council members were religious experts skilled in the Scriptures. They searched the Scriptures because they thought they could find eternal life in them. But they did not find eternal life, for they missed the message of Jesus in the Scriptures. ***"These*** (the Scriptures) ***are they which testify of Me"*** (John 5:39). The person of Jesus is the living Word of God to us!

Peter and the other apostles seemed to be deeply aware of this dilemma. They offered a presentation to the council, following the expositional sermon construction pattern. They begin with a "proposition." It is the entire sermon reduced to a single sentence. This sentence establishes the boundaries of

Part Four: Apostle's Restatement: The Unexplainable

the presentation, with every statement in the message finding its root in the proposition. The proposition is, *"**We ought to obey God rather than men.**"* One must constantly keep in mind the issue at hand. The council did not demand that the apostles offer sacrificial lambs in the temple. The obedience for which the council presses the apostles is not the observance of the hours of prayer. The single issue is Jesus (Acts 4:17, 18; 5:28). Once Peter established the proposition, it became a transitional statement or question: Why should we obey God rather than men and continue to speak about Jesus?

The apostles find the answer in Jesus Himself, and they forcibly declare it! They do not suggest a philosophical or a theological approach. The answer is in the reality of a person, Jesus! Peter and the other apostles first state the "Resurrection." ***"The God of our fathers raised up Jesus"*** (Acts 5:30). The members of the Sanhedrin are familiar with the theology of resurrection. The Sadducees do not believe in the resurrection, while the Pharisees accept this truth. They debate the resurrection consistently, with neither side winning. But the resurrection has moved from a subject of debate to the reality of a person, Jesus. The early Church proclaimed, ***"in Jesus the resurrection from the dead"*** (Acts 4:2). If anyone wants to accept the truth of the resurrection, they must accept Jesus. People who reject the resurrection deny Jesus and ***"the God of our fathers."***

Secondly, they state the "Restoration." ***"Him God has exalted"*** (Acts 5:31). The focus of the Sanhedrin was on the forms and ceremonies revolving around and pointing to God. They led the Israelite nation in this pattern, which was the financial basis for their prosperity. While this process honors God, it does not know Him. The Trinity God has fulfilled all the forms and ceremonies in a person, Jesus. The focus of the Trinity is now the focus of the apostles. Jesus is their supreme authority of life!

Thirdly, they state the "Representation." "***So also is the Holy Spirit whom God has given to those who obey Him***" (Acts 5:32). The high priest with his fellow priests would consider themselves representatives of God to the people and of the people to God. This representation was the high priest's function on the Day of Atonement as he approached the Holy of Holies. But something dramatic took place in the New Covenant, which became the priesthood of every believer. Jesus, the Prince and Savior of all, generously bestowed His Spirit upon all believers. These believers were not mere witnesses to events but had become the body of Jesus for the demonstration of His Person!

The answer is without debate! "***We ought to obey God rather than men.***" In a clarifying manner, God spoke Jesus loudly in the incarnation! The virgin birth, the star in the East, and the singing angelic host all proclaimed His speaking. The visible image of the invisible God lives among us (Colossians 1:15). Did we listen to His message or embrace His Person? The answer is "NO!" "***Jesus whom you murdered by hanging on a tree.***" But God has given us a second chance! The Trinity God raised up Jesus!

Picture an extensive reservoir of all the truth God wants to communicate to us. All the principles by which the universe operates are present in the reservoir. People are sharing the wonders of human relationships and intimacy. The mysticism of the unseen world is a mystery, and we cannot know it unless Someone who knows reveals it. How is this truth going to be told? Will there be seminars of teaching, classes filled with information and data, or simply the chance of circumstances? How will the Trinity God reveal the heart of the universe, which is the nature of His heart? God became Man, and we call Him Jesus! Jesus is not a temporal revelation; for the Trinity God raised Jesus from the dead. He is the eternal revelation! Let's carefully examine this reality.

Part Four: Apostle's Restatement: The Unexplainable

Ceremony
"Incorporate"

Upon examination of the council (upper stratus of Jewish society) contrasted with the apostles (representing the early Church), one might develop concern for the average evangelical church of our day. Are we more representative of the early Church or the council? Paul expressed deep concern over this issue to Timothy. He described the attitude and actions of those who would experience the "last days." He summarized it as ***"having a form of godliness but denying its power"*** (2 Timothy 3:5). The Greek word translated as ***"form"*** is "morphosis," used ironically to refer to that godliness which is merely a form and simply an external appearance. This godliness is a sham and devoid of absolute power, translated from the Greek word "dunamis." In the context of Paul's statement, this is the moving resource of God that breaks the power of sin. Those who practice such religion find the external forms and expressions of worship conducive to their lifestyles. Still, the power of God, Jesus, is violently at odds with sin's internal nature and motive.

This ceremony is a picture of the Sanhedrin who find meaning and value in offering sacrificial lambs to God, but will not embrace the Lamb of God, Jesus. They search the Scriptures, for they believe the Scriptures have eternal life; however, the Sanhedrin will not embrace Jesus, who is the fulfillment of the Scriptures (John 5:39). They readily embrace the activity of fasting twice a week, not for God's approval, but man's approval (Matthew 6:16). Prayer is an important religious ritual. However, they do not communicate with God but pridefully seek to impress men (Matthew 6:5). They have not embraced the heart of the Father. Still, they do charitable deeds for self-glory rather than love (Matthew 6:2). They focused on the ceremony and missed the Person of the ceremony.

Think of the expense and preparation for a wedding ceremony. The wedding gown is beautiful; the suit is impressive. The wedding vows flow without flaw. The reception is lively; the cake is tasty. The ritual is so successful that the couple decides to do it monthly. However, the man and woman never live together. The "one flesh of marriage" never happens because the two lives never share in the details of life. The husband and wife never procreate children; they never experience companionship. Yet the ceremony is faithfully performed. This imagery produces a pathetic sadness.

The council wants to maintain the marriage ceremony between God and man but does not want to experience the oneness with the Spirit of Jesus. They want to drag the apostles back before Pentecost. The New Covenant was a dream as the council performed the ritual. But in Jesus' resurrection, the Trinity God moved us from ceremony to a Person, Jesus. ***"The God of our fathers raised up Jesus."*** Our fathers experienced the ritual; they lived in the dream. We live in the reality of His presence. He is alive within us! Should we obey God, or should we obey men? Everyone understands it is God we should obey. But is He merely the God of ceremonies? Is He Jesus who wants to embrace us and indwell us in the merger? If this is true, it would not be mere ceremonies of accomplishment but an intimate relationship to experience!

Commandment
"Intimacy"

God consistently proposed to His people, ***"I am holy"*** (1 Peter 1:16). We did not understand the meaning or content of such a statement. We appreciated the statement's sincerity but did not comprehend the heart of its intent. So God wrote His holiness in a book. He said, "If I were a man, here is how I would act; this is an expression of my holy nature." The Scripture is the expression of the holy nature of God! We desperately tried to accomplish the great commandments portrayed in the law of the Scripture but experienced consistent failure. Ultimately, we adjusted the law to what we could embrace and maintain in our lives. It became comfortable for us, for we could measure how good we were in keeping the commandments of God.

But when God became man, He revealed the law on a new level. While God revealed Himself through the written Law of the Old Testament, in Jesus, the law suddenly moved from mere activity to the intent of the heart. The commandment of murder no longer focused on action but looked deep into the inner heart's hate, belittling, and anger (Matthew 5:21-22). Adultery no longer consists of a physical act but becomes the intent of the inner being (Matthew 5:28). The strength of an oath is not based on the object upon which you swear but on God, who is involved in all of your words (Matthew 5:37). You are an expression of His Person. Love is not felt and expressed to those you like, but on all, for you are an expression of God's heart (Matthew 5:48).

The high priest and the Sadducees desperately wanted the apostles to return to the "good ole days." They could whitewash the external making themselves appear righteous. No one saw the internal corruption and filth of their inner hearts. But the Trinity God became Man, Jesus! In His death, resurrection, and ascension, He moved us to a New Covenant. Should we obey God, or should we obey men? Everyone agrees we must listen to God. God speaks anew in Jesus. He is the fulfillment of the Law and the Prophets (Matthew 5:17). The council wanted to maintain the Law of God as they had interpreted it. But God gave a new revelation of the law in Jesus. They crucified Him, but God gave them another opportunity. What will they do?

Concrete
"Inspiration"

The physical or concrete aspects of life have always been important to us. No one can deny the consistent interaction and concern for this area. Everything we do is related and demonstrated through the physical. No one discourages the use of the physical or demeans its value in our lives. The difficulty is "focus." The high priest and the Sadducees made the physical aspect their focus. They were very religious; they demonstrated their belief by physically participating in religious activities. No one could criticize their faithfulness to prayer, fasting, and observance of the feast days. The high priest was responsible for guiding all of Israel in the physical activities in the temple.

But Jesus interfered with this physical focus. He shifted the heart of the matter from the physical to the spiritual. The physical is not to be eliminated or downplayed; it must become the expression of the inner spiritual relationship. Should we not obey God rather than men? Everyone understands the answer is "Yes!" But obedience has been elevated to an entirely new level. God imparted a unique aspect to obedience, which radically changed its quality. In the Old Testament, God was outside us; He told us what we should do, requiring us to keep His commandments. We were never able to master that obedience completely. But Jesus came to indwell us. God is not outside telling us what to do, but inside empowering us. He came inside to take what He said outside and make it a reality inside. Therefore, we do not keep the commandments as in mere physical performance, but we are His commandments demonstrating His nature.

The high priest and Sadducees began each day quoting "The Shema." "*You shall love the Lord your God with all your heart, with all your soul, and with all your mind*"

(Matthew 22:37; Deuteronomy 6:5). This is the fulfillment of all the Law and the Prophets. But we cry out, "How do I do this?" There will be physical activities that will express this deep love for God. But the main issue is not physical activities but the passion for love, an abstract, spiritual, or mystical embracing of the Person of God in Jesus! The high priest and Sadducees missed this! The Spirit of Jesus filled the apostles. His indwelt presence was now at the heart of religion, changing everything.

Should we obey God rather than men? The answer is "Absolutely!" But God is not a religion to do but a Person to experience. He is not an activity but a relationship. Jesus is not a prayer to repeat but an intimate whisper in the soul. He is not a religious discipline, but a love passion, not a worship emotion, but a constant inner companion. Jesus is not a counselor giving advice, but the empowerment from the consistent indwelling embrace moving us as He desires. He is not words to read but inner revelation in the depth of our souls, changing our lives. He is not laws to keep but passions of desire expressed in physical activities. The high priest and Sadducees want us to go back before Pentecost and eliminate Jesus, but we cannot!

Acts 5:30

RESURRECTION

"The God of our fathers raised up Jesus whom you murdered by hanging on a tree" (Acts 5:30).

The full weight of the second phase of persecution fell on the apostles. They readily admitted they had not obeyed the desires or instructions of the council. Their explanation for such defiance was simply, **"We ought to obey God rather than men"** (Acts 5:29). Recognize the extreme pressure placed upon the apostles as the Sanhedrin interrogated them for the second time. The full wrath of the leaders of Israel should have crushed the apostles with punishment or even death. No reason offered could appease the apostles' blatant violation of the specific law. There was nothing to do except throw themselves upon the mercy of these seventy controlling men.

They might have pleaded ignorance, saying, "We did not fully understand what you wanted us to do?" Or they could have said, "We had to do what was best for us." They might have even excused themselves by blaming others, "We tried to quiet our followers, but they continued to speak about Jesus. It was beyond our control." The apostles might have requested more time to explain their need to "phase out" the name of Jesus from their program. However, the only reason they offered was the

Part Four: Apostle's Restatement: The Unexplainable

bold statement, *"We ought to obey God rather than men"* (Acts 5:29). They blamed God for their continued declaration of Jesus and aggressive violation of the Sanhedrin's instruction!

The CAUSATION of their disobedience is evident. While the apostles were certainly accrediting God for their disobedience, they focused on the "must" of their actions. It is the Greek word "dei," translated as "must" or *"ought,"* a word we have investigated in previous studies. Peter used this word in connection with the Scriptures in the first recorded business meeting of the early Church. He said, *"This Scripture had to* (dei) *be fulfilled"* (Acts 1:16). Certainly, the emphasis was upon the Person of God, the strength of the cause. However, the absolute necessity of obedience was also stimulated by what the apostles experienced. In the first interrogation, they said, *"For we cannot but speak the things that we have heard and seen"* (Acts 4:20). They interacted with the resurrected Lord for forty days (Acts 1:3), a reality so forceful they could not deny Him. They were not concerned with proper doctrine, ceremonies, or traditions. Out of overwhelming necessity, they must proclaim Jesus. They were not forced by the mystical God, causing them to speak of Jesus. They lived with the resurrected Lord for forty days; He taught, fed, and fellowshipped with them. Now He came to live within them, the reality of the necessity!

The CONTRADICTION of their disobedience is unmistakable. What the council demanded from the apostles directly contradicted what God desired. The Spirit of Jesus that lived within the apostles was the *"Spirit of truth who proceeds from the Father, He will testify of Me. And you also will bear witness, because you have been with Me from the beginning"* (John 15:26, 27). Just before Jesus ascended, He said to His apostles, *"But you shall receive power when the Holy Spirit has come upon you; and you shall be witnesses to Me in Jerusalem, and in all Judea, and Samaria, and to the end of the earth"* (Acts 1:8). Jesus is the focal point of the spiritual war in the seen and unseen world. Everything the council demanded from the apostles was the opposite of the throbbing heart of God!

The COMPULSION of their disobedience is apparent. What Jesus told the apostles in the three verses we just quoted is not a commandment but a compulsion. God would fill them with the power of the Spirit, and they could not resist witnessing Jesus. The merging presence of the Spirit of Jesus and proclaiming the name of Jesus are intimately linked. No one filled can cease to speak about Jesus. If the apostles met the council's demands, they would crucify Jesus afresh in direct rejection of His Spirit (Hebrews 6:4-6). The compulsion about Jesus is not one aspect of Christianity; it is Christianity.

The CONDENSATION of their disobedience is plain. Disobeying God to obey men is ridiculous. For the created to have more authority than the Creator is ludicrous. Paul called those who do such things "fools:" ***"Professing to be wise, they became fools, and changed the glory of the incorruptible God into an image made like corruptible man - and birds and four-footed animals and creeping things"*** (Romans 1:22, 23). They ***"exchanged the truth of God for the lie, and worshipped and served the creature rather than the Creator, who is blessed forever more. Amen"*** (Romans 1:25). Should the council desperately seek with the apostles to discover the complete revelation of the Creator? Jesus fulfilled all traditions, ceremonies, and all past revelations! Should we not bow everything under the new embrace of His Person?

Peter and the other apostles declared they must obey God rather than men. Should not the council consider the same? What is the Jehovah God of the Jews communicating about Jesus? What is the reaction of the Trinity God of the Old Testament to the crucifixion of Jesus? If the Sanhedrin was responsible for the blood of Jesus, what was the power of Jehovah God doing in response? ***"The God of our fathers raised***

up Jesus whom you murdered by hanging on a tree" (Acts 5:30). Let the council carefully examine the actions of God!

Who He Is
"The God of our fathers"

A large crowd gathered, but Jesus' interest was in speaking directly to His disciples. Seated on the mountain, He shared the new level to which He was taking them. It was so radical that no one had ever heard of such teaching. They were astonished (Matthew 7:28)! After explaining the formation of the new Kingdom person through a proclamation of the Beatitudes (Matthew 5:3-12), Jesus began to emphasize "being." He expounded on how the Kingdom person would function in the world (Matthew 5:13-16). It would not be something that he would do, but in the merger with the Spirit of Jesus, he would be a new creature. As Jesus viewed the crowd, by the expressions on their faces, He realized they thought He was starting something new. While it was new, God had been exposing His dream since the fall of man. Jesus did not come to write a new history, formulate a new Bible, or propose a new god (Matthew 5:17, 18). What was happening in the life of Jesus was the dream of the Trinity Jehovah, God of our fathers! He was fulfilling the Law and the Prophets (Matthew 5:17).

If you believe in the God of the Old Testament, you believe in Jesus. Jesus told the Jews who wanted to kill Him, ***"You search the Scriptures, for in them you think you have eternal life; and these are they which testify of Me"*** (John 5:39). Jesus was merely calling Israel to follow the plan of ***"the God of our fathers."*** Jesus is the plan! How could the members of the Sanhedrin miss this reality? We could ask the same question of their ***"fathers."*** Jesus declared "woes" to the scribes and Pharisees! He criticized them for building the prophets' tombs and adorning the righteous monuments. The scribes and Pharisees boldly stated, *"if we had lived in the days of our fathers, we would not have been partakers with them in the blood of the prophets"* (Matthew 23:30). However, they were witnesses against themselves. They testified by their rejection of Jesus that they were sons of their fathers (Matthew 23:31). The author of Hebrews said the same good news God presented to the scribes and Pharisees was delivered to their fathers (Hebrews 4:2). Still, neither the fathers nor the sons embraced the Gospel.

Peter proposed the necessity of obeying God rather than men based upon longevity alone! Men are creatures; God has been sovereign Creator from before time. Men are recently upon the scene compared to God, who always has been. Men are learning the truth, while Jesus is the Truth they should learn. Our Jesus is excellent in His name, above all earthly creation. His glory is above the heavens, for His fingers are the works. He ordains the moon and the stars. In light of this, you must ask, *"What is man that You are mindful of him"* (Psalms 8:4)? Should man's instruction be the deciding fact in my life or the wisdom of Jesus?

The Trinity God established the plan for us before the foundation of the world (Ephesians 1:4). Regardless of the evil one's plotting, our Jesus has never wavered! The Trinity God's steadfastness through the Old Testament, *"the God of our fathers,"* testifies to the certainty of His plan. Has He not proved, again and again, His faithfulness to us? Has God ever falsified His plan for us? Has He promised, failed, pledged, not honored, or hated us instead of loving us? Has God not continually hounded us with His redemptive heart? As He wept over Jerusalem, He wept over us. Contrast the plan of men with the plan of *"the God of our fathers."* Weakness and insufficient wisdom fill our plan. Our self-centeredness has determined its destiny only to find destruction.

No one who understands reality would obey men rather than *"the God of our fathers."* Yet the council demanded such obedience. The authority of men wanted to silence the name of Jesus. At the same time, God's decree *"has highly exalted Him and given Him the name which is above every name, that at the name of Jesus every knee should bow, of those in heaven, and of those on earth, and of those under the earth, and that every tongue should confess that Jesus Christ is Lord, to the glory of God the Father"* (Philippians 2:9-11). Will we obey Him?

What He Has Done
"The God of our fathers raised up Jesus"

We should obey God rather than men because of what the Trinity God is doing in Jesus! He *"raised up Jesus,"* an apparent reference to the resurrection of Jesus. It is amazing how each time Peter proclaims Jesus, he references the resurrection. The Greek word translated as *"raised up"* is "egeiro." At the heart of this word is the idea of gathering together. Therefore, we apply this idea to various settings where God gathers a person's faculties to accomplish a new position or posture. It can apply to an individual who is aroused from sleep or healed. It is noteworthy to consider this word is used fifty-two times as a designation for the resurrection of Christ.

We must see the resurrection of Jesus as a great "success!" If there was any doubt concerning the claims of Jesus and His position as Messiah, the resurrection eliminated them. The resurrection of Jesus placed the council in a place of extreme guilt. If the God of their fathers raised up Jesus, they committed a monumental catastrophe in the crucifixion. Indeed, this teaching intends *"to bring this Man's blood on us"* (Acts 5:28). The plan of God, as seen through the eyes of our fathers,

Resurrection | Acts 5:30

does not find completion without the resurrection of Jesus. We still find ourselves in our sins, for Jesus did not conquer the final destructive wages of sin (1 Corinthians 15:17). If Christ has not risen, He did not ascend to the right hand of the Father. He did not deliver the Kingdom to the Trinity God and establish the new Kingdom person. We are left alone to save ourselves; indeed, we are most miserable (1 Corinthians 15:19). But He has risen from the dead! Our hope is in Him! He completes our destiny!

The resurrection of Jesus is a great "second chance!" The leaders of Israel desperately desired to eliminate the teachings and presence of Jesus. The disturbance to their traditions and the religious system was unbearable. Did Jesus not upset their temple patterns and restore them to a house of prayer (Matthew 21:12-13)? Did He not abolish the offering of sacrificial lambs by becoming the Lamb? In all of its cruelty, the crucifixion did not sufficiently eliminate this threat. Jesus is back in His full glory, the glory of the world beyond. He is raised from the dead! Does this not give all of Israel a second chance? He confronts our lives afresh and anew, for we re-enacted the rejection scene and shared equal guilt with them. Jesus is raised from the dead and is standing before us once again!

The resurrection of Jesus is the certainty of the great "synegeiro" with Christ! "Synegeiro" is the Greek word Paul used to describe what happens to us. It is the same Greek word (egeiro) used fifty-two times as a designation for the resurrection of Jesus. While this word (egeiro) carries with it the idea of "gathered together," it applies more to the faculties of the person involved. In the resurrection from the dead, God gathers all the faculties of the dead person together to present them in life. However, Paul adds the prefix "syn" to the resurrected word. ***But God, who is rich in mercy, because of His great love with which He loved us, even when we were dead in trespasses, made us alive together with Christ (by grace you have been saved), and raised us up together*** (synegeiro), ***and***

Part Four: Apostle's Restatement: The Unexplainable

made us sit together in heavenly places in Christ Jesus" (Ephesians 2:4-6). What is true in the resurrection of Jesus is now true in us! We are together, merged with Him!

Why He Did It
"whom you murdered by hanging on a tree"

The crucifixion of Jesus is horrible in its physical suffering. The central physical issue in crucifixion is breathing. The victim was forced to move up and down the cross, a distance of about twelve inches, to breathe. This breathing process caused excruciating pain and the terror of not getting the next breath. The Roman politician Cicero stated crucifixion is "the cruelest and hideous of tortures."

However, the motivation of the Jewish leaders for crucifying Jesus was not to cause Him physical pain. God had given Israel instructions regarding the defilement of the land: *"If a man has committed a sin deserving of death, and he is put to death, and you hang him on a tree, his body shall not remain overnight on the tree, but you shall surely bury him that day so that you do not defile the land which the Lord your God is giving you as an inheritance; for he who is hanged is accursed of God"* (Deuteronomy 21:22-23). The crucifixion of Jesus would nullify any claim Jesus might have of Messiahship. The law of God curses Him!

Paul clarifies this great truth. *"For as many as are of the works of the law are under the curse; for it is written, 'Cursed is everyone who does not continue in all things which are written in the book of the law, to do them'"* (Galatians 3:10). Jesus hanging on a cross received in Himself the complete absolute curse of the law! Paul continues to give us clarity. *"Christ has redeemed us from the curse of the law, having become a curse for us (for it is written,*

'Cursed is everyone who hangs on a tree'), that the blessing of Abraham might come upon the Gentiles in Christ Jesus, that we might receive the promise of the Spirit through faith" (Galatians 3:13-14).

Jesus embraced the law's curse ***"by hanging on a tree."*** We must think beyond the physical aspect of such a curse. All the spiritual aspects of being cursed, the actual consequences of eternal judgment, must be calculated in this truth! It is not about Him; it is about us! ***"The God of our fathers raised up Jesus"*** from the law's curse, which has redeemed us! Should we obey Him or men? Should we continue praising, honoring, and submitting to Jesus instead of men? Should we cease to spread the redemptive news of everyman's salvation or listen to the ***"God of our fathers"***? Should we not clear the slate of any loyalty except to Him? We must join the apostles in an obsession with Jesus, which will not allow our silence of His name! We must highlight Jesus until every individual is aware of His greatness!

Acts 5:31

RESTORATION

"Him God has exalted to His right hand to be Prince and Savior, to give repentance to Israel and forgiveness of sins" (Acts 5:31).

A foundational understanding of Jesus Christ must always begin with His existence as God! A demeaning or belittling of His position as God twists and confuses His reality. This umbrella overshadows all other revelations of His Person, and there is never a slippage of this position. John firmly established that Jesus never took a posture in which this was not true. ***"In the beginning was the Word, and the Word was with God, and the Word was God"*** (John 1:1). Regardless of whatever may be happening in and through the life of Jesus, this is the undergirding primary truth.

Jesus being God is verified by the focused attack of the demonic forces. They rejoice when men see Jesus as merely another prophet. The demonic forces are overjoyed when Jesus' wisdom promotes Him to a superior rabbi or teacher position. Evil does not fear when Jesus is simply a miracle worker. The consistent demeaning of His name through swearing and cursing pinpoints the intent of the demonic world. All world religions accept Jesus, the man, the prophet, or the teacher, but the issue of His Divinity is the crucial dividing line.

Paul encouraged Titus to keep focused on the hope in the second coming of Jesus, *"our great God and Savior"* (Titus 2:13). Through the prophecy of Isaiah, Matthew pointed to the incarnation as the presence of God among us. ***"Behold, the virgin shall be with child, and bear a Son, and they shall call His name Immanuel, which is translated, God with us"*** (Matthew 1:23). Paul reminded Timothy that in Jesus," ***God was manifested in the flesh"*** (1 Timothy 3:16). To the people of Rome, he said, "***Christ came, who is over all, the eternally blessed God. Amen"*** (Romans 9:5). The writer of the Book of Hebrews is uncompromising in his consideration of Jesus as God. In his first chapter, he recorded the Trinity God saying to Jesus,

"Your throne, O God is forever and ever;
A scepter of righteousness is the scepter of Your kingdom.
You have loved righteousness and hated lawlessness;
Therefore God, Your God, has anointed You
With the oil of gladness more than Your companions"
(Hebrews 1:8-9).

Is there any position superior to or above this? "***For the Lord is the great God, and the great King above all gods"*** (Psalms 95:3). The duplication in thought reads, ***"For You, Lord, are most high above all the earth. You are exalted far above all gods"*** (Psalms 97:9). Jesus as the exalted one is not exalted to the position of God or above God! As a member of the Trinity God, He already holds this status or position. Paul encouraged us, ***"Let this mind be in you which was also in Christ Jesus, who, being in the form of God, did not consider it robbery to be equal with God"*** (Philippians 2:5-6).

If Jesus is already God, how can He possibly be exalted? His exaltation is not about arriving at another position above

Part Four: Apostle's Restatement: The Unexplainable

God. The answer is in the context of our passage! Peter and the other apostles were in their second phase of persecution. They experienced jail, release, and now interrogation. Their release came through the direct intervention of an angel of the Lord (Acts 5:19). Their deliverance was not for safety but the continued proclamation of Jesus' name. There is no denying the apostles' direct and on-purpose violation of the council's orders. The council commanded the apostles *"not to teach in this name. And look you have filled Jerusalem with your doctrine, and intend to bring this Man's blood on us"* (Acts 5:28)! The quick reply of the apostles was, *"We ought to obey God rather than men"* (Acts 5:29). Peter testified to this with a three-fold explanation: The Resurrection (*"God has raised up Jesus"*), the Restoration (*"Him God has exalted"*), and the Representation (*"the Holy Spirit whom God has given"*).

The exaltation of Jesus (the Restoration) is in the context of "the Resurrection." Peter said, *"The God of our fathers raised up Jesus whom you murdered by hanging on a tree"* (Acts 5:30). We must understand the exaltation of Jesus through the perspective of His crucifixion!

Humanity

We must see the exaltation of Jesus as it relates to "humanity!" Look what we have done to Him! Peter framed the exaltation in the crucifixion's background, saying, *"Jesus whom you murdered."* The Greek word "diacheiriso" is translated as *"murdered."* Other translations used "slew" or "killed." This Greek word is only used twice in the New Testament (Acts 5:31; 26:21). It comes from "dia," a prefix intensifying the action of the verb, and "cheirizo," meaning "to lay hands upon, to kill, or slay." It bespeaks the motive of hate and total disregard for worth or value.

In our previous study, we discovered the motivation of the Jewish leaders for crucifying Jesus was not to cause Him physical pain. God had given Israel instructions regarding the defilement of the land: ***"If a man has committed a sin deserving of death, and he is put to death, and you hang him on a tree, his body shall not remain overnight on the tree, but you shall surely bury him that day so that you do not defile the land which the Lord your God is giving you as an inheritance; for he who is hanged is accursed of God"*** (Deuteronomy 21:22-23). The crucifixion of Jesus would nullify any claim Jesus might have of Messiahship. The law of God curses him! Those crucified were cursed and in the worst class of offenders. ***"Golgotha, that is to say, Place of a Skull"*** could be easily identified (Matthew 27:33). Many believe the name came from the many bones and skulls covering the hillside. Those crucified were considered so worthless that they should not be buried. People were left to hang on the cross until the birds ate their flesh, and their bodies fell to the ground. The scavenger dogs would finish eating the flesh, and the bones symbolized their curse.

Matthew highlighted the curse on Jesus with the prophecy of the price of His betrayal. Judas received thirty pieces of silver and, in great remorse, attempted to return it to the leaders of Israel. Matthew said, ***"Then was fulfilled what was spoken by Jeremiah the prophet, saying, 'And they took the thirty pieces of silver, the value of Him who was priced, whom they of the children of Israel priced and gave them for the potter's field, as the Lord directed me'"*** (Matthew 27:9-10). The prophecy was about their consideration of the prophet's worthlessness, allowing them to pay him thirty pieces of silver for his prophetic services. It was a "joke" of ridicule and demeaning.

Consider how humanity (you and me) treats Jesus. He has no value to us! We included Him in the cursed group that society

Part Four: Apostle's Restatement: The Unexplainable

wanted to eliminate, and he has such negative value to us that He must cease to exist. We considered our lives better without Him and sold Him cheap for our self-will, considering ourselves more valuable than Him.

> *"He has no form or comeliness;*
> *And when we see Him,*
> *There is no beauty that we should desire Him.*
> *He is despised and rejected by men,*
> *A Man of sorrows and acquainted with grief.*
> *And we hid, as it were, our faces from Him;*
> *He was despised, and we did not esteem Him"* (Isaiah 53:2-3).

But the Trinity God exalted Him! Listen to the voice of the Father echoing through the heavens, **"This is My beloved Son, in whom I am well pleased"** (Matthew 3:17). Is this not the total approval of God upon a Man we considered worthless? Could any higher state of support be reached? The Father could not resist thundering the same approval statement again at the Mount of Transfiguration (Matthew 17:5). Jesus lived and found His security in this approval from the Father. Jesus described the inner connection between Him and the Father: **"Most assuredly, I say to you, the Son can do nothing of Himself, but what He sees the Father do; for whatever He does, the Son also does in like manner. For the Father loves the Son, and shows Him all things that He Himself does"** (John 5:19, 20). Jesus experienced approval and linkage with the Father. He did not hesitate to say, **"I am in the Father and the Father is in Me"** (John 14:11).

Many Biblical scholars have studied the Book of Revelation titled "The Revelation of Jesus Christ." The central theme is the exaltation of Jesus, "the Lamb," worthy to open and read the scroll (Revelation 5:7). Heaven sings about His worthiness (Revelation 5:9). God exalts the One who opens the seals and directs the final events (Revelation 6:1). Jesus is ***"the Alpha and the Omega, the Beginning and the End, the First and the Last"*** (Revelation 22:12). The Lamb, speaking from His exaltation, says, ***"Surely I am coming quickly"*** (Revelation 22:20)! We must see His place of honor against the backdrop of our demeaning and belittling His Person. The Exalted One is the same Person! He is Jesus of Nazareth, rejected in favor of Barabbas (Matthew 27:15+). The governor's soldiers took Jesus into the Praetorium and mocked His royalty with a crown of thorns, a reed weed scepter, and an anointing of their spit (Matthew 27:27+). He is exalted!

Humility

If Jesus is entirely God, how can He possibly be exalted? There is no position more excellent or beyond the sovereignty of God! We must understand the exaltation of Jesus in the context of His humility. Paul urged everyone to embrace the mind of Christ. He described it as ***"who, being in the form of God, did not consider it robbery to be equal with God, but made Himself of no reputation, taking the form of a bondservant, and coming in the likeness of men. And being found in appearance as a man, He humbled Himself and became obedient to the point of death, even the death of a cross"*** (Philippians 2:6-8).

Jesus, fully God, set aside every advantage He had as God. He did not give up being God but surrendered all the comforts of being God necessary to assume all the aspects of humanity. What Jesus did not assume He could not redeem! He took on the nature, the mind, the emotions, and the will of humanity. Jesus assumed every stage of the life of humanity from conception, toddler, teen, and adult man. The resource of His Divinity did not source His life. He lived through the power of the Holy Spirit

Part Four: Apostle's Restatement: The Unexplainable

(Matthew 3:16). The nature of the Trinity God filled Jesus, the total man, establishing a "second Adam" lineage through which many sons could come (Hebrews 2:10). He lived a life of "faith" in total reliance upon merging with the Holy Spirit. The holy nature of God visibly demonstrated through Jesus revealed the character and heart of the Trinity. It is a bleed, suffer, and die nature that never thinks about itself! Jesus was the visible image of the invisible God (Colossians 1:15). This is now the posture and position of Jesus.

This great humility was not a temporary sacrifice. Jesus did not assume humanity as a token, partial, incomplete, or temporary state but made an eternal sacrifice! He took the death of humanity that He might redeem us (Hebrews 2:14), assumed the sin of man, and embraced the wages of sin (2 Corinthians 5:21). He experienced the resurrection of a human being so that we might follow Him (1 Corinthians 15:20). Without Jesus assuming all of this within Himself, we have no hope. He is one of us!

It is in this position of humanity that the Trinity God exalted Jesus. He sits at the right hand of the Father as one of us! Paul reminds us, ***"Then comes the end, when He** (Jesus) **delivers the Kingdom to God the Father, when He puts an end to all rule and all authority and power"*** (1 Corinthians 15:24). Jesus is not above the Trinity God. ***"Now when all things are made subject to Him, then the Son Himself will also be subject to Him who put all things under Him, that God may be all in all"*** (1 Corinthians 15:28).

No wonder Peter exclaimed to the council, ***"We ought to obey God rather than men"*** (Acts 5:29). Jesus was exalted to the right hand of God! One of us has made it to the throne of God and sits at the right hand! One of us is exalted to the King of the new Kingdom of human beings merged and one with God. They live by God's nature - bleed, suffer, and die. They never think about themselves. They are the demonstration of

God's nature, holiness. We cannot and will not submit to the selfishness of men filled with themselves. God has delivered us in Christ!

Holiness

The Trinity God exalted Jesus as the complete revelation and demonstration of God's holy nature. In the Old Testament, God stated that He is a holy God (Leviticus 11:44). He delivered His law to the Israelites as a statement of this holy nature. If God was a man, He proposed His conduct would follow this pattern. There was a problem with the law, an external proposal that the actual internal nature could only accomplish. The law was a product of the inner nature of God, which only nature could produce. While we were made in (not with) the image of God, we yielded to sin and assumed the devil's nature. We could mentally understand the laws of God but were incapable of accomplishing their activity because of our nature.

The activity of these laws or the basic pattern is to bleed, suffer, and die and never think about yourself. It is a life demonstrating the cross style! Peter declares to the council the absolute necessity of obeying God rather than men (Acts 5:29). The Trinity God exalted His nature through the humanity of Jesus. How could the apostles possibly cease to declare the greatness of the nature of God revealed through Jesus? To deny Jesus, they would have to reject the nature of God, and to deny the nature of God would be to deny God Himself!

The Greek word "hypsoo" is translated in our passage as **"exalted,"** contracted from the Greek word meaning "height." It means "to heighten, raise up, elevate, or lift up." This Greek word is used five times in the Gospel of John directly related to the crucifixion event. Jesus stated to Nicodemus, **"And as Moses lifted up** (hypsoo) **the serpent in the wilderness,**

even so must the Son of Man be lifted up (hypsoo)***, that whosoever believes in Him should not perish but have eternal life"*** (John 3:14). Jesus predicted His departure to His disciples by referring to the cross. *"**When you lift up*** (hypsoo) ***the Son of Man, then you will know that I am He, and that I do nothing of Myself"*** (John 8:28). Jesus promised, ***"And I, if I am lifted up*** (hypsoo) ***from the earth, will draw all peoples to Myself"*** (John 12:32). Those who were listening to Jesus' statement repeated the statement in question form (John 12:34).

The cross was not just an event in the life of Jesus that He was required to endure. It was an expression of the nature of God that filled Him, merged with Him in His humanity, and sourced the manifestation of His physical life. Jesus expressed His nature in the incarnation, washing the disciples' feet (John 13:1-17) and the miracles flowing from His life. He never lived for Himself but always participated in the cross style's bleed, suffer, and die. He never thought about Himself. I must merge with Jesus! Will this be the exaltation of His life in me? Will I become an expression of His nature? To obey the council, we must deny the holy nature of God! We must never live for ourselves instead of Him! To exalt Jesus, we must participate fully in His nature.

Acts 5:31

THE PLACE

"Him God has exalted to His right hand to be Prince and Savior, to give repentance to Israel and forgiveness of sins" (Acts 5:31).

The Sadducees issued a demonic threat to the apostles that they eliminate Jesus from their vocabulary and, therefore, their lives. Since the beginning, the leaders of Israel have been adamant about silencing His name! However, instead of a decrease in the proclamation of Jesus' name, it spread rapidly. In total fury, the council judged the apostles. However, the apostles responded, **"We ought to obey God rather than men"** (Acts 5:29). Their reasoning for such a statement is threefold. The "resurrection" of Jesus is first, **"The God of our fathers raised up Jesus whom you murdered by hanging on a tree"** (Acts 5:30). The "restoration" of Jesus is second, **"Him God has exalted to His right hand to be Prince and Savior, to give repentance to Israel and forgiveness of sins"** (Acts 5:31). The "representation" of Jesus is third, **"And we are His witnesses to these things, and so also is the Holy Spirit whom God has given to those who obey Him"** (Acts 5:32).

God raised up Jesus, and God exalted Jesus. What is the

difference? The Greek word "egeiro" is translated as ***"raised up."*** It focuses on reversing the horrible fact that ***"you murdered by hanging on a tree."*** God raised Jesus from the dead. The Greek word "hupsoo" is translated as ***"has exalted."*** While both words present the element of "lifted up," one focuses on "from," and the other focuses on "unto." God resurrected Jesus from the dead and elevated Him to an honored position! There is an exciting interlinkage of the crucifixion in both of these facts. The cross is incomplete without the resurrection, ***"raised up."*** Victory is in the wholeness of the cross and the resurrection. Jesus conquered death through death (Hebrews 2:14). The resurrection is the act of that victory over death, which is the wages of all sin. But the completion of this victorious work is the exaltation Jesus received from the Father. The Father recognizes in Jesus the complete restoration of humanity through the cross in His exaltation.

Jesus clarified this in His "high priestly prayer" (John 17). In His last hours before the crucifixion, Jesus prayed to the Father in recognition that ***"the hour has come"*** (John 17:1). His singular cry was ***"Glorify your Son"*** (John 17:1). But it was not a self-centered prayer. Rather a desire ***"that Your Son also may glorify You"*** (John 17:1). The Greek word translated as ***"glorify"*** is "doxazo." The word's core meaning is recognition, focus, honor, or perspective. It is the opinion of someone who recognizes, honors, praises, invests with dignity, and gives esteem or honor by putting another in an honorable position. Jesus did not seek self-glory but cried out for the Father to recognize the fulfillment of the Son's destiny in bleeding, suffering, and dying. Jesus fulfilled the redemptive plan of the Trinity God. The accomplishment of this plan is what is exalted! The full exaltation of Jesus to the Father's right hand is not simply about the Person but about the Person crucified. Do not forget that the eternal recognition of Jesus throughout the Book of Revelation is "the Lamb."

The wonder of this is not merely in Jesus but in us. As the Father destined Jesus, He destines you and me. As the Father uniquely equipped and sent Jesus with great purpose, He has uniquely trained and sent you and me. Our glory is not in self-centered accomplishments but in the wonder of His plan flowing through us! Do not dismiss the phenomenon that we are seated in Christ's exaltation (Ephesians 2:6). The Father's perspective of Jesus now includes us. He recognizes us in Him! We have identified with Him in His death and resurrection and share in His exaltation! The Father accomplished His will in Jesus; He now performs His will in us! Who could have imagined that sinful humanity could experience such?

Peter made a bold, declarative statement to the council: **"Him God has exalted to His right hand to be Prince and Savior, to give repentance to Israel and forgiveness of sins"** (Acts 5:31). The action of God's exaltation is focused on **"Him,"** Jesus! In the Greek language, this word is an accusative, direct object. Jesus receives the action of the exaltation. Two secondary direct objects give content to Jesus; they are **"Prince"** and **"Savior."** But Peter provides us with the location of the exaltation, which is equally significant. It is **"His right hand."** In the Greek language, this is a dative, an indirect object. Peter suggests three vital elements to the exaltation of Jesus. There is the PLACE of the exaltation, **"to His right hand." "To be Prince"** highlights the POSITION of the exaltation. The PURPOSE of the exaltation is equally essential, **"and Savior."**

Place of the Exaltation

What I learned as a child, I assumed as a teenager and continued to believe as an adult. I maintained the physical perspective in the perception. In many Biblical references, I quickly concluded a natural progression from the physical resurrection to a physical exaltation. In his great sermon explaining Pentecost, Peter said, ***"This Jesus God has raised up, of which we are all witnesses. Therefore being exalted to the right hand of God, and having received from the Father the promise of the Holy Spirit, He poured out this which you now see and hear"*** (Acts 2:32-33). Peter made the same connection in our passage between the resurrection of Jesus and His exaltation (Acts 5:30-31). However, this naturally causes us to focus on the physical aspect of the exaltation as we did in the resurrection. Since Jesus, who was raised from the dead physically, ascended, we assume a physical location for His destination. I imagined His location as a colossal palace somewhere far above. This palace has a great throne room with a large gold throne covered with multiple jewels. It has royal cushions upon which Jesus sits at the Father's right hand, but you cannot see Him, for the Father is a Spirit. Perhaps there is a physical location at the right hand of God, but is that the emphasis? Are the Scriptures trying to communicate a "spiritual" place of exaltation rather than a "physical" location? Since God is omnipresent, could the right hand of God also be omnipresent? Therefore, it becomes imagery for a spiritual reality! The Book of Psalms establishes the basis of many statements in the New Testament concerning the enthronement of Jesus as a heavenly and messianic Ruler.

> *"The Lord said to my Lord,*
> *'Sit at My right hand,*
> *Till I make Your enemies Your footstool'"*
> *(Psalms 110:1; Acts 2:34-35).*

God exalted Jesus to the place of authority. Consider Jesus in the power of His resurrection, gathering His disciples to commission them to win the world. He began this commission by exerting the exaltation of "the right hand:" ***"All authority has*** been given to Me in heaven and on earth. Go therefore and make disciples of all the nations"* (Matthew 28:18-19). The Greek word translated as *"authority"* is "exousia." It highlights the permission given to Jesus to make decisions and determine the course of events. As He challenges the disciples with responsibility, He also encourages them. Nothing can come to them, but first, it must come to Him. While He does not cause everything, He certainly must allow it. He has all authority!

Can we contain the overwhelming greatness of this reality? One of our kind, One like us, One with our humanity, has been exalted to the highest place of authority. He dwells at the right hand of God, and he has total access to the Father. *"For in that He Himself has suffered, being tempted, He is able to aid those who are tempted"* (Hebrews 2:18). *"Therefore He is also able to save to the uttermost those who come to God through Him, since He always lives to make intercession for them"* (Hebrews 7:25). If this is not merely a physical location at *"His right hand,"* but a spiritual authority, what is its basis or essence?

Cross Place

There are many statements concerning Jesus' exaltation connected with His death and resurrection:

"Who being the brightness of His glory and the express image of His person, and upholding all things by the word of His power, when He had by Himself purged our sins, sat down at the right hand of the Majesty of high" (Hebrews 1:3).

*"Now this is the main point of the things we are saying: We have such a High Priest, who is seated at the right hand of the throne of the Majesty in the heavens, a Minister of the

sanctuary and of the true tabernacle which the Lord erected, and not man" (Hebrews 8:1).

"Looking unto Jesus, the author and finisher of our faith, who for the joy that was set before Him endured the cross, despising the shame, and has sat down at the right hand of the throne of God" (Hebrews 12:2).

"And being found in appearance as a man, He humbled Himself and became obedient to the point of death, even the death of the cross. Therefore God also has highly exalted Him and given Him the name which is above every name" (Philippians 2:8-9).

Jesus' exaltation flows from the crucifixion not because of the actual event of the cross but due to the culminating display of God's nature through Jesus. The nature of God is "holy." The core fiber of such a nature is "bleed, suffer, and die." This nature never lives for itself! It is expressed in the incarnation as Jesus assumes all the frailty of humanity. Jesus expressed the cross style in every encounter as He interacted with humanity. He bent His humanity under this nature to assume the redemptive position of the sacrifice for the sins of humanity. Now, Jesus displays this nature at God's highest level of exaltation to humanity.

Paul described this exalted position. **"He is the image of the invisible God, the firstborn over all creation"** (Colossians 1:15). He continued saying, **"And He is the head of the body, the church, who is the beginning, the firstborn from the dead, that in all things He may have the preeminence"** (Colossians 1:18). John declared that this is not a temporary exaltation, **"and from Jesus Christ, the faithful witness the firstborn from the dead, and the ruler over the kings of the earth. To Him who loved us and washed us from our sins in His own blood, and** *has made us kings and priests to His God and Father, to Him be glory and dominion forever and ever. Amen"* (Revelation 1:5-6).

His exaltation is the context for many to follow in His footsteps, and He includes you and me. The language describes that which God established on our behalf. God did not exalt Jesus because of His incredible feats accomplished on behalf of Himself. We do not praise Jesus for what He accumulated for Himself. If such were the case, Jesus would never have left His throne to make **"Himself of no reputation, taking the form of a bondservant, and coming in the likeness of men. And being found in appearance as a man, He humbled Himself and became obedient to the point of death, even the death of the cross"** (Philippians 2:7-8). He is the firstborn of what we are to be! The exact holy nature of God, "bleed, suffer, and die," now merges with us as it did with Him. "Don't ever think about yourself" becomes our thought as we have the mind of Christ! God exalts the cross-style nature merged and demonstrated through us!

Completed Place

We must recognize that when the Scriptures mention the right hand, the whole individual is claimed, whether in action or suffering. Peter quoted David as saying,

*"I foresaw the Lord always before my face,
For He is at my right hand, that I may not be shaken."
(Acts 2:25; also see Psalms 73:23; 110:5; 121:5;
Isaiah 41:13; Zechariah 3:1)*

Peter emphasized this again in our passage; **"Him God has exalted to His right hand to be Prince and Savior,**

Part Four: Apostle's Restatement: The Unexplainable

to give repentance to Israel and forgiveness of sins" (Acts 5:31). God did not exalt the actions, miracles, or the crucifixion of Jesus. He exalted Jesus! When Jesus' actions are included, the whole Person occupies the exaltation!

We must never forget that the Cross Event is a cross-section of the nature of God existing in the realm of eternity. It is the nature of God displayed in a moment, but is it the entire time? The bleed, suffer and die nature of God (holiness) displayed on the cross, merged with Jesus, engulfs His whole Person and cannot be separated from who He is. Humanity's helplessness, merged with God's nature, defines the new creature. Jesus is the prototype! God exalted this whole Person to His right hand.

The reality of this exaltation highlights the plan of God for us. ***"For it was fitting for Him for whom are all things and by whom are all things, in bringing many sons to glory, to make the captain of their salvation perfect through sufferings"*** (Hebrews 2:10). Our Captain is exalted as the firstborn for it is the pleasure of God to ***"bring many sons to glory."*** We share in the glory of His exaltation, for we are like Him in merging with the nature of God. He is the firstborn of this completed merger between God and man, the new creature of the Kingdom!

With extreme repetition, Paul often records the phrase ***"in Him"*** in Ephesians (1:3-14). He repeats this or a similar phrase fourteen times in these eleven verses. He insists that God wants you and me to possess every spiritual blessing in Jesus! He calls them ***"spiritual blessings"*** (Ephesians 1:3). The content of such blessings is long and inexhaustible; it includes: ***"chose us," "holy and without blame," "adoption as sons," "accepted," "redemption," "forgiveness," "wisdom," "inheritance," "sealed."*** He clusters these blessings around ***"the praise of His glory"*** (Ephesians 1:6, 12, 14). Is ***"His glory,"*** the nature of God expressed on the cross, "the bleed, suffer, and die nature?" The holy nature of God united with humanity and formed the first human being to be the complete living expression of this nature. What the first Adam failed to do, the second Adam accomplished, and the Trinity God exalted Him. We follow in His footsteps and merge with Him in this exaltation!

Comparison Place

One of the fundamental aspects of being placed at the right hand is the intimate connection established with the one responsible for the placement. When a person of high rank puts someone on his right hand, he gives them equal honor with himself and recognizes him as of equal dignity (Matthew 22:44; 26:64; Acts 2:33; 7:55; Romans 8:34; Ephesians 1:20; Colossians 3:1). The Father's approval of the Son resounded from the heavens repeatedly through Jesus' earthly ministry! When the Father filled Jesus with the Spirit at the beginning of His earthly ministry, He ripped the sky open to thunder forth His pleasure. ***"This is My beloved Son, in whom I am well pleased"*** (Matthew 3:17). When Jesus, through the power of the Holy Spirit, defeated the devil in spiritual warfare, the Father sent angels to minister to Him (Matthew 4:11). On the Mount of Transfiguration, the Father descended in a bright cloud declaring, ***"This is My Beloved Son, in whom I am well pleased. Hear Him"*** (Matthew 17:5)! Even in the Garden of Gethsemane, an angel was sent from the Father to minister to Him as He faced the cross (Luke 22:43). Now to complete the redemptive work, the Father drew Jesus through the ascension to an exaltation of honor and dignity.

Carefully consider the tremendous honor Jesus receives in the Book of Revelation! John saw a great throne set in heaven surrounded by twenty-four elders. Four living creatures, night and day, praised God, who sat on the throne. The twenty-four elders cast their crowns before the throne, offering praise (Revelation 4). God received glory, honor, and power; He is Creator, and by His will, everything exists that was created. In His right hand is a sealed scroll that no one can open, but ***"a Lamb as though it had been slain"*** comes and removes the scroll. The Trinity God found Jesus worthy. A new song is written and sung about Him all over heaven (Revelation 5).

"And every creature which is in heaven and on the earth and under the earth and such as are in the seas, and all that are in them, I heard saying:
'Blessing and honor and glory and power
Be to Him who sits on the throne,
And to the Lamb, forever and forever'" (Revelation 5:13)!

Jesus, who the Trinity God exalts, receives glory, honor, and power at the right hand! He is the expression of the nature of God through human flesh. He is the physical expression of the bleed, suffer, die, and never think about yourself holiness of God!

No one proposes that we become God. We are not omnipresent, omniscient, or omnipotent. But we are drawn into His nature. In Jesus, God exalts us to His right hand. In Jesus, God accepts us in the Beloved. In Jesus, we become the expression of God's nature. In Jesus, His essence is revealed and demonstrated to the world. In Jesus, God displays His holiness on the platform of our lives, and the world knows God. Our exaltation is in Jesus, who the Father exalts!

Acts 5:31
THE POSITION - PRINCE

"Him God has exalted to His right hand to be Prince and Savior, to give repentance to Israel and forgiveness of sins" (Acts 5:31).

What do we do when anyone or anything threatens our life? What if the threat is not from natural causes such as a tornado or hurricane, but the source is in the mystical, unseen, spiritual world? Could Paul be correct? **"*For we do not wrestle against flesh and blood, but against principalities, against powers, against the rulers of the darkness of this age, against spiritual hosts of wickedness in the heavenly places*"** (Ephesians 6:12). The threat to our lives is not in the physical but in the spiritual! Do we consistently try to solve our problems with physical answers when the real battle is in the spiritual realm? We must always recognize the spiritual realm manifesting in the physical realm. Therefore, spiritual solutions are the only possibility for effectively altering the physical!

The physical versus the spiritual was the continual conflict Jesus had with the leaders of Israel. While the intent of God throughout the Old Testament was relationship, the leaders became dominated by the law's physical aspect. Jesus made

Part Four: Apostle's Restatement: The Unexplainable

strong statements. ***"For you cleanse the outside of the cup and dish, but inside they are full of extortion and self-indulgence"*** (Matthew 23:25). ***"For you are like whitewashed tombs which indeed appear beautiful outwardly, but inside are full of dead men's bones and all uncleanness"*** (Matthew 23:27). The apostles experienced the same conflict with these leaders.

The leaders of Israel lost physical control over the situation. The crowds in Jerusalem applauded the movement of God through the early Church. The multitude acclaimed Jesus as their Savior and Lord, and the same Divine movement captured other cities outside Jerusalem. The Sanhedrin only had one approach to solve their problem, physical action! They placed the apostles in jail only to find them released through some unknown spiritual source. They threatened the apostles with the only leverage they had, the physical.

Peter answered the council from a spiritual perspective. He said, ***"We ought to obey God rather than men"*** (Acts 5:29). If we are to obey God, we must be constantly aware of God's unseen spiritual direction and movement. Peter and the other apostles believed the movement of God focused on Jesus. The Trinity God did nothing outside of Jesus. Peter boldly proclaimed, "the resurrection." ***"The God of our fathers raised up Jesus whom you murdered by hanging on a tree"*** (Acts 5:30). The Trinity God took the degradation imposed by the leaders and restored Jesus, "the restoration." ***Him God has exalted to His right hand to be Prince and Savior to give repentance to Israel and forgiveness of sins"*** (Acts 5:31). The Trinity God gave consistent testimony through witnesses of these facts in Jesus, "the representation." ***"And we are His witnesses to these things, and so also is the Holy Spirit whom God has given to those who obey Him"*** (Acts 5:32).

Peter made a bold, declarative statement to the council,

referring to "the restoration." ***"Him God has exalted to His right hand to be Prince and Savior, to give repentance to Israel and forgiveness of sins"*** (Acts 5:31). The action of God's exaltation focused on ***"Him,"*** Jesus! In the Greek language, this word is an accusative, direct object. Jesus receives the action of the exaltation. Two secondary direct objects give content to Jesus; they are ***"Prince"*** and ***"Savior."*** But Peter provides us with the location of the exaltation, which is equally significant. It is ***"His right hand."*** In the Greek language, this is a dative, an indirect object. Peter suggests three vital elements to Jesus' exaltation. There is the PLACE of the exaltation, "***to His right hand."*** ***"To be Prince"*** highlights the POSITION of the exaltation. The PURPOSE of the exaltation is equally essential, ***"and Savior."***

The Position
"to be Prince"

Jesus has a position of high honor and exaltation in the Kingdom! He is the ***"Prince,"*** a translation of the Greek word "archegos." "Archegos" is only used four times in the New Testament, a combination of the Greek word "arche," which means beginning or rule, and "ago," which means to lead. In our passage, Peter proclaims Jesus as ***"Prince"*** for the second time. After participating in the miracle healing of the lame beggar, Peter explained to the crowd at Solomon's Porch that Jesus was the only source of the miracle. Boldly he described Jesus as the One they delivered to Pilate, denied His release to embrace Barabbas, ***"and killed the Prince*** (archegos) ***of life, whom God raised from the dead, of which we are witnesses"*** (Acts 3:15). Jesus is the One who led the way to life!

The Book of Hebrews author used "archegos" twice, proposing that God became man to taste death for every person

Part Four: Apostle's Restatement: The Unexplainable

(Hebrews 2:9), charting the course of accomplishment. *"For it was fitting for Him, for whom are all things and by whom are all things, in bringing many sons to glory, to make the captain* (archegos) *of their salvation perfect through sufferings"* (Hebrews 2:10). He calls us to run the race that is set before us, *"looking unto Jesus, the author* (archegos) *and finisher of our faith, who for the joy that was set before Him endured the cross, despising the shame, and has sat down at the right hand of the throne of God"* (Hebrews 12:2).

Each use of "archegos" references Jesus, and Jesus alone fulfills the true meaning of this word. Luke highlights the crucifixion in connection with this position, and he states the resurrection in three passages and Jesus' exhalation to the right hand of the Father in two references. Those statements establish the context by which we must understand the position. The death, resurrection, and exaltation of Jesus bring Him to the position of *"Prince."* His faithfulness in fulfilling the Trinity God's redemptive plan caused the application of this position to Him. We must investigate the content of this position.

Causing

Peter's statement presents a double accusative in the Greek language. He said, *"Him God has exalted to His right hand to be Prince and Savior, to give repentance to Israel and forgiveness of sins"* (Acts 5:31). The subject is *"God."* The main verb is *"has exalted."* The primary accusative or direct object receiving the action of the exaltation is *"Him."* It is challenging yet essential to distinguish between what a person may accomplish and the person's essence. Someone may do a great act that brings them honor, yet their motive is wrong. The honor does not fall upon the person but upon the accomplishment. Jesus is not honored for what He did but for who He is! What He did is essential, but only because it expresses who He is!

The wordage in the Book of Revelation is explosive, consistently referring to Jesus as "the Lamb," expressing what He did. But it is much more, for it speaks to a description of who He is! The word "lamb" is used thirty-two times in the New Testament, and I was amazed to discover only one of those times refers to an animal (Mark 14:12). Jesus is the focus of the word's use. It is also striking that it is used twenty-eight times in the Book of Revelation! The new song sung in heaven is about ***"Worthy is the Lamb who was slain"*** (Revelation 5:12). Several references are about ***"the blood of the Lamb"*** (Revelation 7:14; 12:11).

Indeed contained within the reference is the physical activity of the crucifixion, but it is so much more than just what Jesus did; it is who Jesus is! Jesus completes all the Trinity God desired for His human creation. One Man, the Lamb, fulfilled the destiny of man. He is the first human Man who merged with the nature and the Person of God! He is the prototype of what every Kingdom person will be! He is the "cause" of the new category, "sons of God!" Jesus did not manufacture a solution to our fallen estate and provide it for us apart from Himself. He is not a supply clerk of the great salvation offered to us by God. Everything God dreams for us is in the Person of Jesus.

Jesus is the reason I cannot contribute to salvation through my works. In the whole experience of salvation, Jesus alone is the "cause." We must be careful about our language, never stating salvation in the first person. The moment we say, "I experience salvation because I believe," we have gone astray. If we say, "I repented," or "I have been faithful," we have violated the heart of Jesus. We must always state salvation in the third person, for "Jesus" is the cause. Repentance only takes place because He draws me into Himself. I see who I am in relation to who He is! I am enabled to believe because He touched my life. I find confidence and security in His presence. Outside of His Person, nothing happens.

God exalted Jesus to His right hand, placing honor and glory upon who Jesus is! Should we obey God, or should we obey man? We must obey God because He has become *"the Prince,"* the "cause" of our destiny. Jesus is the essence of my salvation!

Creating

While the position of *"Prince"* may contain the idea of "cause," it is only a start! The Greek word "arches" comes from the primary word "arche," meaning "beginning or rule," and "ago," meaning "to lead." The focus is the concept of the originator, founder, leader, chief, first, or prince. It moves beyond simply being the cause. One may be the cause of something, but not the beginning. "Arche," like "archegos," denotes the founder as the first cause, ruler, or dispenser. The person of Jesus is not only the "cause" of our salvation, but He is the first human being to step into the position of being filled with God! He is the prototype!

In testifying about the miracle healing of the lame beggar, Peter declared Jesus *"the Prince* (archegos) *of life"* (Acts 3:15). He painted an ironic picture of the Jews demanding the release of Barabbas, a murderer, at the same time killing *"the Prince of life."* Jesus not only causes life in the believer by His presence, but He is the beginning or the originator of the existence of that life. In addressing the Church of the Laodiceans, Jesus presented Himself as *"the Amen, the Faithful and True Witness, the Beginning* (Arche) *of the creation of God"* (Revelation 3:14). He is the Founder, the First Cause, Ruler, or Dispenser of the crowning creation of the Trinity. He is an

Agent of the cause but does not have a cause, excluding Himself from being a product of that beginning. Thus His exaltation to the right hand of God!

In our passage, Jesus' position as ***"the Prince"*** is in the context of the resurrection. He is the Founder, the First Cause, Ruler, or Dispenser of the resurrection of those who will follow. Paul determines He ***"has become the firstfruits*** (aparche) ***of those who have fallen asleep"*** (1 Corinthians 15:20). ***"The firstfruits"*** means "the first element in a countable series, understood as the first crop harvested in a season." Paul further explained, ***"For since by man came death, by Man also came the resurrection of the dead. For as in Adam all die, even so in Christ all shall be made alive"*** (1 Corinthians 15:21-22). In this same thought, Paul called Jesus ***"the beginning*** (arche)***, the firstborn from the dead, that in all things He may have the preeminence"*** (Colossians 1:18). Jesus is the Originator, Founder, Leader, Chief, First, or Prince of the resurrection. If God had not raised Jesus from the dead, then there would be no resurrection from the dead.

The proclamation of this fact was the issue that disturbed the Sadducees and initiated the first phase of persecution. The Sadducees captured Peter and John, ***"being greatly disturbed that they taught the people and preached in Jesus the resurrection from the dead"*** (Acts 4:2). The discussion of the resurrection did not disturb them. The Pharisees believed in the resurrection, and the Sadducees did not. There was a constant debate occurring among them concerning this doctrine. Suddenly, Jesus elevated the discussion to a new level. "The resurrection" is now contained in a Person who is the Originator of this reality. He is an Agent who is the cause but does not Himself have a cause! He is not a product of that beginning but originates it within Himself! God exalted Jesus to His right hand as ***"the Prince!"*** Everything God wants for you and me, Jesus is!

Part Four: Apostle's Restatement: The Unexplainable

Conserving

There is a finality in this position, *"the Prince."* The Greek word "Archegos" occurs only four times in the New Testament and is exclusively a Christological title for the exalted Jesus! Christology is the study of the person, nature, and role of Jesus. It describes He, the first, standing at the head and leading! Is His position temporary? Will another come and take His place?

In the Scriptures, it is evident that the Trinity God established a Kingdom in and through Jesus that will never cease but is eternal! God promised, *"I will establish the throne of his kingdom. He shall build a house for My name, and I will establish the throne of his kingdom forever"* (2 Samuel 7:12-13). The Trinity God protected this promise from the conception of sin to the final judgment of all evil. The first Messianic promise established this reality (Genesis 3:15). The long struggle described through the generations of the Old Testament gives credence to the faithfulness of God. Regardless of the intensity of evil, our God will never waver in fulfilling His plan in Jesus!

When sin had accomplished its worst through death, this worst became how the one who had the power of death, the devil, was defeated (Hebrews 2:14). *"The God of our fathers raised up Jesus whom you murdered by hanging on a tree. Him God has exalted to His right hand to be Prince"* (Acts 5:30-31). He is returning in such a position. Listen to His words. *"When the Son of Man comes in His glory, and all the holy angels with Him, then He will sit on the throne of His glory"* (Matthew 25:31). Do you hear the tone of finality in His voice? *"Then the sign of the Son of Man will appear in heaven, and then all the tribes of the earth will mourn, and they will see the*

Son of Man coming on the clouds of heaven with power and great glory. And He will send out His angels with a great sound of a trumpet, and they will gather His elect from the four winds, from one end of heaven to the other" (Matthew 24:30-31).

The incarnation, God becoming man, was established forever. This Man, Jesus, was raised from the dead and exalted to be the leader, originator, and King of the Kingdom! He will return the second time as Man to establish this reign forever. Not only will the permanency of sin's destruction be found in hell, but the permanency of our merger with God in Christ is secured. Jesus is forever one of us! *"Jesus has become a surety of a better covenant. Also there were many priests, because they were prevented by death from continuing. But He, because He continues forever, has an unchangeable priesthood. Therefore He is also able to save to the uttermost those who come to God through Him, since He always lives to make intercession for them"* (Hebrews 7:22-25). Jesus is the guarantor; we are secure in Him!

Can there be any other message, emphasis, or focus? Should not our entire effort be placed into knowing Him? *"Therefore, my beloved, as you have always obeyed, not as in my presence only, but now much more in my absence, work out your salvation with fear and trembling"* (Philippians 2:12). Would not our "work" be knowing Him who is our salvation?

Acts 5:31

THE PURPOSE - SAVIOR

"Him God has exalted to His right hand to be Prince and Savior, to give repentance to Israel and forgiveness of sins" (Acts 5:31).

Jesus as Savior is a radical and dominant theme throughout all the Scriptures. Jesus' name (Greek for Joshua) means "the Lord is salvation." In the angel of the Lord's mission statement to Joseph, he declared Jesus Savior. **"And she will bring forth a Son, and you shall call His name Jesus, for He will save His people from their sins"** (Matthew 1:21). Jesus declared to Zacchaeus, **"Today salvation has come to this house, because he also is a son of Abraham; for the Son of Man has come to seek and to save that which was lost"** (Luke 19:9-10). Nothing outside the boundaries of this mission will occupy His energy, desires, or focus. Jesus came to be the Savior!

Inherent in the term "savior" is the concept of one who saves or delivers from danger to a position of safety. The scope of the threat defines the greatness of the saving. If Jesus came to save us from our sins, we must understand the danger of sin to understand the wonder of salvation given by the Savior. **"The Son of Man will send out His angels, and they will** *gather out of His kingdom all things that offend, and those who practice lawlessness, and will cast them into the furnace of fire. There will be wailing and gnashing of teeth"* (Matthew 13:41-42). What is the content of the *"wages of sin is death"* (Romans 6:23)? We might view the physical content of such consequence. The absolute destruction of physical life is because of sin, and we cannot overlook it in our time. We must include the destruction of relational involvement in the content. Sin tears families apart; hate rules many lives. What is the eternal spiritual death experienced in hell forever? Did not Jesus save me from all this and more that the writer did not describe?

The uniqueness of the Gospel message is that Jesus did not come merely to accomplish deliverance, but He became salvation! Many people have done great acts of sacrifice, benefiting us with freedom and delivering us from great danger. However, they did not become our freedom. Jesus became the *"Prince"* to become my *"Savior."* He is the originator who is the cause of my safety but has never been caused Himself! He is the beginning so that He could be the end of sin in my life.

Jesus could not redeem what He did not assume! In His absolute sovereignty as God, He assumed the lowness of humanity. He did not become a superhuman but assumed the state of our exact likeness. To do so, He relinquished every advantage He had as God, all the benefits of His attributes. He assumed our nature! He assumed conception in His mother's womb; He assumed being born as a baby without knowledge. He assumed his childhood, life as a teenager, and adulthood with everything experienced within such a state. He assumed the struggles, frustration, and utter dependency upon the fullness of the Spirit. In the crucifixion, He assumed the fullness of our sin (2 Corinthians 5:21), death, and total damnation resulting from sin. In being raised from the dead, He assumed the victory of resurrected life. He contained all of this! *"Therefore He*

Part Four: Apostle's Restatement: The Unexplainable

is also able to save to the uttermost those who come to God through Him, since He always lives to make intercession for them" (Hebrews 7:25). He is our Savior!

All Jesus assumed is contained in Peter's confession. ***"We ought to obey God rather than men.*** (The Resurrection) ***The God of our fathers raised up Jesus whom you murdered by hanging on a tree.*** (The Restoration) ***Him God has exalted to His right hand to be Prince and Savior, to give repentance to Israel and forgiveness of sins.*** (The Representation) ***And we are His witnesses to these things, and so also is the Holy Spirit whom God has given to those who obey Him"*** (Acts 5:29-32). In "the restoration," God exalted Jesus to His right hand, which is THE PLACE. THE POSITION of this place is *"Prince,"* and THE PURPOSE of this position is *"Savior."* He cannot be one without the other. Because He assumed who we are as the *"Prince,"* originator, founder, leader, chief, or first, He is now the *"Savior."*

What is the purpose of this ministry as *"Savior?"* Peter precisely said, *"to give repentance to Israel and forgiveness of sins"* (Acts 5:31). The verb *"to give"* is not the main verb but is an infinitive, and it distinctly states the purpose or the result of the main verb's action.

"Him" (direct object receiving the action of the main verb)
"God" (subject) *"has exalted"* (main verb)
"to His right hand" (indirect object of the main verb's action)
"Prince and Savior" (direct objects give content to *"Him"*)
"to give" (infinitive verb stating purpose).

The verb *"to give"* is a translation of the Greek word "didomi." It is the ninth most frequent verb in the New Testament, most often expressing the procedure whereby a subject deliberately transfers something to someone or something so that it becomes available to the recipient. In this case, the Trinity God exalted Jesus to His right hand as Prince and Savior so He can give repentance and forgiveness! This exaltation radically highlights the motive of God's heart! He is not motivated to get or receive but to give and help. Once again, God's love permeates His action toward humanity. His nature of bleed, suffer and die causes Him not to think about Himself but about others. It is the redemptive heart of God revealed to us!

Repentance
"to give repentance"

The Greek word translated as ***"repentance"*** is "metanoia." It involves a change of self (heart and mind) that abandons former dispositions and results in a new self, behavior, and regret over former behavior and tendencies. Repentance is "giving up a former thought to embrace a new thought." The core nature of the individual is involved in such an embrace. However, repentance becomes a lifestyle of openness to all the newness God wants to bring to our lives. Resistance to new revelation, guarding the present against change, and settling for the old is not within the perimeter of repentance. It is an attitude of receptivity in which the believer lives.

Repentance demands change, which may be the most challenging issue of life! Our security is not in the familiar; our security is in Jesus. We must not remain in what we have always known because we fear the risk of the new. Our faith is not in the new but in Him who guides us into the new (John 16:13). Jesus is dangerous, but He is safe! We are not open to every new fad, religion, or cultural wave that comes our way. The issue is Jesus and what He gives us. He is the Savior who gives us repentance!

Repentance is a gift from God, a startling truth! It is a display of the great truth of "prevenient grace!" We often consider repentance a preliminary action to invoke God's forgiveness. Often, we experience as the prodigal son the pig pen of sin (Luke 15:15-16). Finally, repentance begins when we come to ourselves as the prodigal did. We make our way to the Father in godly sorrow and confess our sins. However, this is an arrogant and self-centered approach to repentance. We are incapable of godly sorrow for sin, except the Spirit of Jesus probes deep into our hearts. We have no awareness of guilt except the Spirit of Jesus reveals to us our condition. God must come to us and gives us repentance. We do not repent to receive the movement of God in our lives; the movement of God takes place, and we respond to His presence. Repentance is not something we do but a response to what God is doing! If He gives it, it is not ours. Jesus invites us to participate in that which He owns.

In our passage, Peter directs his statement to the council, the leaders of Israel. God has marvelously moved to bring these leaders another opportunity to embrace Jesus. When Jesus came, how did they respond? They ***"murdered*** (Jesus) ***by hanging on a tree."*** But God reversed their hateful action by raising Jesus! In a sense, they are back to the beginning of the process, confronted with Jesus again. They rejected Him at the crucifixion and in the first phase of persecution. For months the message of Jesus resounded throughout all of Jerusalem. Jesus authenticated His message through miracles. In the second phase of persecution, the leaders drag Peter and the apostles before the council. This same Jesus confronts them again, and they reject Him again. Will they repent?

Salvation is not a product made by Jesus with a time stamp, terminating its use. That would focus on salvation apart from Jesus. Jesus is our Salvation! Salvation is not what He does but who He is, our Savior! Peter boldly declared this in the first interrogation by the council. ***"Nor is there salvation in any other, for there is no other name under heaven given***

among men by which we must be saved" (Acts 4:12). Salvation is ***"in"*** Jesus! If salvation is "in" Jesus, when does it become minimized? When does He deteriorate and become ineffective? Any elimination of salvation from our lives is never on His part but always on ours. If I experience hell, such a state of dwelling will not happen because He has rejected me but because I have rejected Him. It was not on His part but always on mine! Once again, Jesus extended repentance to the leaders of Israel. It was not a second chance, for the opportunities offered were too numerous to count. How many more chances will they have? It is beyond measure! Let it be boldly stated on your behalf as well! Jesus has not discarded you or me. He still gives us repentance without measure, in constant confrontation, and saturated with love!

Reconciliation
"forgiveness"

As ***"Prince and Savior,"*** Jesus gave new content to ***"forgiveness,"*** taking us beyond what we usually experience in forgiveness. Jesus "reinstates" us! "I can forgive, but I cannot forget" is a familiar statement. The offense is always there between us, but we set aside the hatred, desire for revenge, and bitterness. We will never return to the kind of relationship before the offense; it is spoiled forever. We must be astounded by the quality of Jesus' forgiveness! It is a vivid discovery in Peter's denial of Jesus. He blatantly denied any connection to knowing Jesus three times (Matthew 26:69-75). The extreme evil was revealed in his strong declaration to Jesus that He would die with Him before he would deny Him (Matthew 26:35). Peter could not conceive how he could ever have a renewed relationship with Jesus. Yet, in our passage, we hear the declaration of Peter, who has experienced the complete and enveloping forgiveness of Jesus. The forgiveness of Jesus returns the sinful person to the state of relationship before he sinned. Jesus forgives and forgets.

Another aspect of Jesus's new forgiveness content is "review." The depth of forgiveness is in the depth of the offense. If the offense is minor, the forgiveness is minor; if the offense is major, the forgiveness is major. Peter's answer to the council highlights the depth of our guilt. ***"The God of our fathers raised up Jesus whom you murdered by hanging on a tree"*** (Acts 5:30). The leaders of Israel were deeply aware of this, for they said, ***"And look, you have filled Jerusalem with your doctrine, and intend to bring this Man's blood on us!"*** (Acts 5:28). Jesus related this in a comparison within the Parable of the Unforgiving Servant. The evil servant embezzled from the master ***"ten thousand talents"*** (Matthew 18:24). However, the evil servant refused to forgive a fellow servant for ***"a hundred denarii"*** (Matthew 18:28). There are many attempts to calculate this into our currency. I have used the figures of $2,370,000 compared to $16.95, giving us a picture of our guilt.

Peter does not highlight the thirty pieces of silver, the evil plotting behind the scenes, or the blatant denial of the Scriptures. The depth of the leaders of Israel's sin was their rejection of Jesus. Regardless of the act of sin's content, the heart of the sin is always the murder of Jesus. We ***"crucify again for themselves the Son of God, and put Him to an open shame"*** (Hebrews 6:6). Sinful deeds against my fellowman are ultimately a sin against God (Psalms 51:4). We must see all sinful deeds in their consequence to Jesus, not their physical actions! That means all my sin is in my rejection of Jesus, yet He reconciled me with His heart!

Another consideration is the "repayment." I owe Him! The forgiveness of sin always has a price. There is no forgiveness without someone paying the consequences of the sin. If someone steals from me, I may forgive them. However, I must personally pay for the loss of those funds. I can forgive if someone hits me in the face, breaking my teeth and jaw. However, I must endure the pain, go to the dentist, and absorb the expense. Jesus is the Savior who paid the penalty for all my sins! Jesus declares that forgiveness of all sin is no problem (Matthew 12:31). He is the payment for all my sin; forgiveness is in Him.

Rejection
"of sins"

Jesus is the Savior targeting all ***"sins!"*** It is a translation of the Greek word "hamartia," plural in the text. Jesus includes all sins! Jesus is definite in His statement to the Pharisees who accuse Him of being possessed by the devil. He said, ***"Therefore I say to you, every sin and blasphemy will be forgiven men, but the blasphemy against the Spirit will not be forgiven men"*** (Matthew 12:31). There is no unforgivable sin! The only unforgivable issue is blasphemy, a condition of a person's inner spirit. Jesus distinguishes between them. He cannot forgive blasphemy; He must eliminate it. Jesus provided for this by giving ***"repentance."*** "Hamartia" means "missing the mark." We miss God's actual end and scope of our lives because of the inner spirit of rebellion. Self-will and self-centeredness rebel against dependency and abandonment. We missed the mark by being filled with an attitude of independence. We become our god, fulfilling the desires of our self! The Savior completely saves us! He forgives all the expressions of our self-centeredness and gives us repentance.

There is no adequate defense for missing the mark. We all miss the mind and heart of Christ. It is the imagery of the bow and arrow with the assignment to hit the target's bullseye. But how can I possibly accomplish this task? I have no experience in shooting an arrow from a bow. I do not get to practice life.

Part Four: Apostle's Restatement: The Unexplainable

Events totally out of my control are thrown at me regularly without warning. With limited experience and knowledge, I attempt to do my best, only to experience missing the intended target. It is a hopeless possibility in the context of unrealistic expectations. Again this reality only verifies the truth that you and I are helpless. Failure and destruction are inevitable when we live out of our self-centered resources. God did not create us to be independent.

But the task is before us; who can shoot the arrow and hit the bullseye? The answer is our Savior, Jesus! He is the true end and scope of our lives. In merging with His Person, we become a new creature. He always hits the mark! We become the demonstration of Him. Jesus came to save us from the futile attempts of our self-centered righteousness. He does not provide strength; He is the strength. He does not give us instruction or training, so we are adequate; He is truth and wisdom (Colossians 2:3). In merging with His mind, heart, and will, we express His Divine nature. Jesus gives us another opportunity to be His! We can participate in Him to hit the bullseye!

Acts 5:32

THESE THINGS

"And we are His witnesses to these things, and so also is the Holy Spirit whom God has given to those who obey Him" (Acts 5:32).

Let me remind you of the intense threat against the apostles. Jesus' crucifixion was a vivid memory. The leaders interrogating the apostles were the same people who first questioned them. The apostles were guilty as charged. Peter and John with-stood the questioning, returning to the early Church to report the threat against anyone who taught in the name of Jesus. But everyone blatantly disregarded the danger. The council said, **"Did we not strictly command you not to teach in this name? And look, you have filled Jerusalem with your doctrine, and intend to bring this Man's blood on us!"** (Acts 5:28). The apostles faced the most significant threat of their lives from the most powerful men of their hour.

Their response was simple, **"We ought to obey God rather than men"** (Acts 5:29). The leaders of Israel could not deny this truth. All religious training they had received and believed proclaimed obedience must be to God when men contradict it. The issue of the hour concerns the actual commands of God. The Sanhedrin adhered to the traditions of the Old Testament, which God established. The apostles proclaimed Jesus as the fulfillment of all of those traditions. Jesus is the proclamation of all God requires. The New Covenant in Jesus completes the promise of God spoken through the prophets (Jeremiah 31:31).

The same dilemma faces us. We live in a world proposing multiple religious views with numerous gods. Even in Christianity, there appears to be diversity regarding the truth. Everyone quotes the Bible to verify their position. Even the political atmosphere has a religious tone. While we agree we should obey God over lesser authorities, who is God, and what is He saying? It is as simple for us as it was for the apostles. Truth is not a doctrine, theology, or philosophy; the truth is a Person. Jesus is the core issue. Will we come under His authority and allow His Spirit to produce our actions? Will we bend our understanding to His wisdom? Will we open our emotional expressions to Him? Can we fall into Him, submerging in who He is? Can He not just give us life but be our life?

From the council's perspective, the problem rests in the person of Jesus. The apostles swayed the crowds and acclaimed all signs and wonders in His name. The apostles were not simply teaching theology but explaining the Old Testament traditions as fulfilled in Jesus. They no longer taught the law of the Old Testament but the law as fulfilled in Jesus. The council confronted the apostles with **"strictly command you not to teach in this name"** (Acts 5:28). Peter and the apostles responded, **"We ought to obey God rather than men"** (Acts 5:29). The apostles could not possibly obey God without their constant focus on Jesus! Peter and the apostles based this focus on three distinct actions of God. "The resurrection" is dominant. **"The God of our fathers raised up Jesus whom you murdered by hanging on a tree"** (Acts 5:30). "The restoration" is the intent of the resurrection. **"Him God has exalted to His right hand to be Prince and Savior to give** *repentance to Israel and forgiveness of sins"* (Acts 5:31). "The representation" is given by witnesses testifying concerning Jesus. *"And we are His witnesses to these things, and so also is the Holy Spirit whom God has given to those who obey Him"* (Acts 5:32).

God focused His action on Jesus! God raised up Jesus; God exalted Jesus; God gave witness to Jesus! The representation of Jesus is in two witnesses, the apostles and the Holy Spirit. The apostles claimed this position and accredited this function to the Holy Spirit. In the text, there is a stronger emphasis on the apostles' witness than on the Holy Spirit's. The apostles are listed first, with the Holy Spirit added. The Greek word "ego" is translated as *"we"* and is unnecessary because it is the ending of the main verb. It is there twice, giving a double declaration and emphasizing the apostles strongly.

The Holy Spirit's role in witnessing Jesus links with the apostles, highlighting their witness. The Holy Spirit is a witness to Jesus, but He is *"given to those who obey Him."* The Greek word "peitharcheo" is translated as *"who obey,"* used only four times in the New Testament. Two of those times connect with this response from the apostles (Acts 5:29, 32). This word focuses on submission to authority and highlights the authority to which one submits. We must see it in the context of *"God has given"* the Holy Spirit to those who submit to His authority. The individual who embraces his helplessness experiences the resource of the Holy Spirit. In this merger, the witnesses reveal the mind of Christ through their testimony. Likewise, the submitted individual's emotions will begin to demonstrate the life of Jesus. The witness of the Holy Spirit is through the believer. When the Trinity God wanted to bring a complete revelation of Himself to the world, He took on flesh. He wants to do it again through us.

The apostles were *"witnesses to these things."* The grammar of the statement is significant. *"We"* (ego) is the

Part Four: Apostle's Restatement: The Unexplainable

subject; *"are"* (eimi) is the main verb. It presents the quality of a state of being. Therefore, he did not say activities qualified them as apostles, but "who" they are in being filled with the Holy Spirit. The apostles could have claimed unique qualities, such as eyewitnesses to the physical activity of Jesus' ministry, but they did not. They only said what we can claim, *"We are His witnesses!"* The Greek word translated *"to things"* is "rhema." It has a definite article before it, "the" (ho), making it specific! The apostles' witness is within the boundaries of "the rhema."

The Greek words "logos" and "rhema" are often used interchangeably. We are more familiar with "logos" because of John's use of the word (John 1:1). If Jesus is the "logos" of the Trinity, what is the content of such a role? He is the true expression of the thought of the Trinity God. What does God think about children? We see Jesus. *"Then little children were brought to Him that He might put His hands on them and pray"* (Matthew 19:13). How does the Trinity God feel about His enemies? *"Father, forgive them, for they do not know what they do"* (Luke 23:34). Jesus is the visible expression of the invisible God (Colossians 1:15). He is *"the express image of His person"* (Hebrews 1:3). Out of the Trinity God's mouth flows the speaking of His inner heart and nature, Jesus!

"Rhema" is closely related to "logos." All we said about "logos" is also true about "rhema." However, "rhema" represents the subject matter of the word or the things spoken. In other words, "logos" is the document's content, while "rhema" is the document's title. "Logos" is the actual words of the message, while "rhema" is the message's subject matter. Peter and the apostles referred not to the details but to the subject of their teaching, Jesus! The council strictly commanded that the apostles not teach any content connected to the name of Jesus. They did not pinpoint the "logos" of the teaching but the "rhema" of the teaching. They were against the subject and found no value in Jesus! But the apostles cried out that who they are is filled with who He is! They were the expression of the subject, Jesus! Unable to help themselves, they were witnesses of the "rhema," Jesus!

There are several vital issues that we need to highlight.

The Concise Issue

The only issue in Christianity is Jesus! Again Peter and the apostles presented a powerful message to the Sanhedrin. The proposition about which they would agree is that man must obey God even when He is contracted by men. All members of the Sanhedrin, the Pharisees, and the Sadducees, would agree with this statement. But what is the subject matter of which God is speaking? They have not heard from God for four hundred years, and no authentic prophet has come to their nation with the message of God. Finally, John the Baptist, the last of the Old Testament prophets, prepared the way to arrive at the final Subject of God's speaking. For nearly three years, God spoke Jesus to the nation of Israel to introduce this Subject to the world (Acts 2:39; 3:25-26).

Peter asked the council, "How did you respond to this Subject?" They *"murdered by hanging on a tree"* (Acts 5:30). But the Trinity God would not quit speaking about this Subject. *"The God of our fathers raised up Jesus."* The Trinity God exalted this Subject to the highest authority for redemption (Acts 5:31). God filled us with the Holy Spirit, whose function is to reveal Jesus (John 15:26). The Holy Spirit only speaks about Jesus. We also must talk about only one Subject!

Our study of the previous paragraphs in Acts verifies speaking of the one Subject. The leaders of Israel recognize the concise issue is Jesus. The name of the proclamation is

Jesus. The content of the proclamation is the life of Jesus, and Jesus filled the early Church with His Spirit. But the leaders of Israel could not bring themselves to mention the Title of the Book, Jesus. They saw Him as the concise issue whom they must eliminate. In their threats to the apostles, the council keeps speaking about "this name" but never says "Jesus" (Acts 4:7, 17, 18; 5:28)! Peter and the apostles (Acts 5:29-32) keep talking about Jesus. When the council heard this, ***"they were furious and plotted to kill them"*** (Acts 5:33). There was nothing about Jesus the Sanhedrin could tolerate. The problem did not appear to be what Jesus did in three years of ministry or through His apostles; it was who He is! He is the concise issue.

Is that not true for us? The reality of the merger with the person of Jesus confronts us! Could it be the concise issue of the final judgment? What did we do about Jesus? The apostles were very clear in their view of Judas, and they did not list the details of his betrayal; he rejected Jesus (Acts 1:16, 17, 25). Jesus was the entire issue. ***"For by grace you have been saved through faith, and that not of yourselves; it is the gift of God, not of works, lest anyone should boast"*** (Ephesians 2:8-9). The gift is Jesus!

The Central Issue

Life is complex! Are we not consistently confronted with new environments? Different dilemmas face every generation affecting the essence of our lives. One generation's concern is feed for their horses; another is how to pay for gasoline. The Sanhedrin was responsible for the safety of the nation of Israel, facing great difficulties with Roman domination. There were many issues concerning their decisions, the economy, maintaining their traditions, schools training their young men, and many more. The list was long, they had to consider every issue, and Jesus affected everything. He spoke forcibly about their relationship with Rome; He brought tax collectors into His disciple group; He broke their oral traditions and accepted sinners. He seemed to alter and determine every area of their lives!

Jesus proposed, **"If you love Me, keep My commandments"** (John 14:15). He did not suggest a list of rules or new oral traditions. The Greek word translated as **"commandments"** is "entole," referring to direction, charge, or commission. He did not demand the strictness of the law but a relationship with Him that sets the tone for your life's activity. He gave this statement to His apostles in the discourse on the fullness of the Holy Spirit. Jesus is the central issue. If He merges with me, I will begin to feel, think, and desire as He does. He will be the major issue of everything confronting my life.

The apostles faced the Sanhedrin with the same dilemma as Jesus! He disrupted every area of their lives. If His influence was just in compassionate ministry, the council might have tolerated it. They could have admired that He did miracles in the physical realm. But in an exact manner, Jesus altered the Jewish culture before His death, and He was now doing the same through His apostles. Jesus was changing the temple worship; He threatened the loyalty to their oral traditions; such significant change created new friction with Roman authority. The manner of Jewish life, as experienced in the past, was now under siege through the influence of Jesus.

Jesus is the "rhema." He is the central issue in every topic under discussion. The business world must deal with Jesus and can never isolate Him from their practices. His nature will determine and infiltrate my ability to make money. My employment becomes a platform for demonstrating Jesus, for **"we are witnesses of these things."** My sexuality, with all of its expressions, must be an expression of His image. No one filled with the nature of Jesus can discuss abortion without expressing

Part Four: Apostle's Restatement: The Unexplainable

the mind of Christ. Recreation, habits, eating, marriage, and schedule are all under His authority. We are not dominated nor determined by our culture but by Jesus. He is the central issue!

The Core Issue

Peter and the apostles presented the resurrected Jesus to the Sanhedrin. In the first phase of persecution, Peter established the core issue, speaking of Jesus as the cornerstone (Acts 4:11). The cornerstone determines the structure of a building. Jesus is life's cornerstone. Peter declared that the issue is not the doctrine of resurrection or oral traditions but Jesus! We must decide about Him, and then all other decisions become automatic. Peter and the apostles again declared the same in the second phase of persecution. **"We ought to obey God rather than men."** These Jewish leaders would agree with such a premise. God gave the Scriptures from which their oral traditions developed. God gave them the sacrificial system they must maintain and the ceremonial law they must observe. Peter said that none of these was the core issue. Keeping the oral traditions is not the core issue. The core issue is Jesus! Should I continue with the sacrifices? That is not the issue of God's confrontation. I must decide about Jesus! The Trinity God pushed Jesus to the exalted position when He raised Him from the dead. When I decide about Jesus, He will determine my opinion of oral traditions, sacrifices, and ceremonial laws.

What do I believe about baptism? What about social drinking? Where do I stand on the subject of abortion? What about the church and its imposed rules? What do I believe about the inspiration of the Scriptures? God does not challenge you to decide about these issues. The issue is Jesus! What will you do about Him? We must set aside all other matters of life. There is only one issue; it is Jesus. We can argue theology until we create anger and division, but the issue is not a particular theological persuasion but Jesus. Will you and I allow Jesus to embrace us and determine our theology? I do not have to decide about the authenticity of the Scripture; I must embrace Jesus. He brings the Scriptures to life within me! The decision is not baptism's form; it is about Jesus. He will determine my view of baptism. He is the core issue!

Peter and the apostles declared their witness. But they are not witnesses of angelic deliverances. Although a miraculous occurrence happened while the apostles were in prison (Acts 5:19), Peter never mentioned it to the council. While they witnessed mighty miracles in Jerusalem, he never alluded to that in his discourse. Organizational structure was not under discussion. The apostles were witnesses of the "rhema." Jesus is the topic, the theme, and the proposition. He is the core issue that confronts me. Will I be His, or will I not? Will He merge with me so my life can be a platform for demonstrating His life, or will I continue to present myself?

Acts 5:32

LIFE CONSUMING

"And we are His witnesses to these things, and so also is the Holy Spirit whom God has given to those who obey Him" (Acts 5:32).

We are looking at the fundamental proposition of Peter and the apostles' message to the Sanhedrin. The apostles had blatantly disobeyed the leaders of Israel through their continual emphasis on Jesus. The evidence of their disobedience was strong, for ***"you have filled Jerusalem with your doctrine"*** (Acts 5:28). There was no denial! The apostles' defense was ***"We must obey God rather than men"*** (Acts 5:29). While even the Sanhedrin would agree with such a statement, the disagreement concerned what God said. The apostles declared that God is speaking Jesus! The Trinity God was not talking about Jesus, giving information concerning Jesus, or describing Jesus. God was speaking Jesus and His nature into our world. He is the "rhema" of God's speech to humanity!

The Trinity God proclaimed this message, and no one could silence Him. Even after the leaders of Israel crucified Jesus, ***"whom you murdered by hanging on a tree,"*** God raised Him up (Acts 5:30)! He ***"has exalted Him to His right hand to be Prince and Savior, to give repentance to***

Israel and forgiveness of sins" (Acts 5:31). In all of this, the Trinity God left two dominate witnesses operating in union, the apostles and Holy Spirit. It is the unique picture of the merger between God and man, of which Jesus was the prototype. The Holy Spirit, the Spirit of Jesus, came to merge, weld, saturate, and permeate the nature of humanity. The human being would become the demonstration of God's nature to the world. "***We are His witnesses to these things"*** (Acts 5:32).

This unity does not automatically occur but in response to "obedience." "***The Holy Spirit whom God has given to those who obey Him"*** (Acts 5:32). "Obedience" is the pivotal issue. The Greek word translated as ***"obey"*** is "peitharcheo." In previous studies, we discussed this word. Yet, it is profoundly important in this context. It is only used four times in the New Testament, two of which are in this speech from Peter and the other apostles. It means "submission to authority" and is from two Greek words, "peithomai," meaning "to persuade" or "obey," and "arche," meaning "rule or beginning." The emphasis is on the authority that produces something within the obedient one. In other words, obedience or submission to authority is the context in which God created this new thing.

This obedience is the context of the new creature God created to present to the world as a "witness." The apostles were not merely speaking a message of information or data about Jesus. The early Church was not simply a group of people adopting a new belief system based on a Messiah. We discovered this regarding the "resurrection." The Pharisees believed in the resurrection of the dead, while the Sadducees did not. They discussed and debated the issue constantly. There would have been no issue if the apostles had entered such a theological discussion. But the apostles were proposing ***"in Jesus the resurrection from the dead"*** (Acts 4:2). It was not just about the resurrection, but Jesus who brought it into reality. Furthermore, everything Jesus did in His physical life He did through the apostles and members of the early Church. Jesus was alive in them, giving witness by the power of His Spirit. They became obedient instruments demonstrating the life of God as Jesus did! The council saw a multiplication of Jesus' life throughout all of Jerusalem.

Could this be the destiny of God's creation of humanity? Peter spoke of God's *"exceedingly great and precious promises"* to us. He gave promises to us out of His great heart. The purpose of such promises is *"that through these you may be partakers of the divine nature, having escaped the corruption that is in the world through lust"* (2 Peter 1:4). *"Partakers"* is translated from the Greek word "koinonos" coming from the context of "business partners." God and man are investing lives together in a great enterprise. It is the expression of the divine nature to our world. We are His "representation!"

Source of the Representation

How did we receive the privilege of such involvement with God? Did we submit a resumé or application for the responsibility? What have we done, or what profit did we bring to Him that would merit His desire for us? I do not need to convince you that *"by grace you have been saved through faith, and that not of yourselves; it is a gift of God, not of works, lest anyone should boast"* (Ephesians 2:8-9). We have no merit to claim the right to represent His Person. We are helpless, *"poor in spirit"* (Matthew 5:3). BUT He has chosen us! He has *"predestined us to adoption as sons by Jesus Christ to Himself, according to the good pleasure of His will, to the praise of the glory of His grace, by which He made us accepted in the Beloved"* (Ephesians 1:5-6).

We did not begin or accomplish the "representation!"

The testimony of Peter and the other apostles before the council verifies that. The opening proposition of their response undergirds that God is supreme and in charge. ***"We ought to obey God rather than men."*** God created us to receive the means and instruction for our movement. Did we not join all mankind in rejecting Jesus, ***"whom you murdered by hanging on a tree?"*** After all, the wages of our sin is death and destruction (Romans 6:23). But the Trinity, ***"God of our fathers raised up Jesus!"*** If a dead man should live, could He claim his life as his own? If one who has destroyed his life by his destructive action finds himself restored, can he claim such renewal as a product of his own doing?

The Trinity God ***"exalted Jesus to His right hand to be Prince and Savior!"*** God acclaims all repentance and forgiveness in Jesus. God exalted Jesus to the position that everyone must acknowledge Him as the sole source of their lives. But it is not a single action that He accomplished or a mere one-time deed that He did. His exaltation involves the extension of who Jesus is within us! He has given us His Spirit. The reality of His life indwells us. But how else could one ever represent who He is? Any attempt to demonstrate Him without His life's source would be a marred, degraded, and laughable false image. In ourselves, we are a mere joke!

Peter and the other apostles boldly declared, ***"God has given!"*** God is the source of His demonstration, which He has given. Keeping God's sourcing and participation within our humanity's context is essential. We are not skin that He wears or robots that He controls. He did not merely give us orders to obey or commandments to follow. He does not give Himself to us as content within a shell or container. We are essential to the demonstration but never source it, and we participate within the witness but never produce it! The uniqueness of our creation by God, coupled with the saturation of His Spirit sourcing us, brings to life the expression of His image. We see it in Jesus, who is exalted to His right hand. The moment we take the slightest credit or even within ourselves sense pride for our part, we destroy the image! Jesus alone is the source!

Standard of the Representation

The Greek word *"witness"* is "martys" and refers to someone who has information or knowledge of something and, therefore, can give information, bring it to light, or confirm something. However, as this use occurs throughout the Book of Acts and the epistles, the meaning is distinctly increased. Indeed, Peter and the other apostles could state that they were eyewitnesses to the actual physical resurrection of Jesus. They did not see that actual event but experienced for forty days the physical presence of the resurrected Lord. They could give testimony to this fact. However, as Stephen, the first martyr, Paul and others could not be such a witness. Yet, they uniquely experienced Jesus.

The resurrected Lord stated the witness standard on the day of His ascension. He was keenly aware of all those who were to come who did not have the privilege of being eyewitnesses. In the present moment of bringing eyewitnesses, the apostles urged Jesus to establish the Kingdom, **"Lord, will You at this time restore the Kingdom to Israel"** (Acts 1:6)? They wanted to establish a kingdom on the fact of His physically resurrected presence. Jesus tenderly informed them they did not understand nor know what was within the authority of the Father. **"You shall receive power when the Holy Spirit has come upon you; and you shall be witnesses to Me in Jerusalem, and in all Judea and Samaria, and to the end of the earth"** (Acts 1:8). The standard for a witness moved higher than visually seeing the physically resurrected Lord.

The indwelling of the resurrected Lord, merging with the

believer, and manifesting the life of Christ through the physical flesh was far superior to one testifying about something He saw or experienced in the past! That is what perplexed the council. They could not fathom what happened as the influence and the presence of Jesus raised from the dead captured Jerusalem. Perhaps they could crucify the physical Jesus, but what could they do when the resurrected Jesus merged with the physical lives of hundreds of believers in Jerusalem? They had no recourse.

The numerous Scriptures in the Book of Acts, giving bold statements and physical examples, declare this unique merging of God and man as a representation of the Divine Person! On Jesus' day of ascension, He said, *"But you shall receive power when the Holy Spirit has come upon you; and you shall be witnesses to Me in Jerusalem, and in all Judea and Samaria, and to the end of the earth"* (Acts 1:8). The apostles' testimony was about more than merely seeing the physically resurrected Jesus; the Spirit of Jesus empowered them to demonstrate Him throughout the world. They became the flesh of God, making His heart, mind, and emotions present everywhere. The apostles had to demonstrate the resurrected Lord.

During Peter's sermon explaining Pentecost, he said, *"This Jesus God has raised up, of which we are all witnesses"* (Acts 2:32). A surface explanation would note that those filled with the Spirit were eyewitnesses of the resurrected Jesus. Peter said, *"Therefore being exalted to the right hand of God, and having received from the Father the promise of the Holy Spirit, He poured out this which you now see and hear"* (Acts 2:33). God established a consistent pattern connecting the witness, resurrection, and filling of the Holy Spirit. The witness was not merely telling of an event but living the life merged with the Spirit of Christ.

The healing of the lame beggar promoted an opportunity for Peter to proclaim a message at Solomon's Porch. Peter informed the Jews that they *"killed the Prince of life, whom God raised from the dead, of which we are witnesses"* (Acts 3:15). Again, Peter referred to Jesus as the *"Prince."* Jesus is the beginning of a "new creature," which is man merged with God. The Trinity God restored this New Creature, Jesus, by raising Him from the dead. Peter and the others have experienced the same resurrected life indwelling them and are witnesses, a representation of the same.

Are we not in this same heritage, birthed in His life, and declaring Him to our world? No one can be an adequate witness of His resurrection unless God fills him with the life of the Resurrected One! He is the witness's Source, producing the standard for the witness. Without the Source, the witness becomes a theological argument or philosophical debate. A witness turns into a lecture of intellectual data instead of a living Force that moves on other lives. The witness is not in a pulpit but in life experience, and Jesus lives His life through us! Indeed, *"We must obey God rather than men"* because He is sourcing His life through us.

Strength of the Representation

As noted above, the Greek word translated as *"witnesses"* is "martys." It is the source for our English word "martyr." Initially, it refers to one who has information or knowledge of something and, therefore, can give information, bring it to light, or confirm something. However, due to the persecution of the early Church, it quickly became a reference to those who suffered death as a consequence of their confession of Jesus. Paul said, *"When the blood of Your martyr Stephen was shed, I also was standing by consenting to his death, and guarding the clothes of those who were killing him"* (Acts 22:20). In His message to the church in Pergamos,

Jesus said, ***"the days in which Antipas was My faithful martyr, who was killed among you, where Satan dwells"*** (Revelation 2:13). There is a crucial distinction between the word "martys" and the person's death. The martyr's witness was not in their suffering death, but their witness of Jesus becoming the cause of their death.

A self-centered life tends to place the value of every Christian virtue in the action of that virtue. The physical act of prayer does not contain its value. The focus is not on posture while praying, the location where one prays, the length of prayer, or even who hears the prayer. The value of prayer is in the mystical intimacy between God and man. The wonder of faith is not the accomplishment of such a virtue. Moving a mountain, miracles of healing, signs and wonders, or demonstrations of incredible feats are not the essence of faith. Faith focuses on the flowing of God's power and presence within the situation, constantly altering circumstances.

This physical intimacy is the wonder of witnessing or martyrdom! It is not the act of dying or the brilliant display of talent in singing or preaching. The wonder is not in the display of the action; it is the merger between the Spirit of Jesus and the individual, representing the Person of Jesus within the situation. ***"We are His witnesses"*** and ***"so also is the Holy Spirit whom God has given!"*** The purpose of Jesus' Spirit in and through the believer is the representation of Christ's life! The world sees the mind, emotions, and will of Jesus in the believer. As Jesus had His own body in days gone by, now He possesses ours. Indeed, we are His witnesses.

Jesus highlighted this reality by sharing it with His disciples before His crucifixion. ***"Most assuredly, I say to you, he who believes in Me, the works that I do he will do also; and greater works than these he will do, because I go to My Father"*** (John 14:12). The believers ***"greater works"*** is the multiplication of Jesus' displayed in the world! In the middle

Part Four: Apostle's Restatement: The Unexplainable

of the great discussion, Jesus told the parable of the True Vine. ***"I am the vine, you are the branches, He who abides in Me, and I in Him, bears much fruit; for without Me you can do nothing"*** (John 15:5). The ***"fruit"*** to which Jesus refers is the fruit of the Spirit (Galatians 5:22, 23). It is the nature Jesus expressed in His life now displayed through us! Jesus clarified the sole focus of the Holy Spirit in the believer. ***"But when the Helper comes, whom I shall send to you from the Father, the Spirit of truth who proceeds from the Father, He will testify of Me"*** (John 15:26). The only work within the believers is to give witness of Jesus.

Upon the completion of this great discourse, Jesus began to pray. His resounding words to the Father were actually for us. ***"I do not pray for these alone, but also for those who will believe in Me through their word; that they all may be one as You, Father, are in Me and I in You; that they also may be one in Us, that the world may believe that you sent Me"*** (John 17:20, 21). He did not declare the unity among the believers but the unity with Himself and the Father. We are in Him, and He is in us, for the sake of the world seeing and believing in Him. We are a manifestation of His Person.

The question is not "What should I do?" The question is, "What should I be?" I must be His. In merging with His Spirit, my mind, will, and emotions become a display of the Person of Jesus. In this reality, ***"We ought to obey God rather than men!"***

Acts 5:32
JESUS ONLY

"And we are His witnesses to these things, and so also is the Holy Spirit whom God has given to those who obey Him" (Acts 5:32).

This verse has two facts that demand attention. As we look beneath the surface, it seems these facts are yelling. One is the RESPONSIBILITY of the apostles that Peter and the others readily accepted. Their responsibility started when they responded to Jesus' call to be His disciples. It was common in their culture to associate with a teacher to learn from and become like him. When Jesus sent them to be laborers in the harvest (Matthew 9:37), they experienced a more profound realization of their involvement. He gave them power over unclean spirits, sickness, and disease (Matthew 10:1). They indeed became an extension of His life! This call became more evident when the resurrected Jesus commissioned them to **"make disciples of all the nations"** (Matthew 28:19).

The apostles' anticipation of how they would make disciples heightened when the ascending Lord instructed them to wait in Jerusalem for the fullness of the Holy Spirit. They would be witnesses to the entire world (Acts 1:8)! During those days, they felt the need to replace Judas with another apostle. The single motivation for the replacement was *"a witness with us of His resurrection"* (Acts 1:22). As their mission unfolds throughout the Book of Acts, they are not church administrators, overseers of pastoral ministry, or CEOs of an organization. They are "witnesses!"

As we discovered in previous studies, the witnesses were not merely relating data or information but were *"witnesses to these things"* (Acts 5:32). The Greek word translated *"things"* is "rhema," a Greek word related to "logos," two words used interchangeably but with a distinction. John presented Jesus as the *"Word"* (John 1:1). He used "logos," meaning an expression of a thought. The Trinity expresses God's nature through Jesus, and He is the complete revelation of God's nature! While "rhema" definitely relates to this, it focuses on the subject. "Rhema" is the title or theme of the book, while "logos" is the content.

The second central fact in the passage is the ROLE of the Holy Spirit! He is included as a Witness to the Rhema, Jesus! What the apostles proclaimed in our passage, Jesus clearly stated to His disciples in an upper room before His crucifixion. He said, *"But when the Helper comes, whom I shall send to you from the Father, the Spirit of truth who proceeds from the Father, He will testify of Me. And you also will bear witness, because you have been with Me from the beginning"* (John 15:26-27). In the same setting, Jesus continued to describe the role of the Holy Spirit. *"However, when He, the Spirit of truth, has come, He will guide you into all truth"* (John 16:13). He clearly states the content of the truth. *"He will glorify Me, for He will take of what is Mine and declare it to you. All things that the Father has are Mine. Therefore I said that He will take of Mine and declare it to you"* (John 16:14-15). The Holy Spirit is a witness to the Rhema, Jesus.

However, it is essential to note that Jesus and the apostles were not merely saying that there were two witnesses. The apostles were witnesses, and the Holy Spirit was in the role of being a witness. However, they were intimately connected! God gave witness to Himself through creation, miracles, and many additional means. He was not limited. The Holy Spirit's particular role is to witness in connection with us. Peter and the other apostles placed a qualifier on the witness of the Holy Spirit, *"whom God has given to those who obey Him"* (Acts 5:32).

The witness of the Holy Spirit focused on what He will do through the human witness. He will empower (Acts, 1:8); He will guide (John 16:13); He will glorify Jesus (John 16:14); He will declare (John 16:14). We become the platform upon which the Holy Spirit reveals Jesus to the world. We are not a robot or a suit that He wears. He merges with our personality, and the uniqueness of who we are is empowered to declare Jesus. We give expression to the very holy nature of God. This expression is not one aspect of our purpose and calling; it is the entirety of God's design for our lives. We become the visible image of the invisible God!

Humanity

Again in our passage, Peter and the other apostles state a two-fold witness, humanity and the Holy Spirit. Let's begin with humanity. The statement's emphasis is on the human witness of Peter and the apostles, evident from the placement of *"we are witnesses"* in the sentence. The main subject is *"we,"* and the main verb is *"are."* Both are a translation of the Greek word "eimi," which presents a state of being. The focus is not on the action of witnessing but on what the apostles were being. Immediately following the Greek word "martys," translated as *"witnesses,"* is a predictive nominative. *"We"* and ***"witnesses"*** are given a qualitative sense. Peter and the apostles said, "This is who we are!" That was the difficulty with the demands of the Sanhedrin. They asked the apostles and the early Church to be something they were not. The Trinity God merged with each apostle and others to such a degree that they became new creatures and witnesses. It is beyond a requirement of activities, a rule of doing, or a physical function. It is the nature of the Kingdom person. Peter and the apostles could not help who they were in Christ. Jesus expressed this same language! Jesus consistently described a merger with God, the Father, not in the sense of His membership in the Trinity but in the purpose of His humanity. He prayed, **"You, Father, are in Me, and I in You"** (John 17:21). Listen to the words of Jesus. **"Most assuredly, I say to you, the Son can do nothing of Himself, but what He sees the Father do; for whatever He does, the Son also does in like manner"** (John 5:19). Understanding the words **"do"** and **"does"** is essential to grasp the depth of Jesus' statement. The Greek word is "poieo." There is a physical aspect to "doing," which produces physical results, but the emphasis of the word is on the inner resource producing the physical. It is used consistently in the Scriptures for trees "bearing" (poieo) fruit. The fruit is physical, but something is happening within the nature of the tree that determines the fruit. Jesus said this concerning His own life. The nature of the Father, the Holy Spirit, merged with Jesus, producing the Trinity God's image.

The beloved apostle John said, **"And from Jesus Christ, the faithful witness, the firstborn from the dead, and the ruler over the kings of the earth"** (Revelation 1:5). Jesus is a witness; we are witnesses. He was the first witness, the prototype, of what we are to be! He became the second Adam filled with the Spirit. He would not only become the source for all redemption but, through that resource, establish the new category of "witness," expressing the invisible image of God, restoring the purpose of man's creation by God. Throughout the Old Testament, humanity attempted to follow the law of God, an expression of His holy nature. ***"Therefore the law was our tutor to bring us to Christ, that we might be justified by faith. But after faith has come, we are no longer under a tutor"*** (Galatians 3:24-25). We have received the Spirit of Jesus that we might be a witness of God's nature! That is our destiny!

Our destiny is two-fold. First, we are to be THE DECLARATION OF HIS LIFE! There is an emphasis on the linguistic aspect of the witness. We are not silent witnesses and cannot remain on the sidelines watching. That was evident as the early Church proclaimed the Word of God regardless of the council's threats. ***"And when they had prayed, the place where they were assembled together was shaken; and they were all filled with the Holy Spirit, and they spoke the word of God with boldness"*** (Acts 4:31). The concern of the Sanhedrin was the verbal proclamation of the early Church. They said among themselves, ***"But so that it spreads no further among the people, let us severely threaten them, that from now on they speak to no man in this name"*** (Acts 4:17). In the setting of our passage, the council is disturbed about the verbal proclamation. ***"Did we not strictly command you not to teach in this name? And look, you have filled Jerusalem with your doctrine, and intend to bring this Man's blood on us"*** (Acts 5:28).

The apostles and early Church consistently talked about Jesus! The topic of their conversation was the "Rhema." Jesus was the subject! Remember what they had just recently experienced with Him. They spent forty days in His resurrection presence (Acts 1:3). No one could refute His resurrected presence's absolute, infallible proof. They could not stop talking about Him, which compounded the indwelling of His presence through the Holy Spirit. If He had been real in the physical, He was equally

Part Four: Apostle's Restatement: The Unexplainable

real in the inner spiritual realm of their lives! He was their only message, the "Rhema."

Their focus continued throughout the Book of Acts. The apostle Paul clarified the reason for a constant focus on the person of Jesus. Everything God intended for our lives is in Him. The Trinity God put all the spiritual dreams and blessings intended in our creation in Jesus (Ephesians 1:3). Therefore, our focus is not on the blessings or benefits but on Jesus. In Jesus, God fulfilled His dreams for humanity; we are in Him, and He is in us! How can we not constantly speak about Him? Think of the terrible pressure Peter and the other apostles experienced. They must talk about Jesus!

The concern about our personal lives is not that we don't consistently speak about Jesus but that we can comfortably keep silent about Him. We quickly discuss projects, athletics, finances, and jokes; the list is endless. Even in Christian society, we focus on the building project, miracles, gifts, evangelism, and much more manageable. Jesus doesn't seem to be central. The apostles were in a state of being that demanded focus on Jesus. Do we not dwell where they dwelt?

The second phase of our human role is THE DEMONSTRATION OF HIS LIFE. Talk is cheap unless we back it up with action. We see this clearly regarding the ministry of Jesus. Introducing Volume 2, the Book of Acts, Luke summarized Volume 1, the Gospel of Luke. He wrote, **"The former account I made, O Theophilus, of all that Jesus began both to do and teach"** (Acts 1:1). Notice the double emphasis on the link between doing and teaching. Luke not only used the connecting conjunction **"and"** (kai) but also **"both"** (te). He determined that we understand the connection between what Jesus said and what He did. It would be impossible to understand anything Jesus taught without His demonstration. The Gospel writers consistently gave the teaching of Jesus and viewed Him acting out His teaching. The heart of the Sermon on the Mount (Matthew 5, 6, 7) was demonstrated in the action chapters immediately following (Matthew 8, 9). Matthew carefully selected the encounters of Jesus with His world to illustrate the tone and attitude of the Sermon.

A person can aggressively proclaim that God is love, but it nullifies love's existence when hate is present. Jesus said it is worthless when we speak about being forgiven by God yet do not forgive others (Matthew 6:14-15). Words are valueless if my life does not demonstrate what I say. **"If a brother or sister is naked and destitute of daily food, and one of you says to them, 'Depart in peace, be warmed and filled,' but you do not give them the things which are needed for the body, what does it profit"** (James 2:15-16)? The apostles and the early Church impacted Jerusalem because they incessantly demonstrated His life when they spoke about Jesus.

They lived in a state of being that demanded both to do and teach. They merged with the Holy Spirit to form a new creature, their nature and His nature. This merger gave total expression to the person of Jesus in speaking and physical actions. As it took place in Jesus, it happened in the apostles and the early Church. They were not under the compulsion of the law, but Jesus' nature compelled them. They could not be silent about Him, for they were living out His nature in their world.

Holy Spirit

While Peter and the other apostles proposed two witnesses, they combined them. The Holy Spirit is a Witness, but the content of His involvement in this function is defined as, **"Whom God has given to those who obey Him"** (Acts 5:32). The Spirit of Jesus comes to live within the believer! There is no witness without this merger. The apostles will not continue to speak of Jesus or demonstrate His life unless His Spirit fills them.

Part Four: Apostle's Restatement: The Unexplainable

The focus of the Holy Spirit's filling is that the apostles might become witnesses. Jesus said, ***"But you shall receive power when the Holy Spirit has come upon you; and you shall be witnesses to Me in Jerusalem, and in all Judea and Samaria, and to the end of the earth"*** (Acts 1:8).

The council asked the apostles to stop teaching and speaking about Jesus. They did not realize the depth of what they required. There was no possibility the apostles could do what was required because they had merged with the Holy Spirit. His function within the believer was to ***"glorify Me*** (Jesus)*"* (John 16:14). The Greek word "doxazo" is translated as ***"glorify."*** It comes from the noun "doxa," which proposes a perspective honoring or praising someone or something. The Holy Spirit fills the believer to give the perspective of the Trinity concerning Jesus, the "Rhema." All the Father's love expressed in His statements relating to Jesus, He now represents in and through the believer (Matthew 3:17; 17:5). The believer becomes a platform for the praise and honor expressed by the Holy Spirit.

However, the witness is altered in the context of the filling of the Holy Spirit. The intent, intensity, and clarity of the witness of the Spirit through the believer do not change. The Spirit merges with the believer and gives His witness through the believer's personality. Consider the uniqueness of every individual. The fingerprints and DNA of each person are different. The Trinity God intended individuals to speak and demonstrate Jesus through their individuality, which is the picture Paul gave us of the body of Christ (1 Corinthians 12:12). Each person with their unique function and destiny contributes to the full demonstration of Jesus' greatness. Such a demonstration cannot be complete without us all. You are important.

The Holy Spirit merges with those who ***"obey Him."*** The Greek word "peitharcheo," translated as obey, is only used four times in the New Testament. It is two Greek words, "peithos" and "archeo." One means "persuade," and the other means "ruler, first, or chief." These two words together present a picture of conformity and submission to authority. We are to merge in conformity with the Holy Spirit. How He thinks is how we will think; His heart and your heart become one. Our speech and life demonstration become a product of His focus and desires. Jesus is this focus!

The "witness" to which Peter refers is not a result of training, talent, or personality types. It is not memorized Scripture repeated effectively. It flows automatically from the merger with the Holy Spirit. Our sole responsibility is to cling to Him in abandonment *"both to do and teach"* (Acts 1:1)

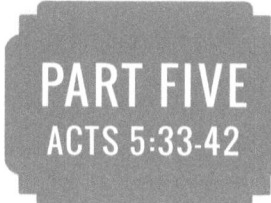

PART FIVE
ACTS 5:33-42

ADVICE REJECTED: AGREEMENT

Acts 5:33-42

AGREEMENT

When they heard this, they were furious and plotted to kill them. Then one in the council stood up, a Pharisee named Gamaliel, a teacher of the law held in respect by all the people, and commanded them to put the apostles outside for a little while. And he said to them: "Men of Israel, take heed to yourselves what you intend to do regarding these men. For some time ago Theudas rose up, claiming to be somebody. A number of men, about four hundred, joined him. He was slain, and all who obeyed him were scattered and came to nothing. After this man, Judas of Galilee rose up in the days of the census, and drew away many people after him. He also perished, and all who obeyed him were dispersed. And now I say to you, keep away from these men and let them alone; for if this plan or this work is of men, it will come to nothing; but if it is of God, you cannot overthrow it - lest you even be found to fight against God." And they agreed with him, and when they had called for the apostles and beaten them, they commanded that they should not speak in the name of Jesus, and let them go. So they departed from the presence of the council, rejoicing that they were counted worthy to suffer shame for His name. And daily in the temple, and in every house, they did not cease teaching and preaching Jesus as the Christ (Acts 5:33-42).

No section of Scripture is a "fill-in" to take up space, relate historical details, or give data. God inspires all Scripture.

Part Five: Advice Rejected: Agreement

"All Scripture is given by inspiration of God, and is profitable for doctrine, for reproof, for correction, for instruction in righteousness, that the man of God may be complete, thoroughly equipped for every good work" (2 Timothy 3:16-17). Approaching this story, we must ask, "Why does Luke include it in this chapter?" We have no understanding until we apply the Scripture to our lives. Each passage is more than information; it is profitable! The profit for my life may come through conviction, correction, or convincing, but it must change my life.

One might like to know the Word of God, but the test of your desire is in your willingness to change. If we study Scripture to validate our beliefs, we hinder God from revealing Himself. Approaching the Scripture to win an argument rather than discovering the life-changing revelation reduces the chance of finding the Truth, Jesus. What is the truth of the passage, and how does it apply to my life? Openness, careful listening, and willingness to change must accompany every encounter with God's Word!

In the fifth chapter of Acts, the second phase of persecution is well underway. All the apostles stand before the council, blatantly guilty of disobedience. The Sanhedrin had one request: they wanted the apostles to eliminate Jesus from all their teachings. ***"Did we not strictly command you not to teach in this name? And look, you have filled Jerusalem with your doctrine, and intend to bring this Man's blood on us"*** (Acts 5:28). Peter, speaking on behalf of all the apostles, states a significant proposition, ***"We ought to obey God rather than men"*** (Acts 5:29). Everyone, including the Sanhedrin, agreed with this statement. The desires of our sovereign God must take priority over the wishes of humanity. Should not a human being, limited in knowledge and wisdom, listen to an omniscient sovereign God?

The twelve apostles and the seventy most powerful men

of Israel agree on this issue! Indeed, ***"We ought to obey God rather than men"*** (Acts 5:29). The issue concerns God's words. The Sanhedrin consists of thirty-five Pharisees and thirty-five Sadducees, and these seventy men do not agree among themselves. The Pharisees believed in the resurrection from the dead and life after death; the Sadducees did not. Paul used this difference to his advantage when they arrested him in the temple. As he stood before the council, he said, ***"Men and brethren, I am a Pharisee, the son of a Pharisee; concerning the hope and resurrection of the dead I am being judged"*** (Acts 23:6). Immediately, a ***"dissension arose between the Pharisees and the Sadducees; and the assembly was divided. For Sadducees say that there is no resurrection - and no angel or spirit; but Pharisees confess both"*** (Acts 23:7-8). Both groups believe in the Old Testament, but they adjusted and adapted the Scriptures to justify their lifestyle!

Peter and the apostles boldly proclaimed Jesus! They proposed that God spoke the Old Testament, and it was about Jesus! Jesus fulfilled all that the law and the prophets proclaimed. The Trinity God opened His mouth, and Jesus came out, the complete, final, and comprehensive speaking of God. God has nothing to say outside of Jesus! Peter proved this point by declaring that when the Sanhedrin murdered Jesus, God raised Him from the dead (Acts 5:30). What God says He cannot silence; He is speaking to them again! God exalted Jesus, His speaking, to the highest position possible, His right hand (Acts 5:31). God filled the believers with His Holy Spirit to represent what He had to say, Jesus (Acts 5:32).

Therefore, God is speaking Jesus again to the council as the apostles bear witness! What will the Sanhedrin do with this continued and renewed speaking?

Part Five: Advice Rejected: Agreement

The Plot
Acts 5:33

The Sanhedrin's response is the same as always. At least they were consistent. They continued to reject anything connected with Jesus. They determined their path and never detoured from it. When Jesus confronted them with God's intent for the Sabbath Day, ***"the Pharisees went out and plotted against Him, how they might destroy Him"*** (Matthew 12:14). What occasion caused such an eruption of violent hate? Jesus' disciples were walking along on the Sabbath Day, plucking and eating heads of grain (Matthew 12:1). How do we compare the apostles eating plucked grain on the Sabbath Day to the Pharisees plotting murder on the Sabbath? Jesus entered the synagogue and discovered a man with a withered hand. He healed the man and violated the Sabbath Day law. Compare the incredible change in a family when the husband is made well to the Pharisees plotting murder on the Sabbath Day! How could the Pharisees be so blind?

Look at the spirit of rebellion gripping the Pharisees and Sadducees, leaving no room for growth, expansion of truth, or the speaking of God. After discussing how to murder Jesus, they returned to the crowd gathered around Him. While they were plotting His murder, Jesus moved into the multitude, and ***"He healed them all"*** (Matthew 12:15). You would think that anyone mingling with the crowd would sense the presence of God and hear the rejoicing of the people for His mercy. The Pharisees only felt the necessity to refute all Jesus was doing. Plotting Jesus' murder resulted in His healing a withered hand on the Sabbath Day; now, He was performing hundreds of miracles on the same Sabbath Day. How did the leaders of Israel respond? After gaining the crowd's attention, the Pharisees discredited Jesus by saying, ***"This fellow does***

not cast out demons except by Beelzebub, the ruler of the demons" (Matthew 12:24). They accused Him of being demon possessed!

After crucifying Jesus, the chief priest and Pharisees, with Pilate's permission, secured the tomb of Jesus. They put a Roman seal on the tomb's entrance and posted a Roman guard (Matthew 27:66). This was no problem for the eternal life of God roaring through the body of Jesus! An angel descended to roll back the stone from the tomb. The bright light and earthquake so frightened the Roman guards they fainted (Matthew 28:4). When they awakened, they ran into Jerusalem to report to the leaders of Israel all that had happened (Matthew 28:11). This group ***"consulted together"*** deciding how to respond. They took a large sum of money and bribed the guards, saying, ***"Tell them, 'His disciples came at night and stole Him away while we slept.' And if this comes to the governor's ears, we will appease and make you secure"*** (Matthew 28:13-14). What could convince them? Blinding lights terrified Roman soldiers, but an empty tomb did not affect them. They plotted murder, lied, and embezzled funds from the church. They simply could not stand Jesus!

The apostles again confront the leaders of Israel with the truth of Jesus. God raised Jesus from the dead and spoke to them again about Jesus. What is missing in the Pharisees? They are not "seeking!" They have no openness to anything outside of what they already decided. Their traditions and cultural environment established an impenetrable block to the presence of Jesus. God spoke Jesus to them repeatedly to no avail. They simply would not listen. While not listening is severe, their self-centeredness drove them to eliminate the speaking they heard. They ***"murder by hanging on a tree,"*** what God is speaking! Now, Jesus fills the apostles and reveals Himself through them. The Sanhedrin plots to kill the apostles as well!

Part Five: Advice Rejected: Agreement

Would it not be amazing if God desires us to listen? Often, the English word "obey" is a translation of the basic Greek word "akouo," meaning "to hear." Am I open? Will I embrace the changes God speaks into my life? Can I know Jesus more and more without altering my life's patterns? Will not the expanded truth of His instruction bring expanded change in my thinking? Has pride so gripped my inner being that I cannot humble myself in submission to the new revelation of His presence?

The Proposal
Acts 5:39

But all is not lost! God has not eliminated them. With all of the council's rebellion and resistance, God speaks Jesus again, which comes from a most interesting source. God did great miracles through Jesus and the apostles, but the leaders of Israel would not listen. The mighty God breathed teaching through Jesus and now the apostles, but the Sanhedrin would not heed. How else could God reveal the truth to this group? He decided to use one of their own, *"a Pharisee named Gamaliel, a teacher of the law held in respect by all the people"* (Acts 5:34). Gamaliel demanded the removal of the apostles to have the council's total attention.

Gamaliel's proposal is simply, *"for if this plan or this work is of men, it will come to nothing; but if it is God, you cannot overthrow it - lest you even be found to fight against God"* (Acts 5:38-39). The intent of his statement is an exact match to the statement of Peter, *"We ought to obey God rather than men"* (Acts 5:29). How can an individual survive in rebellion against God? Does not every man in every religion find it necessary to submit to the will of God? Fighting against God brings ultimate destruction!

Would it not behoove all of us to consider Gamaliel's

proposition? While there is no absolute proof concerning Jesus, there is more evidence verifying His reality than not. There is more historical evidence convincing us of His resurrection from the dead than the evidence concerning George Washington being the United States' first president. The historical accounts accurately recorded are numerous. But beyond physical evidence, there is the wonder of His presence! That was the strength of the apostles' message. What disturbed the priests, the captain of the temple, and the Sadducees was that **"they taught the people and preached in Jesus the resurrection from the dead"** (Acts 4:2). Arguments concerning the resurrection were in abundance between the Pharisees and the Sadducees. One could freely debate if the argument was present in theory or philosophy. But the disciples proposed the resurrection present in Jesus! As they spoke concerning Jesus' resurrection, He came into their midst! Suddenly everyone knew "He is alive!"

What if Jesus is of God? Has the Trinity God spoken Jesus to us? Do the Old Testament and its laws find their fulfillment in the revelation of Jesus? Should we submit our lives to Jesus? Gamaliel is correct; we must carefully consider what the apostles proposed in Jesus. If it is of God, we fight against a sovereign being. If it is of man, we need not worry. This proposition strikes directly at the core of each of our lives. The conflict proposed by Gamaliel is present in us.

The Trinity God opens His mouth and speaks Jesus to us! He speaks at this moment but also in the moments of the past. Repeatedly, the revelation of the Trinity God through Jesus has come to us. We have crucified Him anew, but the Trinity God continues to speak Jesus to us! Amid confusing theology, we see Jesus. God does not speak theology, but Jesus! The person of Jesus embraces us. We are forgiven and empowered by Him. In His love, we experience fullness.

Part Five: Advice Rejected: Agreement

The Persuasion
Acts 5:40

The last section of the story begins with these words, ***"And they agreed with him."*** The Greek word translated as ***"they agreed"*** is "peitho." It means "persuasion, to persuade another to receive a belief, or to convince." Our hearts leap with expectation at the possibility of this governing body of Israel being open enough to consider Jesus as the speaking of God in their lives. If they just seek truth in sincerity, it will change everything in their future. In a few short years, they will experience the destruction of Jerusalem, and their nation will cease to exist. They are desperately fighting to control their national and personal lives. They are blind to any truth outside of what they have already decided. Their resistance to seeking will destroy both their nation and their personal lives.

While they agree with Gamaliel on his proposed principle, they will not apply it to their decisions. They bring the apostles before the group again. They beat them to persuade them of the severity of their desire. ***"They commanded that they should not speak in the name of Jesus, and let them go"*** (Acts 5:40). They do not see that the issue of God's activity and will is Jesus! They do not see that the Trinity God places all His revelation in Jesus. They refrained from murdering the apostles, but they continued in their persistence of eliminating Jesus. If they had agreed, would they not have at least considered Jesus?

But there is an aggressive manner involved in their rejection. Again, the argument between the Pharisees and Sadducees about the resurrection of the dead is merely theological or philosophical. When the last debater has spoken, they fellowship together, working for the betterment of their nation. But there is no tolerance concerning Jesus. Peter said this clearly to them. ***"The God of our fathers raised up Jesus whom you***

murdered by hanging on a tree" (Acts 5:30). He did not say the Romans were involved in the crucifixion and did not include Judas' betrayal in his statement. Peter highlighted the hatred and raging contempt this council had for the person of Jesus. The apostles' miracles were not the issue; they could have tolerated the teachings of Jesus, for there was a variety of diverse teachings in Israel. They simply could not tolerate the person of Jesus!

But Jesus is gone; what is the issue with the apostles? Without fully understanding it, the Sanhedrin recognizes the presence of Jesus flowing in and from the apostles. Jesus has returned! Each time the apostles spoke, it was as if Jesus was speaking again. They now contend with the identical Spirit in the apostles they confronted in Jesus! As the apostles spoke of Jesus' resurrection, His presence was in their midst. It was not about teaching or doctrine; it was about Jesus. The Old Testament law had dramatically changed in its fulfillment in Jesus. It shifted from the believer merely refraining from murder to an expression of love in the person of Jesus (Matthew 5:21-26). They expressed the heart of Jesus. The law focused on adultery, and lust was transformed by Jesus speaking Himself through believers to the opposite sex (Matthew 5:27-30). Marriage exploded into a wife living with Jesus, merging with her husband, and a husband living with Jesus, merging with his wife (Matthew 5:31-32).

The council plotted to kill the apostles, trying to crucify Jesus again! The writer of the Book of Hebrews reveals refusing to listen to God as **"they crucify again for themselves the Son of God, and put Him to an open shame"** (Hebrews 6:6). The attitude and motive resulting in the actual physical crucifixion of Jesus remains the same as the council faces the apostles. But is it not true for our lives? Anything less than a total response to God's heart expressed in Jesus is a crucifixion! My self-centered focus must murder Him to maintain my selfish desires. I cannot live for myself and Him at the same time! The

Part Five: Advice Rejected: Agreement

challenge of the apostles is clear. Indeed, the Trinity God has spoken Jesus. Jesus is the true and total revelation of God to our lives. Will we submit to Him? Will we come under the control of His Lordship? Someone must be crucified. Either I will allow God to crucify my self-centeredness, or I will crucify Jesus by my rejection (Galatians 2:20).

Acts 5:33

TWO REALMS

"When they heard this, they were furious and plotted to kill them"
(Acts 5:33).

Luke sets the stage for the increasing persecution of the early Church. The first phase of persecution focused on Peter and John (Acts 4:1-3). This second phase included the imprisonment and interrogation of all the apostles (Acts 5:17-18). Luke intermingles two concepts in each of these occasions. He intentionally relates the inner attitude of Israel's leaders. **"They were furious,"** before proclaiming their physical activity, **"plotted to kill them."** Their attitude is not a new revelation. The interaction between the spiritual and the physical realm constantly reveals itself. Nothing occurs in the physical realm that does not originate in the spiritual. God created the physical realm to demonstrate and visualize spiritual realities.

Paul highlights this linkage as he concludes his epistle to the Ephesians. He boldly proclaims, **"For we do not wrestle against flesh and blood, but against principalities, against powers, against the rulers of the darkness of this age, against spiritual hosts of wickedness in the heavenly places"** (Ephesians 6:12). The Greek word "pale" is translated as *"wrestle,"* bespeaking conflict, war, struggle, fight, or contest. Paul admonishes us not to focus on the physical, *"flesh and blood,"* but on the spiritual realm where the battle rages. The issue is not with the physical action but the spiritual realm where the physical initiates. We can never solve a problem by making physical changes because they are only symptoms of the inner spiritual realm.

Paul encouraged the Galatians to *"Walk in the Spirit, and you shall not fulfill the lust of the flesh"* (Galatians 5:16). The flesh's domination is in the merger with the Spirit of Jesus. If the physical act is not the expression of Jesus, it is because I am not adequately merged with His presence. The issue is spiritual, not physical! In the same passage, he contrasts *"the works of the flesh"* with *"the fruit of the Spirit"* (Galatians 5:19, 22). *"If we live in the Spirit, let us also walk in the Spirit"* (Galatians 5:25). Being in Christ will determine how we walk in the flesh.

In the Sermon on the Mount, Jesus proposed the same conclusion! We are to treasure *"treasures in heaven,"* not *"treasures on earth"* (Matthew 6:19-21). We must have a single eye focused on light rather than darkness (Matthew 6:22-23). We cannot serve *"God and mammon"* (Matthew 6:24). *"But seek first the kingdom of God and His righteousness, and all these things shall be added to you"* (Matthew 6:33). It is obvious Jesus only recognized two realities, physical and spiritual. His burning desire is our spiritual merger with Him; then, the physical will find proper expression.

Luke contrasts the physical with the spiritual in both phases of persecution. The healing of the lame beggar stimulated the first phase (Acts 3:1-10). News of this miracle spread throughout the temple, drawing a great crowd of witnesses. Peter realized they were crediting him for the miracle. He cried out to the crowd, *"Men of Israel, why do you marvel at this? Or why*

look so intently at us, as though by our own power or godliness we had made this man walk" (Acts 3:12)? Peter began to highlight Jesus, ***"the Prince of life, whom God raised from the dead, of which we are witnesses"*** (Acts 3:15). The resurrected Jesus, in the spiritual realm, just demonstrated Himself through the physical life of the lame beggar!

Luke writes that the priests, the captain of the temple, and the Sadducees came upon them, ***"being greatly disturbed"*** (Acts 4:2). This inner spiritual reaction is a translation of the Greek word "diaponeomai." The basic word is "diaponeo," a combination of "dia" meaning "thoroughly," intensifying "poneo," meaning "to labor or toil." It points to "exhausting, depleting grief which results in piercing fatigue." The leaders of Israel were "worn out" with the miracles and constant preaching of Jesus! Day after day, the apostles proclaimed Jesus as risen from the dead. Finally, these leaders could tolerate it no longer. They captured Peter and John and physically responded to their inner spiritual frustration!

Luke then displays the same dynamic action in this second phase of persecution. These leaders ***"were filled with indignation"*** (Acts 5:17). "Zelos," a Greek word from the root word "ze," meaning "hot enough to boil," filled these leaders. The inner spiritual world of these leaders was at the boiling point! This inner spiritual reality spilled forth with the physical act of capturing all of the apostles (Acts 5:18). When interrogating the apostles, Peter replied, ***"Jesus"*** (Acts 5:29-32). ***"When they heard this, they were furious and plotted to kill them"*** (Acts 5:33). Again, the spiritual realm displaying itself in the physical realm confronts us!

But there is a problem with this concept. There is a clear distinction between the physical and the spiritual realms. From our discussion so far, these two realms appear marked and recognizable. But they are not! They are two sides to one entity, which brings them into unity. While God intended the spiritual to supply the physical, there is backlash from the physical to the spiritual. In a real sense, they intermix!

The Spiritual Realm

Luke describes the unseen, spiritual realm of the council as ***"furious,"*** a translation of the Greek word "diaprio." The Greek word "dia" means "through," and the Greek word "prio" means "cut with a saw." Luke described the emotional state of the council members as "cut all the way through, sawn asunder, split down the center." Indignation, envy, and outrage overcame them. This spiritual condition is not isolated from their physical state. Their blood pressure was undoubtedly high; their faces had a reddish tone; they squirmed in their seats or jumped to their feet. The only way to describe the spiritual realm of the council members is by physical descriptions; this is fascinating. The only means we have to articulate the abstract world is through the concrete world of the physical. However, Jesus found the same limitation: He consistently painted the Kingdom of God with the brush of physical parables.

The physical and spiritual convey to us several essential facts. These two realms are intimately linked; we experience each of them through the avenue of the other. The blessings of the spiritual realm consistently embrace the physical world. The wonder of inner peace, security, and confidence known through faith in our resurrected Jesus is in physical feelings and calmness in the physical disruptions around us. The continual physical provisions and marvelous physical interventions Jesus makes in our physical lives from the unseen spiritual world cause us to wonder at His great love for us. We must also pay tribute to the constant struggle to comprehend the totality of both worlds. The knowledge of the physical has expanded in magnitude in the last fifty years; one cannot describe it; we cannot grasp the physical limits. We must exclaim the same for the spiritual realm. In both the physical and the spiritual, we are on a journey without a known destination!

In light of these thoughts, we might inquire, "What was the physical issue that brought such disruption to the council's spiritual world?" The answer is "Jesus!" Evidence in the first phase of persecution declares the leaders of Israel were ***"greatly disturbed that they taught the people and preached in Jesus the resurrection from the dead"*** (Acts 4:2). A single requirement was demanded upon the council releasing the disciples. ***"So they called them and commanded them not to speak at all nor teach in the name of Jesus"*** (Acts 4:18). The great distress in the spiritual lives of the council is evident in the second phase of persecution. ***"And when they had brought them, they set them before the council. And the high priest asked them, saying, 'Did we not strictly command you not to teach in this name? And look, you have filled Jerusalem with your doctrine, and intend to bring this Man's blood on us'"*** (Acts 5:27-28).

The "saw" that cut the council to their spiritual core was not miracles. They had no concern over the early Church's meetings at Solomon's Porch or suppers in their homes. The compassionate ministry did not upset the inner spirits of the council members. They appreciated the faithfulness of the Christians to the customs in the temple. The single fact that ruined everything in both the physical and spiritual realm was "Jesus!" The council could not tolerate the person of Jesus. Because the Spirit of Jesus and the apostles' spirit merged, the council knew that Jesus was present. They eliminated Him once, ***"murdered by hanging on a tree"*** (Acts 5:30). Each time the apostles spoke of Jesus, the same spiritual realm displayed in Jesus became known again. Whatever was in the spiritual realm of Jesus was now in the spiritual realm of the apostles! The council could not tolerate it!

Part Five: Advice Rejected: Agreement

The intolerance of the council continued to be true. The Greek word describing the spiritual disturbance in the council (Acts 5:33) is only used twice in the New Testament. Stephen was preaching to those from *"what is called the Synagogue of the Freedmen (Cyrenians, Alexandrians, and those from Cilicia and Asia)"* (Acts 6:9). Luke declares that those listening *"were not able to resist the wisdom and the Spirit by which he spoke"* (Acts 6:10). Upon the completion of his message, *"they were cut to the heart* (diaprio)*, and they gnashed at him with their teeth"* (Acts 7:54). The spiritual realm of Stephen's life, the twelve apostles, and Jesus were all the same. A spiritual message spilling forth was far beyond data or information. The presence of the Spirit of Jesus became a "saw" that *"cut to the heart."*

Our resurrected Jesus is not mean or even offensive. He does not desire to hurt or punish. His real intent is redemption! He comes to each of us with His arms open and His heart ready to embrace. But He exposes every aspect of human life contrary to His nature. What is unseen and tolerated in the darkness is made known in the brilliant light of His presence. The spiritual realm reveals protection, self-justification, and anger. *"They were furious."* We must set aside this reaction for the healing forgiveness of Jesus to embrace the spiritual realm. Only in brokenness and openness can Jesus redeem us.

The Physical Realm

The spiritual resolve of the council members quickly displayed itself *"and plotted to kill them"* (Acts 5:33). The intent in the spiritual realm immediately began to make physical plans. *"Plotted"* is a translation of the Greek word "bouleuo." It means "to take counsel, to consult, determine, deliberate with oneself or one another in counsel." The Greek word again highlights the significant spiritual and physical interaction. The physical does not know what action is necessary unless it consults with the spiritual realm. The physical turns to the spiritual, asking, "How do you feel about it? What is your desire?" Therefore, the spiritual condition of the individual determines the physical activity.

The Sanhedrin does not need to "plot." They merely follow the same pattern established throughout their encounters with Jesus. Jesus and His disciples were violating the Sabbath Day laws. The spiritual realm of Jesus displayed itself in activities of mercy, love, and healing in the physical. ***"Then the Pharisees went out and plotted against Him, how they might destroy Him"*** (Matthew 12:14). When confronted by this same group, Jesus told three parables. After hearing the parables, they perceived that He was speaking about them. ***"Then the Pharisees went and plotted how they might entangle Him in His talk"*** (Matthew 22:15). The physical action of this group escalated to attacking Jesus in the Garden of Gethsemane in the middle of the night. They delivered Him to Caiaphas in his palace, questioning, accusing, and physically striking Him. ***"When morning came, all the chief priests and elders of the people plotted against Jesus to put Him to death"*** (Matthew 27:1). Even after Jesus' resurrection, as the soldiers revealed all the details of the event to them, they ***"consulted together*** (plotted)***, they gave a large sum of money to the soldiers, saying, 'Tell them, His disciples came at night and stole Him away while we slept'"*** (Matthew 28:12-13).

The leaders of Israel established a physical pattern of action regarding Jesus. The apostles now confront these leaders with the same Spirit of Jesus. Immediately, they follow through with the same physical pattern, ***"plotted to kill them."*** Often, we establish physical patterns in our lives called "habits." These habits quickly become "addictions." We struggle to break these addictions through various physical activities. However, as it was

Part Five: Advice Rejected: Agreement

true for the leaders of Israel, so it is true for us. These physical patterns are a direct result of the spiritual realm of our lives. First, they are the utmost and produced by the inner spiritual state.

The Trinity God is the same way and created us in His image! The Greek word "bouleuo" does mean to counsel or plot, but there is an undercurrent to the word. It is a word pointing to the predetermined intention that stimulates the plotting, contrasted with the Greek word "thelo," focusing on the desire or wish behind deciding. Within the spiritual state, a craving, desire, or intent (thelo) pushes the individual into planning a physical response (bouleuo). The nature of the Trinity God is redemptive; His desire, wish, and craving is to restore. Therefore, God's physical planning and activities are all determined by this. The cross of Christ was inevitable; His resurrection and ascension had to be! The prevenient grace of God acting upon each of our lives is adjusted not in intent but in physical expression due to our freedom of choice. As we make choices out of an evil heart, He makes choices out of a redemptive heart!

God created us in His image. Our "thelo" determines our "bouleuo." As stated above, these two realms intermix. Often, our physical will influences our inner will and desires. The selfish, self-centered nature of the spiritual world will consistently cater to the physical circumstances of comfort. In this case, the physical realm dictates the spiritual state. However, even in this picture, the problem is not solved by physical change but by spiritual. We only have two options in the spiritual realm, "self" or "Jesus." One or the other must fill, dominate, and drive us.

The self-centered carnal spirit is a survivor. It will fight for control; we cannot conquer, tame, or bring it into submission. The Biblical solution to its domination is "crucifixion!" "***I have been crucified with Christ; it is no longer I who live, but Christ lives in me; and the life which I now live in the flesh I live by faith in the Son of God, who loved me and gave Himself for me***" (Galatians 2:20). As we speak about this selfish spirit, often we refer to it as a "thing." It is not an entity existing independently but an attitude or tendency. While we often refer to Jesus' death as "He died in my place," the reality is His death was the death of my self-centeredness! Jesus encompassed the raw sewage of my selfish nature within Himself, brought it to judgment on the cross, and conquered it in a new life in the resurrection. If I embrace Him, taking sides with Jesus against myself, He can free me from self-domination in the spiritual realm. Self-centeredness is at the heart of every destructive physical act in my life. This selfish nature destroys relationships, bad decisions, and physical addictions. Paul cried, **"O wretched man that I am! Who will deliver me from this body of death? I thank God - through Jesus Christ our Lord"** (Romans 7:24-25).

My wretchedness reveals why Jesus is the single issue in our passage. The leaders of Israel wanted Jesus removed from the ministry of the apostles. The apostles could continue in every ministry activity, but they knew all ministry resulted from Jesus' presence. In the spiritual realm, Jesus captured them and was their single focus. If they eliminated Jesus, all would be lost. The Sanhedrin realized that if "Jesus" reigned instead of "self," this threatened everything they had constructed physically. Either they would crucify self-centeredness, or they would need to crucify the Spirit of Jesus expressed through the apostles. You and I face the same dilemma! It is the critical issue, the only issue, and the final issue of our spirit. What will we do with Jesus?

Acts 5:34

SPIRITUAL WISDOM

"Then one in the council stood up, a Pharisee named Gamaliel, a teacher of the law held in respect by all the people, and commanded them to put the apostles outside for a little while" (Acts 5:34).

The Sanhedrin, or council, was Palestine's supreme ruling body of Jewish affairs. Moses appointed seventy men to govern Israel according to God's instruction (Numbers 11:16). This structure continued throughout the history of Israel until the fall of Jerusalem in A.D. 70. The rulership was divided equally between Pharisees and Sadducees with the High Priest as chairman. This court not only administered civil matters according to Jewish law but also dealt with criminal justice, keeping its police force and making arrests.

The Sanhedrin represented the wealthiest men of Israel. The flourishing business of sacrifice lambs provided the opportunity for a guaranteed market of great flocks of sheep and other items necessary for worshippers. This council protected and secured the required environment to foster their wealth. The conflict they had with the apostles continued from their conflict with Jesus. Jesus' ministry focused on the handicapped, sick, and poverty-stricken people. The early Church continued its growth from this social class. The consistent preaching and teaching concerning Jesus brought guilt and public accusation against the council members. The Sanhedrin accused the apostles of intending *"to bring this Man's blood on us"* (Acts 5:28). The council must eliminate the apostles as they did Jesus! Their interaction with the apostles in the second phase of persecution caused them to be *"furious and plotted to kill them"* (Acts 5:33).

However, *"a Pharisee named Gamaliel, a teacher of the law held in respect by all the people,"* stood up and addressed the Sanhedrin (Acts 5:34). The title "the Elder" was bestowed on him, as it was on his father and grandfather. He was the first of only seven in all rabbinic history to be distinguished "Rabban," meaning our teacher or master. The Jews understood that he was the most significant living authority and revered figure in all of Judaism during the days of Christ. The school of Hillel was the most influential in Judaism, of which Gamaliel was the leader. Paul received his training under the instruction of Gamaliel (Acts 22:3). Paul described himself as *"I advanced in Judaism beyond many of my contemporaries in my own nation, being more exceedingly zealous for the traditions of my fathers"* (Galatians 1:14). Was this not a result of the influential teaching of Gamaliel?

Gamaliel *"stood up,"* which immediately demanded the total attention of the council. He represented the highest level of Old Testament knowledge and tradition of Judaism. All Jews carefully considered His wisdom in applying Jewish traditions to the present cultural influences. His thoughts represented everything sacred in Jewish life's educational, theological, and political arenas. There is no one superior to Gamaliel in Jewish wisdom. The room grew deathly quiet as he began to share his insight.

Compare this to the twelve apostles, who, upon the request of Gamaliel, have been put *"outside for a little while."* Any comparison would be ridiculous even to state. Comic

Part Five: Advice Rejected: Agreement

books compared to theological writings would not begin the comparison. The apostles are all from Galilee, while Gamaliel ministered in the heart of Jerusalem. Gamaliel's background is one of outstanding scholarship, just like his father and grandfather. Many prominent apostles were fishermen, and no decent scholar was in their midst. In interrogating Peter and John, the council *"perceived that they were uneducated and untrained men"* (Acts 4:13).

The fact the apostles are from Galilee is enough to disqualify their opinion. Galilee is far north and removed from the pure, throbbing heart of the Jewish faith. While the Jews established worship in the Galilee synagogues, many compromising practices infiltrated that worship. Many Gentile foreigners traveling the trade routes to the Mediterranean Sea came through Galilee. Bringing their pagan practices with them, they influenced all of Galilee. The priests had not held the Jewish line for tradition and conservative practices. These twelve apostles would not even represent the best Jewish influence from that distant territory.

Then came the issue of Jesus! The apostles have followed Him for three years. Has He not solely influenced their thinking, dominated their education, and determined their manner of life? But even they expressed their suspicion in the early days of discipleship. Nathanael openly declared, *"Can anything good come out of Nazareth"* (John 1:46)? Jesus was not from Jerusalem, nor educated in Jerusalem, and did little ministry in Jerusalem. While He was born in Bethlehem, He was raised and received His education in Nazareth, which is believed to be the worst town in all of Galilee. As one of the officers of the chief priests and Pharisees said, *"Search and look, for no prophet has arisen out of Galilee"* (John 7:52). Numerous times, His teachings were so bizarre many accused Him of being demon-possessed. On one occasion, *"the Jews answered and said to Him, 'Do we not say rightly that You are a Samaritan and have a demon'"* (John 8:48)? After Jesus tried to explain things to them, they reported, ***"Now we know that You have a demon"*** (John 8:52)!

Based on education and theological training, there is no comparison between the apostles and Gamaliel. Why should we even consider anything the apostles said? The screaming message of the Book of Acts answers this question! The Holy Spirit filled apostles but not Gamaliel! While Gamaliel was superior in the knowledge of his culture in Scripture and tradition, he did not know the mind of God! Something happened to the ***"uneducated and untrained men"*** who stood before the Sanhedrin. They spoke with boldness produced not by arrogance or education but by the power of the Spirit of Jesus. Was this not the promise of Jesus in the first chapter of this book? ***"But you shall receive power when the Holy Spirit has come upon you; and you shall be witnesses to Me in Jerusalem, and in all Judea and Samaria, and to the end of the earth"*** (Acts 1:8).

This wisdom of men was the single factor causing Gamaliel to address the council. Peter and the apostles declared, ***"We ought to obey God rather than men"*** (Acts 5:29). Even Gamaliel, the most educated and knowledgeable among the council, agreed. The Greek word translated as ***"obey"*** is "peitharcheo." A picture of a ruler who speaks commands visualizes the word. Other Greek words synonyms of this word are "akouo," meaning to listen, to hear with obedience, and "enotizomai," meaning to give ear, to hearken. However, Gamaliel and the apostles differ in "What is God speaking?" God is not speaking intellectual philosophy or traditional thoughts but is speaking, "Jesus!" The apostles merge with the Spirit of God and reveal Jesus, the Truth (John 14:6). Jesus promised, ***"And I will pray the Father, and He will give you another Helper, that He may abide with you forever - the Spirit of truth, whom the world cannot receive, because it neither sees Him nor knows Him; but you***

Part Five: Advice Rejected: Agreement

know Him, for He dwells with you and will be in you" (John 14:16-17). Jesus continued His explanation to them. ***"But when the Helper comes, whom I shall send to you from the Father, the Spirit of truth who proceeds from the Father, He will testify of Me"*** (John 15:26). ***"However, when He, the Spirit of truth, has come, He will guide you into all truth"*** (John 16:13).

Jesus, in His instructions or Luke in the Books of Acts, never mentions anything about seminars, educational degrees, or worldly knowledge! God, through the Spirit of Jesus, gave us His mind, and we know Truth, Jesus! Paul became a living example of this radical wisdom. He, a student trained by Gamaliel, was the most zealous of all his fellow students for the traditions of his fathers (Galatians 1:14). But a radical confrontation with Jesus transformed his life (Acts 22:6-21). Paul referred to this transformation as ***"reveal His Son in me"*** (Galatians 1:16). When this revelation occurred, ***"I did not immediately confer with flesh and blood, nor did I go up to Jerusalem to those who were apostles before me; but I went to Arabia and returned again to Damascus"*** (Galatians 1:16-17). That is why Paul could boldly declare, ***"But I make known to you, brethren, that the gospel which was preached by me is not according to man"*** (Galatians 1:11).

Paul would write insightful words to the church at Corinth concerning the comparison of man's intellectual knowledge and God's wisdom.

> *"For it is written:*
> *'I will destroy the wisdom of the wise,*
> *And bring to nothing the understanding of the prudent'"*
> *(1 Corinthians 1:19).*

He asked a question concerning the wise: "Where are they?" The members of the Sanhedrin, along with Gamaliel, are included. ***"Has not God made foolish the wisdom of this world"*** (1Corinthians 1:16)? ***"Because the foolishness of God is wiser than men, and the weakness of God is stronger than men"*** (1 Corinthians 1:25). ***"But of Him you are in Christ Jesus, who became for us wisdom from God - and righteousness and sanctification and redemption - that, as it is written, 'He who glories, let him glory in the Lord'"*** (1 Corinthians 1:30-31).

Is this not the message dramatically demonstrated in the story of our passage? Gamaliel and the members of the Sanhedrin, highly educated and filled with the knowledge of their culture, cannot grasp the wisdom of God in Jesus. The uneducated and untrained apostles have the wisdom of God's heart in Jesus. What differed between these two groups? It is the merging, indwelling presence of Jesus within them. Self-knowledge fills the Sanhedrin, but Jesus, the wisdom of God's heart, fills the apostles!

It is remarkable how often this contrast reveals itself in the Gospel story. Nicodemus was a Pharisee, a ruler of the Jews. He recognized in Jesus something he did not have. Jesus confronted him with truth from the spiritual world. ***"Most assuredly, I say to you, unless one is born again, he cannot see the kingdom of God"*** (John 3:3). Nicodemus immediately dipped into his academic education for understanding. He reported to Jesus that such a thing was impossible, for no one could enter his mother's womb a second time. Jesus and Nicodemus operated out of two different realms of knowledge. Jesus was filled with the Spirit of God and knew the heart of God. Jesus exclaimed, ***"Are you the teacher of Israel, and do not know these things"*** (John 3:10)? Nicodemus was an expert on the Scriptures and educated others. Yet, all he knows is earthly wisdom; he does not grasp the wisdom of God's heart. But how could he if the Spirit of God did not fill him?

As this contrast unfolds in our passage, Gamaliel appealed

Part Five: Advice Rejected: Agreement

to the council in the wisdom of men. He gave two examples of individuals with a tremendous following, but it ended and came to nothing (Acts 5:36-37). He was very convincing, for Luke reported, *"And they agreed with him"* (Acts 5:40). While it may have caused the Sanhedrin to beat the apostles instead of killing them, it did not alter their demand. ***"They commanded that they should not speak in the name of Jesus"*** (Acts 5:40). As the story unfolds in the Book of Acts, they will not waver from their intellectual knowledge. More persecution followed, and the nation of Israel was lost.

While Luke vividly established this concept in our verse, he decided to go overboard in its revelation. He concludes his verse by saying, ***"and commanded them to put the apostles outside for a little while"*** (Acts 5:34). The Greek word "keleuo" is translated as ***"commanded."*** This verb is in the indicative mood, not the imperative, meaning Gamaliel did not order the removal of the apostles as a command but as a request. It is a simple statement of fact. He asked for the privilege of speaking to the Sanhedrin without the presence of the apostles. That placed the removal of the apostles in the attitude of Gamaliel's intellectual approach rather than anger or hostility.

Luke placed the action of ***"to put" amid this intellectual approach.*** This verb, an infinitive, is the Greek word "poieo!" I simply could not believe Luke used this Greek word. I searched through many translations only to discover everyone translates it the same. I also learned at least six different Greek words Luke could have used to translate "put." In that list of six, "poieo" is not one of them. As we read the verse, it appears on the surface that Luke is merely telling us the council placed the apostles outside of the council's hearing. However, by using this word, the focus is not on the physical placement but on the spiritual motive of the action! Luke highlighted the intellectual wisdom of the council, which logically wants to eliminate the apostles. The self-centered intellect, the wisdom of men, could not tolerate the wisdom of God in the Spirit of Jesus.

"Poieo" means "to make, form, produce, bring about, or cause." "Poieo" speaks of any external act producing something tangible, corporeal, obvious to the senses, and completed in its action. In the context of our passage, the Sanhedrin commanded and accomplished the removal of the apostles from their presence. But the primary idea connected to this Greek word must always be in its translation. It speaks of a state or condition produced by an inward nature, desire, or will. "Poieo" is always used to describe trees bearing fruit (Matthew 3:10; Luke 6:43). Another Greek word, "prasso," is translated as "do," which refers to the routine, habitual activity of duty or obligation. "Poieo" focuses on the generative power that creates the activity to bring forth, beget, or create. Is Luke using the Greek word "poieo" to focus us beyond the physical level of the action to reveal the inner spiritual motive?

The self-centered intellectual wisdom of men contrasted with the wisdom of God's mind shared through the fullness of the Spirit of Jesus is suddenly the passage issue. Am I going to place the wisdom of God, which He desperately wants to communicate to me, outside the realm of my hearing? My self-centered understanding will not tolerate the constant bombarding of the Truth in the fullness of Jesus. I cannot live out of my understanding and His at the same time. The conflict is destructive. I must accept the fullness of Jesus in my life and knowledge or continue to live in my thinking. I cannot live in both!

Religious people grasp this in viewing the ungodly of our world. The Scriptures help us understand the laws. We can adopt the Ten Commandments through the self-centered intellect of the religious world. The Sanhedrin embraced the ceremonies and traditions established in the Scriptures. They quickly saw the evil of the Roman world through the self-centered intellectual

Part Five: Advice Rejected: Agreement

understanding of their religious tradition. Jesus spoke concerning this group. ***"You search the Scriptures, for in them you think you have eternal life; and these are they which testify of Me. But you are not willing to come to Me that you may have life"*** (John 5:39-40). They only understood the Scriptures through their traditional education and self-centered intellect. If the Sanhedrin, like Paul, would submit their intelligence to the Spirit of Jesus, they would have a new understanding of what God was doing, Jesus!

The resurrected Jesus once again confronts the Sanhedrin. Will He fill their lives? Will they set aside their thinking to embrace His? Will they know His heart? It is the same question for us. We have our own culture, whether it is religious or not. We have been raised in our traditions, which controls our thinking. Who will be filled with the Spirit of Jesus and let Him reveal the Scriptures? Who will abandon their thinking and understanding to the mind of Christ? Is this not what merging with Him means? I want to think like Him; I want to feel like Him; I want to desire what He desires. That is my destiny!

Acts 5:35

TAKE HEED

"And he said to them: 'Men of Israel, take heed to yourselves what you intend to do regarding these men'" (Acts 5:35).

Various instruments of God declare truth to us. God designed them specifically to maximize the possibility of communication. The Trinity God knows our background, language, and emotional barriers. The Scriptures declare we are **"*without excuse.*"** Everyone receives the consistent revelation of the creation through which **"*His invisible attributes are clearly seen, being understood by the things that are made, even His eternal power and Godhead*"** (Romans 1:20). Certainly, this had to be true for the Jewish Sanhedrin. In addition, their religious heritage, the Scriptures, Jesus' ministry, and the apostle's testimonies were all adequate to convince them. Now they live in the new hour of the Holy Spirit's outpouring!

The council stubbornly denied Jesus even with all the Divinely inspired witnesses. But the prevenient grace of God did not cease to pierce these Jewish leaders with the revelation of Christ. Peter and the other apostles once again bombarded them with the message of the resurrected Jesus (Acts 5:29-32). The council again refused to consider truth and **"*plotted to*"**

Part Five: Advice Rejected: Agreement

kill them" (Acts 5:33). However, God was not finished with His witness! He attempted to penetrate their hardened hearts with the revelation of truth. He chose someone they highly respected. They accepted Gamaliel as the most significant living authority and revered figure in all Judaism. While the Holy Spirit did not fill Gamaliel, the Trinity God utilized rebellious instruments to declare His truth!

Gamaliel requested that the apostles be removed from their midst. But Jesus is not limited to the physical presence of the apostles. He will speak this time through Gamaliel. Jesus will use the worldly wisdom of Gamaliel, causing the Sanhedrin to reflect on their inner spiritual lives. Gamaliel's opening statement was, ***"Men of Israel, take heed to yourselves what you intend to do regarding these men"*** (Acts 5:35). In the original language of the Scriptures, this statement is broken into two sentences. The first is ***"Men of Israel, take heed to yourselves."*** The second is a question, ***"What*** (do) ***you intend to do regarding these men?"***

Both of these sentences penetrate the inner spiritual nature of the council members. The solid, unshakable truth of the Scriptures is the interlinkage of the physical and the spiritual. While we focus on a physical problem that is upsetting our physical world, the real issue spills forth from the spiritual realm. The worldly, educated wisdom of the Sanhedrin considered the apostles a physical issue creating a physical problem in the Jewish society, their same reaction to Jesus. He was a physical problem they needed to eliminate physically. Once they physically silenced Him, all would be well. In the worldly wisdom of the council, the apostles continued the physical problem with the proclamation of Jesus' resurrection. Now they must physically silence that as well.

But the problem is not in the physical realm; it is only the platform where the spiritual realm manifests itself physically. The solution for the council was not in the physical but in their spiritual lives. They had a spiritual problem they were ignoring!

Since you and I consistently do the same thing, this should not be a mystery to us. In this opening statement, Gamaliel called the members of the Sanhedrin to consider their spiritual lives.

Focus

Gamaliel's unique command to begin his address to the council was *"take heed,"* translated from the Greek verb "prosecho." It is present tense, active voice, and an imperative mood. Gamaliel commanded the council to persistently take personal responsibility to view their inner spiritual lives moment by moment. Please take a look at your inner motive and heart's passion. "Prosecho" is a combination of "pros," meaning "to," and "echo," meaning "to have." The command of Gamaliel was "pay attention, to hold the mind or the ear toward someone." As a nautical term, it means to hold a ship in a direction to sail towards. In the New Testament, the writers use it to figuratively apply one's mind to something, attend or give heed.

Gamaliel's statement to the council narrowed the focus of their investigation. He instructed them, *"take heed to yourselves."* "Heautou" is a pronoun directing their focus and is translated as *"to yourselves."* Indeed, this should not be difficult for the self-centered council or us! The nature of sin that possesses all of us is self-centeredness. No one needs to encourage us to focus on ourselves, for we constantly live in such a state. Our needs, concerns, and comfort are our life's consistent agenda. This agenda is the issue that gave rise to the imprisonment and interrogation of the apostles. The apostles' constant emphasis on Jesus disturbed the comfort and prosperity of the council members. Their accusation was that the apostles *"intend to bring this Man's blood on us"* (Acts 5:28).

The difficulty with *"take heed to yourselves"* is not in getting the council members to focus on themselves but in

Part Five: Advice Rejected: Agreement

seeing themselves as they are. What is their real motive? What do they desire? What is the actual condition of their inner hearts? However, that is true for all of us! A true self-analysis would most likely demand change and be somewhat uncomfortable. Therefore, our investigation of our inner being becomes filled with self-justification, comparison to others, and denial. One might ask, "Are those filled with themselves capable of seeing their real state of existence?"

Throughout the Gospel accounts, the Pharisees and Sadducees never wavered in justifying their inner motives. They bickered over superficial laws concerning Sabbath activities and yet justified plotting murder on the Sabbath (Matthew 12). They diligently searched the Scriptures only to reject the very One of whom the Scriptures testified (John 5:39). They witnessed the moving power of God in their culture through Jesus only to accredit it to demons (Matthew 12:24). This council labeled Jesus as *"the deceiver"* as they constantly promoted deception in their own lives (Matthew 27:63) and fought for truth as they desired it by promoting falsehoods (Matthew 28:13). Now the Trinity God, through Gamaliel, is pleading with them for a precise, unrestricted examination of their inner heart's motive. But are they capable of such an investigation? Are they so blinded that they cannot see their spiritual condition (Matthew 15:14)? These men now plot how they might kill the apostles and further eliminate the proclamation of Jesus (Acts 5:33).

Should we not ask ourselves this same question? Paul cried out to the people of Corinth, *"But even if our gospel is veiled, it is veiled to those who are perishing, whose minds the god of this age has blinded, who do not believe, lest the light of the gospel of the glory of Christ, who is the image of God, should shine on them"* (2 Corinthians 4:3-4). It is frightening to consider my spiritual state not being as I perceive it! Am I blinded? How can I be sure my self-centered desires are not blinding me?

One might suggest we find the answer in "truth." The difficulty with this answer is that for three years, the Pharisees and Sadducees had exposure to the One who said, ***"I am the way, the truth, and the life"*** (John 14:6). Their act of crucifying Jesus was reversed by the resurrection of Christ, which shook the very culture surrounding them. The same Jesus of truth they eliminated continued to bombard their lives through the apostles. If truth is the great deterrent to all deception, the Sanhedrin would kneel in repentance upon the revelation of their inner depravity. They lived with truth irritating their inner souls and consistently erected protection barriers for their present state.

While no one denies the necessity of Jesus, the Truth, confronting our lives, we must respond with seeking or openness. Even in this second phase of persecution, the council will not fully embrace the instructions of Gamaliel. They refrained from killing the apostles but beat them and continued to resist Jesus with great intensity! How will they ever change without an open response? The dangerous place of arrival, reaching a plateau, ceasing to grow, knowing it all, staleness is destructive.

The author of the Book of Hebrews challenges us, ***"For though by this time you ought to be teachers, you need someone to teach you again the first principles of the oracles of God; and you have come to need milk and not solid food"*** (Hebrews 5:12). This is a description of a "baby." It is not wrong to be a "baby," for we have all experienced such. But there is something wrong when we have been one for 40 years. The author continues to warn us that this pattern of babyishness will become so established in our lives that we will develop patterns that trap our souls. We will end up crucifying Jesus again and putting Him to open shame (Hebrews 6:6). We will continue to quote the Bible, hold to our traditions, and foster our pet beliefs, but the reality of Jesus will be gone!

Luke describes the members of the Sanhedrin in this setting. They handle the truth of the Scriptures, maintain the sacrificial system of the Old Testament, and cling to the Law of Moses, but that has become their death trap. While the Trinity God does not eliminate or destroy the old, He moves beyond it in great revelation (Matthew 5:17-18). Jesus unfolds revelation in their lives! Will they open themselves? *"**Men of Israel, take heed to yourselves**"* (Acts 5:35).

Form

The Greek word "mello" is translated as *"**you intend**"* and is the subject and main verb of the second sentence of Gamaliel's proposal (Acts 5:35). The verb is in the present tense, active voice, and indicative mood. However, an infinitive verb always follows this Greek word, has the same subject as the main verb, and implies purpose. "Mello" means "to have in mind, to intend, or will." When the infinitive verb is in the present tense, it implies duration or continuation. Such is the case in our sentence!

The infinitive verb in our sentence is the Greek word "prasso," translated as *"**to do.**"* Gamaliel instructed the members of the Sanhedrin to look within themselves to consider what they are thinking, intending, or purposing *"**to do**"* regarding the apostles. They must view the inner motive of their hearts, which will determine the physical response to the apostles. In a previous study, I was startled at Luke's usage of the Greek word "poieo," describing what the council already physically did to the apostles. They *"**put** (poieo) **the apostles outside for a little while**"* (Acts 5:34). This Greek word is often translated as "do or done" and refers to physical activity. But the undercurrent of the word emphasizes the inner nature or motive which creates the action. Trees "poieo" fruit. They do not "do" fruit as merely a physical activity; fruit production results from their nature.

Perhaps without even intending to, Gamaliel challenged the members of the Sanhedrin to examine their inner spiritual condition to discover what was producing their reaction. **"They were furious and plotted to kill them"** (Acts 5:33). Gamaliel instructed them to view their inner spiritual condition, creating further physical action toward the apostles. However, in doing so, he changed from "poieo" to the Greek word "prasso," translated as **"to do."** This Greek word focuses on duty, routine, or patterns of practice. The council consistently reacted to the apostles in the same manner; they established a pattern in their lives. From where does this come?

Our inner nature or focus establishes the form or pattern of our actions. The physical is the platform for the activity determined by the spiritual realm of our lives. To effectively change the physical world we create for ourselves, we must begin with the inner spiritual reality of our lives. You will notice the Sanhedrin was not willing to do this. They did curb their physical activity, from murdering the apostles to beating them, but they did not embrace Jesus. Embracing Jesus would have required profound spiritual change within them and upset the physical patterns of their lives.

The issue of embracing Jesus faces us as well! The physical circumstances pressing on our lives require the voice of Gamaliel to ask, **"What you intend to do?"** We must view our internal spiritual relationship with Jesus to determine the future display of the physical circumstances of our lives. It is foolish to consider changing our physical patterns without confronting our spiritual life. We cannot effectively change physical routines (prasso) without uprooting the spiritual conditions (poieo) producing them. The apostles delivered this message to the council, and now Gamaliel echoed it to them again.

Part Five: Advice Rejected: Agreement

Force

Gamaliel completed his second sentence with this phrase *"regarding these men"* (Acts 5:35). The word *"regarding"* is a translation of the Greek word "epi." While writers use this word in various relations, they must maintain two leading ideas in any translation. One is the emphasis of "rest upon, on, or in." The second is "motion upon, to, or towards." The impact of Gamaliel's statement became significant but went unheeded by the Sanhedrin. The Holy Spirit used Gamaliel, who joined the council's rejection of Jesus in a way he did not understand. Gamaliel appeals to the members of the Sanhedrin to look beyond the physical circumstances of their engagement; they must view the deep spiritual motivation gushing forth from their spiritual condition. They must "pay attention" to the continual pattern flowing forth from their inner nature. While they were highly religious in their physical activities, this was a call for internal examination. Although their physical actions of prayer, charitable deeds, and fasting were their weekly routine, the inner spiritual core of their lives was in a state of evil. The focus of the internal examination was personal, *"to themselves."* Each member must view their involvement with Jesus.

As they examine their inner spiritual state, they must view what form this focus manifests in their physical lives. It comes as a question, *"What you intend to do regarding these men?"* The emphasis in his challenge was not eternity, although that was involved. It was the immediate future regarding their physical action toward the apostles. What did their inner spiritual condition *"intend to do?"* Physical activity was required based on the guidance of the spiritual state. The spiritual realm produced the motive that established the physical pattern of action in their lives. There can be no attempt to break such a physical pattern without confronting the spiritual condition.

This physical activity fell upon ***"these men."*** In our passage, Gamaliel referred to the apostles who were ***"outside for a little while."*** Again, a fundamental concept confronts us; our inner spiritual condition will produce a pattern of activity that will rest upon those around us. While Gamaliel referred to the apostles, it was a reference to Jesus. The apostles' single physical action making the council members furious was the proclamation of Jesus. Therefore, the inner spiritual state of the council members was warring against Jesus.

This pattern is for all of us. However, our spiritual state expresses itself in the physical, and whoever may be the physical object of that expression, the real issue is Jesus. I may cry out for Jesus to change the physical circumstances around me, only to discover He wants to change me. I ask Him to change the people closest to me, only to find He starts changing me. When He is at the core of my spiritual life, those close to me are recipients of who He is in me. The apostles focused on Jesus and did not need to change; the council members needed to examine their inner spiritual lives and open themselves to the radical revelation of Jesus. While it did not happen in their lives, it must happen in ours. Jesus was speaking even through Gamaliel.

Acts 5:36-37

A REBELLIOUS PATTERN

"For some time ago Theudas rose up, claiming to be somebody. A number of men, about four hundred, joined him. He was slain, and all who obeyed him were scattered and came to nothing. After this man, Judas of Galilee rose up in the days of the census, and drew away many people after him. He also perished, and all who obeyed him were dispersed" (Acts 5:36-37).

Gamaliel was a member of the Sanhedrin, equally against Jesus, but the Holy Spirit used him to speak truth to the council. The persistence of God's love for us is evident in the consistency of prevenient grace! Why does God not simply eliminate us in our rebellion against Him? How many opportunities is He required to offer us? Have we not all gone beyond our limit? The nature of God's heart finds such value in us He cannot release us to destroy ourselves. He specifically designed His instrument of communication to have the maximum effect on our lives. In this case, it is not the voice of an apostle but the voice of one of the council's own!

Gamaliel begins by challenging them to look into their inner heart, ***"take heed to yourselves."*** He highlights a warning concerning the consistent pattern they have followed regarding Jesus and now the apostles, *"what you intend to do regarding these men"* (Acts 5:35). Each council member's inner core spirit produces (poieo), which is now a routine pattern of reaction (prasso). Gamaliel suggested a new approach. Luke highlights the council's response regarding two other movements within their experience.

The basic approach of the Sanhedrin to these two movements follows the principle offered by the apostles, *"We ought to obey God rather than men"* (Acts 5:29). Therefore, both the Sanhedrin and the apostles agree on this principle. The difficulty is "What is God saying?" Gamaliel suggested the council's approach should be "do nothing," as they did on two previous occasions. If God's speaking produces such a movement, they must not contradict God's words. If God is not speaking, the action is only of men and will come to nothing (Acts 5:38-39). Gamaliel gives a strong warning: let us not fight against God!

Two leaders, Theudas and Judas of Galilee, directed the two movements referenced by Gamaliel. According to Jewish historians and Bible scholars, we have no information concerning Theudas and his followers. During the time of Roman domination, there was much turmoil. According to Luke, Theudas had a following of around 400 men under his authority. The purpose of their movement is not known to us. Theudas died, and without their leader, the movement *"scattered and came to nothing"* (Acts 5:36). Luke said, *"After this man, Judas of Galilee rose up in the days of the census, and drew away many people after him"* (Acts 5:37). There is no dispute among scholars concerning the existence of Judas of Galilee. However, there is strong disagreement about when his movement took place. The purpose of our study is not to seek historical data but to experience Divine truth. Therefore, we will spend no time on the details of such history. Let us simply be open to what God is speaking through Gamaliel.

Part Five: Advice Rejected: Agreement

The Greek text begins with "apo," translated as ***"some time ago."*** Our passage relates to time, meaning "before, earlier than, or prior to." Theudas and his movement occurred within the time bracket of Jesus' life and ministry. Then Luke uses the Greek word "gar," translated as ***"for."*** "Gar" is a causative particle always standing after one or more words in a clause and expressing the reason for what has been before, affirmed, or implied, used in the sense of because or so forth. Gamaliel encouraged the council members to look carefully at their inner motives and the physical patterns developed from them. He based his caution on these two illustrations, Theudas and Judas of Galilee. While these two movements vividly illustrate Gamaliel's statement, we must view the core truth revealed in them.

A Fundamental Principle
"I am in charge"

Gamaliel characterizes both leaders of these movements as ***"rose up."*** It is a translation of the Greek word "anistemi." "Ana" means "again or up," and "histemi" means "to stand." These two words come together to indicate a change in location from a lower position to a higher. It is used in relationship to sick people who are no longer on their sick bed (Mark 5:42; 9:27). Those who move from a sitting position to a standing position give expression to this word (Luke 10:25; John 11:31). Often, it refers to arriving at a position of authority (Mark 3:26; Acts 7:18; 26:30).

The word ***"rose up"*** characterizes Theudas and Judas of Galilee. Gamaliel used an additional phrase to give context to the meaning. He said, ***"Theudas rose up, claiming to be somebody"*** (Acts 5:36). "Lego" is the Greek word translated as ***"claiming,"*** translated throughout the New Testament as "speaking." Initially, it meant "to lay or let lie down;" thus, it meant "to collect." Finally, it developed into "to lay before or relate, recount" and later the meaning of "to say, speak, connected and significant speech equal to a discourse." "Lego" contrasts with "laleo," meaning "to speak," but with an emphasis on the act of speaking, not the content. Therefore, Theudas and Judas of Galilee boldly proclaimed something about themselves.

Gamaliel said they were claiming *"to be."* The Greek word "eimi" means "I am." This Greek word is used for God's answer to Moses's question concerning His name and for all of the "I am" statements of Jesus! These leaders were pointing to themselves, giving expression to their importance. They claimed authority and power within their being. Their wisdom, ability, and plans were the basis of their movements. Their self-centeredness formed a movement whereby others could exert their self-centeredness. The agenda was self-promotion, self-fulfilling, and self-will.

Contrast this with Jesus! He boldly said, *"Most assuredly, I say to you, the Son can do nothing of Himself"* (John 5:19). The Jews quarreled among themselves. Hence, Jesus said, *"As the living Father sent Me, and I live because of the Father, so he who feeds on Me will live because of Me"* (John. 6:57). Jesus cried out in the temple, *"You both know Me, and you know where I am from; and I have not come of Myself, but He who sent Me is true, who you do not know. But I know Him, for I am from Him, and He sent Me"* (John 7:28-29). How could the members of the Sanhedrin miss His message? He *"made Himself of no reputation, taking the form of a bondservant, and coming in the likeness of men. And being found in appearance as a man, He humbled Himself and became obedient to the point of death, even the death of the cross"* (Philippians 2:7-8).

Did the Trinity God speak Theudas or Judas of Galilee?

Part Five: Advice Rejected: Agreement

The answer is NO! They spoke themselves! God spoke Jesus! The message of Peter to the council was God speaking Jesus (Acts 5:19-22). When we silenced God's voice, He raised Jesus from the dead, exalted Him to the position of King of the Kingdom of God, and gave witness to Him through the power of the Holy Spirit. Theudas and Judas of Galilee spoke themselves, displaying their egos and demonstrating their power and ability. Jesus abandoned Himself to the will of the Father and became the prototype for all to follow. Does Gamaliel know the message he is speaking to the council? Is not the Spirit of God using ungodly lips to proclaim His truth again? Will they listen?

But the real question is, "Will we listen?" Have we not repeatedly spoken ourselves? The Pharisees and Sadducees lived righteous lives; it was their righteousness. They spoke themselves. Their faithfulness in charitable deeds, prayers twice a day, and fasting twice weekly were expressions of themselves. Their sin and the sin of Theudas and Judas of Galilee are the same! They *"rose up, claiming to be somebody."* Is this not the heart of every sin? The self-centered nature fills every deed that one might consider evil. Every deed that one might think righteous becomes a sin when filled with this self-centered nature.

No wonder Paul urged us to be crucified with Christ as he was. *"I have been crucified with Christ; it is no longer I who live, but Christ lives in me; and the life which I now live in the flesh I live by faith in the Son of God, who loved me and gave Himself for me"* (Galatians 2:20). No wonder Jesus began His explanation of the New Covenant to His disciples with, *"Blessed are the poor in spirit, for theirs is the kingdom of heaven"* (Matthew 5:3). The Trinity God is speaking Jesus who is the total resource for the helpless person. I must embrace my helplessness and live within the boundaries of my helplessness. Let no one ever say I *"rose up, claiming to be somebody."*

A Fervent Position
"I join"

Gamaliel explicitly stated the power of self-centeredness in both of the movements. Theudas, rising up in his self-will, attracted around 400 others who *"joined him."* Judas of Galilee, through his self-centeredness, *"drew away many people after him."* Self-centeredness attracts self-centeredness. The people who operate from the strength of their self-will and desires stimulate the same passion within those around them. The language Gamaliel used is strong. The Greek word "proskollao" is translated as *"joined."* A combination of "pros," meaning "to," and "kollao," meaning "to glue," form this word, not an expression of casual interest but to commit oneself. Both movements formed a group of people who glued themselves to self-centeredness.

A form of "proskollao" describes the intimate relationship experienced in marriage. In the creation of woman from the rib of man, God pronounced, *"Therefore a man shall leave his father and mother and be joined to his wife, and they shall become one flesh"* (Genesis 2:24). The intent of this statement inseparably intertwines two people. *"Be joined"* is a translation of the Greek word "kollao," the same basic word Gamaliel used for his description. "Kollao" is not a light statement regarding marriage in the Scriptures but is used numerous times (Matthew 19:5; Ephesians 5:31).

Paul described the interaction of the spiritual and the physical. The physical is a stage upon which the spiritual displays itself. Thus, the members of our physical bodies are members of Jesus, who indwells us, possessing our physical. *"Shall I then take the members of Christ and make them members of a harlot? Certainly not! Or do you not know that he who is joined* (kollao) *to a harlot is one body with her?*

Part Five: Advice Rejected: Agreement

For 'the two,' He says, 'shall become one flesh.' But he who is joined (kollao) *to the Lord is one Spirit with Him"* (1 Corinthians 6:16).

Consider this reality in our merger with Jesus! I am "glued" to Him! We become one flesh! Jesus intermixes who He is with who I am until who I am expresses who He is! Jesus energizes me to participate fully, embrace completely, and saturate sufficiently to express His nature physically! This intermixing is the fullness of the Holy Spirit initiated on Pentecost day and the promise of the Father spoken often by Jesus to His disciples (Acts 1:4). Jesus extended this promise, **"But you shall receive power when the Holy Spirit has come upon you; and you shall be witnesses to Me in Jerusalem, and in all Judea and Samaria, and to the end of the earth"** (Acts 1:8). Our nature and His nature are welded together to demonstrate the heart of God in our physical world.

But this was not the case with Theudas or Judas of Galilee. These two men were glued to their followers and themselves. The self-centered carnal mind so dominated them as to give expression in their physical actions. Think about our personal lives! Every thought I have had, I have always thought. I have never gone anywhere that I did not go. Every desire I have ever had, I have had. Whatever I have done, I have always done. I have been so welded, glued to myself, that I participate with myself. I am in constant oneness with ME! Could Jesus fill me in such a manner? Could I be so merged, glued, welded with Him that every thought I think is His? Everywhere I go is an action of Divine purpose? His nature and my nature glue together into "one flesh."

Gamaliel spoke to the Sanhedrin beyond what he knew. He called the Sanhedrin to **"take heed to yourselves"** (Acts 5:35). It is a personal examination consistently focused on who I am **"joined"** to (Acts 5:36). This inner spiritual gluing will give expression in my physical actions, **"intend to do."** It will impact those around me *"regarding these men."* Will I be glued to myself, or will I be glued to Jesus? Only these two choices confront me!

A Fatal Presumption
"I come to nothing"

Gamaliel related the historical facts to the members of the Sanhedrin. While these two illustrations have deep spiritual content, he shares only facts they already know. Fairy tales, visions, or allusions to the unknown were not his approach. Both Theudas and Judas of Galilee came to a physical conclusion, that is, the thrust of Gamaliel's use of their story. Theudas, *"claiming to be somebody,"* gathered around 400 followers. However, *"he was slain, and all who obeyed him were scattered and came to nothing"* (Acts 5:36). In like manner, Judas of Galilee *"rose up"* and *"drew away many people after him"* (Acts 5:37). But a similar conclusion took place, *"he also perished, and all who obeyed him were dispersed"* (Acts 5:37).

It is a startling reality. Self-centeredness is self-destructive. A doctor gave me insight into cancer and described a cancer cell. A cell of the body becomes self-centered. In living for itself, glued to its survival, it eats all the cells around it for its own satisfaction and personal health. Dwelling in the brain, it devours the other brain cells for itself. Residing in the liver, it eats other liver cells for pleasure. It does not seem to realize that its self-centered act destroys the organ in which it dwells. It kills the body in which it lives; thus, it destroys itself. Self-centeredness is always self-destructive.

When a "one flesh" marriage member decides to live for themselves, they destroy the marriage unit. When a church member chooses to live for himself, he destroys the unity and

Part Five: Advice Rejected: Agreement

witness of Jesus within the church. I get fired when I live for myself on my job, no longer serving my employer but utilizing the time for myself. Every area of my life is in destructive mode when I am self-centered. It is a description of "hell!" I refuse to be open and seek a response to find the truth. I adjust the truth to meet my self-centered desires and create a destructive path that comes to nothing.

The members of the Sanhedrin participated in such activities. In rejecting Jesus, refusing the apostles' message, and not listening to Gamaliel, they became cancer cells in their nation. In a few years, a foreign power destroyed the city of Jerusalem, the nation of Israel, and the rulership of the Sanhedrin. What might have happened if they had embraced Jesus, the speaking of the Trinity God?

It is easy to criticize others when I have a beam in my eye (Matthew 7:3-5). There is no fear of being deceived unless I will not, in openness, seek Jesus! He is faithful to guide me into the fullness of being glued to Him. The end of the story is yet to be written, but let me state that the apostles' movement did not come to nothing, as did Theudas and Judas of Galilee. We are recipients of the apostles' selfless seeking of Jesus! This call of Jesus is upon our lives! We cannot serve two masters (Matthew 6:24). There are only two choices, the god of SELF or Jesus!

Acts 5:38-39

THE END RESULT

"And now I say to you, keep away from these men and let them alone; for if this plan or this work is of men, it will come to nothing; but if it is of God, you cannot overthrow it - lest you even be found to fight against God" (Acts 5:38-39).

One of the most startling and essential facts about the Scriptures is extreme honesty! Not one writer ever attempted to cover up or camouflage the truth. They even presented the great heroes of the faith with all their flaws. David rose from humble origins as a shepherd from Bethlehem. He became ruler as Israel's second king and led them to the pinnacle of power and glory. He was the ideal future messianic leader who ultimately found fulfillment in Jesus, a descendant of David. David's failures as a father and king presented him as an imperfect human whom God both chastened and blessed. The Scriptures make no attempt to present David other than he was. Throughout the Gospel accounts, we see the disciples' struggles and failures. Peter declared his loyalty to Jesus, only to miserably fail in denial (Matthew 26:35, 69-75). Paul declared himself Saul of Tarsus, the persecutor and murderer of Christians (Acts 9). The story of the Scriptures is one of redemption!

Part Five: Advice Rejected: Agreement

This reality of truth found in the Scriptures assures us of its revelation of God's call on our lives. The Scriptures do not highlight the blessings of the Gospel and hide the consequence of commitment. Jesus gathered His disciples on the mountain to explain what they could expect, only to declare persecution was inevitable (Matthew 5:11-12). While the heroes of faith overcame all obstacles and fulfilled the call of God's destiny in their lives, it was not without suffering and difficulty. The writers portrayed the heroes of faith. *"Still others had trial of mockings and scourgings, yes, and of chains and imprisonment. They were stoned, they were sawn in two, were tempted, were slain with the sword. They wandered about in sheepskins and goatskins, being destitute, afflicted, tormented - of whom the world was not worthy. They wandered in deserts and mountains, in dens and caves of the earth"* (Hebrews 11:36-38). Would this be the message to enlist people in the Christian faith?

The apostles experienced Jesus' prediction concerning persecution! It is the second phase, as the Sanhedrin captured all apostles. The Sanhedrin's accusations, though not fair, were undoubtedly true. No one criticized the apostles for not providing relief for those in need. The miracles of Jesus changed the physical circumstances of multitudes. The message of hope brought new courage to hopeless people. The problem was the Source, Jesus. The apostles consistently promoted Jesus, resurrected from the dead. They focused their sermons, teaching, and worship on Jesus. The moment a person embraces Jesus, the battle moves from a physical conflict to a massive spiritual war (Ephesians 6:12). While Jesus brings peace, forgiveness, and comfort of hope to the inner life, evil declares war when He is involved.

Gamaliel intervenes, giving the apostles a momentary reprieve. None of the Sanhedrin questioned him, for he was *"a teacher of the law held in respect by all the people"*

(Acts 5:34). After giving two examples from their shared past, Gamaliel suggested, *"And now I say to you, keep away from these men and let them alone; for if this plan or this work is of men, it will come to nothing; but if it is of God, you cannot overthrow it - lest you be found to fight against God"* (Acts 5:38-39).

Gamaliel presented a vivid contrast to the Sanhedrin. He contrasted the works *"of men"* with the works *"of God,"* the same assumption Peter and the other apostles proposed at the beginning of the questioning. *"We ought to obey God rather than men"* (Acts 5:29). This corresponds with Peter's statement during his interrogation in the first phase of persecution. *"Whether it is right in the sight of God to listen to you more than to God, you judge"* (Acts 4:19). The ideas of *"obey"* (peitharcheo) and *"listen"* (akouo) are similar in their challenge. They both promote the idea of coming under the influence and authority of God. Anyone who believes in a sovereign being, God, would undoubtedly advocate coming under His influence rather than the influence of fallible humanity.

Gamaliel was powerful in his advice to the Sanhedrin. He said, *"Keep away from these men"* and then *"let them alone"* (Acts 5:38). *"Keep away"* is translated from the Greek word "aphistemi," a combination of "apo" and "histemi." "Apo" means "from," which is not only the prefix of this Greek word but is present separately in connection with this statement, a double emphasis by Gamaliel to stress this necessity. This verb is also an imperative, which gives it the strength of a command. *"Let alone"* is translated from "eao," which means "to let be or desist." Altogether, Gamaliel's three statements strengthen the urgency of interfering with a movement of God.

It is important to note that the Sanhedrin and the apostles experienced adverse circumstances due to their different perspectives. The Sanhedrin viewed the constant promotion of Jesus as a direct affront to their image. They revealed this in their accusation to the apostles. ***"Did we not strictly command you not to teach in this name? And look, you have filled Jerusalem with your doctrine, and intend to bring this Man's blood on us"*** (Acts 5:28)! The constant preaching in Jesus' name violated the authority of the council and consistently brought them into a position of guilt. They are responsible for Jesus' death. If Jesus was raised from the dead by the power of God, they were wrong! The apostles also faced adverse circumstances. Their ministry, the movement of the early Church in Jerusalem, depended on Jesus. If God did not raise Him from the dead, God was not filling them with His Spirit, there was no truth in their teaching, and they were without the power of God. For the Sanhedrin to require them to cease promoting Jesus was to violate the core of all they know. They had to continue regardless of adverse circumstances.

The Sanhedrin and the apostles had adverse circumstances planted in their midst. You and I constantly battle adverse circumstances. These circumstances may result from physical illness, financial difficulty, relational conflict, marriage struggles, or employment problems, all disturbing standard life patterns. Everything you and I have established will be upset if we allow those circumstances to reach their fulfillment. Did it occur to us that those adverse circumstances may be the hand of God bringing us into the complete design of His plan?

God directly intervened in the lives of the Sanhedrin. Jesus confronted their lives again. We have stated this repeatedly, but it is so important. God speaks Jesus to them. They had experienced three years of His direct ministry carried out against the background of the Old Testament, which Jesus fulfilled. Why did they not recognize Him? Instead of praise and joy, they stood amid adverse circumstances threatening everything they had established. They eliminated this threat by crucifying Jesus, only to discover God raised Him from the dead. God spoke Jesus, and they silenced the voice of God. But God said that He was not done speaking to them. Jesus, the speaking of God, was back, and the adverse circumstances pressed the Sanhedrin again. Now, even one of their own, Gamaliel, warned them to be careful. Was God not speaking through their adverse circumstances, trying to bring them into the complete revelation of His plan?

The apostles faced adverse circumstances. This persecution threatened their ministry. Have they not gone too far to go back now? They set their businesses aside, relocated their families, and changed their life dreams. Did they not experience forty days with Jesus after His resurrection? Was there any question about His resurrection? Did He not fill them with His Spirit and embrace them in a manner far beyond their three years of physical interaction with Him? Is not God pouring out His Spirit in a way only dreamed about in the past? Now, adverse circumstances threaten all of this. But is God not speaking through these adverse circumstances? Is He not driving the reality of Jesus deeper within them? Will this persecution not increase and scatter them over the world? God used adverse circumstances to reveal His destiny for them.

Can we not grasp this truth in our lives? Yes, we are amid adverse circumstances, but God uses those circumstances to reveal Himself to us! L.E. Maxwell wrote a book entitled *"Crowded to Christ."* His premise was that every circumstance should drive us to Jesus. Every temptation should draw us closer to Him instead of defeating and separating us from Jesus. If every adverse circumstance drives us to dependency on Him, intimacy with Him, and revelation of Him, would we not rejoice in the suffering?

There are some basic principles to hold close to in this conflict!

Part Five: Advice Rejected: Agreement

Destruction
Production of Man

It is obvious! That which a human produces will ultimately come to destruction. Gamaliel said, ***"For if this plan or this work is of men, it will come to nothing"*** (Acts 5:38). Consider all the creative ability God has given humanity. According to researchers Hal Varian and Peter Lyman, economists at UC Berkeley, the total production and accumulation of information is increasing 66% annually, which means that all of the knowledge and information in the world is doubling every 18 months. Since this statistic was from their research in 2006, that figure is outdated, and information is already doubling much faster. The Greek word translated as ***"it will come to nothing"*** is "katalyo." "Katalyo" is used in the New Testament as dissolve, destroy, annul, to become useless or out of working order.

Paul vehemently proclaimed the destruction of the wisdom of men to the church at Corinth. He quoted the Old Testament.
"I will destroy the wisdom of the wise,
And bring to nothing the understanding of the prudent" (1 Corinthians 1:19, a quote from Isaiah 29:24).

The difficulty with the wisdom of humanity is not the wisdom itself but the elimination of the source of this wisdom (1 Corinthians 1:20-30). Everything humanity does without dependency upon Jesus becomes useless. Charitable deeds without the permeating source of the Spirit of Jesus produce hypocrisy. Therefore, this religious act becomes a sin and is destructive rather than productive (Matthew 6:2-4). Prayer not involving an intimate relationship with God produces hypocrisy, which is sin. Instead of bringing resources to the praying individual, it brings destruction (Matthew 6:5-7). Likewise, fasting or spiritual disciplines without the embrace of dependency on

Jesus become an expression of self and destroys oneself through hypocrisy (Matthew 6:16-18). There is nothing wrong with any of these activities or man's knowledge. The issue is the exclusion of Jesus from the action or knowledge.

The Sanhedrin excluded Jesus from their actions and knowledge. Their religious and political structure rested on their wisdom and ability. They desperately wanted to protect and guard this structure. Jesus was a threat, bringing a new level of fulfillment to their system. In rejecting Him, they hoped to maintain their old pattern. But the Romans destroyed Jerusalem, "came to nothing," in 70 AD, and the Jewish system ceased to exist as they had known it. Will it be any different for our lives? Operating out of our wisdom and self-effort produces nothing but chaos in our lives. How often do we need to find ourselves in a dead-end alley to know we are inadequate without Jesus?

Destiny
Production of God

In contrast, the early Church found its destiny and thrived during the adverse circumstances of persecution. Stephen became the first martyr (Acts 8:1-3). Saul of Tarsus searched from city to city, bringing Christians to prison and death. James, the apostle, was beheaded (Acts 12:1-2). Did not God utilize this persecution to scatter the early Church throughout the known world? Did they not evangelize every town in which they located? Did not Christianity become known throughout the world? Through Jesus, a group of people found their God-sourced destiny in adverse circumstances. **"If it is of God, you cannot overthrow it - lest you even be found to fight against God"** (Acts 5:39).

While we know few names of those in the Sanhedrin from that time, their contribution to us is **"nothing!"** Does Gamaliel's

Part Five: Advice Rejected: Agreement

life have any lasting effect on you? Whoever the Sadducees were, along with their families, they played no significant role in your lifestyle. But think of the apostles and their influence on you as an individual. While you do not know Peter personally, you now study the scene in which he stood firm; he points you to Jesus, even now. Peter's epistles are a vital part of the Word of God to our hearts! Even in the adverse circumstances of persecution, Peter found the destiny of God unshakable for his life.

Does this not drive us to seek Jesus in a new and more profound way? Must our lives not be sourced entirely by Jesus, or all is lost? Would I dare be my children's father without God's guidance? How can I possibly be the husband my wife needs if Jesus does not energize my life? Will I not fill my life with meaningless activities, which I do unless I am produced by Him? ***"We are His workmanship, created in Christ Jesus for good works, which God prepared beforehand that we should walk in them"*** (Ephesians 2:10).

Dedication
Ponder the Long View

We see this truth correctly only in the long-range view of life! The members of the council could not see beyond their present moment. They only saw the immediate threat to their traditions; they did not view Jesus' open door into the future. Now, the apostles are the same threat to their traditions. What is the blockade to their long-range vision? It is their self-centered carnality. Self-centeredness always focuses on the immediate moment. What can I get now? How will this affect my comfort directly? The pleasure of the moment is the desire of self-centeredness and the core of destructiveness. A moment's happiness cannot grasp the long-range consequence of its immediate desires. The adverse circumstances become its only concern without regard to God's plan for those circumstances.

When Jesus fills our lives, He alters our perspective. We do not suggest we can see into the future and know what will be. We know Him! ***"And we know that all things work together for good to those who love God, to those who are the called according to His purpose"*** (Romans 8:28). Is Jesus not promising that all adverse circumstances under His influence will produce ***"good"*** in our lives? While this may not be the momentary reality, we know Him who has made the promise. He has never failed. Immediately following this promise, Paul gave us the reason underlying such a reality. ***"For whom He foreknew, He also predestined to be conformed to the image of His Son, that He might be the firstborn among many brethren"*** (Romans 8:29). The adverse circumstances are how He conforms us into the image of Jesus. As Christians, we pray, "Oh, to be like Christ!" How can we complain amid adverse circumstances? These circumstances are the fingers of God, shaping us into this likeness!

Gamaliel spoke the truth! Everything in our lives that is not sourced by and participating in Jesus will destroy us; everything in our lives that is sourced by and participating in Jesus will fulfill us. I cannot stop it. I must focus entirely, participate fully, be energized completely, and embrace Him deeply.

Acts 5:38-39

A CERTAINTY

"And now I say to you, keep away from these men and let them alone; for if this plan or this work is of men, it will come to nothing; but if it is of God, you cannot overthrow it - lest you even be found to fight against God" (Acts 5:38-39).

We are studying the second phase of the apostles' persecution. Gamaliel commands that the guards place these men *"outside for a little while"* (Acts 5:34). His impressive message to the Sanhedrin focuses them on their inner motive, *"take heed to yourselves what you intend to do"* (Acts 5:35). We never define sin by the action of the deed, but always by the inner motive of the heart. What is the underlying driving desire? He explains this with two illustrations from their past. Two men, Theudas and Judas of Galilee, *"rose up,"* each with an impressive following but *"come to nothing"* (Acts 5:36-37). The response of the Sanhedrin to these two movements was to leave them alone. In so doing, these movements quickly died of their own accord.

Gamaliel promotes the same response regarding the apostles and the early Church. *"And now I say to you, keep away from these men and let them alone; for if this plan or this work is of men, it will come to nothing; but if it is of God, you cannot overthrow it - lest you even be found to fight against God"* (Acts 5:38-39). Notice the emphasis on *"now,"* translated from the Greek word "nyn." It is a reference to the immediate moment. In the past, we intended to allow those movements of men to bring about their own destruction. Should we not continue in this present moment to have the same motive? Gamaliel strongly urges the council to *"keep away"* and *"let them alone!"*

Gamaliel launches into an explanation behind this action as he says, *"for." "For"* is a translation of the Greek word "gar," meaning "for this reason." He wants them to know the reason for refusing to judge or hinder the apostles. Gamaliel presents two alternatives in two clauses, *"If this plan or this work is of men, it will come to nothing"* and *"if it is of God, you cannot overthrow it."* In the English translation, they appear to have the same grammar construction, but they do not. Let us examine them carefully.

"For if this plan or this work is of men, it will come to nothing" presents a condition of the third class, uncertain but likely. Gamaliel proposes the proclamation of Jesus is likely of men, but it is uncertain. The Greek word "ean," translated as *"if,"* is not conditional but suppositional. It presents a situation they can only know by future experience. The main verb of the first clause is the Greek word "eimi," translated as *"is."* This verb is in the subjunctive mood, which suggests an uncertain possibility. It is also in the present tense. Gamaliel states the uncertainty at the present moment, whether this plan or work is of men. In the second phase of this clause, *"it"* refers to *"this plan or this work."* However, *"it will come to nothing"* translates to a single Greek word, "katalyo," which means painting a picture of a house under demolition. This verb is in the future tense, with a passive voice and indicative mood. The destruction of the plan or work will occur in the future;

Part Five: Advice Rejected: Agreement

the resulting destruction will be due to the action of something beyond the plan or work. This phrase is a simple statement of fact. We might summarize it as follows. Human desire most likely sources the proclamation of Jesus, but it is not for sure. We will know when we see this plan or work cease to exist.

The second clause, **"but if it is of God, you cannot overthrow it,"** presents a condition of the first class. For argument's sake, Gamaliel assumes that what the apostles do is true of God. He begins the clause with **"but,"** a translation of "de," a contrasting and continuation conjunction. The Greek word "ei" is translated as **"if,"** which differs from the first clause. It is a conditional and subjective statement. The verb of the phrase is once again "eimi," translated as **"is,"** but is in the indicative mood and not subjunctive, a simple statement of fact. It is in the present tense, making the consideration a reference to the moment it was spoken with continuation.

The second phrase in this clause, **"you cannot overthrow it,"** contains the main verb **"cannot,"** a translation from the Greek words "ouk" and "dynamai." "Dynamai" presents the idea of ability or power of action in the indicative mood, a simple statement of fact. However, Gamaliel uses an additional verb, "katalyo," the same verb translated in the first clause, **"it will come to nothing."** It is a complementary infinitive used to complete the meaning or force of the main verb. This verb is in the aorist tense and the active voice. The English language has nothing like the aorist tense; it is non-tense. It is a simple snapshot of the verb's action without regard to when it occurs. Gamaliel is saying this is always true regardless of when it may happen. The active voice makes the subject **"you"** responsible for the verb's action, meaning men can never bring the works of God to destruction.

Gamaliel states that human desire most likely sources the proclamation of Jesus, but it is not for sure. We will know when we see this plan or work cease to exist. However, let us assume this proclamation of Jesus is from God. There is no decision or action we can accomplish today that has the ability or power to bring it to destruction. Then he adds the concluding statement, *"lest you even be found to fight against God."* The Greek word "theomacheo" means *"to fight against God"* only in this New Testament passage. It is a combination of "Theos," translated as *"God,"* and "macheo," translated as *"to fight."* Should this statement not permeate the hearts of the council members and result in great fear? Isn't this the core of Peter's reply to their accusations, *"We ought to obey God rather than men"* (Acts 5:29)?

The Sanhedrin's history reveals that the council members followed their father's pattern of continually fighting against God! In the first interrogation of Peter and John, Peter said, *"This is the stone* (Jesus) *which was rejected by you builders, which has become the chief cornerstone"* (Acts 4:11; Psalms 118:22). One of the most moving passages of the New Testament expresses the heart of Jesus as He weeps over Jerusalem at the close of His earthly ministry. He cries out, *"O Jerusalem, Jerusalem, the one who kills the prophets and stones those who are sent to her! How often I wanted to gather your children together, as a hen gathers her chicks under her wings, but you were not willing"* (Matthew 23:37)! We find the foundation for such weeping from the heart of Jesus as He reminds them, *"you are witnesses against yourselves that you are sons of those who murdered the prophets"* (Matthew 23:31). The response of the Sanhedrin follows the pattern of their fathers. What does this mean?

Increased Circumstances

The duration establishes Gamaliel's test for the validity of the proclamation of Jesus' name. His main point to the

Part Five: Advice Rejected: Agreement

Sanhedrin is *"for if this plan or this work is of men, it will come to nothing, but if it is of God, you cannot overthrow it - lest you even be found to fight against God"* (Acts 5:38-39). Ironically, he does not recognize Jesus already passed the test. Jesus is not going away! Peter and the other apostles declared this with great boldness. *"The God of our fathers raised up Jesus whom you murdered by hanging on a tree"* (Acts 5:30). Peter points out two great truths. Even though the Sanhedrin tried to bring Jesus to nothing, He is back! He is raised from the dead and is speaking to them again. Notice this is backed by *"the God of our fathers,"* for Jesus has always been His plan!

Gamaliel and the Sanhedrin should understand this by now! The reality of Jesus is not a new confrontation. They have battled this since John the Baptist first made them aware of the Messiah's presence. John's message was bold and direct when the Pharisees and Sadducees came to inspect the revival at the Jordan River. John cried, *"Brood of vipers! Who warned you to flee from the wrath to come? Therefore bear fruits worthy of repentance"* (Matthew 3:7-8). They needed to set aside their traditions, patterns, and self-centered security. They must embrace the Messiah to which John introduced them. But they would not! Yet, Jesus would not go away, *"come to nothing."*

They argued with Jesus for three years and tried to trap Him with trick questions (Matthew 22). They questioned His authority (Matthew 21:23). They selected the most skilled among them to embarrass Him before the crowds, only to be embarrassed themselves. They just could not eliminate Him, *"come to nothing."* The crucifixion of Jesus was the last resort; what else could they do? They took every precaution at the burial site of Jesus (Matthew 27:62-66). With a Roman seal on the grave and the elite Roman soldiers guarding it, this will *"come to nothing."* But in three days, the Roman guards ran into Jerusalem, reporting *"all the things that had*

happened" (Matthew 28:11). What were those things? They told of the bright light from the angel of the Lord's descent, his rolling the stone away, and their fright, which caused them to faint like dead men. No doubt, they inspected the tomb and found the dead body of Jesus was no longer there. The chief priests assembled the elders and consulted together. They will not merely watch and see if it comes to nothing. They gather money from the treasury and give it to the soldiers, insisting they lie and spread the story that the disciples stole Jesus' body. The leaders of Israel promised to protect the Roman guards if the governor called them into question concerning their failure to guard the body. Yet can the Sanhedrin say Jesus has ***"come to nothing?"***

Why don't they ask some of their members? Nicodemus, a ruler of the Jews, came to Jesus in the night and said to Him, ***"Rabbi, we know that You are a teacher come from God; for no one can do these signs that You do unless God is with him"*** (John 3:2). Nicodemus brought about 75 pounds of myrrh and aloes to prepare Jesus' body for burial (John 19:39-42), an amount of spice necessary to royally bury a king. This same account recognizes Joseph of Arimathea, a member of the Sanhedrin, as a disciple of Jesus (John 19:38). Jesus just does not go away, ***"come to nothing."*** These Jews have had hundreds of years of prophetic proclamation concerning Jesus, three years of His ministry to them, and now an expanded time of His resurrection presence through the apostles. Jesus has not ***"come to nothing!"*** Why won't they embrace Him?

Could the same not be said for us? Jesus is not a new event in our lives. He has bombarded us with His truth and presence through His prevenient grace. Jesus has not ***"come to nothing"*** but continues to call us into His embrace! Does He not pass the test?

Part Five: Advice Rejected: Agreement

Increased Consequence

One of the great emphases of Gamaliel's statement is the consequence of men's works. Men's productions ***"come to nothing."*** That was the conviction of Gamaliel, verified by two illustrations from their recent history (Acts 5:36, 37). It was the teaching of Jesus. He illustrated it in the Parable of the True Vine (John 15:1-8). If we are the branches and Jesus is the vine, we produce no fruit without the intimate connection between the two. He said, ***"Abide in Me, and I in you. As the branch cannot bear fruit of itself, unless it abides in the vine, neither can you, unless you abide in Me"*** (John 15:4). While this is a negative statement, Jesus also immediately states it in a positive statement. ***"I am the vine you are the branches. He who abides in Me, and I in him, bears much fruit; for without Me you can nothing"*** (John 15:5). There is no possibility of any positive result without Jesus, all will ***"come to nothing."***

Jesus told three parables with this same truth for a more substantial impact, all in the same setting. He began with the Parable of the Lost Sheep (Luke 15:1-7), continued with the Parable of the Lost Coin (Luke 15:8-10), and concluded with the Parable of the Lost Son (Luke 15:11-32). While the sheep did not lose its value as a sheep, it lost its purpose in its separation from the shepherd. The coin retained its value but had no meaning in separating from the woman. When separated from the Father, the lost state of the son was a pig pen. In each case, in their lost state, they came to nothing.

The Greek word "apollumi" is translated in each parable as *"lost!"* "Apollumi" is the primary word "ollumi" and the prefix "apo." The force of "apo" is "away or wholly." In its simplest form, "ollumi" means "to destroy." However, with the prefix "apo," the verb is much stronger. There is a severity connected to "lostness" in each case, which goes beyond *"coming to nothing."* When applied to Gamaliel's statement, *"it will come to nothing,"* it becomes much more severe. That which is a product of man will ultimately disappear. It will evaporate like it never existed; however, the consequence of man's production is much greater. There is the condition of being alone on the side of the mountain with the wolves howling around you as a lost sheep; there is the darkness of the crack in the floor where you have fallen as a lost coin; the pig pen with all of its stench consumes your life as the lost son. Consider the hard work of a lifetime where God is not involved. All such productions *"come to nothing."* The smell of the pigs, the awful waste of energy and effort of an entire life, and the danger one inflicted upon himself and those around him overshadow the *"come to nothing."*

But even these parables do not begin to complete the picture of *"come to nothing!"* Again, consider Gamaliel's statement. ***"And now I say to you, keep away from these men and let them alone; for if this plan or this work is of men, it will come to nothing; but if it is of God, you cannot overthrow it - lest you even be found to fight against God"*** (Acts 5:38-39). We must never accept that there are plans or works of men that do not fight against God! If God does not direct or empower the work, it is because men have rebelled against God to live for their own plans or work.

In the Parable of The True Vine, Jesus reported fruit is a result of the branch abiding in the vine, ***"for without Me you can do nothing"*** (John 15:5). However, the result is much more than just not bearing fruit! ***"If anyone does not abide in Me, he is cast out as a branch and is withered; and they gather them and throw them into the fire, and they are burned"*** (John 15:6). Jesus expounded this truth in the Sermon on the Mount. He warned us about charitable deeds done without God's involvement. When a man

Part Five: Advice Rejected: Agreement

does charitable deeds out of his ego and pride, he becomes a hypocrite (Matthew 6:2). He appears to be generously giving, but in reality, he wants to receive the applause of men. He gets what he wants, but his hypocrisy makes his religious deed a sin: fighting against God. Those who are faithful in prayer need to be very careful. They *"love to pray,"* but it is not God they love but themselves (Matthew 6:5). This makes them hypocrites. They have their reward, which is the applause of men and the exclusion of God. Their prayer becomes a sin that has destructive power. The spiritual discipline of fasting is no different. The hypocrite disfigures his face, not wanting to be noticed, when men's recognition was the purpose of his action (Matthew 6:16). His fasting becomes a sin with terrible consequences!

Gamaliel says much more than he recognizes. All works and plans that are a product of men will *"come to nothing,"* meaning they are void of the empowerment of God. The lack of God's power is why they *"come to nothing."* But they are not merely void of God's involvement. These works and plans are warring against God. The council does not seem aware that their plans and efforts are of men. Are they not warring against God as they demand silence concerning Jesus? They crucified Jesus to silence Him, only to have God raise Him from the dead. Jesus is back, speaking through hundreds of Spirit-filled Christians. God's power will defeat them at every turn, and the consequences of their rebellion will be extreme!

Here is a lesson for us. We must not live for ourselves; in doing so, we fight against God. We must not design our destiny from the selfish desires of our heart, for that will place us in a position of war against God. In submission, we must abandon ourselves to His plan and work!

Acts 5:40

WHO IS IN CHARGE

"And they agreed with him, and when they had called for the apostles and beaten them, they commanded that they should not speak in the name of Jesus, and let them go" (Acts 5:40).

The action of the Sanhedrin fills this verse. They demonstrated their internal motive in their external action, clarifying their character. This verse paints a descriptive picture of the inner soul of these Sadducees and Pharisees. Often, Jesus spoke of a tree's fruit, declaring its inner nature (Matthew 12:33-37). While this verse gives us insight into the inner core of the council, the following two verses allow us to see the heart of the apostles. What a contrast! The Sanhedrin is angry; the apostles rejoice! Negativity and condemnation come from the Sanhedrin; positivity and encouragement flow from the apostles! The Sanhedrin makes demands; the apostles humbly accept suffering as honor! The Sanhedrin continually desires to eliminate Jesus; the apostles do **"not cease teaching and preaching Jesus as the Christ"** (Acts 5:42).

Our study verse demonstrates the revelation of the character of the members of the Sanhedrin. Their physical actions do not correlate with their apparent agreement. Deception, producing hypocrisy, is happening within the Sadducees and Pharisees. But hypocrisy is not new to either of these groups. They boldly condemn the healing of a man with a withered hand on the Sabbath but have no problem rescuing one sheep who fell into a pit (Matthew 12:9-14). They recognize the miracles of Jesus as delivering people from Satanic destruction, yet they accuse Jesus of being demon-possessed (Matthew 12:22-24). They experienced the massive number of miracles performed by Jesus but still asked for a sign of proof (Matthew 12:38).

Jesus exposed the Sanhedrin's hypocrisy in the Sermon on the Mount. They appear to be generous with charitable deeds, yet their real desire is to receive the praise of men (Matthew 6:2). They strictly pray twice a day, planning their daily schedule to pray on the busiest street corner to be seen by men. While appearing to pray to God, they were speaking to others for their approval (Matthew 6:5). They would disfigure their faces during times of fasting to hide who they were when their real desire was for everyone to recognize their spiritual superiority (Matthew 6:16). Their hypocritical spirit continues into our verse!

They Abused

It is essential to note the physical actions of this group! **"And when they had called for the apostles and beaten them"** (Acts 5:40). The primary Greek word translated as **"beaten"** is "dero." It means "to skin or flay." Often, the penalty was scourging, the Greek word "mastizo." It comes from the Greek word "mastic," meaning "a whip," one of the methods of "dero." In our passage, the verb **"beaten"** is a participle in the aorist tense, giving us no time frame for the actual event but focusing on the act of beating. Luke may be expressing the severity of the beating given to the apostles. Since this is the second phase of persecution, the tension and frustration of the council members are undoubtedly high. One must conclude the beating was severe, and the pain and suffering were extreme. They must have remembered the words of Jesus from the last beatitude, **"Blessed are those who are persecuted for righteousness' sake, for theirs is the kingdom of heaven"** (Matthew 5:10).

In the first phase of persecution, the Sanhedrin commanded Peter and John never to mention Jesus again. This command led the apostles to pray to the sovereign God for boldness to continue preaching in the name of Jesus. They have blatantly disobeyed the only request of the council, that they eliminate the person of Jesus. In the second phase of persecution, the Sanhedrin included all the apostles. They strengthened and enforced the prohibition concerning Jesus with this beating. How will the apostles respond? Leaving the council with their backs cruelly lacerated and bleeding, they were **"rejoicing that they were counted worthy to suffer shame for His name"** (Acts 5:41). They were honored to be dishonored. They received grace to be disgraced.

The devil has never given up his attempt to destroy the church by force. From Christ's crucifixion to our generation's last martyr, he expressed himself through some council. Christians, including Paul and Peter, were imprisoned and executed in 54-68 (AD). During 81-96 (AD), Domitian demanded all people pay him the divine honors he demanded. Christians were persecuted, including John, whom they exiled to Patmos. During the reign of Marcus Aurelius (161-180 AD), his followers scattered outbreaks of mob violence against Christians. He believed that Christianity was dangerous and immoral; therefore, he turned a blind eye to the persecution. What was scattered and sporadic soon became organized and intentional. Under Decius (249-251 AD), thousands of Christians died, including Fabian, Bishop of Rome, for refusing to sacrifice to the imperial name. Diocletian issued four edicts in 284-305 AD to eliminate Christianity. He ordered churches to be burned, Scriptures to be confiscated, clergy to be tortured, and Christian civil servants to be deprived of citizenship and, if stubbornly unrepentant, executed.

The martyrs continue even in our day! Many still harass the church; will it get worse? We need not fear for the survival of Christianity. Tertullian, addressing the rulers of the Roman Empire, cried out, "Kill us, torture us, condemn us, grind us to dust.... The more you mow us down, the more we grow, the seed is the blood of Christians." Bishop Festo Kivengere said in February 1979, on the second anniversary of the martyrdom of Archbishop Janna Lawn of Uganda: "Without bleeding the church fails to bless." Persecution will refine the church, but not destroy it. As it did with the apostles, so it will do for us; it leads us to prayer and praise, to an acknowledgment of the sovereignty of God and our merger with Jesus in His sufferings. However painful, we welcome it!

Think of the contrast in our passage between the Sanhedrin and Jesus. Both are calling the apostles! According to Gamaliel's instruction, they **"put the apostles outside for a little while"** (Acts 5:34). Now, **"when they had called for the apostles,"** they beat them. **"When they had called for"** is translated from the Greek word "proskaleo." "Pros" means "to," and "kaleo" means "call." "Proskaleo" is the exact Greek word used for Jesus calling disciples, multitudes, and others to Himself (Matthew 10:1; 15:10, 32; 18:2; 20:25). While there may be little difference in the method of the call, the motive and intent is extremely different!

The Sanhedrin lounges in physical comfort and ease, intending to bring the apostles into suffering and pain. The motive of their heart is the protection of their materialistic comfort, threatened by the fulfillment of the Messianic promise. Everything would change, including their authority and power, if Jesus is the Messiah. Thus, lounging in their self-centered comfort, they call the apostles to suffer and pain. However,

Jesus is also calling the apostles. He calls them in the midst of crucifixion so they may enter His life. He invites us to life out of bleeding, suffering, and death! Can we not see? The demonic invitation is always for destruction and ruin. Jesus' invitation is always for construction and safety. *"For whoever desires to save his life will lose it, but whoever loses his life for My sake will find it"* (Matthew 16:25).

They Announced

Luke states, *"They commanded"* (Acts 5:40). One understands the severity of the command, for it is not new. It is the reason for this second encounter with the Sanhedrin; the apostles disobeyed this command, a renewal of the previous command, *"that they should not speak in the name of Jesus"* (Acts 5:40). The issue of the command is simple: eliminate Jesus. It is not about the resurrection, a constant discussion between the Pharisees and Sadducees. However, the apostles were not discussing a philosophical view of the resurrection but *"taught the people and preached in Jesus the resurrection from the dead"* (Acts 4:2). The Sanhedrin appreciated the miracles and helping others. Still, Jesus was at the heart of every miracle. The daily gathering of the church was not a threat to the council, but the church gathered and proclaimed Jesus. The council had no resistance to compassionate ministries among the poor, but they objected to the apostles always doing it in the name of Jesus. Jesus was the issue!

If you have questions about the depth of the Sanhedrin's commitment to eliminating Jesus, view their history. Did they not crucify Him? They did not ignore or merely argue against Him; they eliminated Him. Now the apostles intend *"to bring this Man's blood on us"* (Acts 5:28). In all of their sermons, they seem to identify Jesus as the One *"whom you crucified,*

Part Five: Advice Rejected: Agreement

whom God raised from the dead" (Acts 4:10. See also Acts 3:15, 5:30). Will they not eliminate the ones who are proclaiming Jesus now? The beating of the apostles gives us an indication of the commitment of the Sanhedrin!

We can also see their commitment in the Greek word "parangello," translated as **"they commanded."** "Para" means "to the side of," and "aggello" means "to tell or declare." "Parangello" is a proclamation or announcement. The heart of the word is not the idea of a specific action to be taken, although the Sanhedrin may have assumed that. It is the idea of direction or instruction. For instance, could the apostles merely change the name of Jesus and call Him "Christ?" They could simply refer to the same person and preach the same message, only renaming Jesus. The Sanhedrin demands more than eliminating the use of His name. They want the emphasis of Jesus as the Messiah, resurrection, and redemption gone.

We must understand the Greek word "parangello," not merely as a specific act such as a law but as the direction and overall intent of the command. The command from the Sanhedrin is not just to eliminate the name of Jesus but also everything connected to Him. Miracles were acceptable if they had no connection to the power of Jesus. The discussion of the resurrection would have been fine if Jesus were not involved. Biblical teaching would be pleasing only if Jesus were eliminated, but that produced an obstacle for the apostles. Everything touching their lives connected them to the Person of Jesus. They are filled with His Spirit and live in the expression of His person. There is not anything they do or are involved in that is not a result of Jesus. Jesus is not "an add-on" to their life; He is their life! They cannot function without Him.

What about your life does not involve "you"? Every thought, every action, and every desire are expressions of "you." Where you go and what you say are all determined by "you." The supreme authority of your life is "you." Can you imagine someone asking you to eliminate "you"? Is this not the essence of a merger with Jesus? The command of Jesus is not a law to keep or an action to do. It is a shift in the authority and direction of my life. I must involve Jesus in my life as I have involved myself!

They Agreed

Now, the hypocrisy appears! Gamaliel is a Pharisee, a ***"teacher of the law held in respect by all the people"*** (Acts 5:34). While the Sadducees were involved, the dominating force behind the crucifixion of Jesus was the Pharisees. They were the protectors of the law, the oral tradition. Jesus obeyed the law of God but certainly discounted the Pharisees' interpretation of that law. Now, after Pentecost, the Sadducees have come to the forefront. Jesus, in His resurrected presence, cannot be tolerated by them either.

Gamaliel proposed to the Sanhedrin the conviction Peter had already presented, ***"We ought to obey God rather than men"*** (Acts 5:29). Gamaliel gives validity to this statement by reminding them of two individuals who led movements of rebellion in Israel (Acts 5:36, 37). Both movements disappeared without any effort from the Sanhedrin. Gamaliel argues, ***"for if this plan or this work is of men, it will come to nothing; but if it is of God, you cannot overthrow it - lest you even be found to fight against God"*** (Acts 5:38-39). This argument was not a superficial suggestion but a strong demand. Gamaliel demanded that the Sanhedrin leave the apostles alone. The risk of fighting against God was too significant! Allow the apostles to continue in ministry and see what results.

"And they agreed with him" (Acts 5:40). In principle and logic, the Sanhedrin understood and agreed with Gamaliel. The Greek word "pietho" is translated as ***"they agreed,"*** meaning "to persuade another to receive a belief, meaning to convince." In this case, the verb is passive since Gamaliel is acting to persuade the Sanhedrin. Certainly, Gamaliel's appeal to the Sanhedrin affected them; they did not stone the apostles to death but merely beat them. However, this does not qualify as **"*let them alone*"** (Acts 5:38). Mentally, the Sanhedrin embraced Gamaliel's logic. Still, in practice, all they can do is beat the apostles and continue to demand the elimination of Jesus from their lives.

Do I believe that Jesus is Lord? I do! I loudly sing songs about His Lordship with an upraised hand. Am I willing to recognize areas where He is not Lord in my life? In practice, I continue to exert my sovereignty and strength. Do I believe that Jesus is adequate for every situation? Absolutely, I do! Then why is my life often filled with anxiety and stress over problems beyond my control? I readily embrace the reality of "Jesus never fails!" But far too often, I panic over circumstances beyond my ability.

"And we know that all things work together for good to those who love God, to those who are the called according to His purpose" (Romans 8:28). This is the testimony I share with others. Mentally, I have accepted this statement in my belief system, but is this my reality in daily life? Why do I complain and blame? Far too often, there is a disconnect between my agreement and my life's physical activity and expression. Think of proclaiming the love of God and continuing to hate others. Consider our proclamation of the unity in the body of Christ, yet the divisions are so blatant in our everyday lives.

Our passage explains the hypocrisy of the Sanhedrin as a rejection of Jesus. They will not embrace Him as their Messiah; the necessity of change in their practical living, created by His presence, fosters their resistance. How do I translate this conclusion into my personal life? Can I agree with Jesus in my spirit and resist the results of that agreement in my everyday life? Can I proclaim Him Lord in my heart without allowing Him to be Lord in my practical living?

They Assigned

Our passage ends with, *"They commanded that they should not speak in the name of Jesus. and let them go"* (Acts 5:40). This action followed the beating and the command of the Sanhedrin. It was the full intent and expectation of the council that the apostles would cease from any expression concerning Jesus. While the Sanhedrin imposed this command on the apostles, they also gave expression to their intent, revealing their hypocrisy again. They were never open to God speaking Jesus to them. If they agreed in spirit and practice with Gamaliel, would not the prevenient grace of God bring a renewed vision of Jesus? The remaining chapters of the Book of Acts would be radically different!

But it is true in our lives as well! Might our agreement with Jesus be present both in spirit and in practice? I will not allow the influence of past tradition, current philosophy, or cultural practices to hinder the flow of His presence in my life! I will bend my practical daily life under the Lordship of His Spirit in my heart! I want no disconnect between what I believe and how I live! Only when I release the fullness of Jesus in my total life can I experience His Lordship in my life!

Acts 5:41

WHAT?

"So they departed from the presence of the council, rejoicing that they were counted worthy to suffer shame for His name" (Acts 5:41).

"Foxe's Book of Martyrs" was published in March of 1563. It was my constant companion, retrieved from my father's study while growing up. It gave details in story form to the images presented by the writer of the Book of Hebrews. The great "faith chapter" highlighted a list of individuals so lengthy that the writer placed them in categories (Hebrews 11). They were tortured, mocked, scourged, placed in chains, imprisoned, stoned, sawn in two, slain with the sword, destitute, afflicted, tormented - **"of whom the world was not worthy"** (Hebrews 11:38). These people experienced such love and intimacy with Jesus nothing could hinder their faithfulness to Him!

Each occurrence of temptation in my life caused me to face the martyrs' loyalty compared to mine. How could I be so easily swayed? Did they have a relationship with Jesus? I did not. How could I embrace Jesus as they did? Their commitment compelled me to spend two years reading every book I could locate on the great saints of the church. I concluded that Jesus completely possessed them. He was so real in their lives nothing could distract them from Him! Their passion for Jesus overshadowed every other circumstance in their lives. Stubbornness or "bare-knuckled" hanging on was not their experience. They passionately loved Jesus, and every situation caused them to love Him more!

Our passage faces me again with a challenge. Twelve men, placed in the common prison, slept on a dirt floor in the body waste and stench of the other prisoners. An angel of the Lord delivered them from this situation and commanded them to return to the temple and preach Jesus (Acts 5:20). This was not freedom to escape but to be captured again. These uneducated men are inferior to the wealthy, sophisticated members of the Sanhedrin. The single issue of contention between them is Jesus. The apostles need only to cease any mention of Jesus. They could continue their compassion and church organization ministry if they only downplayed Jesus. The Sanhedrin threatened their lives! Could they not pledge a more strenuous effort to obey the council?

The apostles cannot escape this confrontation without consequences. The Sanhedrin released them, but only after they beat them (Acts 5:40). In the heated frustration and anger of the council, we know it was a strenuous beating, perhaps the scourging of forty save one. Will this end their loyalty to Jesus? Can their love for Jesus survive such punishment? Indeed, some of them will recant and disown Him. But they rejoiced *"that they were counted worthy to suffer shame for His name"* (Acts 5:41).

Were they not so wholly merged, glued to Him, that separation was impossible? Had their walk with Him for three years been crowned with forty days of His resurrected presence (Acts 1:3)? How could they possibly deny the reality of His presence? Their testimony was *"That which was from the beginning, which we have heard, which we have seen with our eyes, which we have looked upon, and our hands have handled, concerning the Word of life - the life was manifested, and we have seen and bear witness, and declare to you that eternal life which was with the Father and was manifested to us - that which we have seen and heard we declare to you"* (1 John 1:1-3). Were they not filled with His presence so that He moved from a physical embrace to the merger in the spiritual realm of their lives? Did they not know Him from the outside to the inside? Was He not now their inner resource of life?

The Sanhedrin had nothing but circumstantial, doctrinal, and philosophical thoughts. Jesus was not in this realm. His belief system was not for argument or up for debate by the most clever individual. The apostles had encountered Jesus. But it is more than an encounter, for He merged with them! He was more significant than the threat of the council. Their passion for Jesus was beyond the beating of the Sanhedrin.

The apostle Paul testified to Jesus' belief system. Some desired to kill him; did he tremble in fear at their threat? *"I have been crucified with Christ; it is no longer I who live, but Christ lives in me; and the life which I now live in the flesh I live by faith in the Son of God, who loved me and gave Himself for me"* (Galatians 2:20). How do you threaten a man with death, when he is already dead to himself? Some threatened to take everything Paul had. *"Yet indeed I also count all things loss for the excellence of the knowledge of Christ Jesus my Lord, for whom I have suffered the loss of all things and count them as rubbish, that I may gain Christ and be found in Him"* (Philippians 3:8-9). How do you take from an individual when he has already given everything he has away?

The Cause for Rejoicing

The grammar structure of the statement is no doubt intended to make a bold statement. *"They"* is a translation of the Greek word "hoi." However, we find this same pronoun at the end of the main verb, **"*departed,*"** giving a double emphasis focused on the twelve beaten apostles. **"*They*"** must be linked with the main verb in the imperfect tense. It is translated from the Greek word "poreuomai," **"*departed.*"** This tense refers to something happening in the past with continuing action and no regard to when it is completed. One can only speculate on the depth of the meaning of this focus. The council threatened the apostles' after they beat them, and they made their way from the presence of the Sanhedrin. But there appears to be something more indicated than just a physical action. While there may have been some hope for reconciliation with the council during the first phase of persecution, were the apostles utterly aware of the reality of the threat of the Sanhedrin? The council was not going to alter their position or lessen their threat. The division between the apostles and the Sanhedrin was only going to widen. While they had enjoyed peace and success during these early days of growth, the early Church was at war with the same demonic forces that crucified Jesus!

The apostles may have experienced some inner rejoicing in escaping the Sanhedrin with just a beating. But they were not foolish enough to consider the issue settled. Their loyalty to Jesus was still an issue of contention. Their Jewish culture, along with the Roman world, would not tolerate the Man Jesus! The Sanhedrin again forced the apostles against the wall over one central issue: Jesus. They could continue with ministry, miracles, helping the homeless, suppers, preaching, and all the activities established through the church, but Jesus was the council's only issue! Our culture is no different. We can adjust our methods to fit our culture to be accepted by our generation, but we are driven face to face with the issue of Jesus. The demonic forces did not tolerate Jesus then, and they will not tolerate Him now. Are we going to cling to Jesus, present Jesus, and live in Jesus? If we do, we will need to "depart" from our personal Sanhedrin, which will not tolerate Jesus!

Part Five: Advice Rejected: Agreement

"Rejoicing" is translated from the Greek word "chairo." This verb is present tense, in which the writer portrays an action in process or a state of being with no assessment of the action's completion. The apostles were feeling not just immediate relief from escaping the Sanhedrin but ***"rejoicing"*** continued through the days ahead, forming their attitude within the battle in which they were engaged. The highlight here is that ***"rejoicing"*** is a participle, making it an adverb modifying the sentence's main verb. If their departing was more than a physical action but was an awareness of the separation between them and the Sanhedrin causing increasing conflict, they continued to rejoice in such resistance!

While this may be true, Luke points to an additional cause of rejoicing. He interjects a purpose clause, introduced by ***"that,"*** translated from "hoti." Luke is marking the deep cause of their rejoicing. He declares it as ***"that they were counted worthy to suffer shame for His name."***

The Counting of Joy

Luke attempts to display the depth of the rejoicing within the apostles. This rejoicing was not a light, superficial, or emotional feeling quickly changing as other things attracted their attention. It was not a childlike rejoicing over some new toy. The apostles have discovered the profound reality of the presence of Jesus. They understood the wonder of all the provisions in His person. They surrendered to the embrace of forgiveness and acceptance found only in Jesus. They experienced moment-by-moment within themselves the power of God their forefathers knew when the death angel delivered them in Egypt through the sacrificial lamb. This power was the Spirit of Jesus enveloping their lives. When Solomon finished building the temple in Jerusalem, he conducted a grand dedication ceremony. ***"Fire*** *came down from heaven and consumed the burnt offering and the sacrifices; and the glory of the Lord filled the temple. And the priests could not enter the house of the Lord, because the glory of the Lord had filled the Lord's house"* (2 Chronicles 7:1, 2). The apostles comprehended the reality of this Presence in Jesus. In this same way, He had come to them (1 Corinthians 6:19)!

The Greek word "kataxioo" is translated as *"they were counted worthy."* The basic Greek word is "axioo," meaning "to be worthy, consider something worthy." In classical Greek, this word had to do with tipping or balancing the scales. When two entities are compared and found of equal weight, they are "fitting." When "kata" becomes a prefix of "axioo," it intensifies the meaning. "Kataxioo" is only used four times in the New Testament (Luke 20:35; 21:36; Acts 5:41; 2 Thessalonians 1:5). I searched diligently through numerous translations and discovered each one uses the word *"counted"* or "considered." A primary thrust of "kataxioo" is not merely being worthy, but worthiness results from the discovery. Placing the issue on the scales and finding it balances results in the conclusion.

This verb *"counted"* is in the passive voice, meaning the subject is being acted upon and is not responsible for the verb's action. The apostles did not make this judgment concerning themselves. Someone else placed them on the scales of value and judged them worthy. Who came to their lives and found worthiness in them? The answer is *"to suffer shame for His name."* Jesus considered, evaluated, understood, went through the process of placing them on the scales, and found them worthy. Their worth was in and by Jesus!

The author of the Book of Hebrews declares we are worthy while angels are not (Hebrews 2:16). When God cast the sinning angels out of heaven, they were not worthy of *"aid."* The immense redemption in Jesus was released when we sinned because we are worthy. We are worthy to share in His life, worthy to be His brother (Hebrews 2:11), worthy of a merciful and faithful High Priest (Hebrews 2:17), worthy of Jesus partaking of our flesh and blood (Hebrews 2:14), worthy of release from that which all our lifetime subjected us to bondage (Hebrews 2:15), worthy of propitiation of our sins (Hebrews 2:17), and worthy to be sons (Hebrews 2:10).

How could this be true? We are worthy of only death, destruction, and eternal damnation! We are incapable of accomplishing one deed or work that could be considered worthy. *"We all once conducted ourselves in the lusts of the flesh, fulfilling the desires of the flesh and of the mind, and were by nature children of wrath, just as the others"* (Ephesians 2:3). We had no hope and were without God in the world (Ephesians 2:12). How could He find us worthy? *"But now in Christ Jesus you who once were far off have been brought near by the blood of Christ"* (Ephesians 2:13). Jesus is our worthiness. He has set the scales. All the Trinity God required is placed on one side of the scale. God placed Jesus on the other side, and it balances! We are in Jesus!

Yes, the apostles rejoice, not as a child who found a new toy. They are in a state of rejoicing that seems to increase with every experience of their lives, even suffering shame for His name.

The Connection of Shame

There is a strong twist when using "kataxioo," *"they were counted worthy."* There is a great sense of being unworthy among the apostles. Our passage presents the apostles as being surprised that as they view their unworthiness, the Trinity God finds them worthy to participate in the sufferings of Christ! That is the constant tension in which Christians dwell, constantly aware of their sinful past from which God has saved them. The inability to merit, deserve, and earn a position of worthiness is consistently present. All that we can do has no weight to balance the scales. So, the foundation of rejoicing within the apostles is the deep awareness of being unworthy.

The absolute helplessness of our lives becomes the basis by which we can rejoice. This reality has always been the conflict between the message of our world and the gospel. We rejoice in losing our lives; the world rejoices in saving their lives. We rejoice in finding our lives; the world's rejoicing evaporates because they have lost their lives (Matthew 16:25). Our blessing comes from our helplessness (Matthew 5:3). The world finds no pleasure in such helplessness but always exerts self-centered efforts to compensate for their weakness, resulting in the constant exposure of their helplessness. However, we rejoice in our helplessness because it is the essence that allows God to fill us with His Divine strength! We readily embrace our unworthiness, the basis of being *"counted worthy"* by Jesus!

The apostles are *"rejoicing that they were counted worthy to suffer shame for His name"* (Acts 5:41). This is an oxymoron, a paradox, or a contradiction. They are honored by dishonor; they are graced by disgrace; they are blessed by cursing; they are commended by condemnation. *"To suffer shame"* is a translation of the Greek word "atimazo," meaning "to dishonor." What was the *"shame?"* The beating received from the Sanhedrin is the focus of dishonor. The apostles blatantly disobey the council who desire to eliminate Jesus and His name. The Sanhedrin treats them as criminals who are not in the class of ordinary, decent human beings. Therefore, the *"shame"* and "suffering" are beyond the physical pain of the beating but in the stigma surrounding the name of Jesus. Everything connected to the rejection of Jesus by the Jewish world is now attached to the apostles. Remember, the crucifixion of Jesus occurred in recent days. The memories are fresh and still spoken.

The *"shame"* reflects the description Peter gave to the Sanhedrin concerning their treatment of Jesus, *"whom you*

murdered by hanging on a tree" (Acts 5:30). He placed the blame on them, not on the Romans. Peter depicts their guilt in words describing the worst of motives and actions. Now, the apostles are privileged to experience those same motives and similar actions imposed upon them, placing them within the boundaries of Jesus' suffering. Singing the song *"Oh to be Like Thee"* might occur. Would we be rejoicing? ***"That I may know Him and the power of His resurrection, and the fellowship of His sufferings, being conformed to His death"*** (Philippians 3:10).

Is our goal and purpose to merge with Him above all other things? Knowing Him in the depth of His mind, embracing His heart, and experiencing the accomplishment of His will might not be comfortable. How will He accomplish this in and through me? In abandonment, I surrender to Him for such a life regardless of the consequences! How else will I know His righteousness? My honor will come from being dishonored, and I will experience grace by being disgraced!

Acts 5:42

NO CHANGE

"And daily in the temple, and in every house, they did not cease teaching and preaching Jesus as the Christ" (Acts 5:42).

Our verse is a simple statement, but it was at the heart of the life of the early Church. Luke concludes the second phase of persecution; however, we must view this conclusion as a synopsis of the early Church's history (Acts 1-5). Luke began with the "Foundation for the Spirit" (Acts 1). The resurrection of Jesus has welded the members of the early Church together. After spending forty days with Jesus (Acts 1:3), they are beyond doubt. They experienced three years of ministry with Jesus that cemented their relationship with His reality. The presence of the resurrected Jesus clarified the principles of truth, the explanation of the Old Testament, and the revelation of the New Covenant! They were beyond dispute and disbelief. One hundred and twenty believers set all other activities aside, waiting **"for the Promise of the Father"** (Acts 1:4).

In a few days, the "Filling of the Spirit" exploded in their lives (Acts 2). While the experience of the physically resurrected Jesus was earth-shattering, the indwelling merging Spirit of Jesus was beyond description! During Peter's first explanation

Part Five: Advice Rejected: Agreement

of the indwelling Christ, ***"about three thousand souls were added to them"*** (Acts 2:41). The early Church was on its way to impacting all Jerusalem with His presence. ***"So continuing daily with one accord in the temple, and breaking bread from house to house, they ate their food with gladness and simplicity of heart, praising God and having favor with all the people"*** (Acts 2:46-47).

The number of believers continued to increase. Luke writes about the miracle of the lame beggar's healing, introducing the continual "Flow of the Spirit" (Acts 3). This miracle is the single event that the Sadducees could not tolerate; therefore, the first phase of persecution began. The council imprisoned Peter and John and interrogated them the next day (Acts 4). After threatening the apostles, the council released them to return to the early Church and expected them to eliminate Jesus as the focus of their ministry. However, their ministry remained the same and increased in intensity and boldness (Acts 4:31). The number of believers increased and became a ***"multitude"*** (Acts 4:32).

The apostles aggressively maintained the necessary commitment to Jesus, even though a married couple in the church tried otherwise (Acts 5:1-11). The Spirit of Jesus was moving, and the ministry expanded outside Jerusalem (Acts 5:16). The high priest and Sadducees were indignant at the blatant disobedience of Peter and John (Acts 5:17). The Sanhedrin brought all the apostles before them, even though there was interference from an angel of the Lord and a respected teacher of the Law, Gamaliel (Acts 5:18-39). They did release the apostles, but not before reinforcing their demand by beating them. They treated the apostles like common criminals. Yet, the apostles rejoiced in being honored by dishonor and graced by disgrace.

What is the conclusion of all that has taken place? ***"And daily in the temple, and in every house, they did not cease teaching and preaching Jesus as the Christ"*** (Acts 5:42). Has the focus, the heart, or the intent of the early

Church changed? Has their culture changed their desire, lessened their passion, or altered their approach? Is this not a restatement of Luke's previous report (Acts 2:46, 27)?

Subject of the Ministry

"To whom He also presented Himself alive after His suffering by many infallible proofs, being seen by them during forty days and speaking of the things pertaining to the kingdom of God" (Acts 1:3). The Greek word "tekmerion" translated as **"infallible proofs"** is only used by Luke in this verse. It is a scientific term presenting absolute certainty and proof. A new idea, theology, philosophy, organization, method, meditation, emotional feeling, or solution did not capture the apostles. It is the person of Jesus! Jesus is alive! All they can speak about is Him! Their security is in the reality of His resurrected person. They remain in Jerusalem to experience Jesus' promise because of Him. Jesus contains all the ceremonies, sacrifices, feast days, and law!

While the physically resurrected presence of Jesus was beyond what they could imagine, the indwelling presence of His Spirit took them to a new level! Forgiveness, acceptance, destiny, purpose, and victory were all in Jesus. There was no secret formula or mystical methodology. Peter declared, *"Therefore being exalted to the right hand of God, and having received from the Father the promise of the Holy Spirit, He poured out this which you now see and hear"* (Acts 2:33). If Jesus captured them during His resurrection appearance, they are now moment-by-moment overwhelmed with Him! The Person of Jesus within them fulfilled all expectations of God from the Old Testament. They merged with Jesus! Their only message is the reality of His Person!

Jesus is solely responsible for the healing of the lame

Part Five: Advice Rejected: Agreement

beggar. Peter is horrified the gathering crowd would think he was responsible (Acts 3:12). His message to this crowd ***"greatly disturbed"*** the priests, the captain of the temple, and the Sadducees because the apostles ***"taught the people and preached in Jesus the resurrection"*** (Acts 4:2). When interrogated by the council, Peter emphatically, ***"let it be known to you all, and to all the people of Israel, that by the name of Jesus Christ of Nazareth, whom you crucified, whom God raised from the dead, by Him this man stands here before you whole"*** (Acts 4:10). The Sanhedrin understood how central Jesus was to the message of the apostles, for He is the only element they want eliminated.

The second phase of persecution occurred because the apostles blatantly disobeyed this single request of the Sanhedrin. Now, having been threatened and beaten, ***"they did not cease teaching and preaching Jesus as the Christ"*** (Acts 5:42). Nothing has changed! The single reason for the ministry of the early Church was Jesus. Not a belief system about Jesus, an organization for Jesus, or even a movement concerning Jesus, but the Person of Jesus! Everyone in the early Church was captured and filled with the Person of Jesus. The only threat to the demonic opposition was Jesus. Perhaps the only scheme of the Devil is to get us sidetracked from Jesus. Any other emphasis will please him. Programs, methodology, social causes, compassionate ministry, and recovery programs only have value when Jesus is central. ***"Nor is their salvation in any other, for there is no other name under heaven given among men by which we must be saved"*** (Acts 4:12).

Sequence of the Ministry

Luke emphasizes the consistency of the teaching and preaching about Jesus. The main verb of our passage is ***"did not***

cease, *"* a translation of the Greek words "ouk epauonto." The negative "ouk" expresses direct and full negation, independently and absolutely. Therefore, it is objective, different from the Greek word "me," also translated as "not," which implies a conditional and hypothetical negative. Therefore, it is subjective. The early Church ***"did not cease"*** to focus on Jesus; this is not a matter of opinion. No one could disagree with such a statement. The Sanhedrin verified it by accusing the apostles (Acts 5:28).

"Epauonto" comes from the basic Greek word "pauo," meaning "to stop, pause, make an end." However, Luke includes this absolute, beyond opinion, negative ***"not"*** (ouk). No one could question the consistent, unstoppable, without-rest emphasis on Jesus! This verb is in the indicative mood, meaning a simple statement of fact. The imperfect tense declares this action in the process, occurring in the past with no assessment of the action's completion. This verb controls two present participles, supplementing its meaning. Therefore, the content of the action is in the ***"teaching and preaching Jesus as the Christ."***

Luke further emphasizes the ***"teaching and preaching Jesus as the Christ"*** by using the word ***"daily,"*** translated from "pas" and "hemera." "Pas" is the Greek word meaning "all," and "hemera" means "day." When was the early Church not speaking of Jesus? What service could you attend where Jesus was not declared? What social activity did they experience when Jesus was not the central theme? Miracles were abundant, and they gave validity to the message of Jesus! The early Church cared for those in need, but their sharing focused on giving Jesus (Acts 4:32, 34). They ate together from house to house only to share Jesus (Acts 2:46). They were consistently in the temple, not to offer sacrifices, but to embrace the sacrificed and resurrect One!

Christians have no difficulty declaring His name, for they bear His name. While we must accomplish daily physical issues, everything is under the control of Jesus. If He is not central in the physical action, it ceases to be Christian. That is the experience of being filled and merged with the Spirit of Jesus. We are a new creature; He redeemed us in newness in Himself. We are new because He merged with us; the new creature combines Him and us! Would this not mean that every action of the new creature would be an expression of Jesus? The voice of the new creature gives constant expression to His glory! The vine gives life to the branch, which becomes an extension of the vine. The fruit is not a product of the branch alone or the vine, but both! We have become one with Jesus in nature. Our teaching and preaching are not a declaration of doctrine or theological perspective but the declaration of a Person, Jesus! Since this is true, it is a daily accomplishment, a moment-by-moment life experience! The question is not "When should we teach and preach Jesus?" The question is, "When do we not teach and preach Jesus?" The moment we cease is the moment we are not Christian!

Sphere of the Ministry

Luke is precise about the platform of the apostles' teaching and preaching. It was **"in the temple, and in every house"** (Acts 5:42). The apparent base of ministry for the early Church was in the temple. Luke concludes his gospel account with this information. After the apostles received the final instructions from Jesus and experienced His ascension, they returned to Jerusalem **"and were continually in the temple praising and blessing God"** (Luke 24:53). They experienced Pentecost. They continued their witnessing in the temple to the great crowds that gathered twice daily for prayer and sacrifice. They adopted Solomon's Porch in the temple as their place for meeting together. Luke refers to the early Church as **"they were all with one accord in Solomon's Porch"** (Acts 5:12). After the great miracle of the lame beggar's healing, the great crowds gathered together in Solomon's Porch to see the healed beggar and hear the testimony of Peter (Acts 3:11).

Luke's words specifically state *"in,"* a translation of the Greek word "en." "From" is a movement term indicating a change of location. "Into" refers to movement, but *"in"* is fixed, no movement! It is the abiding, remaining concept. Speaking Jesus was the consistent, constant ministry of the early Church. The temple was the heart of the city of Jerusalem; the ministry of the early Church was not isolated but at the core of all the activities in Jerusalem. When the angel of the Lord delivered the apostles from the common prison, the angel commanded them, **"Go stand in the temple and speak to the people all the words of this life"** (Acts 5:20).

The Bible applies this to our lives as Paul reminds us, **"Do you not know that you are the temple of God and that the Spirit of God dwells in you? If anyone defiles the temple of God, God will destroy him. For the temple of God is holy, which temple you are"** (1 Corinthians 3:16, 17). Are not our personal lives a constant platform for proclaiming Jesus' redemption? Is there never a time when the Spirit of Jesus is not declaring Himself through our flesh, the temple of God?

But Luke quickly adds, *"in every house"* (Acts 5:42). Evidently, small groups would gather in the homes of the members of the early Church. **"So continuing daily with one accord in the temple, and breaking bread from house to house, they ate their food with gladness and simplicity of heart"** (Acts 2:46). Included in these meals in their homes, they observed the Lord's supper. Their homes became a stage for the demonstration of Jesus. Notice that in the Greek text, Luke does not use the word *"in"* regarding the meetings in homes. He refers to "kata," meaning "down upon, down from, down in." In this case, he suggests the idea of motion throughout every part of the whole.

Part Five: Advice Rejected: Agreement

While the Spirit of Jesus is fixed in the temple, merging with the believer, the base of operation is the physical aspect of life. It is in the home where we live together physically. We eat, interact, fellowship, love, and participate in essential physical functions. That is the physical demonstration of the spiritual reality of His presence merged with us. Is there not constant ministry manifested through the physical life of the believer? We see Jesus in every activity!

System of the Ministry

"Teaching and preaching" describes how the apostles declare *"Jesus as the Christ."* Our involvement in this verse does not allow us to study this dynamic phrase thoroughly. The Greek word "didasko," translated as *"teaching,"* has inherent in it the intent to influence the understanding of the person receiving the teaching, which is not present in "euangelizo," *"preaching."* In our passage, Luke presents "didasko" in the active voice, meaning the apostles are responsible for and participate in the activity. We must understand this in the context of Peter's statement to the Sanhedrin, *"And we are His witnesses to these things, and so also is the Holy Spirit whom God has given to those who obey Him"* (Acts 5:32). Are not the apostles united with the Spirit of Jesus manifesting a single witness? What the Spirit of God reveals or teaches the apostles is now being taught by them to others. Luke does not propose an academic approach to teaching. This teaching is not merely about data or information but a deep understanding of what they are experiencing in merging with Jesus!

The emphasis of "euangelizo" is somewhat different. It comes from "eu," meaning "good or well," and "aggello," meaning "to proclaim or tell." The word's intent is to evangelize, proclaim the good news, and preach the gospel. The verb "euangelizo" is in the middle voice, signifying the subject of the verb is affected by its action or is acting upon itself. Again, this highlights Peter's statement to the Sanhedrin. The Holy Spirit is acting upon and within the apostles. The good news from their preaching is what the Spirit does within them as He merges with them. That is the first time this word (euangelizo) is used in Acts describing the activity of the early Church. The emphasis on "good news" spills forth from the context of persecution! After the martyrdom of Stephen (Acts 7:54-60), Saul began to persecute the church. **"Therefore those who were scattered went everywhere preaching** (euangelizo) **the word"** (Acts 8:4). Luke continues to highlight this (Acts 8:12, 25, 35, 40).

We must understand that these two, **"teaching and preaching,"** are not exclusive of one another. The Holy Spirit may use the same presentation to do both simultaneously. The teaching or preaching ability of the proclaimer does not determine the effect on the listener of what the Spirit of Jesus is doing in and through the believer. Still, it results from the engaging of the Spirit of Jesus projected through the proclaimer. The Spirit of God will teach and declare good news to the inner heart of the listener as He desires. We merely receive His indwelling, which projects what He is doing and reveals it to others through us. Is it good news (euangelizo)? Does it instruct (didasko)? Could it not do both at the exact moment? Do we not rejoice in the privilege of being a platform of His revelation?

ABOUT THE AUTHOR

Stephen Manley has found through the saturation of the Word the message of the cross. It is beyond an event; it is a style. Thus, the cross is not a piece of wood or an emblem, but it is the heart of the person of Christ. Cross style is the Christ style. He must be central. As an international evangelist, Stephen has taken this message to the world.

Stephen's life, testimony, and preaching has been used throughout the last eight decades to touch, influence, and transform the lives of countless people around the world. For Stephen, his life is wrapped up in a total saturation of Jesus and the Word of God. Time in the Word is more than an activity or duty to schedule in his day. It is the delight of his heart and the focus throughout his day because it draws him deeper into intimacy with Jesus Christ. He wants his "moment-by-moments" saturated with the Person of Jesus and the Word. He longs for Jesus to ever increase and expand in and through His life. As he once wrote:

> *"Jesus is present in every situation of my life.*
> *There is no conversation in which*
> *I do not feel His presence.*
> *He participates in all my recreation.*
> *He is everywhere I go. Who would want to be*
> *without Him? He is the protection for my life.*
> *He is the fragrance I constantly smell.*
> *He is the flow of my spiritual blood*
> *giving me life. He is my constant*
> *nutrition making me healthy.*

I cannot survive without Him.
I am a Jesus pusher!!!!

I want to push Him on you.
I want you to join me in this obsession.
You do not have to work at it;
it is not a discipline.
It is as natural as breathing.
Please let Him pull you to His heart."

Learn more about Stephen Manley
and the ministry of Cross Style at:
CrossStyle.org

www.ingramcontent.com/pod-product-compliance
Lightning Source LLC
Chambersburg PA
CBHW030733250426
43671CB00034B/56